# SOCIOBIOLOGY, SEX, AND SCIENCE

SUNY Series in
Philosophy and Biology

David Edward Shaner, Editor

# SOCIOBIOLOGY, SEX, AND SCIENCE

Harmon R. Holcomb III

## STATE UNIVERSITY OF NEW YORK PRESS

Production: Ruth Fisher
Marketing: Bernadette LaManna

Published by
State University of New York Press, Albany

For information, address the State University of New York Press,
State University Plaza, Albany, NY 12246

**Library of Congress Cataloging-in-Publication Data**
Holcomb, Harmon R., 1954-
  Sociobiology, sex, and science / Harmon R. Holcomb III.
    p. cm. — (SUNY series in philosophy and biology)
  Includes bibliographical references and index.
  ISBN 0-7914-1259-8 (ch.) — ISBN 0-7914-1260-1 (pb)
  1. Sociobiology.   2. Human evolution.   3. Social evolution.
4. Sex.   I. Title.   II. Series.
GN365.9.H65  1993
304.5—dc20                                                91-41478
                                                              CIP

10 9 8 7 6 5 4 3 2 1

To my Mother and Father
For all their love and support
In cultivating the life of the mind

# CONTENTS

# ACKNOWLEDGMENTS

My first look at sociobiology came when I studied as a graduate student with Elliott Sober at the University of Wisconsin–Madison. By 'philosophy of science', he had understood general questions about the nature of science as a whole, realizing that there were also questions internal to certain theories in physics and psychology. Given this outlook, his book, *The Nature of Selection*, did something new; it addressed questions internal to the system of theories in evolutionary biology. Elliott's teaching and his book combined to provide me with a model for doing philosophy of biology. Sober's innovation became my standard. I thank him for pointing me in the right direction.

I took it for granted, then, that philosophy of science treats both general questions about the character of science as a whole and questions specific to the various sciences. However, these two sorts of questions are usually handled separately, as evident from two courses I have regularly taught at the University of Kentucky. When I taught *Philosophy of Scientific Method*, I dealt with such topics as theories and observations, explanation, testing, realism and instrumentalism, and scientific change in a general way. When I taught *Biology and Society*, I dealt with such topics related to sociobiology as the very idea of a biological basis to human nature; culture and biology; the reasonableness of sociobiological theory or lack of it; the state of the evidence for that theory; and the ideological affiliations that motivated bold claims within and about sociobiology. I would have liked to present the connections I saw between these two courses. But I realized that it is beyond the scope of a single course to teach my students evolutionary theory and sociobiology, to teach them general philosophy of science, and to explore the connections between them.

Even so, it troubled me that people continue to evaluate sociobiology without using the resources in the legacy of philosophy of scientific method and that people continue to hold general ideas about scientific method that fail to do justice to the research situations of sciences like sociobiology. This book is an attempt to remedy the situation, arguing that we need to expand our image of science in order to evaluate sociobiology adequately. I thank the University of Kentucky for enabling me to teach courses that dovetail with my research and for a leave during the 1989 fall semester to work on this book.

I wish to thank Elliott Sober, Barbara Horan, Paul Thompson, Bill Harting, and a number of anonymous referees for their carefully thought out comments on the manuscript. I thank my father, Harmon R. Holcomb Jr., for good judgement about what to include and what not to include. I thank my mother, Sylvia Holcomb, and my wife, Sara Holcomb, for examining the manuscript word by word, catching mistakes of word choice and grammar. While my errors are, of course, my own, what remains is much better for their help.

# PART I

The Quest for Explanatory Completeness

# CHAPTER

# 1

## THEORIES AS THE UNIT OF ANALYSIS

### 1.1 On Assessing an Emerging Science

### The Sociobiology Controversy

Sociobiology, rooted in Darwin's (1872) legacy, is the branch of evolutionary biology that studies social behavior in all social species. Applying evolutionary theory to the human species has always provoked heated controversy, and contemporary sociobiology has amply fulfilled this historical role. In the 1970s a fresh wave of publicity, excitement, and shock followed E. O. Wilson's (1975) encyclopedic systematization of work on nonhuman species. Impressed by the success of past work, he conjectured that evolutionary explanations could transform our understanding of human behavior, and early enthusiasts tried prematurely to explain almost everything about the human condition. When initial speculations were reported to the public as a set of assumed-to-be-true explanations that tell us what human nature really is, thereby establishing biological limits to social change, the debate became rancorous. In the late 1970s and 1980s, people struggled to come to grips with the idea of a biology of human society that strives to be a science whose validity is independent of its social context and yet which influences and is influenced by the society of its practitioners.

Advocates glorified the field and critics condemned it. Feeling that sociobiology hurts people, critics fought it in order to protect society from bad science and bad ideology. Feeling that sociobiology had been unfairly put on trial, advocates defended it in order to

3

protect science from misguided political criticism. Each side claimed to be misinterpreted by the other side and regarded the other's case as exaggerated. Dispute became polemical and accusatory. "The sociobiology debate" became well known among evolutionists, social scientists, and the academic community (Caplan 1978; Leeds and Dusek 1981–82; Kitcher 1985). Polarization led to a stalemate between advocates and critics on the basic issues of sociobiology's validity and significance.

Animal and human reproductive behavior is here chosen to bear the burden of our examination. The reason for focusing on a single phenomenon is that it facilitates detailed comparison of various theories of scientific validity. Reproductive behavior is chosen because it is an important property of societies, i.e., groups of individuals of the same species organized in a cooperative manner. It is also chosen because it is a crucial test case: if anything specific about human sociality can be explained by the theory, it can. Recall the bare outlines of the underlying theory.

Typically, social behaviors are explained as reflecting a history of evolution by selection. All life on earth is connected by an ancient chain of reproduction. As a result, organismic behavior is designed to result in reproductive success. Throughout the animal kingdom, females tend to be more selective and discriminating than males in their mating choice (Darwin 1871). Why? The theory of sexual selection posits that males and females maximize their fitness differently (fitness is the probability of reproductive success, often calculated using a strategic design analysis). Males and females in ancestral populations encountered different reproductive opportunities and constraints. Hence, their different behaviors can be explained as reflecting the outcome of different fitness strategies and historical patterns.

Darwin conceived of natural selection as imposed by environmental demands and of sexual selection as imposed by the demands of species members. However, both operate through the mechanism of differential reproductive success. In the background are statistics about who lives, who reproduces, and who dies. Organisms vary. Some leave more offspring than others. Therefore the traits inherited from the parents more successful at surviving and reproducing increase in frequency in the next generation. The mechanism Darwin had in mind introduces fitness-related biases into these statistics. There is normally much variation in morphology, physiology, and behavior within each species. Such variations often yield different aptitudes for reproductive success (fitnesses). These variations are often inherited. In ideal conditions, the type of organism with the most fit variations will increase in the population from one generation to the next. In brief, heritable variation in fitness results in evolution by natural selection. Selection acting on variation within a population in each generation results in change in the population from one generation to the next. The evolutionary record of adaptations to local environments and to other organisms is explained as the cumulative result of selection.

Sociobiology's *raison d'etre* is to help complete an evolutionary picture of life. By definition, evolutionary theory would be incomplete if it could not explain phenomena that it should explain. At issue is whether it should be expected to explain various specific facts about animal and human behavior in the same breath, and if so, how to do so rigorously. Can it be complete without explaining the origin of the double standard between the sexes? As an example of how sexual selection theory can be provocative and incite scientific, political and moral debate, take Barash's (1979, 53) "insight":

> Compare these two situations: (1) you are a male animal, paired with a single female, and your "wife" goes around copulating with other males; (2) you are a female animal, paired with a single male, and your "husband" goes around copulating with other females. In which case is your fitness likely to be lower? In the first situation, if you (as male) remain faithful to your "swinging" spouse, she will eventually conceive offspring via other males, and you will have lost out in the evolutionary sweepstakes. However, in the second case, if you (as female) remain faithful to your mate, you can still breed successfully despite his philandering, provided he includes you among his girlfriends. This is the basic biology of the double standard: males are expected to be sexually less discriminating, more aggressive and more available than females. They are also expected to be more intolerant of infidelity of their wives than wives will be of the infidelity by their husbands.

On first impression, the message of this somewhat jaunty version seems to be that men are by nature promiscuous while women are naturally prone to be faithful. So we debate whether the explanation is scientific fact or sexist drivel. Such matters can be decided only if the explanation's meaning is clear. Organisms enhance their fitness equally by copulating successively with the same or different members of the other sex, if offspring number and quality are the same. Promiscuity and faithfulness are selectively equivalent in that sense. So the explanation is compatible with both men and women being promiscuous, both being faithful! Despite the male-oriented presentation, promiscuity is just as advantageous as faithfulness for women in the above scenario. And when the promiscuous woman reproduces, her husband may not.

What is explained is not a certain number of sexual partners in either sex, but a relative difference, whatever degree of "faithfulness" or "promiscuity" a species exhibits. The evolutionary import of the fact that women, not men, bear children is this: men and women have evolved differently because a woman can transmit her genes to the next generation only through her own body, whereas a man can transmit his genes through the bodies of multiple women. "The more mates, the more potential offspring" holds for men, not women. The sex investing more potential reproductive output in an offspring should be more careful in choosing mates. The bearing of offspring by women makes their investment heavier. Women put a far greater amount of reproductive potential at risk with every copulation or fertilization than men. These conditions set up an asymmetry in mate-choice strategies. Other things being equal, selection favors greater mate quantity in men. They may not be equal, e.g., if the current mate is suboptimal, females may benefit from multiple mates. The story is complex and depends on the current forms of selection theory.

It is easy to see why loosely phrased statements of sociobiological explanations fire emotional responses stronger than the normally tepid strictures of scholarly disagreement. The following claims and charges are distillations of actual assertions from a variety of sources cited in the bibliography. They capture the point and counterpoint driving the debate.

Advocates claim that sociobiology: "offers an intellectual revolution" which "unites the biological and social sciences," "lays the foundation for social theory," "offers a scientific basis for social policy," "explains culture and history," "shows that social institutions grow out of individual interactions," "provides the key to human nature," "identifies the ultimate reasons for why we do what we do," "undermines the received dichotomies between nature/nurture, genetic/learned, and biological/cultural," "can be rejected only at the price of rejecting evolution," and "is the first genuine application of scientific method to human behavior"!

Bold promises invite scepticism. Critics typically retort sociobiology is simply "bad science with politically dangerous implications." They claim that sociobiology: "has contributed nothing of value," "attacks the social sciences," "offers a scientific excuse for dangerous social policy," "pretends that what is cultural and historical is really biological and natural," "disregards the autonomy of social institutions from biological predispositions," "uses a human nature ideology to justify status quo inequalities between races, sexes, and classes as natural, genetic and inevitable," "projects human attributes onto animals and reads them back onto humans as pseudo-explanations," "assimilates nurture to nature, learning to genes, culture to biology and so forth through a one-sided perspective," "replaces the role of God in producing perfect adaptation in nature with natural selection," "extends evolutionary theory where it has no business being," and "collapses into a caricature of science"!

Each side finds the assessment given by the other side unjustified and irrational. We need to make sense of the fact that an array of intelligent, informed thinkers can arrive at starkly opposed conclusions. Is the sociobiology of sex a science?

Among advocates, the commitments of sociobiology are straightforward. They are: to bring the standards of rational validity associated with the sciences to bear upon the extension of well-established biological knowledge to animal (that is, nonhuman) sociobiology and human sociobiology. By calling some work "scientific," we normally think of it as valid, established science. Evolutionary biology has long been an established science, and animal sociobiology is now an established science, whereas human sociobiology is not. Some work in human sociobiology is now far more rigorous than the early sensationalized edicts about human nature. By focusing on the presentation of human sociobiology to the public, the critics neglect the rigorous work in the scholarly journals (such as *Ethology and Sociobiology, Behavioral and Brain Sciences, Human Evolution, Journal of Social and Biological Structures,* and *Behavioral Ecology and Sociobiology*).

The critics think that this is only part of the story. They charge that the very content of the explanations which allegedly result from "the scientific method" is molded by intellectually unworthy ideologies. These include: biological determinism (all human events are biologically, genetically determined through evolution); naive reductionism (social science is reduced to biology just because humans are evolved organisms); vulgar adaptationism (all behaviors are assumed to be optimally adaptive); neo-Social Darwinism (e.g., the double standard between the sexes is inevitable and hence justified because it is an evolved genetic adaptation); and panbiologism (biology is the single privileged key to human nature). Indeed, the allegedly "scientific aims and results" are merely rationalizations of these "isms."

The pendulum had swung from too easy acceptance in the mid-1970s to overly harsh rejection in the mid-1980s. Whereas some had accepted sociobiology on Wilson's authority, others came to reject it due to criticisms of Wilson's work. Sociobiology does not stand or fall with Wilson's scientific approaches or his claims about its import. In practice it takes a variety of forms, many quite different from Wilson's work and unanticipated by past criticisms. Still, it is important to be clear about what Wilson was getting at in his attempt to complete the Darwinian revolution through a new sociobiological synthesis.

The discussion evolved in the 1980s to the point of fruitfully reassessing evolutionary explanation in general. Some advocates have retracted their most ambitious, extreme claims on behalf of sociobiology (e.g., Wilson, Trivers, Barash). Some critics find hope for better work in the future (e.g., Maynard Smith, Kitcher) or are satisfied that their concerns have been generally appreciated (e.g., Gould, Lewontin). A new body of serious, improved explanatory work in human sociobiology is being produced and will be reviewed throughout the book (e.g., Betzig, Borgerhoff Mulder, Turke, Buss and Barnes, Lancaster, Hrdy, Daly, Hawkes and Hill). In the effort to meet well-taken criticisms, Wilson embarked on a new program, one in which the significance of mind and culture for population genetics and population ecology are directly addressed. As of 1990, there were a wide variety of research programs for producing a unified evolutionary account of cultural change and genetic change. Many invoke a complex psychology in order to meet well-taken criticisms showing that traditional evolutionary explanations could not fulfill their task. For example, Barkow (1989c) shows how mind, self-consciousness, culture, and human choice intervene in the explanation of social patterns from genetic evolution. The research programs of Alexander, Boyd and Richerson, Tooby and Cosmides, and others will be identified and discussed where pertinent throughout the book.

The cooling down of the debate is due more to fatigue, to tolerance, and to a desire to get on with one's work than to a resolution of the issues or even to a better grasp of how to argue them. Sociobiology's ambitious aim to bring human sociality under the explanatory tenets of evolutionary theory was bound to bring ideological and political concerns to the fore. This accounts for the heat, but the stalemate also stems from lack of agreement about the routine topics of philosophy of science: e.g., the role of theories, tests for accepting hypotheses, the structure of explanation, and the aim and scope of the science (see Brody 1970; Kourany 1987).

This book has no interest in spreading news of a "sociobiological breakthrough" or in puncturing "sociobiology's scientific pretensions". Nor shall it try in vain to turn critics into advocates or advocates into critics. To participate in that debate would be to continue to obscure an even more fascinating role for sociobiology. The sociobiology controversy provides a splendid opportunity to reflect on the adequacy of the methods by which we reach our evaluative conclusions about emerging sciences, whatever those conclusions may be. If at times the attention paid here to the foibles of advocates and critics seems excessive, the motive is to make full use of a striking test case for philosophies of scientific method and to transform the debate by changing the very terms and assumptions which have guided it.

Let us put to advocates and critics alike the question, "What is required for sociobiological explanations to count as acceptable scientific explanations?" A question central to the debate over the scientific status of sociobiology, it calls for an evaluation-centered approach to the philosophical study of science. This book is evaluation-centered and will present a model of the criteria, the analytical tools, intellectual structures, and goals which bear upon an answer to our question. A moderately complex model is needed if questions aren't to be forever begged, and our model will differentiate the roles of theories, research programs and conceptual frameworks, and will use these to refine the evaluations.

## Evaluating Explanations: The Three-Unit Model

The preceding perspective alerts us to the need to utilize a relatively rich conception of evaluation in order to assess projects such as human sociobiology. It inspires us to replace the impoverished image of science most people employ in reasoning about science with one that does justice to the richness of its characteristic structures and procedures of decision making. What makes our image impoverished is that it is blind not only to the subtle interplay between science and ideology, but also to the deep structure of explanatory inquiry, the aims of science and the way they bear on emerging sciences, and the full array of criteria which enter into the determination of what counts as an acceptable scientific explanation.

As a step in the right direction, we here propose what may be called the "three-unit model" for analyzing and evaluating science. Everyone admits that there is more to science than observation. How much more? The traditional answer is "theory"; call that the "one-unit model." The recent answer is "theory, and in addition, research programs"; call that the "two-unit model." The proposal here is "theory, research programs, and conceptual frameworks." We are ready to state the bare bones of this three-unit model, realizing that it will be elaborated by application to sociobiology throughout the book.

The three-unit model has two main components: a view of the scientific enterprise and a view of how explanations should be evaluated.

The model postulates that the scientific enterprise involves three kinds of activities: (a) the use of logic and facts to verify or falsify a hypothesis; more precisely, setting up plausible explanatory and predictive hypotheses based on one or more theories and then checking them against observed facts to see whether the hypotheses are confirmed or disconfirmed; this aspect of science has been thoroughly investigated by traditional logical empiricist philosophies of scientific knowledge (Carnap, Hempel, Quine, etc.); (b) the continual revision and changing of hypotheses; more precisely, continually proposing, revising, or discarding plausible explanatory and predictive hypotheses and theories as motivated by evidential and nonevidential considerations under the guidance of one or more research programs; this aspect of science has been thoroughly investigated by recent philosophies of scientific change (Lakatos, Kuhn, Laudan, etc.); (c) the determination of the research value of hypotheses within the current research situation; more precisely, the determination of the aim-oriented conceptual roles of explanatory and predictive hypotheses in terms of their underlying conception of the explanatory problem addressed, the phenomena to be explained, and the factors doing the explaining; this aspect, involving a conceptual framework irreducible to the basic concepts of a theory, is here identified as something worthy of investigation by philosophies of research structure.

In the sociobiology controversy, what is at issue is not evolutionary theory in general, but the way it is extended to explain animal and human sociality. This kind of research situation occurs often in science; an established underlying theory is extended to new domains. So instead of talking about validating theories, it is more appropriate to talk about validating explanations and analyzing the criteria of their validity in terms of their basis in theories, programs, and frameworks. The model postulates that explanations in cases of this kind should be evaluated in the following manner: (d) the unit of achievement and the object of validation is the particular explanation or explanatory hypothesis; (e) the commitments arising from accepting an explanation are induced by the explanation's role in the quest for completeness, which contours one's commitment to an affiliated theory, an affiliated research program, and an affiliated conceptual framework; and (f) the scientific status of these explanations is properly assessed by evaluating particular explanations in terms of these three units, as described in (a), (b), and (c).

Completeness is a basic property of theories, a relation between a theory and its domain. The degree of completeness is the extent to which the theory covers its domain. By definition, an established theory would be explanatorily complete if it explained everything in its domain in need of explanation. If evolutionary theory were complete, it would explain each behavioral fact that is evolutionarily significant and so in need of evolutionary explanation. Before the advent of sociobiology, evolutionary theory was incomplete in practice but complete in principle: the evolution of social behavior in animals and humans could not yet be explained by the theory of the forces that govern evolutionary change.

On the present view, the current image of science that recognizes only observation, theory, and research programs, and not conceptual frameworks as distinct from them, is impoverished. To see why, we have to argue that scientific practice is richer than the customary image of science admits. It will be argued, in part 1, that the issues over sociobiological observations, theories, and research programs turn on matters involving conceptual frameworks, by showing that completeness is the fulcrum upon which evaluations in terms of observation, theory, and programs turn. Then it will be argued, in part 2, that these matters are connected to matters that directly concern conceptual frameworks built around the concept of completeness. Chapter 6 puts the cumulative results of all previous chapters together so as to show how the evaluation of sociobiology is appropriately conceptualized according to an integrated employment of all these units of analysis.

The model postulates that a justifiable evaluation of explanations in an emerging science must take into account not only the surface structure of an explanation (the way it answers a why question), but also the deep structure of explanatory inquiry (the context of assertions and ideas in which it is embedded). Our review of the sociobiology debate has already given credibility to the model's assertion that the deep structure includes three kinds of elements: theory (evolutionary theory in general, mate selection theory), research program (gene-culture theories and related aims and methods), and conceptual framework (conceptualization of what aspects of social behavior are or are not evolutionarily significant).

We are now ready to exhibit the way the three-unit model will be developed. We will connect the structures of explanatory inquiry with issues in evaluating sociobiological explanations in the designated chapters. An explanation's theoretical structure embodies the way it attempts to help show that social facts are neither independent of nor incompatible with the theory (chap. 1). An explanation's programmatic structure embodies the way its guiding assumptions embody choices about how to make biological fitness, natural selection, genes, and so forth relevant to and consistent with sociality in nonhuman and human organisms (chap. 2). An explanation's conceptual structure embodies the way the quest for completeness orients decisions about the way it connects evolutionary theory with social facts: choice of the explanatory problem it addresses (chap. 3), choice of the facts it explains (chap. 4), choice of the factors it employs to explain (chap. 5), and choice of the specific explanatory task of acting as the target for evaluating its performance (chap. 6).

We will develop a working concept of the differences between theories, research programs, and conceptual frameworks sufficient to handle issues in sociobiology, revealing the ways in which reference to them arbitrates issues it raises. That is, instead of providing a logical analysis of these units of thought in the traditional sense of analytic philosophy, we will provide a concrete identification of their differences as revealed in and by scientific practice. To get on with the project of identifying conceptual frameworks, it will be assumed that we know the sort of thing we are talking about when we talk about theories, lest we become bogged down in the usual debates over theory structure. Gene-culture theories act as presuppositions guiding explanatory work on particular explanations, as theoretical cores of research programs. The interacting components of research programs are intertwined theory, methods, and aims that guide selection, evaluation, and revision of explanations. A conceptual framework of commitments regulates the direction of a sequence of research programs and theories as it provides a system of intellectual controls over the conceptualization of explanations.

Chapters 1 and 2 go to show that standard views of science emphasizing theories or research programs require connection to the quest for completeness in order to apply appropriately to sociobiology. Traditional logical empiricist views that analyze science in terms of theories alone are illustrated by applying the views of Hempel on explanation (chap. 1), Popper on disconfirmation (chap. 2), and Quine on plausibility (chap. 2). The Rudner-Jeffrey-Hempel debate about standards of confirmation will be applied (chap. 1). Recent historicist views are illustrated by briefly applying the views of Lakatos on research programs, Kuhn on paradigms, and Laudan on research traditions (all in chap. 2). These are, primarily, philosophical applications, not philosophical summaries or analyses. By showing that the usual evaluative methods are misleading unless completeness is given center stage, the need for analysis in terms of a conceptual framework built around completeness is motivated.

Ensuing chapters identify criteria for evaluating the explanatory role of explanatory activities in the quest for completeness. To understand their explanatory role, we must understand how an explanation's distinctive features—its goals, development, scope, modality, resources, kind, power, and limits—are characterized by its relation to a conceptual framework. These distinctive features are not normally recognized in philosophy or biology as systematically integrated. Explanatory work is well-articulated only if it clearly presents its claims in relation to these distinctive features. Chapters 3 through 6 individually elucidate relations between the distinctive features of explanation and each component of an explanatory framework. By unduly neglecting an explanation's conceptual structure, evaluations miss their target and distort what a given piece of explanatory work means, presupposes, implies, is expected to accomplish, and contributes to ongoing research.

Problem specification, addressed in chapter 3, answers the question "How should we formulate problems addressed in extending evolutionary theory to explain features of sociality left out of our picture of evolution?" Domain specification, addressed in chapter 4, answers the question "How should we formulate statements of the evolutionary facets of the behaviors to be explained?" Disciplinary structure specification, addressed in chapter 5, answers the question "How should we marshal the resources of the evolutionary subfields to formulate statements of the explanatory factors?" Performance-evaluation specification, addressed in chapter 6, answers the question "How should we formulate evaluations appropriate for assessing progress toward completeness by speaking to the type of explanation and type of evidence pertinent to the explanatory study being examined?"

The structures and procedures of thought used in asking and answering these questions form a conceptual framework: *As specific studies solve problems in achieving the completeness of evolutionary theory (problems) by applying explanatory factors from various subfields in evolutionary biology (disciplinary structure) to various topics concerning animal and human sociality (domain), the resulting explanations are evaluated for research value (performance evaluations) in order to make revisions that promote completeness.* Chapters 3 through 6 develop this idea in detail.

Now we are ready to explore the idea that we and all other social species are connected by the undeniable fact that we are evolved organisms, and as such, we use our social abilities to behave in ways which enable us to survive and reproduce. In order to develop explanations of sociality from the evolutionary theory of differential reproduction, many more kinds of research decisions are made than are usually recognized. The focal point for understanding how all these decisions fit together lies in its chief aim. Sociobiology, whether animal sociobiology or human sociobiology, should be evaluated as an extension of the revised, updated Modern Synthesis into the realm of sociality in order to complete evolutionary knowledge.

## 1.2 Explanatory Completeness

### Confirmationist Methodology

Suppose we grant that a causal source of behavioral differences among males and females in many species is that natural selection favors greater mate quantity in males. Critics attack sociobiology by saying that the explanations generated by this idea do not satisfy scientific standards for being well-developed, correct explanations. Advocates defend sociobiology by insisting that the explanations so far proposed are based on explanatory insights. What would justify evaluating a sociobiological explanation as an acceptable scientific explanation? We will begin by examining the implications for our answer of the traditional view that the scientific enterprise consists basically of the use of logic and facts to verify or falsify a hypothesis; more precisely, setting up plausible explanatory and predictive hypotheses based on a theory and then checking them against observed facts to see whether they are confirmed or disconfirmed.

Many evaluators of sociobiology, upon hearing the question "Sociobiology is fascinating, but is it science?" think to themselves, "Is it supported by the evidence?" If you evaluate the scientific status of sociobiology in terms of evidential support and only in terms of evidential support, then we shall say that you employ a "confirmationist methodology." Is a confirmationist methodology adequate for assessing sociobiology as a science? If our answer is to appeal to mainstream philosophy of science, then we cannot afford to overlook the once-dominant school of logical empiricism, whose insights can often be taken on their own merits quite independently of the excesses of positivist philosophies.

Confirmationist methodology is an attitude, a preoccupation with confirmational success, that can be made precise and represented through an associated postulate. Let us define confirmationist methodology as a method based on 'confirmationism', a class of views of validation that treat the validity-making property of being well-confirmed as a necessary and sufficient condition for acceptability. Confirmationism postulates that explanations in sociobiology, as in any science, are acceptable scientific explanations if and only if they are (sufficiently) confirmed by the observational evidence.

Confirmation is itself a celebrated mine-field in need of remapping and renewal, but that is not our task. We want only to consider what difference, if any, the notion of explanatory completeness would make to confirmationist methodology.

This chapter argues for the three-unit model by showing that the concept of completeness acts as the glue, so to speak, which holds together evaluations in terms of standards for satisfying criteria for acceptability related to theories, research programs, and conceptual frameworks.

The following themes connect the arguments of the rest of this chapter to various aspects of confirmationism. The concept of completeness is clarified so as to make sense of Wilson's view of sociobiology as a New Synthesis, revealing that the scientific legitimacy and scientific significance of sociobiology lie in the quest for a synthesis that achieves explanatory completeness. The character of scientific explanation is clarified in relation to completeness, using Hempel's model of sound explanatory reasoning. Brought to bear on Barash's explanation of male-female differences, the model implies that we use the right assumptions to reach explanatory conclusions and that what counts as confirming evidence depends on the inferential structure of the explanation under study. A summary of Betzig's evidence for these conclusions shows that there is some respectable confirmation, raising the question of whether the evidence is sufficient for accepting them. In the face of Kitcher's appeal to high standards of sufficient confirmation due to the political risks incurred in accepting sociobiological explanations of human nature, it is argued that the dispute over human nature is irrelevant to the scientific validity of sociobiology and premature if separated from the quest for completeness. Clarification of acceptance shows that standards for acceptance are relative to the current state of research aimed at completeness and specific to the use of explanations in inquiry, belief, or action and that their use in inquiry turns on their generative potential for promoting completeness.

Explanatory completeness in biology has never received sufficient attention. In the rest of this section, 1.2, we will do so in three ways: in a historical sense, in an intuitive sense, and in a metalogical sense.

## The Historical Context of Completeness

Evolutionary theory has to be made applicable to and true of all the main kinds of phenotypic traits (e.g., sociality) in all the main kinds of species (e.g., the social species, including humans) in order to be complete. Hence, completeness demands the principled legitimacy of both animal and human sociobiology as sciences. Completeness, however, only provides the rationale for doing sociobiology, not a justification of its results.

Sociobiology should be analyzed as a means of completing the best version of evolutionary theory we have, given by the legacy of the Modern Synthesis as currently revised. To see the scientific significance of sociobiology as a culmination of the scientific history of evolutionary biology, consider the fact that the persistence and character of adaptation is to be explained in part by the theory of evolution by natural selection. This theory has undergone three phases of maturation, whose broad outlines will be described in a way pertinent to sociobiology.

In the original Darwinian revolution triggered by Darwin and Wallace, natural selection was conceived as a natural process that tends to cause the survival of individuals and groups best adjusted to the natural and social conditions under which they live. So the idea of sociobiology in this sense is not new at all, but, rather, a part of Darwinism from the beginning, as evident from Darwin's writings on the descent of man and on the evolution of the emotions and even morality. Darwin anticipated the sociobiological viewpoint that, "we were selected for the capacity for culture (Spuhler 1959), and the societies generated by our cultures were the environment to which natural selection adapted us." (Barkow 1989c, 143).

However, widespread Darwinism did not begin with Darwin. In the latter half of the nineteenth century, many theorists were converted to evolutionism without Darwinism. Still under the influence of Lamarkian ideas, they regarded evolutionary change as a guided, purposeful process. Darwin had some Lamarkian ideas about the inheritance of environmentally produced variations, e.g., his theory of pangenesis. But he posited that evolutionary change moved in no preordained direction through a series of developmental stages. It was due to a relatively mechanical process of sorting among variations produced in ways undirected to organismic needs according to the differential effects of variant traits on survival and reproduction. Undirected variation was followed by natural selection among variants within a population. Evolution was to be explained by variational explanation, not developmental explanation (for details, see 5.3).

Darwin applied natural selection to the struggle for existence of organisms within a population. Social Darwinists reapplied it to the struggle for existence and power between races, classes, and nations. Current uses of selectionist theory to explain male-female differences envisage struggle for power between the sexes, "a battle of the sexes" (Dawkins 1975). Each sex is selected to control the sexuality of the other sex and to overcome control by the other sex, resulting in relentless intersexual conflict (Barkow 1985, 337). In species as diverse as insects and humans, males and females face different reproductive constraints, females with limited eggs and males with virtually unlimited sperm. These differences lead to competition between males for access to females and between females and males to control mating success. Such competition is a causal source of social behaviors.

In the modern Darwinian revolution triggered by the Modern Synthesis of Darwinism and Mendelism, genes were found to provide the sort of undirected variation required by Darwinism. Genes also provided a continual source of new variation, so that selection was not merely a temporary process, sorting quickly among a few existing variants and leaving nothing further to operate on. Natural selection was conceived as a natural process that not only had the tendency to produce local adaptation, but also to both perpetuate genetic qualities transmitted through reproduction and eliminate untransmitted genetic qualities in ways affected by other forces of evolutionary change, such as mutation, migration, and immigration. Sociobiology attempts to connect forces of cultural and biological evolution in a unified scheme, on grounds, for example, that the species-specific behavioral abilities, skills, motives, and goals presupposed in culture itself have already been subjected to the effects of biological evolution. So the project of unifying biological and cultural evolution in terms of an evolved psychology is not new, but, rather, an extension of the project to connect the forces of biological evolution in a unified theoretical scheme (for details, see 2.4).

When isolating mechanisms were added to this list of evolutionary forces, it became possible to understand the origin of species and macroevolution as an outgrowth of microevolution insofar as it involves within-population change. However, the role of natural selection in the origin of new species and higher taxa has been subject to continuing debate, e.g., any radical changes required intermediate variants that were adaptively neutral or maladaptive. So concerns over sociobiological methods that take social behaviors to be made optimally adaptive as a result of natural selection is not new, but, rather, an outgrowth of similar worries about macroevolution. In any case, the experimental crossing of many forms, either within or between species, gave rise to the sorts of hybrids and intermediary forms postulated by evolutionism. Where the Modern Synthesis sought to complete Darwinism by connecting natural selection to macroevolutionary phenomena, sociobiology's New Synthesis seeks to complete Darwinism by connecting natural selection to social phenomena (for details, see 3.1).

Unless evolutionary theory is incomplete, variation in social behavior within and among species should also be explained in ways that conform to evolutionism. As with the Modern Synthesis, the debate has centered on the role of natural selection in the evolution of sociality. To make evolutionary theory in the legacy of the Modern Synthesis empirically adequate, adequate to explain the available social facts, the role of natural selection is being reconceptualized. We will highlight two themes here.

First, there is a reconceptualization of the genetic basis of selection. An influential theme is that natural selection has been maximizing the perpetuation of genes, including the effects on copies of genes in one's own body and in other bodies. This has given rise to the idea of the selfish gene: we are motivated to behave in whatever ways maximize the survival of copies of our genes, regardless of whom we help or hurt to do so (non-kin, kin, or self), providing we can launch more copies of our genes into succeeding generations by doing so than by some available alternative.

There are numerous variations on this theme. Altruism to progeny is favored by Darwinian individual selection when it perpetuates (copies of) one's genes better than alternative behaviors. Altruism to kin is favored by kin selection when benefits to kin perpetuates one's genes better than alternative behaviors. Altruism to non-kin is favored by reciprocal altruism when benefits to non-kin are reciprocated so as to perpetuate one's genes better than alternative behaviors. Manipulation of progeny to provide altruism to siblings is favored by parental manipulation when benefits to siblings perpetuates the parent's genes better than alternative behaviors. Altruism to the group is favored by group selection when benefits to one's group better perpetuates one's genes than alternative behaviors. The phrase "better than alternative behaviors" has been made specific for a tremendous diversity of evolutionary scenarios by application of various models that specify mathematical values for all the relevant variables and constants. Actual evolutionary scenarios are likely to involve several of these selection processes at the same time, as well as interacting selection forces and other forces of evolutionary change (for details, see 3.2, 3.3).

In addition, there is a reconceptualization of the social effects of selection. An influential theme is that natural selection affects nongenetic variations in sociality. These selection processes concern effects of behavior on genes, not the effects of genes on behavior. Between genes and behavior there is the brain (or the mind), and so we don't expect one-to-one gene-behavior effects. Behavior is learned, but learning has been subject to genetic evolution; the brain has evolved specific information-processing capabilities to handle environmental, experiential, or cultural data pertinent to specific adaptive problems. Natural selection is conceived as a natural process that not only has the tendency to produce adaptation in the sense of the Darwinian revolution and the tendency to produce genetic change in the sense of the Modern Synthesis, but also the tendency to screen nongenetic variations in social behaviors, social roles, and social organizations for their harmony with evolved social motives (for details, see 2.4, 4.2).

If we put these two themes together, we arrive at the projected New Synthesis of both natural and social causes and effects. The phenomena to be explained are observed patterns of connections between variations in social behavior and variations in reproductive success. The factors doing the explaining are psychological skills used to screen social variations for their concord with evolved social motives directed to achieve genetic selfishness. Since selection has established in us the goal of attracting mates likely to maximize our genetic fitness, we seek mates with qualities that are fitness-enhancing and the psychology of mate attraction functions as the array of proximate mechanisms we use to perpetuate our genes. In the sense of such efforts, efforts not yet validated, sociobiology aims to create a New Synthesis that is both a theoretical and an empirical completion of the Darwinian revolution (for details, see 3.1).

In this research situation, the idea of completeness eventuates in the idea of a synthesis. Evolutionary biology would be complete with respect to the general scientific goal of explaining nature in terms of natural processes if it describes all significant evolutionary processes and forces so as to explain all kinds of evolutionary phenomena in need of explanation. Now, the core of evolutionary theory posits that the various types of animals and plants have their origin in other preexisting types and that the distinguishable differences are due to modifications in successive generations. It is necessary for evolutionary theory to be able to explain not only the evolution of the bodies of organisms, but also the evolution of organismic behavior. Given the work of the last fifty years following the Modern Synthesis, evolutionary theory can do this, although there are always unsolved problems to work on. So, it is almost complete.

We say "almost complete" because it must also explain the evolution of social behavior and any other evolved aspect of sociality. To do so, it takes two available bodies of information and puts them together: evolutionary theory and social data. Evolutionary theory must cohere with social data if the range of explanatory results in evolutionary biology is to be complete. The degree of success that may be achieved in carrying out this task is constituted by the degree of coherence achieved. Sociobiological reasoning is aimed at creating a synthesis of theory and data, a rational unification whereby theory and data fit together in a suitable, orderly, cohesive, logical manner.

In this way, the concept of completeness leads directly to the concept of the "new synthesis," a culmination of the Darwinian revolution, that E.O. Wilson proposed as the fundamental conception of sociobiology. This concept, as derived here, is a relatively unproblematic idea of sociobiology's scientific aim, although even an unproblematic scientific aim is sociopolitically problematic. We can accept it without being logically committed to any of Wilson's excessive claims that have been so polemically debated, although we shall expend much effort at figuring out what commitments it suggests. It is a conception of sociobiology's basic scientific aim that should be acceptable to advocates and critics of sociobiology alike, a conception pivotal for moving the examination of sociobiology well beyond the confines of the usual debate.

## The Intuitive Sense of Completeness

Intuitively, such a synthesis would consist in creating coherence between the accepted theory and the accepted data. The proper conception of the test situation essential to sociobiology's aim is radically different from the standard one found in confirmationist methodology. Normally, we think of testing theories by means of data. We know what the theory is and how it is supposed to apply to the data. We test the expectations for observation induced by the theory by making observations. The issue in question is whether old and new observations conform to or violate those expectations. However, in cases like sociobiology, we know what the theory is and we know what the data is. What we don't know is how the theory is supposed to apply to the data. We are not testing the theory, since it is already well established. What we are testing, first and foremost, are assertions about the way in which the theory is supposed to apply to the data. The expectations for observation induced by the theory are not taken as a fixed background for testing the theory. Rather, those expectations are the objects of the test. We are not theory-testing, but application-testing. The issue is whether the statements that intervene between the given theory and the given data are appropriate for creating a coherent relationship between them.

Intuitively, such coherence consists in explanatory relevance (application of theory to data in a way that creates a logical connection between them) and explanatory consistency (the statements of theory and data used in the application do not contradict one another, and so form a consistent set). If sociobiology succeeds in helping to achieve explanatory completeness, it would rule out all sources of irrelevance or inconsistency between the explanatory factors of evolutionary theory and the social data in need of explanation. Explanatory relevance would vindicate our faith in the lack of total independence of sociality from the fact, course, and processes of evolution (a distinction made in Ruse 1979). Explanatory consistency would vindicate our faith in the lack of incompatibility between social facts and evolutionary theory.

The utility of this concept will be given philosophical defense by showing that it makes sense of, focuses, and clarifies the issues surrounding sociobiology. For example, reconsider Wilson's (1975, 2) opening statement that altruism is the central problem of sociobiology, one basically solved by the new selection processes of kin and group selection. The very selection of altruism as a primary problem is motivated by its logical subordination to the goal of completeness, as is evident in the following tacit but influential research-generating reasoning. Given the many ways organisms give aid to others at their own expense, some sort of altruism is a precondition for observed animal and human sociality. Hence, a completed evolutionary theory would explain altruism. But Darwinian individual selection, understood through the theory of the Modern Synthesis of Darwinism and Mendelism, cannot explain altruism. Darwinian individual selection "helps those who help themselves." In this context, the observed altruism just doesn't make evolutionary sense; we cannot understand how it could have possibly evolved. Either the observed altruism is irrelevant to selection or it is inconsistent with selection. That is, prior to sociobiology, applications of Darwinian selection theory to altruism result in relations of irrelevance or inconsistency between statements of the explanatory factors and statements of the phenomena to be explained.

Likewise, what counts as a proper solution to the problem of altruism is constrained by the quest for completeness. If Darwinian selection theory exhausted all the selection processes of evolutionary theory, evolutionary theory would remain incomplete. So let us develop new theories of the way selection processes work and associated methods, data, concepts, and hypotheses that extend the Modern Synthesis to cover altruism so as to attain explanatory relevance and explanatory consistency. No other sort of solution would be adequate. Kin selection theory shows how behavior that benefits other organisms sharing one's genes but hurts one's own chances for reproductive success can be selected for and evolve by selection. Group selection theory shows how behavior that benefits the group but hurts one's own chances for reproductive success can be selected for and evolve by selection. The cumulative result of achieving such extensions for the main social mechanisms in the main social species would be a New Synthesis, a completion of an appropriately revised and updated Modern Synthesis.

When we appeal to the principle of completeness, we need to be sensitive to the difference between evaluating exploratory science-in-process and evaluating rigorous, established science. When Wilson treated altruism as a solved problem, he treated it as if a completed evolutionary theory were at hand. He mentioned kin and group selection. More is involved. We just reviewed the basic ideas of Darwinian individual selection, kin selection, reciprocal altruism, parental manipulation, and group selection. The relations between such processes are still being clarified. There is still little consensus on the relations between altruism and the selection processes of individual selection, kin selection, group selection, and genic (pronounced "gene-ic") selection. Some evolutionists think that all group selection involves selection for altruism toward the group. Others model group selection in ways irrelevant to altruism (recall Wright's model). Some evolutionists find that the "selfish gene" theory of selection processes has nothing to do with altruism. Others insist that all selection is ultimately genetically selfish in an evolutionary sense. Astute thinkers (Voorzanger 1984) have produced plausible arguments showing that the issue of the relevance or irrelevance of evolutionary altruism to the sorts of altruism found in human morality is quite unsettled (for details, see 3.1, 3.2, 4.2).

The debate over human sociobiology has not done justice to the character of the research situation in emerging sciences. Common preconceptions prevent behavior involving mind and culture from being regarded as a product of natural selection and genetic evolution. How can statements expressing what we know about behavior, mind, culture, natural selection, and genetic evolution be made mutually relevant and consistent? Advocates ignore manifest incompleteness, presenting initial speculations as if they were finished results, while the critics have not taken into account the stumbling nature of any new quest for completeness, expecting hypotheses to meet the standards for conclusions. Thus, to decide whether human and animal sociobiology stand or fall as sciences, we need to be clear about how to make decisions about progress toward explanatory completeness.

Judgements of progress, with or without regard to compleness, involve four levels of statements. At the base level, there are actual explanations in human (and in animal) sociobiology. We ask such questions as, "What is the biological basis of the double standard between the sexes?" This question is factually and ideologically charged, thereby setting the stage for critical comment. At the second level, there are evaluations of our answers. We ask such questions as, "Is any explanation of human reproductive behavior an acceptable scientific explanation?" This question applies norms to factual statements, the sort of question on which much of the sociobiology debate focuses. The ongoing debate cries out for clarification, setting the stage for metascientific reflection. At the third level there are applications of psychology, sociology, history, and philosophy of science to assess the institutional and epistemic condition of human sociobiology. We ask such questions as, "Does Popper's falsificationism reveal that explanations of human reproductive behavior in sociobiology are unfalsifiable, and hence unscientific?" Since there are many philosophical theories of validation to choose from, we should not take any of them for granted, thus setting the stage for critical and innovative philosophical analysis. This book, pitched mainly at the fourth level, asks such questions as, "Which theory of scientific validity, if any, employs an adequate method for assessing the research value of explanations in human sociobiology?"

The concept of completeness adds an important nuance to these questions: (1) How should evolutionary explanation be completed, eliminating apparent irrelevance or contradiction between evolutionary theory and social data? (2) Which explanations satisfy and which violate proper methodological rules, where the standards for satisfying or violating the rules take into account the fact the proposed explanations may contribute to research aimed at completeness even if they are not validated according to high standards of rigor? (3) What basic criteria of explanatory success at the core of these rules are necessary and sufficient for judging acceptability, where acceptability means an acceptable contribution toward completeness? and (4) How does each criterion fit with the totality of criteria pertinent for judging the validity and import of explanations in a science whose quest is to complete an established science but which is not itself yet established?

In order to lay the groundwork for addressing these questions, we need a better idea of what would count as a completed theoretical system in evolutionary biology.

## The Metalogical Analogue to Completeness

Logical empiricists use modern logic as a tool for making the idea of completeness clearer and more precise. Metalogic can be used as a resource for doing metascience. Perhaps we can exploit an analogy between the concept of completeness as used in modern metalogic and its use in sociobiology.

> Definition. A formal system S with language L is complete with respect to the class of all truth-functional tautologies if and only if (1) L is adequate for the expression of any truth function and (2) every tautology of L is a theorem of S.

This definition (Hunter 1971, 92) is a particularly useful definition of completeness because most logicians talk about (2) but tacitly assume (1). Logicians have proved that propositional logic is complete in this sense. The language of propositional logic is adequate for naturally representing every truth-function. Every well-formed formula of propositional logic that is a logical tautology, according to the semantics for propositional logic, can be derived as a theorem, according to the proof procedures for propositional logic. Now, the happy match between semantics and syntax exhibited by metalogic is obviously not the issue in sociobiology. However, logical empiricists customarily think of a science in terms of its observational language and its theoretical language, and they think of explanation as a relation between theory and observation. What evolutionists are after is a happy match between theory and observation.

This suggests the following way of making completeness more precise. Evolutionary theory would be complete if it could both express any evolutionarily significant fact and could explain any fact it could express. Our previous analyses of completeness in theoretic terms, historical terms, and intuitive terms supply argument-sketches for thinking that social facts are among these facts, arguments which could be filled out in response to queries and objections. These argument-sketches together with our metalogical analogy provide the following definition:

> A theoretical system T in evolutionary biology which contains an observation language O is complete with respect to the class of all evolutionarily significant social facts if and only if (1a) O is adequate for the expression of any evolutionarily significant social fact and (2a) every available fact expressed in O is or can be explained by T.

This clarifying definition calls attention to an important difference in the situations of metalogic and sociobiology. Other writers in metalogic define completeness in terms of (2) and ignore (1); they strive to prove that (2) is true, taking for granted the fact that the truth of (1) is well known. In sociobiology, both (1a) and (2a) have been ignored by advocates and critics. Both (1a) and (2a) are going to be extremely hard to prove true. And before a proof is possible, sociobiologists are going to have to work on developing the requisite theoretical system T, observation language O, and the body of observational facts to be explained by T. Since any development must make use of the evolutionary theory and social data at hand, sociobiologists have to work on extending both the observational and the theoretical languages and claims of evolutionary biology. From completeness, it follows that sociobiology's problems are problems of extension.

The present study of what is involved in such an extension reveals that the theoretical system T is going to have to be complex. To satisfy (1a), it includes explanatory theories and research programs guiding the character of the extensions of observation and theory. To satisfy (2a), it includes frameworks providing reliable (not "effective" in the metalogical sense) procedures for conceiving of what count as evolutionarily significant social facts. Without one, judgments of the form "Social Fact F has evolutionary import," are undecidable. To satisfy (1a) and (2a) jointly, it requires frameworks for conceiving the explanatory problems imposed by efforts at extension, for conceiving the extended domain of observable phenomena, for conceiving the extended array of theoretical explanatory factors that structure the subfields of the discipline, and for conceiving the role of individual pieces of explanatory work in contributing toward the extension.

To sum up, our use of the concept of completeness has led to the identification of the components of a conceptual framework proposed by this book: interconnected decisions in conceptualizing problems, domain, disciplinary structure, and performance evaluations. It has argued for the adoption of the three-unit model for evaluation proposed by this book: evaluating explanations in terms of a differentiation of the structure of theoretical systems into theories proper, research programs, and conceptual frameworks. The thesis of this chapter that completeness is the source for integrating analyses in terms of theories proper, research programs, and frameworks has been given a conceptual argument.

This view of completeness adds another view of theory structure to those in philosophy of science. At present there is some dispute over the syntactic (or: statement) views of theory structure and the semantic (or: concept) views of theory structure. A persistent point of contention has been whether theories automatically come with a fixed delimitation of their domains. It is easy to think of objections to this view of completeness based on either of these rivals. By defeating the justification of inferences of the form "If such-and-such view of theory structure is true, completeness is not a problem," that concept will be further clarified.

On the traditional "syntactic" view rooted in Carnap's logical empiricist legacy, statements of theory are to be syntactically and semantically represented in quantificational logic as partially interpreted formal calculi. The truth-values of existentially or universally quantified sentences are expressed relative to a fixed universe of discourse or domain. The theory is said to explain those observable objects in its domain by subsuming them under generalizations. Such a view might lead us to object that domains are defined by what a theory explains, and so every theory is complete. Therefore, completeness is not a real problem.

For instance, the interpretation of $(x)\,(Fx \rightarrow Gx)$ is relative to a domain of objects over which the variable x ranges. Unless theoretical predicates are interpreted, directly or indirectly using variables placed within the scope of quantifiers, sentences using those predicates have a syntax but no "empirical meaning." That is, theoretical predicates (i.e., Fx, Gx) are to be interpreted directly (i.e., Fx signifies x is male, and Gx signifies x is selected to be promiscuous) or indirectly (i.e., Fx and Gx are logically connected to other terms directly interpreted). Variables (i.e., (x)) are placed within the scope of quantifiers (Fx is bound to (x)) that range over observable objects in the theory's domain (i.e., actual organisms). We might interpret $(x)\,(Fx \rightarrow Gx)$ with respect to the domain of all evolved sexually reproducing organisms as "For each x, where x is an organism, if x is male, then x is selected to be promiscuous."

So it is objected that if a theory explains the traits of organisms, then the theory is complete with respect to the domain of organisms. However, this idea does not take account of the fact that science searches after the truth. False generalizations do not produce ideally correct explanations; only true generalizations do. If the above generalization is false, it does not enable sociobiology to completely cover its domain in the way we wish. So the objection is mistaken since we have said all along that evolutionary theory has to be made applicable to and true of sociality in social organisms in order to be complete. We do need to supplement our definition of completeness with reference to truth and standards of truth, which will be done later.

Moreover, note that mere recourse to logic does not decide the issue of how to understand theoretical completeness. In metalogic, completeness is understood, intuitively, in the sense that a complete formal system is one that would give you all the proofs you want or need. In particular, a complete formal system of quantificational logic is one from which we can derive all the tautologies (logical truths) of quantificational logic, since those are the ones we want or need to derive. So if we take our cue from metalogic rather than logic, a complete theoretical system of evolutionary biology is one from which we can derive all the evolutionarily significant facts, since those are the ones we want or need to derive.

On the recent "semantic" view, theories are represented as one or more (mathematical) model(s), each defining a kind of system (Giere 1983). The domain of applicability of that kind of system is left entirely open by the statements of theory. In a sense, the theory is not a set of statements, a set of generalizations over a observable domain at all. It is a concept, a concept of a kind of system that obeys the relationships postulated in the model. The semantic view differs from the received view on the way the empirical and the theoretical parts of a theory are related. The semantic view holds that the theory is represented without recourse to a domain since the domain is to be determined independently of the resources of the theory itself. Instead, its domain is specified according to theoretical hypotheses of the form, "such-and-such is an instance of the kind defined by the theory." The domain is specified extrinsically to the theory proper.

For instance, we can rewrite Barash's explanation as defining a kind of system, using a rough qualitative model. It defines a kind of ideal system, a population of males and females subject to natural selection on two scenarios: one with a faithful male and a promiscuous female and a second with a promiscuous male and a faithful female. It supplies a generalization about this kind of system: the fitness of males will be higher in the second scenario, that the fitness of females will be equal in both scenarios (provided the female is a mating partner with the promiscuous male), and that due to this fitness differential, males will be selected to be more promiscuous than females. Notice that this model contains reasoning, an inferential structure. In this ideal case, the selectionist result is logically derivable from the propositions about the kind of system.

This reasoning does not dictate any particular domain of application. It might apply to all species among those that reproduce sexually, to some, or to none at all. That is why theoretical hypotheses, quite independent of the theory here, are needed to suggest how to apply it. We might hypothesize that "human populations instantiate this kind of scenario." We might hypothesize that "certain nonhumans, but no humans, instantiate this kind of scenario." Or we might hypothesize that "nothing at all is an instance of this kind of scenario."

So it is objected that it makes no sense to say that a given theory of male-female differences should be applied to animals and humans in order to completely cover its domain, as it has no domain. However, we did not say that a given theory within the theoretical system of evolutionary biology should completely cover its domain. We said that the entire theoretical system of evolutionary biology itself should do so. Mere recourse to models does not decide the issue of how to understand theoretical completeness. There is no empirical point in constructing an explanatory model in the first place unless there is some data to be explained. At present there is an array of models in evolutionary biology. There are optimality models, of which Barash's model is a crude example. There are models of evolutionarily stable strategies. There are inclusive fitness models. There are models of population trajectories in population genetics. There are models of group selection, individual selection, and genic selection. And so on. Is this array of models sufficient to capture all the evolutionarily significant facts? This is a question about the adequacy of the array of models to completely cover the intended domain of evolutionary biology. The activity of modeling tacitly recognizes a range of facts that need to be explained, facts in terms of which we frame theoretical hypotheses. And that is the idea of the range of evolutionarily significant facts, an idea already incorporated into our concept of the completeness of a theoretical system.

What these arguments suggest is that the feature of theories we are concerned with here differs from a feature which divides the syntactic and semantic views of theory structure, i.e., whether the domain is intrinsic or extrinsic to the theory. We will argue from scientific practice that the determination of completeness within evolutionary theory's intended domain turns on the justification of taking something to be its intended domain. That is what the human sociobiology debate is about, e.g., whether specific human behavioral patterns of mating are properly part of the domain of evolutionary theory. A full resolution ultimately involves all four components of a conceptual framework for completing evolutionary theory with respect to sociality: problem conceptualization, domain conceptualization, discipline conceptualization, and performance conceptualization. A justifiable determination of what would count as a completed evolutionary theory with respect to sociality, and hence of whether the one we have is complete, requires us to consider the sorts of decisions we will identify as falling into these categories.

## Three Views of Explanation

Confirmationists need to decide what, exactly, we are trying to confirm in order to tell how well explanations are confirmed. Even though our definitions of explanatory completeness presuppose an understanding of what counts as an explanation in the first place, they do suggest constraints on what model of explanation is pertinent to sociobiology's research situation. Our intuitive definition suggests that a pertinent model would invoke logical conditions to establish relevance (a logical connection between statements of theory and statements of fact) and empirical conditions to establish consistency (the statements of theory, true facts about the experienced world, and their connections can be asserted together without contradiction). Our metalogical definition suggests that a pertinent model would invoke a logical derivation of the statements of fact from statements of theory.

Hempel's well-known model of explanation fulfills these desiderata, as is evident from its conditions for adequate explanations: logical derivability, lawhood, empirical content, and truth. (If there were a well-worked-out model of explanation based on the semantic view, it would have been used as well.) Indeed, our discussion of the relation between a theory and its domain led us to emphasize the condition of truth as well as the presence of inferential structure. Let us turn our attention toward Hempel's model, its relation to other views of explanation, and its utility for evaluating sociobiology.

What is a scientific explanation? Kourany (1987, 20ff) distinguishes three competing conceptions of scientific explanation. On the inferential conception, an explanation is a logical argument. On the causal conception, an explanation is a causal account. On the erotectic conception, an explanation is an answer to a why question. Of these three, logical empiricists have favored the inferential conception, as it is worked out in Hempel's model of explanation. Hempel's model has been extensively criticized, but it can be defended against many criticisms (F. Wilson 1985). In the spirit of a practical evaluator, we can ground our evaluations in Hempel's model without going on to claim that it captures the nature of explanation. By applying Hempel's model, we need not endorse the inferential conception, just restrict the model's role to that of a tool for capturing logical structure. Whatever the nature of explanation is, explanations do have an internal inferential structure.

Scientific explanations gain import for common sense when expressed as "because" answers to "Why did such-and-such happen?" or "How did such-and-such happen?" questions and their variants. However sophisticated and technical scientific language gets, we always end up relating back to everyday language in order to upgrade our common-sense explanations of things. In this sense, the root conception of an explanation, whether scientific or ordinary, is the erotectic conception. Thus, when we say that sociobiological explanations are properly evaluated in terms of theories, research programs, and conceptual frameworks, we are thinking of explanations as sets of explanatory questions and explanatory answers. In science, though not usually in everyday life, such question-answer sets have no research value unless they involve controlled observation and explicit theories.

In sociobiology, the explanatory questions are never of the vague form, "Why do we behave as we do?" Sociobiology does not explain behavior per se. It explains the evolution of behavior, that is, the evolution of behavioral preconditions (whether physical or psychological) and their effects on behavior. This limits sociobiology's scope, placing limitations on its proper implications (see 2.3, 4.3). To identify when its assertions are within its limits and when they go beyond its limits is difficult. Even the excessive claims for and against it have a useful role. In emerging sciences, scientists find out what the limits are by ambitiously going beyond them and by returning to work within them upon reflecting on devastating criticism.

Why have males and females evolved different ways of competing for and selecting mates? Because natural selection has favored different strategies of competition with members of the same sex for mates and selection of members of the opposite sex as mates. The same principles apply to insects, fish, birds, mammals, etc. Our question above is formulated using an observation language sensitive to evolutionarily significant social facts, not just social facts as given to common sense. Our answer is formulated using a theoretical language designed to explain social evolution, not social facts expressed apart from an evolutionary time scale. Sociobiology is not a novel answer to common-sense questions about behavior we already had. It alerts us to new explanatory questions and answers, deepening our understanding of social behavior by expanding the dimensions of what we take it to involve. The questions "How did X actually evolve?" or "How is X actually influenced by what did evolve?" call for how-actually explanations. Some doubt that questions of these forms could apply to humans. The more basic questions "How could X possibly evolve?" or "How could X possibly be influenced by what did evolve?" or "Given that X is mentally produced and culturally variable, how can it also be biologically evolved and genetically adaptive?" call for how-possibly explanations.

When related to the content of theoretical systems, formulations of explanations merely in terms of questions and answers do not suffice to capture their internal reasoning unless combined with formulations in terms of arguments. What makes an evolutionary "because" claim true is a reasoned relation between theory and data, one in which theory explains data. The "because" claim proclaims that there is a connection between the explaining theoretical hypothesis and the explained data. What is the connection? To identify the connection made, we need to reconstruct the internal inferential structure of the explanation.

Those thinking of the connection as a linguistic connection are thereby motivated to adopt the inferential model. Those thinking of the connection as a real connection in nature are thereby motivated to adopt the causal model. Let us construe the connection as a connection in our thought when we represent nature to ourselves. When we represent nature to ourselves, we make causal inferences whereby we draw inferences from statements of cause and effect. In this respect, there is no need to choose between the inferential and causal conceptions of explanation (Sober 1987a). Indeed, Hempel intended his model to capture causal explanation, where causal relations are expressed in terms of subsumption of events under laws. Evolutionary explanations yield causal arguments in virtue of evolutionary theory's purpose to explain transitions in population states over successive generations (for details, see 5.2). Unlike the inferential mode, the causal model denies that noncausal laws have explanatory power. It will be argued that the causal model does not capture lawful functional explanations in sociobiology, which concern capacities and dispositions rather than events (see 5.3).

The point made here is that evolutionary biologists do in fact present explanations as arguments about selective causes and evolutionary effects (Sober 1984). For example, Betzig (1988) states the core of many explanations of reproductive behavior as such an argument, with explanatory theoretical hypotheses stating relations among causal variables and the explained observational generalizations stating evolutionary effects:

> How much reproductive effort should be spent on mating or parenting depends on how much effort is devoted to each by the opposite sex (see e.g. Darwin 1871). Where the amount of parental effort offspring need stays the same, one sex may benefit by devoting more effort to mating to the extent that the other devotes more effort to parenting. This argument has been used to explain why females and males evolved: as eggs devoted more effort to nurturing offspring, sperm devoted more effort to seeking out eggs (Parker et al. 1972). In almost every case, males can benefit reproductively by mating with more than one female, while females cannot benefit by mating with more than one male (Bateman 1948). More females than males will, then, contribute to the next generation: the effect will be a polygynous breeding system; (see Daly and Wilson 1980, discussion in Wade and Arnold 1980 and Clutton-Brock 1983; reviews in Partridge and Halliday 1984 and Vehrencamp and Bradbury 1984).

In his landmark work, Hempel (Hempel and Oppenheim 1948) invoked both logical and empirical conditions of adequacy for scientific explanations in general. From a logical point of view, any explanation is associated with an argument whose premises, called the "explanans," are sentences stating what is supposed to explain the phenomena under study, and whose conclusion, called the "explanandum," is a sentence describing the phenomena to be explained. A correct scientific explanation contains reasoning that can be reconstructed as a sound argument, an argument whose premises are true and whose conclusion follows logically from the premises, where the explanans functions as the premises and the explanandum functions as the conclusion. Call this the "sound-argument model of explanatory reasoning." What bearing does the sound-argument model have on confirmationism? It has a favorable implication and an unfavorable implication for confirmationism.

The favorable implication is that appeal to Hempel's model furnishes a justification for viewing confirmation as a validity-making property. Hempel's model requires that the explanans is true. Since the derivation of the explanandum from the explanans presumably follows the truth-preserving rules of modern deductive logic, whether propositional or quantificational logic, the explanandum is true as well. Now, the obvious way to justify taking validation to depend on confirmation is to realize that what it means for an explanation to be confirmed by the evidence is for the truth of the explanation to be confirmed by the evidence. Evidence consists in facts that favor a decision about the truth-values of statements. Why should we care about confirming the truth of an explanation? Because a correct explanation is true, that is, one having both a true explanandum and a true explanans. That is why an explanation's confirmaton is crucial to its acceptability.

The unfavorable implication is that Hempel's logical empiricist model of the ideal scientific explanation shows that sociobiology's validity turns on more than evidence. The model is not epistemological in the sense that it concerns what qualifies something as a correct explanation. Even so, the model shows that confirmationism is false. Confirmationism fails to incorporate any logical condition into its conception of acceptability, but recognizes only the empirical condition of truth. Confirmationist judgements about whether sociobiology is valid or invalid recognize that explanations should be well-tested, but fail to recognize that they should also be well-articulated. To decide the latter, we need to reconstruct its internal reasoning. So we formulate it as an argument, a set of premises leading to a conclusion. A well-articulated explanation is one whose inference from premises to conclusion is deductively valid or conforms to respectable nondeductive rules of inference.

The emphasis on evidence to the exclusion of articulation inherent in confirmationism is unfortunate since matters of evidence can be decided only on the assumption that the hypothesis, or explanation, or theory being tested is clear in the first place. You need a good idea of what claims are being tested and what the logic of the reasoning that binds them together amounts to in order to decide what the test results show. Thus, appeal to the sound-argument model reveals that although confirmational success is a necessary validity-making property, it is insufficient. We need not only good reasons for thinking that the explanans and explanandum are both true, but also good reasons for thinking that they logically connected in the right way. In even stronger terms, we shall see by applying the sound-argument model to Barash's explanation that it is neither empirically confirmable or disconfirmable unless it has a surprisingly tight logical structure.

Confirmationist evaluations also fail to consider the big picture. The validity and significance of our explanations reflect the way we specify the relevant problems posed by incomplete unification, specify the relevant augmented domain, specify the relevant explanatory factors taken from available fields, and specify what results would and do count as an improvement in completeness. Decisions made in expanding and limiting the domain are reflected in the character of the explanandum. Decisions made in choosing and combining relevant explanatory factors are reflected in the character of the explanans. The explanandum and explanans were constructed to address an explanatory problem, and their evaluation will lead to reformulating that problem or identifying new ones. In this sense, the components of a conceptual framework orient the construction, revision, and evaluation of theoretical explanation. We need to evaluate explanations in terms of their conceptual context: the way we conceive explanatory problems, explanatory domains, explanatory resources, and explanatory roles in contributing to further research. Thus, one cannot adequately evaluate explanations, as answers to why questions, in terms of theories without going on to evaluate them in terms of conceptual frameworks.

Efforts at confirmation validate particular explanations. According to the definition of completeness interpreted via Hempel's model, sociobiology will do its part in completing evolutionary theory when:

> (1b) every social fact is representable by the observation language in such a way as to formulate it as an explanandum, and (2b) for every such explanandum there is an explanans based on evolutionary theory, and (3) the explanandum and explanans in each explanation satisfy appropriate logical and empirical conditions of adequacy.

Confirmationist evaluations ignore the fact that the success of sociobiology depends on cogent arguments that sociobiology is successful in achieving (1b), (2b), and (3). Success at confirmation, if divorced from success at logical structure, does not by itself give us the needed arguments.

In this way our former historical, intuitive, and metalogical definitions of explanatory completeness have been supplemented with a view of explanation that takes what is useful from the question-answer model, the causal model, and the inferential model, and lays the basis for understanding what is involved in confirming sociobiological explanations.

## 1.3 Explaining Sexual Selection: Theory and Data

### The Illogic of Explanation

Confirmationists will ask what the application of the sound-argument model reveals about the explanations sociobiologists propose. Hempel's model tells us that unless an explanandum is logically tied to a true explanans stating regularities and initial conditions, no actual fact has been explained. This is typically the case in sociobiology. Barash's explanation is chosen as a simple example to make general points that hold for better versions and for other explanations.

Let's reconstruct the logic of Barash's explanation of why males generally, though not always, have more mates than females, despite tremendous variation among species in how males and females come together to produce offspring. A conclusion about mating patterns is to be derived from evolutionary premises. Premise one: A faithful male paired with a promiscuous female may not bear offspring since she may conceive offspring by means of other males. Premise two: But a faithful female paired with a promiscuous male will always bear his offspring, provided he includes her in his mating partners. Intermediate conclusion: So, it pays in an evolutionary sense for males but not for females to be promiscuous. (It is unclear whether this is about conception, child bearing, or child caring.) Final conclusion: Hence, males are relatively promiscuous compared to females.

Because it is abstracted from particular species, this argument entails no conclusion about mate choice in any particular species. To deduce either specific facts or regularities of human mating, theoretical and observational assumptions must be added. The logical gap opens the door to criticism.

Hempel's first logical condition of acceptability is that "the explanandum must be a logical consequence of the explanans" (1948, 31). The argument generates an inference from the first two premises, which state facts linking physiology and behavior, to the third premise, which makes a claim about adaptive significance (fitness). Here is a pertinent set of assumptions for justifying this inference: sex-roles are universal and do not vary essentially within or between species and do not differ from gender roles; complete faithfulness or complete promiscuity are the only available strategies; the case of both partners being promiscuous or faithful need not be considered; the adaptive value of these behaviors is independent of other parental investment such as parental care and independent of environmental variation; there are no other beneficial or costly results of these traits or trade-offs with other traits in promoting reproductive success; the adaptive value of these behaviors is independent of cultural influence and independent of whether the human society is hunting-gathering, pastoral, nomadic, agricultural, industrial, or highly technological. If any of these assumptions is false, the inference from sexual dimorphism to differential adaptiveness of promiscuity is blocked. All these assumptions are false, that is, inconsistent with known facts and theory.

This set of assumptions is sufficient to close the logical gap. Some assumption in each category is necessary to close the gap. Whether these specific assumptions are necessary is debatable. If unnecessary, the falsity of these assumptions does not render the explanation false. However, the explanation is indefensible in the absence of further articulation that includes local (even "nonbiological") conditions in the explanation itself.

Another tacit assumption or set of assumptions is needed to deduce the conclusion, which refers to actual behavior patterns, from the premises, which refer to hypothetical situations. Barash (1979, 25) presents it earlier, since he uses it in all his explanatory hypotheses: "A guiding principle of sociobiology is that individuals tend to behave in a manner that maximizes fitness." Since statements of tendencies do not imply that all actual cases conform to the generalization, one cannot deduce that "humans behave so as to maximize fitness" but at most "probably, humans behave so as to maximize fitness." But this is an "adaptationist" assumption, i.e., it ignores all the situations known to interfere with fitness maximization.

The conclusion holds: only insofar as genes are the most significant biological factor on sexuality, only insofar as genes have phenotypic effects contoured by natural selection, only insofar as the selection of alternative alleles motivates individuals to act optimally with respect to genetic fitness, only insofar as other factors of evolutionary change such as random genetic drift do not interfere with the maximization of average fitness in the evolving population over many generations, and insofar as selection at levels of organization other than the individual organism do not interfere with the effects of individual selection. Current consensus in evolutionary biology has it that each of these assumptions about evolutionary processes is often violated in nature! Barash has not investigated any of them to find out whether they happen to hold in the case of human mating practices.

What has gone wrong? Hempel's model reveals that one must combine (lawlike) generalizations with statements of initial (antecedent) conditions in order to derive statements of particular facts. Barash's "derivation of the double standard" is no derivation at all since it omits the antecedent conditions, expressed by a complex array of auxiliary assumptions. If we had used the semantic or definitional model of explanation, we would express the same point in different terms. We would say that the organisms to which Barash applies his theoretical model of male-female differences are not instances of the kind specified in the theory, and so his theoretical hypotheses are false. Either way, the basic statement under test, "this is how to apply evolutionary theory to male-female differences" is false, for the application is full of logical holes.

Hempel's second logical condition is that "the explanans must contain general laws, and these must actually be required for the derivation of the explanandum" (1948, 31). There is much debate over whether biology contains laws and over what makes a statement lawlike. Let us finesse this issue with the liberal interpretation that includes strict laws, probabilistic and universal generalizations, and general statements about processes. This is why we are treating Hempel's model as the "sound-argument model," rather than as "the covering-law model." Barash's explanation invokes generalizations about the adaptive significance of sex-typical mating behavior and general statements governing evolutionary processes. But he does not distinguish (a) general statements about how selection works to guide evolutionary change from (b) singular statements about contingent events in the past involving fitness, selection, genotypes, and phenotypes during the evolutionary past. The explanation violates both the conditions of derivability and lawlikeness. The price is that no actual fact is explained! Yet he applies his "insight" directly to a host of species, claiming to explain the diversity as variants of adaptive behavior maintained by selection. Falling far short of that, the explanation's role is to say how it is possible that males generally have more mates than females.

We must add to his "insight" the initial conditions and generalizations needed to infer actual behavior patterns from what behavioral differences would be favored by selection in idealized situations. (Or, we must recast it as an explanation of higher-order generalizations where boundary conditions play a logical role analogous to initial conditions.) At least the initial conditions vary from species to species. This omission of initial conditions, stating the cumulative results of all the forces governing evolutionary change as they operate in divergent historical circumstances, makes the explanation verge on a direct derivation of facts from a seeming universal law of nature. This omission prompts critics to call it a "just-so" story. Instead, the idealization is characteristic of how-possibly explanations, which provide the basis for constructing how-actually explanations: when the gaps in how-possibly explanations are filled in, they turn into how-actually explanations (Brandon 1990; see also 4.1). Only then are actual behaviors explained.

Hempel's third logical condition is that "the explanans must have empirical content; i.e., it must be capable, at least in principle, of test by experiment or observation" (1948, 31). The testability condition is implicit in the derivability condition. The explanans has empirical content only if sentences expressing the results of observation or experiment are derivable from the explanans. Since the derivability condition is violated, it has no empirical content; the explanatory claim is not yet testable. It is not confirmable, and hence, not testable in the sense of a formal account of empirical content.

Hempel's sole empirical condition of adequacy is that "the sentences constituting the explanans must be true" (1948, 31). He requires that the explanans must be true rather than merely well confirmed in order to capture adequacy conditions for correct explanations (modeled as sound arguments). False explanations don't really explain, even if confirmed. Do we have sufficient reason to think that the explanation is true, that is, to judge that the sentences constituting the explanans are sufficiently confirmed? No, the auxiliary assumptions needed for the deduction are dubious or false.

## Explanation and Prediction

Hempel's model adopts the symmetry thesis, a demanding requirement on explanation: the argument used to rationally reconstruct the explanation could serve equally as well to predict the phenomena as to explain the phenomena. Explained phenomena are shown to be expected by inference from the explanatory facts. The symmetry thesis is controversial. Two related intuitions favor the symmetry thesis: (a) The fact that in explanations the phenomena are already known whereas in predictions the phenomena are not yet known does not make a difference for the quality of the inference; (b) If the explanatory premises lead to the expectation of an occurrence but do not rule out incompatible occurrences by their logical structure, we won't know why that occurrence rather than an incompatible one took place.

With respect to (a), the activities of explaining and predicting are different, as many objections to the symmetry thesis show. The symmetry thesis is not invoked here as a conception of the nature of explanation, but as a constraint on the reasoning in an ideal explanation. Although we can often correctly identify the cause of an event only after the event occurred, and could not have predicted it beforehand, this does not refute the symmetry thesis. Merely identifying the cause does not qualify as a well-reasoned explanation. Unless we can identify the cause and the contextual conditions that enable us to infer the statement(s) describing the effect from the statement(s) describing the causal scenario, we have not understood why the causal connection in fact obtained, and thus we have not understood why the event did happen rather than not happen at all.

We can use metalogic to develop this point. A formal system is simply consistent if we cannot derive both a sentence and its negation from it. Analogously, a theoretical system is explanatorily consistent if none of its explanatory techniques are such that they could both explain a fact taken to be evolutionarily significant and an incompatible fact. One purpose of the symmetry thesis is to rule out explanatory inconsistency by creating a sufficient condition for ruling out explanations of fact F and of fact not-F using the very same set of explanatory resources. Thus, we want from sociobiology a theoretical system that is both explanatorily complete and explanatorily consistent with respect to sociality.

Now apply this point to the proposed unification of animal and human sociality with each other and with the rest of evolution that constitutes explanatory completeness. To judge whether the unification of the facts of animal and human behavioral diversity is genuine or spurious, we reconstruct the explanatory arguments associated with theoretical explanations. The connection between theory and facts found in genuine unification satisfies the symmetry thesis; if not, it is spurious. Barash's insight may correctly identify a causal source of evolved male-female differences. That is a necessary first step, not an achievement of explanatory unification.

We can understand the motivation for the symmetry thesis as part of the logical empiricist view that scientific explanations are empirical in character. Even though theories cannot be logically reduced to statements of observations, theories induce expectations that make an observational difference. The symmetry thesis makes sense of how we use observations to confirm scientific explanations. Think of various levels of generalizations: theoretical generalizations, involving the forces of evolutionary change, and empirical generalizations, involving observed patterns of sociality. Further, picture a hierarchy of statements of increasing generality and distance from experience ranging from bottom to top: particular observed facts at the bottom, empirical generalizations above, and theoretical generalizations on top. Explanation, on the sound-argument model, moves inferentially from the top down, using suitable auxiliary statements: the observed facts follow from the theory, assuming the theory is true. Evidence, as confirmation, moves inferentially from the bottom up, using suitable auxiliary statements: the theory's truth follows from the truth of the observed facts. The symmetry thesis makes explanation and confirmation coincide in this way since we confirm an explanatory theory by confirming its observable predictive consequences. Although there is no adequate formal account of empirical content, this is a useful account of a formal feature of empirical content.

Do all scientific explanations have predictive content that rules some observations in and others out? Evolutionary explanations are confirmed mainly by applying the comparative method to natural (and, sometimes, laboratory) populations. Exit the myth that "the scientific method" is only "the experimental method." Barash (1982, 37) distinguishes four kinds of explanations resulting from four approaches that use the comparative method: historical, evaluative, correlational, and predictive.

Explanations resulting from the historical approach explain by identifying behavioral phylogenies, reconstructing the evolutionary history of the behavior. Historical explanations are tested against evidence about the chronology of events during the evolutionary past. Explanations constructed by the evaluative approach explain by evaluating the adaptive significance of observed behavior patterns. Evaluative explanations are tested against evidence about the genetic causes and reproductive effects of the behavior. Explanations formulated with the aid of the correlational approach explain by correlating behaviors and environments and determining the correlation's adaptive significance. Correlational explanations are tested against evidence about the match between behavior and environment. Explanations formulated as a result of the predictive approach explain by starting with a general theoretical postulate. Predictive explanations are tested against evidence about the expectations induced by applying the theoretical postulate to the case at hand.

Barash's scheme suggests that some evolutionary explanations lack predictive content, being designed to explain particular facts in their particularity rather than to unify them under generalizations. If so, either they are unscientific or the symmetry thesis is not universally true. In any case, Barash's explanation of the double standard is a how-possibly predictive explanation, based on his postulate (1982, 42) that "when a behavior under study reflects some component of genotype, animals should behave so as to maximize their inclusive fitness." Hence, we are justified in taking Hempel's adequacy conditions to apply to such explanations, but only in capturing what it takes to transform a how-possibly into a how-actually explanation. An explanation is well-tested only if it is confirmed by the sort of evidence pertinent to the kind of explanation it is. Evidence for how-possibly explanations is only supposed to make them plausible, not true (see 2.2, 4.1).

Moving to intuition (b), Salmon (1984) has objected, roughly, as follows: (1) Suppose that to explain an event is to render it expected; (2) We cannot predict unexpected events; (3) So, the symmetry thesis entails that probabilistic theories cannot explain anything. This argument falsely assumes that improbable events are unexpected. Since some events are probable only if other events are improbable, probabilistic theories lead us to expect that probable events occur and to expect that improbable events occur in proportion to their relative probabilities in the long run. Suppose trait A gives its carriers a greater probability of reproductive success than does trait B. We expect the frequency of A to increase on the average relative to B according to the selective differential (1 minus s). In the simplest case, take an indefinitely large number of populations all with allele frequencies of A 1/2 and B 1/2. Let all the populations run for a very long time compared to generation time. In a random sample of populations, we expect the frequency of A to increase on the average relative to B, other things being equal, (an average decrease is an incompatible occurrence). Due to our physical inability to do experiments over evolutionary time scales for most of the social species we study, we make predictions about frequencies in a large number of species. Studies of interfering factors using the comparative method decide whether expectations are met. Betzig's explanation leads us to expect polygynous breeding systems in species where males benefit more from multiple mates and females benefit more from single mates. Barash's explanation leads us to conclude that "males are expected to be sexually less discriminating, more aggressive and more available than females."

The anecdotal style of Barash's popularized presentation of the whole range of sociobiological explanations precludes any detailed elaboration of his explanation that would render it well-articulated and well-tested. As pop sociobiology, we don't expect it to satisfy Hempel's conditions of proper explanation or confirmation. Hence, the well-warranted initial reaction to explanations like Barash's was that human sociobiology is long on theory but short on evidence. Hempel's conditions, and the symmetry thesis they embody, do indicate what has to be done to turn what he rightly called only an "insight" into a correct, well-reasoned scientific explanation.

Let us grant that the sound-argument model and the symmetry thesis characterize an ideal of explanation difficult to achieve and so often not achieved in science. Should we give up the ideal? Not at all. First, it is the nature of ideals that we fall short of them. Second, reference to the ideal helps us point out flaws, which we recognize as shortcomings independent of the ideal, e.g., the false assumptions behind Barash's explanation. Correcting efforts that bring us closer to the ideal are often recognized as improvements independently of the ideal, e.g., finding better assumptions. Third, the kind of explanations Barash and other sociobiologists have proposed are notoriously ad hoc; whatever the facts happen to be, one can always invent an evolutionary explanation for them. Typically, ad hoc explanations have a loose logical structure. It is highly unlikely that we could routinely construct explanations that both are viciously ad hoc and also satisfy the ideal. If we strive to achieve an alternate ideal of explanation whereby we freely violate the symmetry thesis, remain unable to predict the phenomena purported to be explained, and fail to logically derive the allegedly explained facts from the theory, then we are setting ourselves up for ad hoc explanations that we could construct whatever the facts are.

In sum, the sound argument model can be, within limits, motivated and defended. So the explanations that violate the model are shown to be invalid as how-actually explanations, relatively independently of evidence. Still, those explanations are valuable as how-possibly explanations in initial stages of development of the field, as ways of countering irrelevance arguments (Brandon 1990, 184). Confirmationists often miss these points.

## Kinds of Confirming Evidence

Ruse (1979) distinguishes three kinds of positive evidence for explanations in sociobiology: direct, analogical, and indirect.

By "direct evidence" he means "evidence that might be obtained of the genetic control of social behavior by immediate reference to and experiments upon humans" (127). Of course, it is morally wrong and technically difficult to obtain evidence that genes control such human behavioral differences as "males compete and females select" and "males are sexually less discriminating, more aggressive and more available than females." So the direct evidence is nil or weak, as Ruse and most evaluators agree. According to Mill's and Hume's account of scientific method, a causal hypothesis is unjustified if we cannot identify the cause independently of the effect. By this standard, sociobiological hypotheses are unjustified. However, the standard is inappropriate. It would rule out the justifiability of any theory that postulated theoretical (or: unobservable) causes. It would rule out much of experimental method in physics, which concerns unobservable microentities. It would rule out much of evolutionary biology, anthropology, and history, which concern technically unobservable causes in the past. That is why direct evidence, although proper when available, is unnecessary. Instead, the standards for confirmation are to be suited to the comparative method.

The reason the lack of direct evidence creates problems in human but not in animal sociobiology is that an obvious alternative explanation exists for human behavioral differences but not for most other species, namely, mind and culture as separated from biology. This fact bears out the point that judgements of evidential success involve more than a two-place relation between the explanation tested and the data, namely, a many-place relation involving all available rival explanations. If rivals are not considered, as often done in popularized reports about sociobiology's revolutionary breakthrough in understanding human nature, then the conformity of data to the explanation tested has little confirmational power.

By "analogical evidence" Ruse means evidence that permits one to "argue legitimately from the animal world to the human world" (141–2). Barash's (1979) book is full of animal-human comparisons. Even though basic theory spans animals and humans, the specific applications to humans are chosen in virtue of analogies with allegedly similar behaviors in animals. Ruse makes the point that "inasmuch as one has relevant similar properties one has a stronger analogy and inasmuch as one has relevant dissimilar properties one has a weaker analogy." Now, many people think that there is no evolved biological behavioral basis for what we do and that all human behavioral differences of the sort with which Barash is concerned are due to mind and culture. In the idiom of completeness, they don't think that a completed evolutionary theory would have to explain these behavioral differences, presuming that biology is irrelevant to them. Since the goodness of an analogy presupposes relevance and since relevance is denied, it follows that none of the analogies presented in pop sociobiology are evaluated as good ones. Thus, no one who thinks this way would ever be impressed or persuaded by the analogical evidence, no matter how detailed and extensive.

That is why so many critics view the comparisons lurid and laughable, where the alleged similarities are category mistakes. The anthropomorphic misapplication of human behavioral categories to animals (e.g., duck "rape," elephant seal "harems") destroys the objectivity of animal sociobiology's observation language. The misapplication of animal cause-effect categories to humans destroys the objectivity of human sociobiology's theoretical language (e.g., claims that our genes cause male promiscuity and female faithfulness reflect "genetic determinist ideology, not the facts"). The practitioners can challenge such critics to prove their assumption that mind and culture make biology irrelevant to human sociality in a way that precludes any legitimate sociobiology. But the critics have never done so in any way that persuades the practitioners because they haven't delivered a satisfying alternative picture of the way human sociality relates to evolutionary processes. Given this stalemate, the issue, "Can evolutionary theory be complete without applying to humans in the ways sociobiologists claim?" remained unsolved.

By "indirect evidence" Ruse means "the kind of evidence that one has for a theory when it leads to true predictions or implications." Although such evidence was scant when Ruse wrote his (1979) book, there is now a respectable and growing body of evidence. The explanation has been tested against improved cross-species comparative evidence (Daly and Wilson 1983; Eible-Eiblesvelt 1989) and improved cross-cultural evidence (Symons 1979; Betzig, Borgerhoff Mulder, and Turke 1988).

A strong case can be made only by combining all the types of relevant evidence with strong research programs. Brandon (1990, 165) identifies five kinds of information found in an ideally complete adaptation explanation:

(1) Evidence that selection has occurred, that is, that some types are better adapted than others in the relevant selective environment (and that this has resulted in differential reproduction); (2) an ecological explanation of the fact that some types are better adapted than others; (3) evidence that the traits in question are heritable; (4) information about the structure of the population from both a genetic and selective point of view, that is, information about patterns of gene flow and patterns of selective environments; and (5) phylogenetic information concerning what has evolved from what, that is, which character states are primitive and which are derived.

Research programs in which gene-behavior links are mediated by a complex psychology typically regard these types as behavioral preconditions, not behaviors. But behavior remains crucial; behavioral preconditions which do not lead to successful reproductive behavior, on average, would be selected against.

## Statistical Evidence

Actually, what we have called "Barash's explanatory insight" or "Barash's explanation" is not supposed to be something that explains behavior all by itself, but is only the citation of a well-known explanatory factor. It expresses the theory that mate-selection strategies of males and females reflect the fact that males can produce offspring by means of the bodies of multiple females at the same time whereas females can produce offspring only in their own body. Although this selection pressure would lead to males having more sexual partners than females, other counteracting selection pressures could lead to quite different results. In any case, Barash (1979, 74) combined that theory with a theory that three concerns govern the mate-selection strategies of females. One is genetic quality (the mate has the best possible genes to combine with her own). A second is access to resources (the mate gives her access to the best possible combination of food, defense against predators, protection from other males, and so on). A third is behavioral tendencies (the mate behaves in ways that help provide food for offspring, defend offspring against predators, teach offspring how to survive, and so on). Males are not free to pursue their own mate-selection strategy regardless of female choice but must mold their behavior to fit female preferences. The observed evolutionary effects reflect various compromises.

Sexual selection theory leads us to expect that behavior will not reflect any single selection pressure. It will reflect the complex interaction of many selection pressures in historical circumstances that involve many other items affecting evolution. For instance, the theory that each organisms's reproductive effort is divided into mating and parenting effort predicts that actual behavior reflects the interaction of both sorts of selection pressures. Because we cannot observe evolution in the sense of making observations that span significant trends on an evolutionary time scale, we cannot know the numerical values of the theoretical variables and parameters which determine the relative effectiveness of each selection pressure in nature. This is no failure on the part of evolutionary biology, but a consequence of being the sort of organisms we are. Sociobiology, like other areas of evolutionary biology, will remain a theoretical science in the sense that we are in no position to obtain the sort of evidence we need to definitively confirm the sort of complex selectionist explanations of social behavior ultimately developed from simplistic insights. Historical explanations remain speculative.

Betzig (1988) summarizes the evidence gathered over the last decade, which offers statistically significant generalizations based on carefully constructed quantitative studies in human mating patterns. In the idiom of completeness, this data base extends the observation language and observation statements of evolutionary biology so that it can apply consistently and relevantly to the human species. Unlike the earlier popularizations, it identifies evolutionarily significant human social behaviors and patterns largely without using animal-human comparisons.

The selection theory tested states that, although both males and females have evolved to compete with members of the same sex for members of the opposite sex and to choose members of the opposite sex for certain traits, males and females have different strategies of competition and choice. Here are the theoretical generalizations. Males are selected to compete for as many females as possible ("promiscuity"), to compete so as to exclude others from resources needed to raise the children of other males and to acquire resources needed to raise their own children, and to choose women according to indicators of their potential success in bearing and raising children. Females are selected to compete for as few males as possible ("faithfulness"), to compete so as to exclude other females from males and to keep males for themselves, and to choose males according to indicators of their potential for providing quality genes, access to resources, or behaviors that enhance success in bearing and raising children.

Betzig finds good confirmation in the comparative studies she reviews for each of these predictive implications for the human case: male/female differences in mating behavior robust over a wide variety of historical, cultural, social, and ecological contexts; the reproductive significance of these differences; and the specific adaptive strategies previously postulated by the theory. The human subjects studied run the gamut: contemporary Americans, fifteenth-century Portuguese elite, Persian Yomut Turkmen, Venezuelan Yanomamo, rural Trinidadans, Paraguayan Ache foragers, Micronesian Ifaluk, nineteenth-century Utah Mormons, twentieth-century Kenyan Kipsigis, modern Iranians, Nigerians, African Ife, New Guinea Highlanders, rural Bangladesh, and so on.

These studies support the following empirical generalizations about male-male competition: (1) "Men with fewer resources may be more likely to undertake risk, in order to increase their access to resources, or, more directly, to women"; (2) "Measures of success in male-male competition, including dominance, status, and wealth, positively correlate with measures of reproductive success, including fertility to date, age-specific or completed fertility, and mechanisms promoting fertility"; (3) "Dominance, status and wealth have all been positively associated with a variety of mechanisms promoting men's reproductive success, including number of serial or simultaneous conjugal unions, number of reported extramarital liaisons, age at first marriage or reproduction, spouse's age at first reproduction, interbirth intervals, longevity, offspring survival, and probability of cuckoldry"; (4) "The correlation most often demonstrated has been between measures of success in male-male competition and number of (legitimate or illegitimate) conjugal unions" (Betzig 1988, 4–6).

These studies support the following empirical generalizations about male and female choice of mates: (5) "Women choose men for the provisions they offer"; (6) "Dominant men successfully sequester the youngest, and 'prettiest' women", since "attractiveness in women might signal youth, health, and other important components of reproductive potential"; (7) "Men choose faithful mates," since faithfulness enhances paternity confidence; (8) "Men with a lot to offer choose wives for various indices of reproductive potential, especially youth and lack of children by another spouse" (Betzig 1988, 6–8).

Evaluators should assess the body of decisions that lead to these generalizations. How? Our previous discussion shows that each supporting study must be examined individually with a close, detailed, thorough analysis of whether the logic of its argument is sufficient to yield rigorous connections between theory and data. In addition, tests of explanatory hypotheses carry their own characteristic points of evaluation.

Since we used an example about mating previously, let's pick one about parenting. Inclusive fitness, roughly, is one's fitness as calculated by factoring into one's reproductive output both one's own offspring and the offspring of others who share one's genes. In this way, aid to relatives can be seen to enhance one's inclusive fitness even if it detracts from one's personal fitness. Turke tested the hypothesis that "daughters born early in their parents' reproductive careers serve, at least for a time, as helpers at the nest (1988 173)." Turke's work, like the other work in this book, exemplifies good science in the sense that it makes its case with great methodological sensitivity. It attempts to justify its decisions about: (a) the theory employed (review of inclusive fitness theory in general, relation of the hypothesis to be tested to that theory, description of the circumstances in which offspring and parents maximize inclusive fitness by turning help to parents into greater parental reproductive output), (b) the method of data collection (descriptions of the Ifaluk site, of how interviews were used to collect demographic and genealogical data, of how participant observation and behavioral scans were used to collect behavioral data and compute fitness benefits/costs, measurement of reproductive success), and (c) the test results (claims of statistical significance, identification of proximate mechanisms, reasons against rival hypotheses, generalizability).

Consider just one facet of statistical significance. The hypothesis is said to be confirmed by the data that the total reproductive success of women who bore two daughters (DD) first is significantly greater than that of women who bore two sons first (SS), and both are significantly greater than that of women who bore either a daughter first and a son second (DS) or a son first and a daughter second (SD). Differences involving the sex of the helping juvenile are expected from facts about the particular culture (daughters live in the parents' home throughout life, whereas sons leave the home). The explanation incorporates facts about different life styles of males and females particular to the culture studied and does not try to derive them directly from "biology," as critics who charge "sexism" assume. Standard error equals the standard deviation divided by the square root of the number (45) in the sample: DD (.6), DS (.6), SD (.4), SS (.3). Correcting for standard error, the upper and lower bounds are: DD (8.86 + or − .6 = 9.44; 8.26), DS (6.93 + or − .6 =

7.53,6.33), SD (4.87 + or − .4 = 5.27; 4.47), (DD (5.09 + or − .3 = 5.39; 4.79). Statistical significance is upheld.

As expected, some of the studies are more rigorous than others, each having its good points and bad points. Recognition of flaws in recent results does not diminish the obvious fact that confirmation has improved and so progress has been made. This raises the issue of what determines judgements of whether there is "sufficient confirmation," not just "some confirmation," the topic of the next section. And other problems will be addressed later, such as the fact that we might expect the generalizations to be true even if the sexual selection theory employed is false. Suppose the reason why parents with helping daughters have more offspring is that they have more free time and in their free time they decide to copulate more often. Would that count against or in favor of sexual selection theory? That depends on the way one conceives the relation between biology and culture, genes and mind.

Our discussion of kinds of evidence and of the statistical evidence mitigates against (purely) confirmationist methodologies. Even good evidence for or against an explanatory hypothesis is unpersuasive and will probably not change the minds of advocates or critics if they think in terms of the viewpoints of rival research programs. Ironically, although critics chide sociobiology on the basis of its lack of evidence, improved evidence is unlikely to provoke their endorsement of sociobiology. This is one reason why the sociobiology debate has resulted in a stalemate. To extract ourselves from this stalemate, we need to direct evaluation explicitly to research programs. If you are committed to evaluating explanations in terms of evidence in relation to theories, then you are also committed to push your evaluation to locate its presumptions pertinent to research programs concerning biology and culture, genes and mind.

## Implications

We will conclude by drawing some lessons that combine our use of Hempel's model of explanation to examine Barash's explanation of mating patterns and our use of Betzig's anthology to illustrate the state of the evidence for similar explanations of mating and parenting patterns.

Hempel's model of explanation is particularly informative because it shows that whether a sociobiological explanation is well-articulated or well-tested is intimately related. The derivability condition is a way of capturing the criterion that correct explanations be well-articulated. The empirical adequacy condition states the rationale for requiring that correct explanations be well-tested. Application of the model to sociobiology reveals a novel respect in which Hempel's conditions for finished science suggest imperatives for science-in-process. When we improve logical structure by filling in logical gaps with appropriate auxiliary assumptions, the assumptions should be confirmed independently of the cases said to be explained by the explanation. Independent confirmation is a standard practice in scientific modeling, an additional constraint on confirmational success. The studies Betzig reports would have to be examined for independent confirmation and a representative variety of instances.

The specific manner in which Barash's explanation violates Hempel's conditions of adequacy supports the conception of completeness previously developed. Explanatory consistency and explanatory relevance between evolutionary theory and human social data were not achieved. Why not? Lacking appropriate initial conditions, it violates derivability. Since derivability is a logical condition of relevance, its violation reveals the irrelevance of theory to data. Suppose we add the tacit assumptions needed to satisfy derivability. Since they connect general processes to actual patterns by appeal to false generalizations, they violate lawhood, which makes the theory and data inconsistent. So either irrelevance or inconsistency remain. Due to the generality of the type of assumptions, this result holds generally.

To generalize, sociobiology faces a serious dilemma: if the data can be derived from the theory, at least one false assumption is typically present (explanatory inconsistency with known facts and theory), but if all the assumptions are true, the data typically cannot be derived from theory (explanatory irrelevance to known facts). Hence, explanations like Barash's in these respects may reduce but do not eliminate obstacles to unification. Recent statistical work on human reproductive behavior improves the amount of confirmation for empirical generalizations, but these are not shown to follow from the theory plus antecedent conditions. Without all the needed intervening assumptions, inferences from theory to facts make the theoretical explanations unempirical and data supporting empirical generalizations are not empirical tests of the explanatory theory!

The evaluation of evidence itself turns on the extent to which the explanations have an appropriate logical structure. What we have is empirical generalizations establishing relations between behaviors and their expected or actual effects on reproductive success. In the absence of the theories tested, we would expect that some such relations obtain; of course reproductive success is not random with respect to all categories of behaviors. Confirmational power lies in confirming that the specific relations which actually occur as cross-cultural regularities are the specific relations that are expected on the basis of evolutionary theory, and not expected without it. What these extensions of evolutionarily significant observations do not tell us is in what conditions we should expect human behavior to be adaptive and to what extent those conditions are fulfilled in actual populations. This is the role of auxiliary assumptions used to deduce the prediction. The fact that the evidence seems to show behavior to be adaptive is not telling unless the theories tested contain sound explanatory arguments that satisfy the symmetry thesis through the use of true auxiliary assumptions. Thus, confirmationist methodology fails to adequately evaluate the validity of the explanations when it bypasses logical structure.

None of the explanations produced in human sociobiology so far, strictly speaking, manage to satisfy all the logical and empirical conditions for well-reasoned, correct explanations. If future explanations are to more closely approximate the ideal, the name of the game is to work on the auxiliary assumptions and intervening variables that bridge basic theory and observed behavioral patterns. A key to success is to find the right auxiliary assumptions for jointly achieving consistency and relevance.

Nevertheless, human sociobiology has progressed. It started from simple popular edicts about the double standard, which are suggestive, entertaining, and ideologically provocative but lack any confirmational success. It has arrived at more refined versions of the same explanation, which are given some confirmation by both qualitative and quantitative cross-species and cross-cultural studies. Thus, it is false that "there is no evidence whatsoever" for explanations in human sociobiology. But improved evidence is not enough. Acceptability turns on logical structure internal to explanations in addition the external relation they bear to the experienced world.

# 1.4 Standards of Evidence and Human Nature

## The Politics of Accepting Explanations

Suppose the explanations of human mating behavior were revised so that they satisfy all appropriate conditions of logical structure. Many philosophical arguments have shown that, for any scientific theory, no amount of evidence is sufficient for logically proving it true; there is always some conceivable way in which the positive evidence could be true and yet the theory be false. This unnerving situation is known as "the underdetermination of theory by data." Biologists rightly don't expect evolutionary theory or particular evolutionary explanations to be subject to logical proof, i.e., their truth is never uniquely determined or guaranteed by the data. Rival explanations that seem to fit the data are always possible. The studies Betzig reports argue that the hypotheses tested are better confirmed than the particular rival hypotheses they consider plausible.

In what conditions, if any, is the observational evidence sufficient to validate an explanation in human sociobiology as acceptable? Both advocates and critics claim that sociobiology is a theory of human nature. Here we find an intrusion of politically explosive views of human nature into science. We will critically examine the use of politically explosive views of human nature as reasons or standards for accepting explanations.

A purported strength of confirmationism is that it directs us not to succumb to the temptation to rely on political preferences. When political preferences and evidence conflict, evidence gives the stronger argument. Ideology, it seems, has loomed large in the acceptance and rejection of sociobiological explanations of gender differences. Advocates who hold male chauvinist ideas about innate gender roles reason from political premises to the acceptability of Barash's explanation. Human sociobiology has been adopted by The New Right, The National Front, and other conservative groups (Beckwith 1981–82). The *New York Times* cited sociobiology as showing that biology places limits on change toward sexual equality (Gould 1980). Barash's pop sociobiology (1979) may not be actively sexist, advocating social inequality for women, but it is passively sexist, paving the way for uncritical adoption and sexist misinterpretation of evolutionary explanations (as exposed by Bleier 1984). The following extreme example should document this point and display in no uncertain terms the continuing vulgar abuse of science that causes so much uproar, rage, and passionate denunciation of sociobiology.

The *Playboy* articles (Morris 1980; Hutchison 1990) exploit science to justify sexist preconceptions: its inevitable and right for men but not for women to cheat on their sexual partners. Morris writes about male promiscuity: "Some men invoke the double standard: A man's got to do what a man's got to do; its natural." Then he "justifies" such vulgar excuses by invoking Barash's explanation: "Males are also driven by their genes to reproduce: They tend to be more promiscuous because, in the past, that was their best way to reproduce the most offspring. If you get caught fooling around, don't say the Devil made you do it. It's the devil in your DNA."

Morris's title caption blares: "It has been said that a man will try to make it with anything that moves—and a woman won't. Now the startling new science of sociobiology tells us why." Hutchison follows Morris in citing scientific evidence and hypotheses against "feminists pursuing sexual equality": differential brain chemistry (serotonin, testosterone) creates men's stronger sex drive, the proximate mechanism for carrying out evolutionary imperatives that make men the seekers and women the gatekeepers of sex. The language has been cleaned up in the years from 1980 to 1990, but the sexist message remains. We saw that a host of assumptions are needed to apply the basic theory of mate selection to the data. The popularizations overlook the need to justify the auxiliary hypotheses. Instead, they hastily substitute the first applications that come to mind for careful work on case-specific differences in intervening assumptions and antecedent conditions. Morris admits: "men may be more promiscuous than women, but they are extremely unpromiscuous in comparison with virtually every other type of male animal. The love-'em-and-leave-'em strategy is effective for most species, but not for men. Sometime after our ancestors split off from the other primates, males who tended to love and stay must have begun to produce more offspring than those who loved and left."

These examples epitomize the sense in which sociobiology reflects and perpetuates sexist ideology. Any science can be used to support the status quo. Whether the science of sociobiology is being abused or whether sociobiology is an abuse of science remains unclear. In emerging sciences, where speculation is rampant and their status as science is at issue, the temptation to construct explanations reinforcing prior views of human nature is hard to resist. Sociobiology does not tell us what human nature is; we have to already know what human nature is in order to explain its origin. One version of an explanation is used to explain/justify male promiscuity, another to explain/justify male faithfulness.

When the evolutionary reasoning is developed sufficiently to satisfy the sound-argument model of explanatory reasoning, the initial message is transformed. As further factors are added, the relation to issues over sexual equality changes. The theory is so loose that explanations can be constructed to support sexism or egalitarianism. Barkow's addition (1989c 326–27) lends itself to egalitarianism:

".. . The standard sociobiological portrait of human sexuality need(s) to be modified in the case of males seeking longer-term relationships with females, females in whose offspring they would be likely to invest parentally. The greater total parental investment available (one assumes), the higher the number of surviving offspring likely to result. Thus, for longer-term relationships, males should prefer females whose above-average ability to produce or control resources permits them to provide more parental investment than do other females. Female prestige systems should therefore in many ways resemble those of males, and male-female mate selection strategies should be more similar to each other in long-term than in short-term relationships. In the former case, human males, too, should tend to be fairly discriminating, seeking mates who not only appear likely to be fertile and provide paternity certainty but who also show evidence of being able themselves to produce and control resources.

Variations in formulation and theory are congenial to radically diverse political orientations. Although we cannot justifiably identify sociobiology with any one political stance, some political stance or other is waiting in the wings. Whether sociobiology is judged politically dangerous or benign depends on the explanation evaluated and on the evaluator's own politics.

To the extent that the explanations are underdetermined by the evidence, ideology and preconceptions move in to direct us about what to accept. Reacting against the traditional view that scientific explanations have no political significance, people now claim that the scientific and political debate over sociobiology are one and the same. How can the logical empiricist distinction between science and ideology be maintained? To answer this question, some distinctions are needed: between the political and the scientific status of an explanation, criteria and determinants of acceptability, and the ontology of a scientific theory and metaphysics.

Is sociobiology "politics by other means" (Harraway 1984)? Yes and No. Yes, science is an institution in our society, as subject to politics as any institution. Sociobiology is a projection of culture and ideology.

In the historical, philosophical, and social studies of science, it has become commonplace to note that "facts" depend on the interpretive framework of theory, and that theories are loaded with the explicit and implicit values of the theorizers and their cultures. Thus, all facts are laced with values. (Harraway, 79)

In what sense are "facts" dependent on theory, theory on values, and thus facts on values? People would regard such-and-such proposition as a fact unless they interpreted it according to a theory. People would not create those theories unless they were motivated by having certain values. Harraway adds that values are story-laden. What is interesting is to identify the ways explanatory facts involve complex, historically specific storytelling practices that reflect culture and ideology (as Harraway does). What is a truism is that the content of every sociobiological explanation is laden by culturally and ideologically influenced choices about goals, topics, language, selection scenarios, leaps from causal factors to facts, and so on.

> And there would be no stories, no questions, without the complex webs of power, including the tortured realities of race, sex, and class—and including people's struggles to tell each other how we might live with each other. (Harraway,80)

In what sense are explanatory stories dependent on the struggles of race, sex, class, and so on? The practices of performing explanatory acts would not exist unless existing people struggled in these ways.

Whether an explanatory hypothesis is confirmed depends on the relation between the truth-values of the propositions involved in stating the hypothesis, the evidence, and background information. To conflate this sense of dependence with Harraway's is a category mistake. Logical empiricism studied explanatory and evidential relations in the sentences themselves, not our acts of constructing or evaluating the explanatory and evidential relations (Holcomb, 1987b). It stipulated that by "science" it meant the sentences themselves, not including the social arrangements from which the sentences arise (which it ignored but did not deny). Hence, the latter, but not the former, is within the scope of the sociology of scientific knowledge. An explanation's scientific status concerns relations among the products of thought. The psychological, political, cultural, ideological, or historical status of an explanation each concern the relation between products of thought and explanatory acts of people. To assert or deny that "science is insulated from cultural and ideological pressures" is to confuse categories like 'the content, form and truth of the explanations' with categories like 'the relation of explanations to explanatory acts'. There is no conflict between logical empiricist norms of method and macrosocial (e.g., ideological) or microsocial (e.g., everyday-life) elements in the construction of science.

So, science and nonscience are conceptually distinct. Ironically, that allows them to be totally interpenetrating when it comes to matters of what people do. Strictly speaking, there is no such thing as a "scientific explanation." There are just explanations. Each sociobiological explanation has both a scientific status and an extra-scientific status. To evaluate an explanation's scientific status is not the same thing as to evaluate its political status. The concept of an acceptable scientific explanation reduces to the concept of an explanation that meets various criteria for being well-articulated and well-tested according to certain standards. That concept includes no reference to explanatory acts or to relations between explanatory acts and their social context. Conformity to one's political preferences is not one of the criteria. So it is not rational to accept or reject the derivation of a double or of a single standard because it fits or violates one's political preferences in judging its scientific status.

Most advocates and most critics hold that the scientific rationality of accepting or rejecting Barash's hypothesis depends on the quality of the evidence. Kitcher (1985, 8) writes, "We come to the central theme of this book: The dispute about human sociobiology is a dispute about evidence." In the trial over whether human sociobiology is guilty of being bad science, as in many legal trials, the evidence is contested. There is strong disagreement on such decisions as: what is admissable as evidence, what evidence is relevant, what relations obtain among the pieces of evidence, what are the relative weights of various pieces of evidence, and what standards of evidence suffice for acceptability. Hence, advocates find good evidence where critics find none at all. Scientific disputes over fundamentals are not resolved by simple appeal to "the facts." Even when there is a measure of agreement about the facts, conflict over these issues prevents consensus. Simple appeal to confirming instances has had little success as a way of sifting out acceptable scientific explanations.

Here, logical empiricism finds its limits. One limit is that there can be no logic of confirmation in the sense that Carnap and others sought. Carnap's formalized logic of confirmation is of no use in resolving debates over evidence. Indeed, these sorts of judgements cannot be reconstructed without loss in a formalized, canonical language. Another limit is that even if political preferences do not operate as criteria for acceptability, they operate as determinants of judgements of acceptability, whether made by scientists or non-scientists. This limit is the other side of what we said about the political debate about sociobiology. Expressed in terms of determinants-as-causes, our metaphysical, ideological, and political views cause us to make these decisions in one way rather than another, leading us to different evaluations. Expressed in terms of determinants-as-reasons, people strive to have a unified belief system and so cannot help but use the coherence of their metaphysical, ideological, and political commitments as reasons to make these decisions, leading some to regard an explanation as acceptable and others to regard it as unacceptable. Any attempt to separate science from metaphysics, ideology, or politics involving explanatory acts (or acts of judgement about the validation or significance of scientific explanations) violates the spirit of logical empiricism. Even the failed hard-core positivist attempts at demarcation concerned sentences, not acts.

Presuppositions lurking in the ideological context of an explanation can make a difference in evaluative conclusions, resulting in dissensus. It does not follow that they must issue in conflicting conclusions. Kitcher (1985) proved through painstaking, detailed study of a variety of explanations what had been obvious to most evolutionists all along, despite a diversity of extrascientific orientations. He proved that sociobiology's alleged import for human nature was not at that time backed up by well-confirmed explanations or sound evidential methods. We can state the significance of this result in terms of the perspective of the quest for completeness.

## Completeness and Human Nature

Evolutionary theory at present can explain the evolution of all kinds of phenotypic traits except social behavior. Suppose we had to sum up our present evolutionary knowledge. *The Book of Rigorous Evolutionary Explanations* is incomplete: it has headings of social behaviors followed by blank pages. This is an intolerable situation for working evolutionists. In both animal and human sociobiology, we have data in search of theory and theory in search of data. Why, then, do we regard animal sociobiology as valid science and human sociobiology as not yet valid science? There are some cases in which relevance and consistency have been achieved, by usual standards of success. We know how to bring data and theory together so as to achieve relevance and consistency in these and other cases (see the journal *Behavioral Ecology and Sociobiology*). So animal sociobiology is not only legitimate in principle, it contains results that validate it in practice.

In human sociobiology, even the best empirical work—where variables are measured, controls are used, statistically significant results are well argued, discrepancies between expected and observed outcomes are pursued, and so on—is based on problematic proposals for how to connect fitness, selection, adaptation, genes, and so forth to existing social patterns. So sociobiology tends to be far less rigorous in practice when explaining human behavior than when explaining animal behavior. Critics infer from the lack of equally rigorous results that human sociobiology is invalid as a science. Advocates infer from the need to explain human sociality and the effort to emulate the success of animal sociobiology that human sociobiology is valid as a science. Everyone can agree that animal sociobiology is legitimate in principle (it has good goals) and valid in practice (it has a body of significant, good results) whereas human sociobiology is legitimate in principle (it has essentially similar, good goals) but not often or never valid in practice (most of its results are flawed by dubious assumptions or unrigorous explanatory or evidential methods).

Kitcher finds in human sociobiology a potential science since the strategy and techniques of Lumsden and Wilson (1981) are legitimate, but not an actual science since the applications are disastrously flawed (Burian 1989). Kitcher's findings bring us to the point where we can identify a serious, unresolved issue. Advocates of human sociobiology are right that we can think of explanations which, if relevant and true, would have exciting implications. Critics of human sociobiology are right that the explanations so far produced might be irrelevant or false. Since doing rigorous human sociobiology is far more difficult than doing rigorous animal sociobiology, we will probably remain in this research situation for some time. The real issue, then, is not over the existence of severely flawed explanations that would have exciting implications if relevant and true, but over how to evaluate their scientific worth with an eye to improvement in the match between goals and results. Their scientific worth is a function of whether they promote or hinder progress toward completeness.

Instead of continuing to judge the legitimacy and validity of human sociobiology primarily by debating its implications for human nature and other fields (external utility), let us get back to the basic scientific goal and debate its prospects and effectiveness for completing evolutionary explanation (internal utility). In a sense, this evaluative perspective substitutes the aim of attaining completeness within evolutionary biology for the aim of using evolutionary biology to illuminate human nature. Because about everyone thinks of sociobiology as a theory of human nature, many will resist the idea. Let us reconsider Kitcher's main point.

Simplified, the argument goes as follows. Pop sociobiology as conceived by Wilson and others "stands in a long tradition of attempts to discern the elements of human nature in the behavior of nonhuman animals and thus to justify the ways of man to man" (1985, 13). A necessary condition for accepting pop sociobiology's view of human nature is that it is backed up by validated science. Critical examination reveals that the so-called science is not valid. Since the technical arguments do not support the nontechnical conclusions, the pop sociobiological view of human nature is unjustified.

The argument does not show that view to be false, but merely unjustified by science. The argument does not show it to be less justified than other pop views of human nature, its rightful competitors. The argument also ignores completeness. Is it necessary for a completed evolutionary theory to deliver some view or other of human nature? No. Kitcher has shown that human sociobiology is invalid. The implication of this fact is it does not scientifically support any view of human nature, regardless of whether that view is politically viable or repugnant. The treatment of human sociobiology as pop sociobiology masks the possibility of a human sociobiology aimed at goals internal to evolutionary biology, not requiring such metaphysics. If you insist on supplying a metaphysical interpretation in terms of human nature, then do so only after taking into account its internal goals. It is not necessary for a science to support a view of human nature in order for it to be a legitimate and valid science. To see why, distinguish metaphysics from ontology, a distinction in the Quinean tradition.

The sense of human nature used in Kitcher's argument is metaphysical: the essence of being human, the human condition, what it is to be human, or some such idea. The ontology of a scientific theory is merely a description of what the entities (processes, states, etc.) to which the theory refers must be like in order for that theory to be true. The theoretical claims on which correct explanations are based are true, according to the sound-argument model. It follows that commitment to the theoretical basis of an explanation brings with it commitment to the ontology of the theory. Human organisms must be evolved organisms, governed by the forces of evolutionary change, and so forth in order for evolutionary theory to be true. You may call those characteristics "human nature," if you wish, but the point is that the ontological concept is not the same concept as the metaphysical concept.

In the ontological sense, every theory about humans, whether as superficial as a theory about clothing fads or as deep as a theory about evolution, is a theory of "human nature," i.e., the nature of the items the theory is about insofar as the inference holds that "if the theory is true, then those items have certain features." Now, if evolutionary theory were complete, it would explain the evolved behavior of all species of organisms, but this task does not require it to disclose the metaphysical nature of everything it says exists. So the dispute over the metaphysics of human nature is irrelevant to the validity of sociobiology aimed at completeness.

However, the validity of sociobiology aimed at completeness is not irrelevant to constructing a metaphysics of human nature. To see why, reconsider our use of metalogic to clarify completeness. Suppose we were interested in understanding the nature of deductive validity in logic. Let's distinguish two ways of doing so. First, we could take whatever logic was being proposed at the time and draw out its implications for what it is for a proof to be deductively valid. Similarly, sociobiologists drew implications for human nature from initial explanatory hypotheses. Then the critics had a field day. Second, we could take our best, fully developed logic and draw out its implications. Of course, the latter approach is preferable. Since in sociobiology we don't have any fully developed evolutionary biology of sociality, we have not been in a position to adopt the preferable approach.

What sort of logic do logicians envisage as ideal? It would be one that satisfies the metalogical constraints of being complete, consistent, and decidable. Both standard propositional and predicate logic were designed to satisfy these constraints. It turns out that logicians were able to construct a propositional logic that is complete, consistent, and decidable, whereas even the best predicate logic is complete, consistent, but undecidable. The undecidability of first-order predicate logic and of elementary number theory is one of the greatest discoveries in modern logic and mathematics. It would be unthinkable to try to understand the nature of deductive validity without taking into account the literature on this result (e.g., on Godel's proof of undecidability). Similarly, the debate over sociobiology and human nature is not well grounded unless it takes the quest for completeness into account. The lesson is: first try to construct a consistent, complete, decidable theory of social evolution, then talk about human nature.

We can understand why sociobiologists did get involved in talking about human nature. First, everyone is interested in human nature, in the sense of wanting to know why we are the way we are. In our haste to draw implications of sociobiology for human nature, we ignore the fact that a given science's ontology can only supply raw materials that need considerable conceptual processing before they can be combined with other sources of insight about human nature. Second, there is a tempting glamour to dress up one's views about our species as views about human nature. In our haste we ignore the critical point that to conceive 'the nature of the human species' as 'human nature' presupposes the unbelievable claim that the conceptual apparatus of biology is sufficient to identify what is or is not human nature.

Third, and most importantly for understanding emerging sciences, when sociobiologists initially speculated about the behavioral repertoires of human populations from an evolutionary point of view, they encountered resistance due to traditional ideas. Whenever they tried to explain some specific behavior, people complained, "But that's not biological . . . we aren't just like animals . . . genes don't determine behavior in humans . . . we don't do things just to reproduce and pass on our genes." And so on. These issues seemed so basic to our concept of ourselves and our place in or out of nature that it seemed appropriate to think that sociobiology's validity turns on whether it transforms our conception of human nature. A complete theory of human nature would incorporate sociobiology, but it is unwise to turn a source of resistance into a goal.

The conception of human nature usually employed in the sociobiology debate is ambiguous. It equivocates between being an epistemic concept (any view about humans considered particularly revealing is said to be about human nature), a stylistic concept (a concept used to dramatize what is being asserted), a metaphysical concept (about our real nature), and a concept about the ontology of theories (about the qualities of items insofar as they are the objects referred to by theories). The fact that views about human nature are obstacles to the acceptance of explanatory aims, methods, and results internal to a science does not imply that we must take on the project of illuminating human nature in order to construct acceptable scientific explanations. The debate over human nature has gone off on a tangent.

To dramatize the change in perspective, recall that Copernicus was said to induce a revolution. Instead of taking the sun to revolve around the earth, he posited that we should take the earth to revolve around the sun. Let us reorient the discussion of sociobiology by calling for a "Copernican revolution" in the way we ground our standards for evaluating it. Instead of devising standards for endorsing or rejecting evolutionary theory's import for human nature, let us devise standards for endorsing or rejecting the import of human sociality for the completeness of evolutionary theory. Let us work on deciding how programs for connecting the fitness, selection, adaptation, genes, and so forth to the kind of sociality found in organisms with flexible behavior, culture, and mind contribute to unifying evolutionary theory with its domain. Attempts to draw and test implications for human nature are premature if not grounded in the results of unifying strategies.

The courageous can go even further. We should do for sociobiology and its "isms" what Fine has already done for physics and the struggle between the adherents of realism and the adherents of antirealism. Fine said that the answer is "not realism, and not antirealism either." Similarly, let us say, "not biological determinism, and not biological indeterminism either," "not reductionism, and not antireductionism either," "not adaptationism, and not antiadaptationism either," not "neo-Social Darwinism and not anti-neo-Social Darwinism either," and so forth for any further "isms" that become the targets of debate as sociobiology develops. In that sense, let us proclaim the death of The Sociobiology Debate.

Suppose that human sociobiology developed so that its explanatory results were properly validated. Would it be correct in that situation to say that human sociobiology is a validated theory of human nature? Would it be correct to portray the general orientation of that theory as some "ism," as a scientific philosophy? Not if we adopt what Fine (1984, 366–67) calls the natural ontological attitude, which dissolves the idea of interpreting science to which we have become so accustomed:

> The attitude that marks NOA (the natural ontological attitude) is just this: Try to take science on its own terms, and try not to read things into science. If one adopts this attitude, then the global interpretations, the "isms" of scientific philosophies, appear as idle overlays to science: not necessary, not warranted and, in the end, probably not even intelligible.

The usual critiques of sociobiology presuppose that it is necessary for a science to be validated for it to support a view of human nature. Indeed, advocates and critics alike think that it would be a good thing if sociobiology were to produce a breakthrough in the effort to understand our place in the scheme of things. If that means showing how human and nonhuman organisms evolved and are evolving as social beings in ways governed by evolutionary processes, then that is what the project of completing evolutionary explanation is all about. But if it means something more, some ability to capture the Truth or the Reality or the Nature or some such Ultimate Character of The Human Condition, then we are trying for a pie-in-the-sky justification of metaphysics by science. Indeed, we already have seen that views of Human Nature are projected onto sociobiology, not derived from it. The concept 'human nature' is not part of its theoretical or observational language. The idea of a science justifying a view of human nature is incoherent; you can't make a sow's ear into a silk purse. Striving for such a grand science is itself a "vaulting ambition, which overleaps itself." Fortunately, it is not necessary for a science of humans to support a vision of Human Nature or for a science of animals to support a vision of Animal Nature in order to be valid or significant.

Scientists may or may not do better research when they think they are trying to illuminate human nature. Psychologists of science can study the results of motivational essentialism: the idea that our motivating goal is to illuminate the nature or essence of social beings. If that psychological crutch has good results, it is prudent to retain. But the object of scientific study is not to capture the nature of humans, of animals, or anything else. Science is not in need of metaphysical interpretation, or any scientific philosophy for that matter. The practice and evaluation of sociobiology in the image of such "isms" should be exposed, showing that the "isms" are externally imposed onto it, not warranted, and hardly intelligible. Discussions throughout this book of the "isms" will bear out this challenging point. They function as a call for therapy, not a disproof convincing to those enamored of talking in terms of those "isms."

## Standards of Evidence

Kitcher (1985, 9) answers the question of standards:

Everybody ought to agree that, *given sufficient evidence*, for some hypothesis about humans, we should accept that hypothesis whatever its political implications. But the question of what counts as sufficient evidence is not independent of the political consequences. If the costs of being wrong are sufficiently high, then it is reasonable and responsible to ask for more evidence than is demanded in situations where mistakes are relatively innocuous. . . . if we are wrong about the bases of human social behavior, if we abandon the goal of a fair distribution of the benefits and burdens of society because we accept faulty hypotheses about ourselves and evolutionary history, then the consequences of a scientific mistake may be grave indeed. . . . The rationality of adopting, using, and recommending a scientific hypothesis depends not merely on the probability that the hypothesis is true, given the available evidence, but on the costs and benefits of adopting it (or failing to adopt it) if it is true and on the costs and benefits of adopting it (or failing to adopt it) if it is false. The abstract principle is familiar to us from many concrete cases. Drug manufacturers rightly insist on higher standards of evidence when there are potentially dangerous consequences from marketing a product.

Rudner (1953) initiated a debate, one predating the sociobiology debate, over the pragmatics of accepting scientific hypotheses. Familiarity with that debate puts Kitcher's proposal in its proper philosophical context. Rudner argued that sufficient evidence is a function of both the evidential probability of the hypothesis and "of the importance, in the typically ethical sense, of making a mistake in accepting or rejecting the hypothesis." He claimed that what properly counts as sufficient evidence has both a cognitive component (weight of the evidence) and a valuational component (analysis of the ethical consequences of mistakes). Whereas empiricism offers the cognitive component as both a necessary and sufficient condition for rational acceptance/rejection, Rudner treats it as a necessary but insufficient condition.

Rudner motivated this position with a well-chosen example. He considered a pharmaceutical firm which has to decide whether to manufacture a new drug on the basis of the hypothesis that the new drug is both safe and effective. Perhaps Kitcher is committed to the position espoused by Rudner. His language and choice of the drug-manufacturing example gives that impression. Perhaps he is committed only to something that is philosophically less loaded than Rudner's position. He may mean only that we should be just as rigorous in evaluating evidence when theories are about ourselves as we are when they are about other things and that the importance of being rigorous varies with the pragmatic consequences of acceptance or rejection. That makes good sense.

In fact, many critics have adopted Rudner's position. They become quite sceptical of explanations in human sociobiology, thus raising their standards for sufficient evidence to a high level of rigor, as a result of their evaluation of the field as bad, dangerous ideology. Whether or not Kitcher is one of them, we need to decide whether that sceptical attitude is warranted. Once again, science meets politics, so that proper assessment of explanatory hypotheses turns on relations between the ideological and scientific status of those hypotheses. Rudner proposes that even if we should not accept/reject explanations in human sociobiology on the basis of arguments from premises expressing our political preferences, we should accept/reject them on the basis of standards raised/lowered according to our political preferences.

Jeffrey (1956) countered that Rudner's example does not concern acceptance of a given hypothesis as such, but with the practical consequences of adopting a hypothesis as a guide to action. Jeffrey did agree with Rudner that the acceptance/rejection of a hypothesis is an action. He agreed that potential costs and benefits, including those of a moral character, of the consequences of that action are relevant to the rationality of performing that action. So Jeffrey ended up defending the position that "it is not the business of the scientist as such . . . to accept or reject hypotheses," but merely to assign them evidential probabilities.

Hempel (1981) found a way to incorporate the insights of Rudner's and of Jeffrey's position without thereby incurring their faults. He agrees with Rudner and Jeffrey that the acceptance of an explanatory hypothesis is an action, whose consequences are relevant to the rationality of performing that action. He maintains, against Jeffrey's noncommittal attitude, that scientists as such do not just rule on how well supported a hypothesis is but do go on to accept or reject hypotheses. He holds, against Rudner's departure from empiricism by invoking ethical factors, that rules of evidence are rules of inductive acceptance/rejection for pure or basic research, not for any consequences of applied science. Thus, the scientist as such does indeed make value judgements (with Rudner, against Jeffrey), but they are not of a moral kind (against Rudner, with Jeffrey).

Hence, we should not accept Rudner's pragmatic condition of acceptability uncritically, but should realize that arguments by Jeffrey (1956), Hempel (1981), and others (Levi 1960) have subjected it to searching criticism. There are several important issues distinctive of the application of Rudner's position to human sociobiology.

Kitcher never does specify what practical actions he has in mind in raising the spectre of abandoning "the goal of a fair distribution of the benefits and burdens of society because we accept faulty hypotheses about ourselves and our evolutionary history." With the most heinous interpretations of the theory T of mating and parenting in mind, let explanatory hypothesis H be the hypothesis that women are less promiscuous than men for sociobiological reasons. Let action A be promoting laws allowing men to be granted a divorce for their wife's infidelity but not permitting women to be granted a divorce for their husband's infidelity.

## Refutation of Politically Based Standards

One serious doubt concerns the link between T, H, and A. The same theory T may be developed to assert the hypothesis H* that men's care for wives and children improves children's emotional well-being, which makes their children more attractive mates later on. Then action A* might be promoting laws allowing both men and women paid leaves of absence from work after they bear offspring. Here T inspires hope and equality, not fear and inequality!

Another serious doubt concerns the link between hypothesis H and action A. Critics select, from all politically relevant actions one might undertake on the basis of its hypotheses, just the subset of actions that promote status-quo inequalities between sexes, races, classes, and so forth. This choice unwittingly perpetuates politically conservative misuses of human sociobiology by reaffirming their false assumption that a justified sociobiology would justify conservative politics. Critics (Sociobiology Study Group 1975, 1976, 1978a, 1978b; Kitcher 1985) find the field dangerous because people treat biologically based social behaviors as "genetic" and hence as "a fixed part of human nature" and so "we cannot help but behave that way."

Consider the inference "If Behavior B is explainable by sociobiology, as a result of evolution by selection on its genetic basis," then B is "inevitable," or "irreversibly fixed," or "changeable only with great difficulty," or "changeable only at the price of giving up other desirable behaviors," or "changeable but the new condition will be unnatural and so will demand continual conscious monitoring." People do make such inferences, but such inferences are unjustifiable. Even hypothesis H does not imply that men cannot remain faithful to their mates once they have vowed fidelity with wholehearted devotion. The psychological states involved are part of the conditions for applying H to actual human cases. When ignored, H is no more linked to A than to not-A. If we apply H on the assumption that selection favored those individuals who altered their reproductive strategies in response to changing conditions, then we might expect great individual, historical and cross-cultural variability in sexual behavior (see Barkow 1989c, 346).

The changeability of a human behavior depends on which behavior it is. Behaviors known to be changeable do not become fixed just because we place them in an evolutionary perspective. Nor does the ability of sociobiology to explain a behavior require that the behavior is inevitable, fixed, etc. Logically, concern over biological limits to social change arise because of the assumption that what is genetic is part of human nature and that human nature is unchangeable. The proper way to discuss the related charge that sociobiology is necessarily committed to genetic determinism is in terms of gene-culture research programs, not in terms of disciplinary affiliation. Typically, they claim only that genes affect the probability of a behavior and don't determine it, and they deny genes the role of an overriding proximate cause.

What this shows is that inferences from scientific facts to social norms are not inherent in the explanations themselves, but in the identification of the facts explained as part of human nature. The concept of human nature is doing all the political work, not anything unique about sociobiology. Since the concept of human nature is not a scientific concept, the judgement that a sociobiological explanation qualifies as an acceptable scientific explanation contains no commitment to the pragmatic consequences of adopting claims about human nature. Rather, claims about human nature are externally imposed on sociobiological explanations. Related judgements about social and political policy are never logical consequences of the explanations themselves if properly articulated, but logical consequences of the combination of premises expressing the explanations, premises expressing concepts of human nature arrived at independently of the explanations, and policy premises as well. Sociobiology itself has no implications for human nature.

So there is no rationale internal to the logic of the hypothesis H for choosing between A and incompatible actions, such as actions promoting sexual equality, as the pragmatic effect of accepting H. Yet Rudner's proposal depends on being able to identify the pragmatic effect of acceptance of H with A rather than not-A, since the costs and benefits of mistakes in acceptance and rejection cannot be calculated otherwise. Since there is no subset of "political implications" fixed on scientific grounds, sufficient evidence cannot depend on standards fixed by political effects.

As a solution to the problem that no one explanation is uniquely determined by the evidence, Rudner's proposal fails. In reaction, standards for sufficient confirmation were located in political/moral consequences of accepting the explanation. But no one sort of political/moral action is uniquely determined by regarding something as an acceptable scientific explanation. The evidential problem is not solved, just postponed. With alert critics like Kitcher, Gould, and Lewontin watching, we don't need Rudner's proposal to reduce political misuses of the explanations. Showing that the evidence does not warrant believing the explanations does that job.

Another serious doubt about Rudner's proposal arises over whether there is one practical action A that is properly linked to hypothesis H. H may be put to use in different courses of action. The moral seriousness of a mistake may vary according to the particular use it is given. In such cases there is no one level of evidential support high enough to warrant acceptance of H.

For instance, H may be used to change divorce laws or change job opportunities or change advertising strategies. We would require a higher level of confirmation of H for making female but not male infidelity grounds for divorce than for exploiting differential reactions to infidelity to sell products. The hypothesis that men are by nature more promiscuous than women is so general that the number and variety of uses to which it may be put is antecedently inestimable. Again, the underlying problem is a preconceived notion linking a single action or class of actions—actions that perpetuate and promote status quo social inequalities—to a given hypothesis. For a given hypothesis, there is an indefinitely large and antecedently unspecifiable class of actions to which it may somehow be practically relevant. The various mathematical calculi in decision theory are of no help in such situations. Hence, choosing to accept a hypothesis is not equivalent to choosing to act on the basis of that hypothesis relative to some specific objective whose costs and benefits are antecedently calculable.

Another serious doubt concerns a precondition for applying Rudner's view to human sociobiology. For logical reasons, the pragmatic condition breaks down in cases where the utility values vary with the truth value of the hypothesis. Suppose we undertook and achieved A on the basis of H, but that H is false. Suppose we conceive human nature as fixed or unchanging. How high are the costs?

Suppose we infer that if it is false that women are by nature less promiscuous than men, then actions perpetuating the double standard about promiscuity have dire consequences. Then we would have to infer that if it is true that women are by nature less promiscuous than men, then actions perpetuating that double standard would have good consequences. On such suppositions, the costs of A are high if H is false but low if H is true. When costs/benefits are truth-value dependent according to the value system presupposed in their assignment, evidential standards cannot be determined.

Critics too often take human sociobiology to have dangerous political effects in virtue of their belief that its claims are false. What is so bad about abandoning the goal of a fair (equal) distribution of the benefits and burdens of society among the sexes? Abandoning that goal is costly if the sexes have equal aptitudes for the various benefits and burdens but beneficial if the sexes have unequal aptitudes. Critics who portray the field as "another dangerous biological determinism" arrive at the charge "dangerous" upon presupposing that the hypothesis "specific human social behaviors have a biological behavioral basis" is highly improbable. Why? It is assumed that human social behaviors are entirely culturally conditioned and that "biology cannot explain culture." These cost/benefit assignments beg the question against the truth of improved versions of H in assuming that the costs of adopting H when H is false far outweigh the benefits of adopting H when H is true. An agent who makes a rational decision on pragmatic grounds must already know a lot; such putative knowledge is exactly what is at issue.

The preceding objections refute the thesis that standards of confirmation sufficient to rationally warrant acceptance of explanations in human sociobiology are a function of the risk that it will perpetuate social inequalities. Why, then, did it seem reasonable? It is a truism that when the effects of accepting an explanation are important, as in consequences for social equality, we need to be quite clear about the degree of confirmation of the explanation. Normally, we would not adopt the explanation as a basis for social policy unless the degree of confirmation is high. No one infers from the truism that political commitments are reasons to believe or disbelieve the explanation. The method of counting political preferences as reasons to accept or reject a given explanation in human sociobiology is obviously an inadequate method for evaluating its scientific status. However, it is tempting to conclude from the truism that standards of acceptance have their source in political preferences.

Suppose we decided to change divorce laws concerning infidelity on the basis of incorporating H into our belief systems. Different people have incompatible belief systems. Egalitarian scientists would demand high standards for acceptability. Inegalitarian scientists would demand low standards for acceptability. The allegedly pragmatic rationale for standards yields a very impractical result. To achieve uniform standards in a science, scientists would have to first agree on politics and morality. Obviously, such consensus is neither likely nor relevant. Some critics use potentially harmful political effects as reasons to raise the standards of acceptance to a high level. They forget that, by parity of reasoning, potentially beneficial political effects would count as reasons to lower the standards of acceptance to a low level, which some advocates have done. You can't put both illogical attitudes together and make sense. This reduces to absurdity the idea that standards of acceptable scientific explanations rise and fall in proportion to the overall balance of bad and good political effects.

The methods of assessment by politically motivated reasons and by politically motivated standards are defeated on the same grounds; they fail to do justice to the autonomy of scientific evaluations from political evaluations. Both methods confuse distinct sorts of rationality: prudential rationality and epistemic rationality (Pollock 1986, 7–8). It may be prudent for us to accept hypotheses for which we have no good evidence and imprudent for us to accept hypotheses for which we have good evidence. We have no good evidence that live lobsters feel no pain when immersed in boiling water, but it is prudent for us to believe that they feel no pain. A dying man might have the best medical reasons to believe that he will die tomorrow, but that belief might be so psychologically crushing that it is prudent for him to believe he will live for another day. As distinct types of rationality, problems involved in epistemic rationality are not solved by matters pertinent to prudential rationality. Evidence has to do with grounds for holding a hypothesis on the basis of whether it is true or false. Prudence has to do with grounds for holding a hypothesis on the basis of whether holding it has good or bad effects. These are distinct matters.

## Use-Specific Acceptance

What, then, are proper grounds for deciding how high the standards of evidence must be? We can reconcile insights found in the answers given by Rudner, Jeffrey, and Hempel, in an effort to do justice to the political debate over human sociobiology. The premise of this solution is that to accept an explanation is to make a kind of commitment; otherwise acceptance would not have serious pragmatic consequences that make it an important decision. To clarify the pragmatic content of the concept of an acceptable scientific explanation, we should ask, "If we were to regard something as an acceptable scientific explanation, to what would we be committing ourselves?" The answer depends on what kind of commitment we are making. Are we thinking in terms of commitments relevant to inquiry, to belief, or to deeds (especially, political action)? Validation of scientific explanation involves three contexts of commitment that embody different kinds of knowledge: the context of inquiry (knowing as ongoing disciplined inquiry), the context of belief (knowing as holding a true justified belief), and the context of action (knowing as engaging in effective action).

Each context marks a distinct sort of use or purpose to which an explanation may be put. The concept 'acceptable scientific explanation' has different justification conditions in each context. We are justified in accepting an explanation in the context of inquiry if further thought in terms of that explanation helps solve important intellectual problems. We are justified in accepting an explanation in the context of belief if that explanation is worthy of being regarded as true. We are justified in accepting an explanation in the context of action if deeds based on that explanation bring about the changes we expect them to make.

The use of 'action' in two senses may cause confusion. Human beings are agents. Acceptance of an explanation is an action (the first sense), since anything an agent does is by definition an act or action. To what use are we to put the explanation, once accepted? Acceptance for the purpose of further inquiry is an act; an inquiry is an act of searching for information in the manner of a systematic investigation. Acceptance for the purpose of belief is an act; a belief is an act of assenting to something whereby the item believed is regarded as true. Acceptance for the purpose of action (the second sense) is an act; an action is something done or effected whereby one brings about an alteration in self, society, or nature.

Debate over sociobiology has blurred these contexts, ignoring the fact that acceptance is use-specific. Let H be any explanatory scientific hypothesis in sociobiology. People accept or reject H by taking its acceptance to imply that H is fruitful for research, that we are justified in believing H, and that H is a tool for social control. When Kitcher (1985, 9) says that "the rationality of adopting, using, and recommending a scientific hypothesis" depends on both evidence and political consequences, he employs an incomplete concept. We should ask, "adopting, using, and recommending a hypothesis for what use?"

Surely we often use H in our research without believing H; indeed the attitude of believing or disbelieving H interferes with adopting it as a working hypothesis to be tested for its truth or falsity. Surely we often believe H without making H the basis of social policies to be acted on; if people's preconceptions about human nature lead them to treat any behavior explained by sociobiology as irrevocably fixed, it would be imprudent to use H as a source of social policy. We normally would not make H the basis of a social policy to be enacted unless we believed H to be true or highly probable, but if we must have a policy about something and the factual assumptions behind all rival policies are doubted, we would enact some policy even without believing it. We normally would not believe H unless H had already shown its research value, but many of our beliefs are arrived at through socialization and have never been subjected to scientific study. These obvious truths reflect the fact that we must already take different sets of attributes of explanations as relevant for their use in inquiry, belief, or action.

The evident fact that the contexts of research, belief, and action are distinct provides a perspective for seeing that philosophy of science has overemphasized the context of belief. It based its view of scientific method on the concept of knowledge ("scientia" means "knowledge" in Latin). Hence, by "science" it meant "the systematic pursuit of knowledge," and by "scientific method" it meant "the principles and procedures for the systematic pursuit of knowledge." So far, so good. Problems arose in taking from modern philosophy in general the narrow conception of knowledge as true justified belief and in taking from empiricist theories of knowledge an even narrower conception of justification. Logical empiricism interpreted "justified" as "sufficiently confirmed by the observable facts," as if every reason to think a theory true must ultimately be a deductively valid or an inductively strong inference from sensory data. Since standards of evidence are not observable, it tried in vain to ground the standards of evidence on modern quantificational logic. If observation and logic do not ground the standards of sufficient evidence, how else, if at all, can they be grounded in a way that prevents them from being altogether subjective?

Jeffrey answered that, given the underdetermination of the truth or falsity of theory by data, explanations are confirmed or disconfirmed but neither accepted nor rejected, which assumes that standards cannot be rationally grounded. Rudner tried to ground standards of evidence in values, claiming that effects judged costly/beneficial in ethico-political terms alone determine when the evidence is sufficient for acceptability. Hempel countered that effects judged costly/beneficial in terms of research utility alone determine evidential sufficiency.

## Hypotheses and Theories

The terms of this debate are vexed because they each emphasize distinct contexts of use, but fail to make them explicit. Ordinary language analysis, we shall argue, reveals that the distinction of contexts is inherent in the way we commonly understand the meaning of the terms "hypothesis" and "theory" for analyzing science. Each context is a context of analysis. Units of analysis have different meanings in each context.

Sometimes by "hypothesis" we mean "an interpretation of a practical situation or condition taken as the ground of action." And by "theory" we mean "a belief, policy, or procedure proposed or followed as the basis of practical action." When we construe hypotheses and theories in this way, we take the point of view inherent in the context of action. We are thinking of the effects we can bring about by adopting (or using or recommending) the hypothesis or theory. In this context of analysis, the optimal hypothesis or theory is one that reliably produces the effects we want to bring about. Rudner's view emphasizes the use of hypotheses or theories for practical action. The ensuing claim that conditions of acceptability include both assessments of empirical support and political effects is appropriate for the context of action but inappropriate for the contexts of research and belief.

Other times by "hypothesis," we mean "a formulation of a natural principle based on inference from observed data." And by "theory" we mean "the general or abstract principles of a body of fact, a science, or an art" or "the analysis of a set of facts in their relation to one another." When we construe hypotheses and theories in this way, we take the point of view inherent in the context of belief. We are thinking of the systematic relation among the truth of claims we antecedently hold induced by the adoption of the hypothesis or theory. In this context of analysis, the optimal hypothesis or theory is one that is itself true or best enables us to recognize systematic relations among claims antecedently regarded as true. Jeffrey's view emphasizes the problem of inferring truth from any degree of confirmation, leading to his claim that hypotheses need not be accepted or rejected.

Now, we should distinguish between whether the evidence rationally permits or obligates us to believe the hypothesis true. If by judging the hypothesis acceptable we are rationally obligated to believe it to be true, Jeffrey's position makes good sense. But surely we are only rationally permitted, not obligated, to do so. Epistemic norms are norms of permissibility, not obligation (Pollock 1986, 7–8). The significance of this distinction is to proclaim the autonomy of the context of research from the context of belief. The hypothesis may be acceptable as a tool for research, a working hypothesis to be subjected to further testing and articulation, quite apart from whether it is acceptable or unacceptable for augmenting our bundle of beliefs.

Other times by "hypothesis," we mean "an assumption or concession made for the sake of the argument" or "a tentative assumption made in order to draw out its logical and empirical consequences." And by "theory" we mean "an ideal or hypothetical set of facts, principles, or circumstances." When we construe hypotheses and theories in this way, we have already taken the point of view inherent in the context of inquiry. We are thinking of the ongoing learning in disciplined research potentially achievable by adopting the hypothesis or theory. In this context of analysis the optimal hypothesis or theory is one that best enables us to undertake the further thought needed to actualize those virtues of the hypothesis or theory which are now only potential. Hempel's view emphasizes the use of hypotheses or theories for future research, and so it is appropriate for the context of research.

Indeed, this view best expresses the normal view of scientific method which emphasizes the fact that when a hypothesis is tested, scientists tentatively reject it if it is disconfirmed and tentatively accept it if it is confirmed, always standing ready to change their judgement as new evidence arises. The scientific attitude is not dogmatic, rigid, and close-minded. It is critical, flexible, and open-minded. Instead of belief and disbelief, there is tentative acceptance and tentative rejection. This view of the scientific enterprise identifies the fundamental context of evaluation as the context of research, not the context of belief or action.

Although science strives for explanations that have research value, belief value, and practical value, distinguishing which value orients an evaluation of science dissolves the Rudner-Jeffrey-Hempel debate. Their positions are irreconcilable, taken on their own terms, but are reconcilable, once we distinguish these contexts and note their relations. The present terms are preferable to theirs because the very concept of acceptance implies some use or purpose to which acceptance is relative, because they had different uses in mind in talking about acceptance and because hypotheses and theories should meet different standards according to these uses.

Hempel's (1981, 398) statement of the pragmatic condition of acceptance is readily applicable to sociobiology, evaluated in the context of inquiry: A given explanation in sociobiology is acceptable in the present knowledge situation if and only if the acceptance of that explanation possesses greater expectable value for promoting the aims of basic sociobiological research than does the acceptance of any rival available explanation. This is a suitable standard of acceptance for all criteria of acceptable explanations.

## Implications

This solution to the problem of grounding standards has implications for the ideas of sufficient evidence and aim-oriented science, the debate over science and ideology, and the emphasis on belief in philosophy of science.

If the only condition of acceptability is degree of confirmation, then it makes sense to say that an explanation is acceptable if and only if it is sufficiently confirmed. Suppose we add a logical condition of acceptability. If two explanations satisfy all appropriate logical conditions, such as lawhood and derivability and empirical content, then we can rationally choose between them when one meets the standard of evidence sufficient for acceptability and the other does not. But what if the situation is reversed and both explanations satisfy all empirical conditions but one satisfies and the other violates the standards of logical structure? Do we then need a standard of logical structure "sufficient" for acceptability? What if both explanations violate some empirical condition and some logical condition necessary for meeting each standard of sufficiency? What if the list of kinds of conditions relevant to acceptability includes many more conditions?

Pluralism about conditions of acceptability renders incoherent the very idea of talking about "sufficient x for acceptability," where x is a kind of condition such as confirmation and derivability. There is no completely general overall condition which is so privileged that only it determines when the explanation is acceptable. Rather, the only completely general overall determinant of acceptability is utility for promoting the aims of basic research. To first lay down standards of confirmation, logical structure, and so forth, and then decide whether an explanation is acceptable on the basis of whether it meets those standards is to put the cart before the horse. Instead, we must get clear about the basic justifiable aim(s) of sociobiological research, then figure out what qualities and standards enable available explanations to best promote that aim, and on that basis regard as acceptable the explanation which best exemplifies those qualities and standards. Explanatory knowledge in science consists of acceptable explanations—those that best fulfill the total list of criteria according to standards specific to the current research situation in the field, i.e., its best examples of explanatory work.

This conception of acceptability is justified by a persuasive intuition:

> That valuational considerations should play an essential role here is hardly surprising: how could a procedure like the adoption of a hypothesis be qualified as appropriate or rational except in consideration of the objectives of scientific inquiry, i.e. in consideration of the contribution that the adoption of the hypothesis is likely to make to furthering the objectives of inquiry? And that contribution is expressed in the epistemic utilities or values assigned to the possible scientific consequences of the adoption. (Hempel 1981, 398)

This conception has implications for realism and pure/applied science:

> One important consequence of introducing values into an account of scientific inference is that it automatically relativizes the acceptance of a theoretical hypothesis to the scientific context characterized by those values. This relativization eliminates what has often been regarded as a fatal objection to the idea that hypotheses are ever "accepted" as being true. The objection is that it would be irrational to regard any hypothesis as true for all purposes or in any possible context. Thus Laplace may have been convinced of the truth of Fresnel's hypothesis, but it would have been irrational to stake the fortunes of the whole French nation on this conclusion. On our analysis, however, Laplace's commitment to the truth of the hypothesis would be restricted to the scientific context, leaving open the question

whether the hypothesis was sufficiently well-tested to presume its truth if other values were at stake. This makes the relationship between "pure" and "applied" science more complicated than is often supposed, but that, I would argue, is an added virtue of this approach. (Giere 1983, 223–24)

We can now make rational sense of both pro and con positions in the sociobiology debate. We have critiqued Barash's explanation of the double standard based on Hempel's model of explanation, finding that it violated the model's specific conditions and ignored its basic distinctions. Being an explanation-sketch rather than a full-fledged explanation, it is not yet suitable to be a worthy object of belief or a source of political action. Critics are right that the explanations produced so far are not worthy of acceptance in the contexts of belief and action, the contexts of assessment pertinent to the political debate over human sociobiology. Advocates are right that explanations produced so far in human sociobiology may be worthy of acceptance when evaluated in the context of inquiry, the context pertinent to scientific research as such. Whether a given explanation should be accepted or rejected for purposes of scientific research as such turns on whether it promotes or hinders completeness. Since that sort of decision is often problematic, opposing conclusions are reasonable. Hence, the dissensus found in the sociobiology debate is rational.

Since validation is tied to aims, we need to identify an overarching aim by which explanations in sociobiology should be evaluated with respect to the context of inquiry. This is the need or aim to extend the Modern Synthesis to achieve completeness by becoming applicable to and consistent with facts about the range of social traits in all the main kinds of animal species and especially the human species. The crux of the sociobiology debate, then, lies in whether sociobiology completes the synthesis and whether completeness is desirable. Even though Barash's explanation is not rigorous according to Kitcher's and Barash's own standards of rigorous science, its presentation did contribute to reducing incompleteness more than rival explanations that merely recognize a "biological capacity for culture in general" (Spuhler 1959) available at the time. Organisms whose cultures did not include specific strategies for enhancing reproductive success would have gone extinct; our ancestors must have had genetically adaptive cultures. Barash's sketch of how evolutionary considerations about adaptiveness and natural selection might bear on sex-specific mating practices is testimony to the applicability of the neo-Darwinist synthetic theory to animal and human social behavior. This does not imply that anything goes as long as it somehow connects Darwinism and human behavior. As new rivals are constructed and evaluated as better than previous rivals, the standards for acceptability automatically go up.

In this way we can acknowledge the critics' point about the "lack of (sufficient) evidence" (for use as beliefs that generate political action) without implying the lack of scientific legitimacy of its explanations (for use in scientific research). The explanation-sketches found in Wilson's (1975) chapter on humans should be evaluated as acceptable or not in terms of their rivals. The standard of success was which explanation-sketches best promoted completeness by identifying preliminary steps for making evolutionary theory applicable to human sociality. For instance, Hinde (1974) articulated the relevance of biology for human behavior better than Wilson (1975), though Hinde's is work far less publicized (see Hinde 1982).

Much philosophy of science confuses belief/disbelief and acceptance/rejection. Acceptance is a use-relative or purpose-relative concept broader than the concept of belief. The Rudner-Jeffrey-Hempel debate and the political debate over sociobiology are vexed because they neglect this point in blurring contexts. Assessed in the context of inquiry, explanation is never final knowledge, but always open ended, as the border between known and unknown shifts. We never have final explanatory knowledge. Final knowledge is an end-point that leaves nothing to be learned, but in science learning never ceases. In this situation we need a concept of acceptability not designed for final knowledge as opposed to utter ignorance but for the the ever-changing edge of research, where knowledge and ignorance mingle.

We do not need to identify an absolute unchanging threshold that establishes sufficient evidence for acceptability in order to do justice to science as such. The scientific value of an explanation as such is its research value. To reduce its research value to its value as belief arises from a standpoint external to science, namely, a focus on how the results of science are incorporated into our belief systems. No scientific journal requires its contributors to believe (that is, accept as true) the results of their studies, but to portray accurately the degree of confirmation and other features of the hypotheses under investigation. Religion in the West usually requires belief in some set of doctrines or other, not science. Such practices indicate that belief is irrelevant to scientific research as such. Acceptance of a hypothesis does not entail belief that the hypothesis is true, just the decision that the hypothesis is the best among available alternatives, and hence the most fit for guiding further study.

To draw the contrast between the traditional approach and the one proposed here as sharply as possible, consider the situation in which no explanatory hypothesis in a science is highly confirmed. By usual standards, this is the case in human sociobiology at present, but some explanations in animal sociobiology are highly confirmed. The traditional approach would have us conclude that there are acceptable explanations in animal but not in human sociobiology, and so animal sociobiology as practiced is legitimate, actual science but human sociobiology is not legitimate as actual science but only as potential science. The traditional approach is correct when restricted to the context of belief; explanations in human sociobiology are unworthy of belief, but some explanations in animal sociobiology are worthy of belief. The traditional concept of acceptance is fine for those not engaged in human sociobiology, who evaluate it from the outside to see if it should lead them to change their belief system. But the traditional concept of acceptance is most unhelpful for practitioners of science. This leaves us with a problem: Which unacceptable explanations should be used as models to guide further inquiry, as applications of evolutionary theory that set the standard for further inquiry? The answer demands another concept of acceptability, the relative concept proposed here, one suitable for the changing course of research where our commitment to completeness forces us to apply evolutionary theory in some way or other.

The concept of acceptance proposed here is designed for internal assessment of science relevant to its process of operation, regardless of whether outsiders can use it to change, support, or discredit their belief systems. The logic of "the best among available alternative explanations" implies that if there are any available rival explanations for some phenomenon, at least one of them must be the best available (sometimes more than one will share the highest score given by multiple criteria). Given commitment to completeness, we are committed to some view of how to explain sociality, and so if there is an explanation that articulates our general view, then there is at least one acceptable explanation for the phenomena to be explained. If a faulty explanation in human sociobiology is the best available one among rivals, then it has be used to guide further work in the sense that it provides its best example of such explanatory work to date. When further work supplies higher confirmation for a revised explanation than before, the more highly confirmed version of the explanation may displace the previous one as an acceptable explanation. As standards satisfied rise, explanations previously judged acceptable are later judged unacceptable.

The proposed relative concept of acceptance is therefore "pragmatic" with respect to scientific research as such in the best sense of the term. The working scientist who extends an established science operates with some such concept of acceptance in order to make decisions about how past critical evaluations are to guide future inquiry. This concept makes rational sense of the debate. Both animal and human sociobiology are legitimate sciences containing acceptable explanations (as the practitioners hold), even though many explanations in either field are unworthy as beliefs or the as bases of social policy and social action (as the critics hold). Of course, even legitimate science is sociopolitically problematic, and so when we say that sociobiology contains some acceptable explanations, we are talking about acceptability with respect to their scientific status, not their sociopolitical status. And we are taking for granted the fact that completeness is a desirable goal, as initially motivated in section 1.2 and as will be further justified in section 3.1.

The explanations proposed in science are not given to us by nature, but are constructed by us. All our reasons for or against explanations are socially constructed. This holds no matter whether the explanations are accepted for purposes of further investigation or as items to be believed or as factors of social policy. However, the statements expressing facts of the social construction of science are not reasons to think that explanations are true or false, acceptable or unacceptable, worthwhile or wrongheaded. Nor are the statements expressing the social construction of science standards of truth or falsity, acceptability or unacceptability, worth or worthlessness. Statements about the social construction of scientific assertions, decisions, and facts are not premises useful in scientific arguments, but serve to identify the status of what science has wrought. In scientific research, an explanation is something to be investigated rather than an article of faith demanded by one's world view. And this investigation may benefit from socially sensitive evaluation.

In conclusion, sociobiological explanations count as knowledge (in one important sense of the term) just in case they satisfy an aim-oriented standard better than available rivals. The acceptability of a sociobiological explanation (or explanation-sketch) with respect to the context of inquiry is determined by its relative pragmatic utility for promoting the aim of completeness, a function of at least two sorts of conditions, namely, logical structure and confirmation. Evaluative conclusions arising from methods of assessment that ignore or conflate contexts of explanatory commitment or that invoke criteria without standards are unjustifiable. Standards of acceptability for sociobiological explanations depend on the goals of the field and the particular role an explanation plays in fulfilling those goals. Since its goals ultimately derive from the aim of completeness, acceptability depends on the structure and procedures of inquiry involved in the completeness project as manifested in the explanation's role in unifying evolutionary theory and its domain.

# CHAPTER
# 2

RESEARCH PROGRAMS AS THE UNIT OF ANALYSIS

## 2.1 The Unfalsifiability of Adaptationism

In chapter 1 we drew some implications for sociobiology of the traditional logical empiricist view that the scientific enterprise is basically constituted by the use of logic and observed facts to verify or falsify a hypothesis; more precisely, by setting up plausible explanatory and predictive hypotheses based on theories and then checking them against observed facts to see whether they are confirmed or disconfirmed. In this chapter we will draw some implications for sociobiology of the historical presuppositionist view that the scientific enterprise is basically constituted by the continual revision and changing of hypotheses; more precisely, by continually proposing, revising, or discarding plausible explanatory and predictive hypotheses or theories as motivated by evidential and nonevidential considerations under the guidance of research programs.

In order to open the way for the three-unit model of theory structure for evaluating science, we should note that science involves both of these sorts of activities. No sophisticated compatibility argument is needed to see that they can be combined compatibly into a single scheme which recognizes both units of theoretical thought: theories and research programs.

As scientists, we construct plausible explanatory hypotheses (or explanations). We make observations and check our hypotheses against the observed facts to find out the ways in which they are confirmed or disconfirmed relative to rival hypotheses. We decide which rival hypothesis is the best available hypothesis. Each hypothesis in the set of rivals is evaluated for its acceptability. Then we decide which hypotheses to work further on using evidential and nonevidential considerations about how best to conduct future research. Some old hypotheses are revised. Other old hypotheses are discarded. Some new hypotheses are proposed. Work on theoretical hypotheses, observational evidence, and evaluation of relative acceptability lead to changes in each.

The direction of change is regulated by presuppositions, some of which we are critically aware and others of which have to be pointed out by critics. These presuppositions are important factors of what counts as plausible and thus of what to do in the face of successes and anomalies. We may decide that progress in research is best served by working on underlying scientific theories, on scientific approaches like approaches for studying adaptation or approaches for applying the genetic theory of natural selection to cultural organisms. We debate about the adaptationist research program or about gene-culture research programs. Or we may decide that progress in research is best served by working on underlying ideological orientations or belief systems, on becoming sensitive to the influence on research of underlying conceptions of human nature, of sexism, or reductionism, of biological determinism, of neo-Social Darwinism, of panbiologism. How to improve research involves a multitude of interrelated judgements of our research situations that span evidential and nonevidential considerations.

In this chapter we will show how the criteria for acceptability such as disconfirmability, plausibility, theoretical progressiveness, and problem-solving success involve both theories and research programs. We will continue to emphasize that the significance and persuasive force of evidence about the genetic basis of behavior or lack of it, about the adaptiveness of social behavior or lack of it, and so forth is influenced by research programs for relating genes to culture, for relating behavior to reproductive success, and so forth. And we will continue to emphasize ideologies.

Evidence has two poles: confirmation and disconfirmation. Confirming evidence indicates the truth of some proposition. Disconfirming evidence indicates the falsity of some proposition. We have already examined confirmationism. Philosophy of science has shown that decisions about the falsity, and not just the truth, of scientific explanatory theories are never logically conclusive. That is why logical empiricists eschew talk of "verifying or falsifying theories" in favor of talk of "confirming or disconfirming" theories. So falsifiability is best interpreted as 'disconfirmability'. If you evaluate the scientific status of sociobiology solely in terms of falsifiability, that is, disconfirmability, then we will say that you are employing a "disconfirmationist methodology." So let us examine 'disconfirmationism': Explanations in sociobiology are acceptable scientific explanations if and only if they are disconfirmable, have undergone severe attempts at disconfirmation, and yet have not been found false.

Our previous results have direct implications for disconfirmationism. First, consider criteria and standards. Evidence is an empirical condition of acceptability. No set of empirical conditions is sufficient for acceptability. Hence, as views of what is sufficient for acceptability, confirmationism and disconfirmationism fail for the same reason. Logical conditions matter, too. The issue of appropriate standards for "sufficient confirmation" has a parallel in the issue of appropriate standards for "sufficiently severe efforts at disconfirmation." Sufficient for what? To decide when the goal of achieving an established sociobiology that completes evolutionary explanation is reached, a standard of absolute disconfirmational success is needed. To decide when a version of an explanation is the best rival explanation in sociobiology's current research situation, a standard of relative disconfirmational success is needed.

Second, confirmational problems have a mirror image in disconfirmational problems. Hempel's inferential model of ideal explanation suggests the basic character of problems in achieving well-articulated and well-tested explanations. Completeness will never be achieved if logical derivability and empirical adequacy are not jointly satisfied. The dilemma for confirmation is that: (a) if the data can be derived from the theory (relevance is achieved), the auxiliary assumptions are typically false (inconsistency remains); and (b) if the auxiliary assumptions are true (consistency is achieved), the data typically cannot be derived from the theory (irrelevance remains). This problem is heightened by the fact that auxiliary assumptions typically refer to events in the evolutionary past which are not subject to direct testing.

Similarly, Popper's falsificationism suggests that spurious unifications due to theoretical inadequacy will never be recognized if the inconsistency of the theory with the data or the irrelevance of the theory to data is never a possible inference from a failed prediction. Theories are insulated from possible falsification when error is always attributed to the auxiliary assumptions rather than the theory. This happens when: (c) in recognizing that the data cannot be derived from the theory (irrelevance remains), the auxiliary assumptions are judged false (in effect, the theory is held to be consistent with the data); and (d) in recognizing that the data cannot be rendered consistent with the theory (inconsistency remains), the auxiliary assumptions are judged false (again, in effect, the theory is held to be relevant to the data). Lack of sufficiently severe assessment permits evaluators to regard their favorite version of evolutionary theory as true, even if it is false, and to regard all social data as relevant to the theory, even when it is irrelevant.

This happens in pop sociobiology, when the neo-Darwinist theory of the Modern Synthesis is uncritically applied to any piece of data about human sociality that strikes our fancy. For instance, adaptationist explanations explain animal and human sociality as adaptive outcomes of natural selection. The natural selection theory it applies ignores limits to natural selection in optimizing adaptation (the theory is false). Not all social behaviors are evolutionarily adaptive (the data are irrelevant). Thus, the practice of uncritically constructing adaptationist explanations hinders completeness.

To counteract the tendency toward insufficiently severe tests, Popper suggested that we develop theory in a manner that enables us to envisage specific situations which could possibly contradict expectations induced by applying our theory to those situations and then go on to find out whether they do. Here, we have another analogue between metalogic and metascience. In metalogic, simple consistency means that from a deductive system we can never derive both a sentence and its negation (Hunter 1971). Both propositional and predicate logic were constructed to be consistent in this sense and both successfully satisfied this ideal. In metascience, simple epistemic consistency means that when applying a theory to an actual situation, the expectations induced by the theory could possibly, but never actually do, contradict the results of observation. Just as an ideal logic would be both complete and consistent, so an ideal sociobiology would be explanatorily complete, explanatorily consistent, and epistemically consistent.

Adaptationist explanations violate simple epistemic consistency since they are constructed so that whatever the results of observation may be, there is some adaptive explanation of them. That is, the expectations induced by the theory never actually do contradict the results of observation only because those expectations are constructed so that they could never possibly contradict the results of observation.

## Adaptationism

Criticism adopting the inference "explanations in sociobiology are adaptationist, hence unfalsifiable, hence unscientific" is quite common. This line of criticism has to justify each step in its reasoning: a meaningful statement of what adaptationism is, the attribution of adaptationism to sociobiology, and the judgement that sociobiology is invalid because it is unfalsifiable. Consider each.

Lewontin (1979, 6) defines the adaptationist program as follows:

> I call that approach to evolutionary studies which assumes without further proof that all aspects of the morphology, physiology, and behavior of organisms are adaptive optimal solutions to problems *the adaptationist program*. It is not a contingent theory of evolution or hypothesis to be tested since adaptation and optimality are *a priori* assumptions. Rather, it is the program of explanation and exemplification in which the purpose is to show *how* organisms solve problems optimally, not to test *if* they do. . . . Sociobiology is one manifestation of the adaptationist program, concentrating on the behavioral aspect of the phenotype.

Now, to justify the charge of adaptationism, the charge itself needs to be formulated using an adequate definition of the adaptationist program (Sober, 1987b). In fact, it is meaningless to assert or deny that "all aspects of the phenotype are adaptive." 'Adaptiveness' is a many-place predicate, denoting a complex relation, not a property (Van der Steen and Voorzanger 1984). To call trait T "adaptive" may be to say that (1) trait T is adaptive as compared to trait T\*, both of which are found in present populations, or (2) trait T is adaptive as compared to trait T\* found in an ancestral population, or (3) trait T is adaptive in environment V as compared to environment V\*, or (4) trait T is adaptive relative to criterion of fitness F but not F\*, or (5) trait T is adaptive in effects E as compared to effects E\*, and so forth. To call a trait "adaptive" without stating such relations is as meaningless as saying that I am "taller" without stating whom I am taller than.

Lewontin's definition of adaptationism makes sense only by having us think of two categories of traits, adaptive traits and nonadaptive traits. A trait can be adaptive as compared with one trait but maladaptive as compared with another trait, adaptive in one environment but maladaptive in another environment, adaptive in the present population but maladaptive in the past population, adaptive with respect to one but not another fitness factor, adaptive in one effect but maladaptive in another, and so on. More precisely, it is meaningless to assert or deny that a trait is adaptive except with respect to a background of contrasts specifying such relevant relations.

Lewontin (1976, 1977a,b) speaks for many in regarding sociobiological explanations as vulgarizations, caricatures, or pseudoscientific applications of evolutionary theory. He is well aware of the comparative nature of adaptiveness, but this awareness is not vis-

ible in his formulation of the adaptationist program. Similarly, practitioners of sociobiology are well aware of the ongoing study about
limits to natural selection, at least after Lewontin's critique was
widely circulated. But their awareness is not always visible in their
formulation of explanations, leaving them open to the critics' tendency to assume the worst interpretation.

The fact that one has not incorporated an important factual,
theoretical, methodological, or conceptual limitation into an explanation does not mean that the explanation implies that the limitation does not exist. No one expects a single explanation to be specified so as to take account of all possible background conditions to
which the effectiveness of natural selection is relative. The absence
of certain limitations and the presence of others help define the
specific explanatory role of the explanation in reducing incompleteness, a role explicit in well-articulated explanations.

The same considerations apply to the attribution of genetic
determinism to sociobiology (Lewontin 1977b). Genetic determination, or more generally, genetic causation, is a many-place predicate.
There are not two sorts of traits, those genetically determined and
those not genetically determined. Trait T may be genetically determined when comparing past and present populations, but not when
comparing subsets of present populations, e.g., females/males,
blacks/whites, rich/poor. A difference between trait T and T* is genetically caused relative to a particular background of traits, population, environment, and circumstances. Change any background
condition to which genetic causation is relative and the trait may
switch from seeming genetically caused to seeming not genetically
caused. More precisely, it is meaningless to assert or deny that a
trait is genetically caused unless the relevant relations are specified
(Van der Steen and Voorzanger 1984).

To justify attributing excessive adaptationism to sociobiology,
one has to show, not only that it constructs adaptive explanations,
but also that the main form of adaptive explanation used is an
uncritical adaptationism. Study of the articles that make the charge
(Sociobiology Study Group 1976, 1978a; Gould and Lewontin 1979;
Lewontin 1979) reveals no such argument. Instead, there are critiques of the adaptationist program, examples of adaptive explanations in the field, but very little effort at showing that sociobiologists
think in the terms that define the program.

Another method of unjustified criticism is to ignore counterevidence. Consider the charge (Kitcher 1985, 237) that "Barash's assertions about optimal compromise simply reflect Panglossian faith"

(that all traits are either optimal or optimal compromises between various factors of fitness). He cites as evidence statements from the first edition of Barash's textbook, ignoring its second edition (1982), which contains a chapter on obstacles to optimality and concludes: "Many of the foregoing obstacles lead to the irrevocable conclusion that perfect optimality will not be achieved" (55). In passing, we will identify the reasons both against perfect optimality and for using optimality models (for a fresh view, see the end of 5.3).

Barash correctly reminds us that a behavior may not be optimally adaptive if any one of the following situations holds: allele A is fixed in the population by natural selection but it mutates back to allele A at a significant rate; an adaptive allele is linked on the same chromosome to a neutral or maladaptive allele; a single allele has multiple effects not all of which are adaptive; genetic diversity underlying phenotypic diversity is selectively neutral; environments to which a trait is adaptive vary and so adaptive values change; selection maximizes average fitness in the population but not the fitness of each individual; evolutionary change lags behind rates of environmental change; resistance of a species to the acquisition of adaptive traits because of the species' prior evolutionary history; adaptive groups of genes are broken up each generation during sexual reproduction, interaction of genes so that the effect of one gene is dependent on the effect of other genes; the maintenance of diversity by selection; trade-offs among adaptive traits because of competing needs; adaptively neutral by-products of other traits; and traits are adaptive only in a relative sense.

Culture tends to reduce genetic fitness when environments alter but cultural ways of life remain the same, when immediately beneficial cultural practices have maladaptive long-term effects, when we have false beliefs and teach them to our children, and when elites make cultures serve their own genetic interests to the exclusion of others (Barkow 1989c, 320).

Adaptation may not be optimized by selection when such situations occur (Dawkins 1982a), when the selection scenario involves multiple alleles (Kitcher 1985, 215), when the results of selection alone are changed by interaction with other evolutionary forces of change: mutation, random genetic drift, meiotic drive, migration, and immigration (Gale 1980), and when other constraints limit selection (Mayo 1985). Given the array of explanatory factors in evolutionary theory, it is unlikely that any explanation invoking only a few factors is a true, full explanation. The methodological pluralism Gould and Lewontin call for is grounded in the theory itself.

In this situation, assuming that social behaviors are aimed at maximizing fitness carries both risks and opportunities. Critics emphasize research risks, inferring that "optimality theory is a complete waste of time" (Pierce and Ollason 1987). Advocates emphasize research opportunities, inferring that "evolutionary insights should not be wasted" (Stearns and Schmid-Hempel 1987). Even though ontological adaptationism (all traits are optimally adaptive) is false, ". . . the assumption of optimality provides a first approximation of substantial predictive and analytic power" (Barash 1982, 62). Assuming optimality in the methodological sense is justified because many features are used to diagnose adaptiveness (Tooby and DeVore 1987), because fitness-promoting effects are unlikely to arise from something other than selection (Cato and Borgerhoff Mulder 1987), because optimality modeling is a structured, contingent, and partial entry to inquiry (Winterhalder 1987), and because certain simple selection models supply good initial predictive approximations as compared to other approaches (Sober 1987b).

Thus, the literature shows that researchers are critically aware of what is involved in assumptions about optimal adaptation. Still unresolved are debates over rival explanatory methods we should use in this situation. For instance, some advocates hold that we should start by constructing deliberately oversimplified explanations of the main kinds of human social phenomena and gradually develop them in detail and complexity as the data permits. Some critics hold that we should start by constructing explanations of a few kinds of human social phenomena and only move on to other explanations after we have done justice to the details and complexity involved. Both strategies eventually arrive at the full range of detailed and complex explanations. Much debate about whether sociobiology is bad science or pseudo-science is a misleading overstatement of legitimate disputes over rival, rational strategies of progressive research.

# Falsifiability

Gould and Lewontin (1979 587–88) portray sociobiology as pseudo-science on the grounds that adaptationist explanations are unfalsifiable:

> We would not object so strenuously to the adaptationist program if its invocation, in any particular case, could lead in principle to its rejec-

tion for want of evidence. But if it could be dismissed as failing some explicit test, then alternatives would get their chance. Unfortunately, a common procedure among evolutionists does not allow such definable rejection for two reasons. First, the rejection of one adaptive story usually leads to its replacement by another, rather than to a suspicion that a different kind of explanation might be required. Since the range of adaptive stories is as wide as our minds are fertile, new stories can always be postulated. And if a story is not immediately available, one can always plead temporary ignorance and trust that it will be forthcoming. . . . Secondly, the criteria of acceptance of a story are so loose that they may pass without proper confirmation. Often, evolutionists use consistency with the data as the sole criterion and consider their work done when they concoct a plausible story. But plausible stories can always be told. The key to historical research lies in devising criteria to identify proper explanations among the set of plausible pathways to any modern result.

This sounds like Popper's falsification criterion. Expanded, the criticism maintains that sociobiologists usually look for confirming instances for adaptive hypotheses, rarely or never for falsifying violations. This method of explanation testing will not reveal that the explanation is false, if it is false. By not undertaking attempts at falsification as severe as possible, attempts to explain everything end up explaining nothing at all. The explanations are constructed so that no real testing is possible. Explanations are acceptable only if in principle rejectable; otherwise they are pseudo-scientific. The critics conclude that sociobiology is a pseudo-scientific vulgarization of evolutionary explanation.

Has the notion of falsifiability been properly understood and used in a way to warrant such a damaging characterization? Unfortunately, the attack on sociobiology as unfalsifiable obscures two crucially distinct conceptions of falsifiability. To appreciate the significance of the difference, we must mention the philosophical context of Popper's work.

Popper interpreted falsification in a way designed to solve Hume's problem of induction. The problem of induction confronts all theories of validation that admit confirmation. In brief (Watkins 1984, 3), Hume believed that (a) there are no synthetic a priori truths about the external world, that is, factual claims known independently of all sensory experience whatsoever; (b) any genuine knowledge about the external world must ultimately derive from sensory experience; and (c) only deductive derivations are valid, since inductions from past regularities to future regularities or laws are suspect for a variety of reasons. It is always possible that the future will be unlike the past, that what is not experienced will not conform to what is experienced. Scepticism, as the denial that we can justify our claims to knowledge, follows from the conjunction of (a), (b), and (c).

Popper proposed to finesse scepticism by denying Hume's assumption that factual claims are positively controlled by experience. Instead, he asserted that factual claims are only negatively controlled by experience. Experience has no power to indicate the truth of factual claims. There is no such thing as genuine confirmation. Experience has power only to indicate the falsity of factual claims. The paradigm case is when a lawlike statement having the form of a universal generalization is refuted by a single negative instance or counterexample. Thus, science operates by the method of conjecture and refutation. Though its hypotheses, theories, and explanations are unprovable, they are controlled by experience (observation and experiment) designed to see if they stand up to demanding attempts at falsification. If a theory or explanation has stood up to every demanding test so far, we are not entitled to infer that it has been confirmed (it has a nonzero chance of truth) or that it is not false (since if it is not false, it is true) but only that it remains a viable option. It is not confirmed, but just corroborated.

Now we can see that the Gould-Lewontin critique is un-Popperian. They say that "the criteria of acceptance of a story are so loose that they may pass without proper confirmation." Popper's theory of falsifiability has no place for confirmation; he holds that Hume's problem of induction reveals the impossibility of genuine confirmation. They say that "evolutionists use consistency with natural selection as the sole criterion." This is supposed to be an improperly low standard, but apparent consistency (apparent lack of contradiction between theory and data) is the most we ever get on Popper's theory. Popper would formulate the point by saying that adaptationist methods fail to test selection theory severely, rendering it badly uncorroborated.

We have required that sociobiology be "consistent" in two senses of the word. First, there is the sense bound up with the concept of a correct explanation: all the statements in the explanation are true. Statements of theory, facts, and auxiliary hypotheses that make theory applicable to the facts do not produce any contradictions. This is required by the sound-argument model, on which false statements don't explain, even if apparently consistent with the data ("empirically adequate"). Second, there is the sense bound up with testing for whether the explanations proposed are correct explanations, namely, apparent consistency with the data.

The struggle to achieve completeness imposes a far more demanding standard of evidence than the one criticized by Gould and Lewontin. A well-tested explanation is one such that (a) attempts to confirm it are successful, where a well-developed body of evidence indicates that all the pertinent statements of theory, data, and auxiliary hypotheses are true, and (b) attempts to disconfirm it are unsuccessful, where a well developed body of evidence indicates that attempts at disconfirmation could possibly show statements in each of these categories false but in fact do not disconfirm any of them. This concept raises the issue of the relation of confirmation and disconfirmation in the context of Popper's views.

## Confirmation and Disconfirmation

One approach, Popper's, states that confirmation is neither sufficient nor necessary for acceptability, on the grounds that genuine confirmation is impossible. This book does not address the problem of radical scepticism, but shares the consensus in mainstream philosophy that Popper's solution is unsatisfactory and that there is genuine confirmation. Both confirmational and disconfirmational success are crucial for achieving well-tested explanations. Note in passing that Popper motivated his view on the basis of saying that "It is easy to obtain confirmations, or verifications, for nearly every theory—if we look for confirmations" (Kourany 1987, 141). Yes, it is easy, providing we have low standards for what counts as a definitive confirmation. No, it is quite difficult, providing we have high standards that incorporate rules about statistical significance, data collection techniques, independent testing of auxiliary assumptions, and other factors that discriminate strong from weak confirmation. These controls on confirmation defeat the presumption that high standards for acceptance can only be found in disconfirmation and not in confirmation.

Another approach, Kitcher's (1987, 67), states that confirmation is necessary for acceptability, where to confirm is to find independently justified case-specific constraints that enable us to eliminate rival "Darwinian histories" (recall the kinds of explanation). "Successful pursuit of adaptationist hypotheses already presupposes just that attention to rival possibilities that Gould and Lewon-

tin urge upon their colleagues. Significant confirmation of adaptationist hypotheses is possible—but only if biologists are prepared to
undertake the investigations necessary for articulating claims
about allometry, pleiotropy, and so forth" (Kitcher 1985, 233). In
contrast, Popper holds that explanations are disconfirmable but not
confirmable. That is, inferences to their falsity are justified when
deductively valid, but inferences to their truth are always unjustified.

On the concept of evidential success used here, a well-tested
explanation is one thoroughly tested such that the evidential reasons for judging it true are better reasons than the evidential reasons for judging it false. This concept naturally combines the criteria of confirmation and disconfirmation, acknowledging the fact that
we can normally find reasons for and reasons against any explanatory hypothesis that scientists have worked on. Such reasons employ
evidence but do not reduce to formalizable inductions or deductions
from observation statements alone. Deductively valid reasons and
inductively strong reasons aren't the only sorts of legitimate reasons
in science or everyday life; we normally and legitimately employ
prima facie reasons (Pollock 1986).

The hypothetico-deductive method has a positive form, whereby increased number and variety of confirming instances yields increased indication of truth, and a negative form, whereby constructing a set of rival explanations and confirming one by eliminating
rivals is the key to truth. Which form we use is not a matter of
logical principle, but of the economy of research: use whatever evidential methods are most efficient and effective for attaining the
best quality of positive and negative reasons, where we arrive at
considered judgements of truth and falsity as quickly as possible.

This view of evidence has an implication for what counts as a
good criticism of an explanation. Critics do not show an explanation
to be unacceptable merely by thinking of ways in which it might be
false. That would only be revealing it to be falsifiable in principle.
Nor do they show it to be unacceptable by going on to show that tests
of its falsity have not been carried out. That would not rule out its
status as the best available alternative hypothesis since its rivals
may not fare any better. Arguments for unacceptability must show
that a rival explanation fares better with respect to arguments that
the reasons for thinking it false are better than the reasons for
thinking it true. The reasons appeal to more than simple observation; they involve matters of theory, programs, and frameworks.

Some evaluators (e.g., Kitcher 1985, 58) have derided appeals to Popper's falsificationism in order to evaluate sociobiology. Their criticism is that no scientific claim is provably false, where provability is a logically impeccable inference from impeccable sensory data or a single observation statement. The criticism is baseless since it caricatures Popper's views. Popper (Lakatos 1970) agrees that theories are not falsifiable in that sense. Falsification for him is just disconfirmation.

Kitcher attacks falsifiability as a "red herring" on the grounds that no statement incompatible with any scientific theory is one whose truth or falsity can be ascertained by relatively direct observation alone. For instance, Darwin said his theory would be falsified by demonstration that some existing complex organ "could not possibly have been formed by numerous, successive slight modifications." No relatively direct observation could establish a statement of that sort. This example does make its point, one Popper didn't deny. Popper is well aware that no observable fact by itself logically falsifies a theory since he stressed that theories have observational consequences only in conjunction with auxiliary hypotheses. Popper claims that, before testing, one must conceive of some set of (1) statements about observable situations and (2) appropriate auxiliary hypotheses, which would count as a reason for thinking it false, and then go on to devise tests that in some way embody the situation. When theoretical expectations are violated, one can identify the source of error in the falsity of the observation statements, the auxiliary assumptions, or the theoretical statements. Popper realized that nature can't tell us which judgement to make and that such judgements are debatable. His critical method advises us to debate them. Popper's view of falsifiability is less extreme and more sophisticated than is generally recognized (Schilpp 1974).

## Implications

The preceding discussion of falsifiability and adaptationism can be filled out by drawing some implications for the character of scientific debate, what theories are about, demarcation of science and nonscience, the critical attitude, and the objects of testing. Consider each in turn.

Because claims about adaptive significance and genetic causation are relational in character, attempts to confirm or to disconfirm them must be sensitive to the comparisons that give them meaning.

For the same reason, dispute over "adaptationism" and "genetic determinism" remain ill-defined pseudo-issues. They are labels for conceptual confusions of those who don't know much evolutionary theory. Criticisms of the alleged "unfalsifiability" of sociobiological explanations are unjustified when they ignore the various sorts of confirmation and disconfirmation, their relation, and invoke Popper's name but violate his analysis of falsification. Critique takes the form of name calling (being "unscientific" is like being "un-American") or parody of opponents' aims (no one advocates "vulgar adaptationism"). Scientific debate about real issues concerning adaptation are routinely carried out in terms of focal-point caricatures and obituary notices. At issue is the degree to which selection has been effective in the actual past, given the constraints imposed by historical contingencies.

Darwin's claim that theory falsification would require showing that something "could not possibly" occur indicates that theories are not falsified by statements about what is actual, but about what is possible. It is a short step to see that theories are not just about the actual world, but are also about possibilities. Observation statements are singular statements designed to express facts about what is actual and so are tested against other observation statements about what is actual. Theoretical statements are general statements designed to express facts about what is possible and so are tested against other theoretical statements about what is possible. Since the actual is possible, observations are indirectly relevant to theory-choice. This is why observation logically underdetermines the truth or falsity of theories. This also enables us to distinguish how-possibly explanations (explanations of how something could have evolved) from how-actually explanations (explanations of how something did in fact evolve). When sociobiologists seem to give poor how-actually explanations expressing extreme adaptationism, they often are sketching how-possibly explanations.

Evolutionary theory explains observations of human mating behavior by joining theoretical and observation statements so that actual mating behavior is embedded in and projected from the array of evolutionary possibilities. Evolutionary explanations are tested against statements about what is actual and what is possible (see 4.1 and 5.1). Brandon (1990, 183) shows by example that how-possibly explanations "can be rigorously formulated so that they have testable consequences." There are rival thermoregulatory hypotheses about the adaptive value of proto-wings during the transition from wingless to winged insects. By experimentally manipulating physical models, statements about what can result from intervening changes are tested. Computer simulations offer a way of testing how-possibly social hypotheses.

Popper claimed that the method of falsification he endorses acts as a criterion which demarcates science from nonscience. The kernal of truth here is that some sort of difference-making quality is implicit in the concept of an acceptable scientific explanation. Science differs from nonscience in that scientific work is aimed at the goals of science. Explanatory work aimed at these goals comes in various degrees of quality that grade into each other. To add to Kitcher's gradations, there is a slippery slope from excellent, to good, to average, to bad, to dreadful, and to pseudoscience in various versions of an explanation of mating behavior. Sociobiologists are engaged in explanatory work deserving the title "scientific" if they are effective in striving to improve the array of currrently acceptable scientific explanations, as given by the totality of appropriate criteria and standards for their fulfillment. If not, their work is "unscientific" in a criterial, normative sense even if "scientific" in a sociohistorical sense.

A core of truth in Popper's falsificationism is that a necessary quality of the scientific attitude is that we do not deliberately protect explanations from the threat of criticism (Kitcher 1985, 61). Explanations are advanced in the cause of scientific inquiry so that every feature is potentially subject to criticism. The critical attitude is particularly heightened in science, but not unique to it. Presumably, it is part of rational inquiry as such. Adaptationism is only one feature of the hardened Modern Synthesis subjected to extensive critical scrutiny. Of course, sociobiology should take as its point of departure both the best-received version of evolutionary theory and its body of critical scrutiny. Sociobiology has in fact confronted the most potentially fatal putative counter-examples to the completeness of evolutionary theory. In animal sociobiology a prime example is altruism. In human sociobiology every social behavior having evolutionary significance is a counterexample, with reproductive behavior being potentially fatal. Practice in sociobiology has attempted to turn these potentially refuting counterexamples victoriously into examples. For instance, the fact that humans have sex while practicing contraception reduces fitness, seeming to refute adaptive explanation. But it only goes to show that the past connection between sex and reproduction is now broken and that we have been selected to seek the pleasure of copulation, not reproduction per se. This response treats the problem as a puzzle to be solved, for if such problems cannot be solved, then the adaptive approach is in trouble. The very recognition that evolutionary theory had been inconsistent or irrelevant with social data embodies a heightened critical attitude. These choices of problems indicate that the critical attitude is inherent in the rationale for sociobiology.

What is tested by evidence and accepted or rejected on that basis is not evolutionary explanation of sociality in general, a given explanatory approach, or an explanation abstracted away from its various versions as the research situation changes. Those items would be "unfalsifiable" in the usual sense. The proper objects of testing are particular formulations of particular explanations. The criticism that sociobiology is an unfalsifiable adaptationist program misconstrues the proper objects of testing. Programs are not the sort of things subject to direct confirming/disconfirming tests.

An explanation in sociobiology is an acceptable scientific explanation, judged in the context of inquiry, if it is the best of rival available explanations for promoting completeness according to at least three kinds of conditions: logical conditions (reasons for thinking that the conditions of derivability, lawhood, and empirical content are satisfied), confirmational conditions (evidence indicating the truth of particular formulations of the explanandum and the explanans), disconfirmational conditions (evidence indicating the falsity of particular formulations of the explanans and explanandum). Common evaluative methods fail to utilize all the forms of confirmation and disconfirmation that qualify well-tested explanations.

## 2.2 Sexist Sexual Hypotheses

### Plausibilism

Most scientists won't expend the time, energy, and effort needed to thoroughly test an explanation if they deem it implausible. Even though particular versions of hypotheses in sociobiology may be "falsified" by tests, their root insights are often deemed plausible enough to be revised accordingly. Decisions to abandon core insights are not made lightly, e.g., that females have limited eggs and males have virtually unlimited sperm must be important for nonhuman and human evolution. It is common sense to demand higher standards of evidential success and lower standards of evidential failure for implausible than for plausible explanations. If you evaluate the scientific status of explanations in sociobiology solely in terms of whether they are plausible, then you are adopting a "plausibilist methodology." So let us examine "plausibilism": Explanations in sociobiology are acceptable scientific explanations if and only if they are plausible.

Plausibility is obviously an insufficient criterion of acceptability. Telling plausible "adaptive stories" is the first of successively more rigorous phases in fulfilling completeness. Moreover, rigor in judging evidence is wasted if there is no rigor in judging plausibility. A precondition for trying to disconfirm each rival explanans in a set of plausible explanations is that one must already have sorted the plausible from the implausible explanations. Plausibility judgements themselves need to be backed up by good reasons.

There are at least five criteria of plausible explanatory hypotheses treated as virtues of scientific hypotheses: conservatism, modesty, simplicity, generality, and disconfirmability (Quine and Ullian 1970). As one plausibility factor among several, disconfirmability is not merely an end in itself but a factor of something more essential to assessment. Therefore, it is false that the only empirical condition of acceptable explanation is to pass the test of observation alone. Instead, we attain a wider perspective on empirical adequacy: "All our contemplating of special virtues of hypotheses will not, we trust, becloud the fact that the heart of the matter is observation. Virtues I through V are guides to the framing of hypotheses that, besides conforming to past observations, may plausibly be expected to conform to future ones. When they fail on the latter score, questions are reopened" (Quine and Ullian 1978, 80).

Of course, the emphasis on plausibility is grounded in Quine's views about testability in science. Quine and Duhem endorsed a holistic theory of evidence, one emphasizing that no hypotheses are tested in isolation from other related bodies of theory and observation. They argued against the early empiricist view that the results of evidential tests definitively confirm or disconfirm a given hypothesis. Definite confirmation is impossible in cases when the results of test fit our hypothesis since those results do not permit us to reliably infer that they fit our hypothesis because our hypothesis is true. Alternative hypotheses can be made compatible with the evidence by tinkering with their auxiliary assumptions about how they would apply to the test case. Definite disconfirmation is impossible in cases when the results of test do not fit our hypothesis since those results do not permit us to reliably infer that they do not fit our hypothesis because our hypothesis is false. The hypothesis can always be claimed to be true and the error can always be claimed to lie with the auxiliary assumptions about how it is to be properly applied to the test case.

Popper thought that disconfirmation could be definite only because he thought of the auxiliary hypotheses as being fixed, purposely fixed by conscious efforts to falsify the hypothesis under test. Quine and Duhem emphasized the logical freedom of the scientist, no matter what the evidence may be, to make adjustments at any place in a holistic web of judgement and belief. The web, ultimately, spans everyday beliefs, scientific doctrines, and even mathematics and logic (recall Quine's attack on the analytic/synthetic distinction). Since evidence itself does not logically rule in or rule out any hypothesis, the role of nonevidential criteria for acceptability looms larger in hypothesis-choice than admitted by previous logical empiricist philosophies of science. If evidence seems definitive, it is because plausibility judgements guide decisions about what to praise as true when things go right and what to blame as false when things go wrong.

A sociobiological explanation is an acceptable scientific explanation only if it is plausible, where plausibility is faithfulness to past and future observations as filtered through the criteria of conservatism, modesty, simplicity, generality, and disconfirmability. Application of these criteria is to be made in accordance with our vision of what a completed evolutionary theory would be like. Prior to rigorous testing, an explanation has to be judged sufficiently plausible to be worthy of being tested in the first place. The function of trying out hypothetical adaptive stories is to develop trained judgements of relative plausibility. As the list of available explanations expands and as each explanation is developed in detail and complexity, higher and higher standards of plausibility are used.

Even if evolutionary explanations of human reproductive behavior were well-tested, critics would continue to regard them with scepticism when holding on to initial reactions of disbelief and implausibility. For instance, explanations that seem sexist or adaptationist are thereby deemed implausible. To eliminate such appearances, we need to identify exactly where sexism and adaptationism can enter explanations of male/female differences, even if we judge their scientific and not their political status. We do so, not because of bad consequences for social policy (effects on political action), not because sexism and adaptationism beget biased belief (effects on systems of belief), but because of obstacles they engender in progress toward fulfilling the goal of completeness (effects on future scientific inquiry).

Prior beliefs have the role of constraints on the sort of explanandum and explanans constructed. "In order to explain the happenings that we are inventing it to explain, the hypothesis may have to conflict with some of our previous beliefs, but the fewer the better. Acceptance of a hypothesis is of course like acceptance of any belief in that it demands rejection of whatever conflicts with it. The less rejection of prior beliefs required, the more plausible the hypothesis—other things being equal" (Quine and Ullian 1978, 66). How do we acquire these prior beliefs? "Actually we inherit the main ones, growing up as we do in a going culture" (Quine and Ullian 1978, 81). Much opposition to sociobiology has arisen because it has seemed to ignore or conflict with social facts known either from everyday life or traditional social science.

Scientific method critically processes particular cultural beliefs, but cannot transcend them as a whole. Since our culture is pervaded by various ideologies, they affect our prior beliefs. Since our prior beliefs affect our explanations, ideologies affect what we count as an acceptable scientific explanation. The same goes for beliefs gained in scientific training. In this simple point we find a source for understanding how it is possible for cultural ideologies (sexism) and scientific ideologies (adaptationism) to influence acts of constructing, revising, and accepting explanations.

# Ideology and the Content of Explanations

In the sociology of science, a recent trend has been to emphasize the fact that ideology influences the very content of science. There are various schools of the sociology of scientific knowledge that propose to demonstrate these influences in various ways. Scientists often find this fact embarrassing, something that threatens to destroy the objective validity of science. If the cultural and scientific ideologies that affect explanatory inquiry are not critically examined by scientists, then science will be their hostage. It should be part of scientific method to identify and critically reflect on the points of entry whereby ideology influences the actual content of scientific knowledge. Ideology affects the general theory that females have a greater stake in each reproductive act than males, the way general theory and specific data are mixed to suggest general behavior patterns robust across species and the application of general behavior patterns to humans. Consider each.

Let's examine the infamous "Sperm are cheap. Eggs are expensive" argument, showing how a logical explanation is also ideological:

> Sperm are cheap. Eggs are expensive. Accordingly, females have a much greater stake in any one reproductive act. Biologist George C. Williams points out that in virtually all species males are selected to be aggressive—sexual advertisers—while females are selected to be choosier—comparison shoppers. Again these behaviors follow directly from the biology of what it is to be male or female. For males, reproduction is easy, a small amount of time, a small amount of semen, and the potential evolutionary return is very great if offspring are produced. On the other hand, a female who makes a "bad choice" may be in real evolutionary trouble. If fertilization occurs, a baby is begun, and the ensuing process is not only inexorable but immensely demanding. . . . Small wonder that females in virtually every species are more discriminating than males in the choice of sexual partners. (Barash 1979, 48)

Is this plausible? Think about the logical structure involved. One logical gap to be closed is from "Sperm are cheap. Eggs are expensive" to "females have a much greater stake in any one reproductive act and in each child." Differential size of male and female gametes is a factor making female gametes more expensive to produce. But this doesn't imply that female investment actually is greater than male investment in each act. There are other relevant factors. The far greater numbers of sperm than eggs (e.g., millions to one in humans) is an opposing factor of relative investment. "Would male expenditures per zygote then be less or more than female expenditures per zygote? We do not know. Indeed, we do not know what would be relevant to deciding" (Richardson 1984, 416).

This query can be turned into an argument for implausibility. We would expect that the quantitative measure of the relative male and female investment due to all such factors varies from species to species and in humans from culture to culture. Suppose there are at least two explanatory hypotheses about the very same state of affairs that are logically incompatible and yet equally likely given background information. To choose one of these hypotheses rather than any other is arbitrary. As a rule, if the hypothesis is chosen arbitrarily, then it is implausible. This rule extends the force of the demand for explanatory consistency to plausibility judgements: Do not use the very same resources to explain incompatible states of affairs. If we did so, we could explain both a fact and an incompatible fact and any choice of one or the other would be arbitrary. Without such a rule, any hypothesis that might be true, given the background information, would be plausible, and plausibility would not effectively rule out any hypotheses. Here, the human species is arbitrarily hypothesized to have higher female investment, yet higher male investment is equally likely, prior to study of factor interactions. Hence, the hypothesis is implausible.

Perhaps whichever sex has smaller gonads (male testes versus female ovaries) is the sex that invests less (Williams 1966). Perhaps not, since we have no good reason to think that gonad size will correlate to parental investment (Richardson 1984). Further, if males expend significantly more energies in excluding other males than do females, that factor would increase male investment. Why do sociobiologists ignore such misgivings? Why assume factors favoring male investment to be outweighed by factors favoring female investment, e.g., the greater cost to potential reproductive output of having an egg go unfertilized as compared to the sperm of one ejaculation? The issue is which explanation they give and why it is commonly regarded as plausible. An answer is that in our society it is commonly believed that males are sexually aggressive and promiscuous whereas females are sexually choosy and faithful. If so, an ideologically influenced belief about human sexual differences penetrates to the construction, revision, and acceptance of a particular explanans intended to apply to all species. Similarly, why do women writers more often emphasize risks of injury or disease in copulation and risk of death in pregnancy in explaining why women are more selective? The answer would presumably lie in differing individual experiences.

Another logical gap obtains from 'females have a greater reproductive stake in any one reproductive act and each child' to 'natural selection favors females who are coy and faithful whereas it favors males who are fast and philanderers'. According to the game-theoretic analysis in terms of evolutionary stable strategies, no pure strategy of this sort is stable (Richardson 1984, 415). That is, a population adopting any given pair of these strategies can be invaded by a population adopting some other pair of these strategies. On these theoretical grounds, we have no reason to think that male-female differences should conform to Barash's and Williams's expectations. Why do people have such expectations, rather than expecting more variation across species? A reasonable but untested answer is the prior culturally induced belief that males and females by nature differ that way.

Consider the way general theory and animal data are mixed to suggest general behavior patterns in animal species. General theory specifies in what conditions a behavioral difference would be favored by selection or would be expected to evolve. Knowledge of actual initial conditions must be mixed with general theory to imply sentences about actual behavioral patterns. Causal arguments are not well-articulated if they confuse general statements about how evolutionary processes work with singular statements about the course or result of evolutionary history. Statements of the form "The theory of male-female differences states that in some species . . ." violate this condition of acceptable logical structure. Barash's (1979) explanations blur claims about how selection pressures work with claims about historical events: ". . . in virtually all species males are selected to be aggressive . . ." (48); "It is clear that women (indeed, females of nearly all species) necessarily invest more in each child than do men, quickly reaching a point where they exhaust their potential and can invest no more" (56).

Sexist preconceptions and illogical thought combine to yield explanations that underestimate diversity within and between species (making sex roles falsely seem universal, inevitable, unchangeable). In some species demand for parental investment by males is low. In others demand is high. Logically and politically sensitive assessment alerts us to what research is needed to test explanations, e.g., actual levels of male and female investments.

Judgements of plausibility on the grounds of conformity with evolutionary theory are tricky because of subtle theoretical differences. The degree to which it is necessary for males to give aid to females in order that they can successfully rear their young prevents males from all-out pursuit of mating success (Trivers 1972; Lancaster 1985). This postulate leads to the following expectations in species where demand for paternal investment is high: monogamous mating patterns; low levels of sexual dimorphism in body size and weapons of aggression; equivalent behavioral levels between the sexes in aggressiveness, territoriality, nurture of young, sexuality, and bond formation (Lancaster 1985). If we assume that the demand for paternal investment is high in humans, we will treat explanations that posit greater promiscuity in men than women as "bad science, caused by and perpetuating male bias." Yet the sex allocating the smaller portion of reproductive effort as parental effort benefits most from competing for mate quantity (Bateman 1948; Trivers 1972; Wade 1979; Betzig 1988). That postulate leads to the expectation that in species where males allocate less reproductive effort to parenting, polygyny will evolve. If we assume that men allocate less reproductive effort to parenting than women, we will treat the same explanation as "good science, free from male bias."

Consider the application of general behavior patterns to humans:

> There is even direct evidence from our anatomy and physiology suggesting that polygyny is the biologically "natural" state of *Homo Sapiens*. Except for our genitalia, the physical differences between men and women are much more associated with fighting than with copulating. Among animals, monogamy is almost invariably found among those species that have little differences in size between the sexes. Foxes, coyotes, eagles, geese, swans, ducks, sparrows, bluebirds and warblers all tend to be monogamous, with males and females growing to approximately the same size. If we consider some polygynous species—elephant seals, deer, elk, moose, gorillas—the typical social system is one male mating with several females, and, not surprisingly, the males are considerably larger than their consorts. Among human beings, although some women are larger than some men, there is no question that, on the whole, men are the larger sex. (Barash 1979, 64)

Is this animal-human comparison plausible? Some culturally inherited views about male aggressiveness and polygyny lead us to answer in the affirmative. But each aspect of the comparison needs to be studied before we regard it as plausible. Is the statistical difference in size between men and women large enough to be significant with respect to polygyny? Are differences in bone structure and muscularity large enough to be significant with respect to differential aggressiveness? How do differential size, bone structure, and muscularity produce a link between differential aggressiveness and polygyny? What rival comparisons exist? "In fact, human sexual dimorphism in body size, stature, and muscularity is relatively minor by mammalian standards, but we have one system in which sexual dimorphism is prominently developed: The storage of energy in fat deposits. The storage of energy is so important that its deposition as fat affects both the sequencing of pubertal events and the establishment of fertility" (Lancaster 1983, 14). Perhaps males selected females for large breasts even when their fat reserves were low, where enlarged breasts confused males about ovulatory status and so weakened male control over female sexual activity (Barkow 1989c, 340).

Let us consult Quine and Ullian's criteria to decide the plausibility of Barash's and Lancaster's explanations. Barash's explanation fulfills all of Quine's criteria. In a sense, it is conservative: it offers an explanans for an explanandum widely regarded at the time in our society as a fact, namely, that our social system reflects the tendency of males to search out more sexual partners than females. It is modest: it makes as few assumptions as possible. It is general: it aims to encompass human institutions and human nature, animal behavioral patterns across all species, and general evolutionary mechanisms in a single scheme. It is simple: it uses a few general theoretical claims about sexual dimorphism, which behaviors are selected for or against given that sexual dimorphism, and evolutionary principles together with common conceptions about the animal kingdom to yield statements of these supposed differences. While not testable, strictly speaking (in Hempel's sense), it is testable in an important sense: work along the lines of Richardson, Lancaster, Bleier, and Hrdy can refute it.

Lancaster's explanation fulfills only the last criterion. It is not conservative: it explains facts not yet regarded as facts in our society, i.e. a feminist version of differences in the nature of men and women. It is immodest: it makes a unique set of auxiliary assumptions, e.g., about the relative effectiveness of different selection pressures for each species in order to apply evolutionary theory to that species. It is not general: different explanations are given for each species whereby seemingly small details may have great evolutionary significance. It is complex in three ways: it combines theories of sexual selection, parental investment, K- and r-strategies of reproduction; it unites a host of studies of sex differences in dominance, mating behavior, sexual assertiveness, attachment to home range and the natal group, ecological and social correlates of sex differences in body size; it combines the implications of fieldwork and species comparisons among primates to deal with the complexities of actual behavior. It is testable and well-tested, by ordinary standards: it integrates multidisciplinary data from primate fieldwork, social ecology, human social anthropology, and evolutionary, reproductive, and developmental biology.

Quine's criteria gave the result that Barash's explanation is plausible and Lancaster's implausible. But we know independently of those criteria that the reverse is true. What went wrong? Our application of Quine's criteria failed to distinguish relative from absolute standards for their application. Quine intended those criteria to be applied in a relative sense; other things being equal, of two hypotheses, the one that is more conservative, more modest, simpler, more general, and more refutable is more plausible than the other hypothesis. But we don't want to create a hypothesis so conservative, modest, simple, general, and refutable that it hardly has a chance of being true. We want to create one as conservative, modest, simple, general, and refutable as needed to give it a good chance of truth. Then we try to reduce a set of such hypotheses to one through efforts at confirmation and disconfirmation. Kitcher's maxim, "The truth is rarely simple," and Lewontin's maxim, "The truth is in the details," capture this point.

## Scientific Development

Early advocates (e.g., Wilson, Barash, Trivers) and early critics (e.g., Sociobiology Study Group) succumbed to the temptation to sensationalize sociobiology by attributing to it all sorts of fantastic implications about human nature. The ensuing debate focused on the idea that certain human nature ideologies were scientifically grounded and others scientifically undermined. An assumption on both sides is that features of our species constitute human nature (e.g., Gribbon and Gribbon 1988, 1). But why expect human nature to be revealed by one science rather than others or by science rather than, say, poetry?

The political debate over biological limits to social change is confused over what it means to explain behavior in the human species. Sociobiological claims about human nature are untestable in the obvious sense that no observational tests could decide whether a behavior or a psychological mechanism is accidental or essential to being human. Human nature is not a variable subject to experimental controls. No scientific arguments could possibly determine whether a set of theoretical variables contains variables whose values constitute human nature. So the assumption that some essential human nature is or could be revealed by evolutionary biology is unjustified. Claims about human nature are nonscientific and yet are bound up with ideologies that influence scientific explanations.

The production, revision, and acceptance of explanations insensitive to the ideological content of science risk uncritical assessments of plausibility. For instance, Barash's explanation of the double standard in terms of predispositions for male sexual aggressiveness and female sexual passivity leads readily to his statement that "it should surprise no one that women almost always are sexually coy relative to the more available men" (1979, 48). Sociobiology cannot afford to continue to identify its explananda uncritically, through the use of cultural stereotypes, lest it explain presumed facts that are not facts and underestimate variation:

> For over three decades, a handful of partially true assumptions were permitted to shape the construction of general evolutionary theories about sexual selection. These theories of sexual selection presupposed the existence of a highly discriminating, sexually "coy" female who was courted by sexually undiscriminating males. Assumptions underlying these stereotypes included, first, the idea that relative male contribution to offspring was small, second, that little variance exists in female reproductive success compared to the very great variance among males, and third, that fertilization was the only reason for females to mate. While appropriate in some contexts, these conditions are far from universal. Uncritical acceptance of such assumptions has greatly hampered our understanding of animal breeding systems particularly, perhaps, those of primates. (Hrdy 1986, 119)

Hrdy, a feminist sociobiologist, goes on to show the origin of Trivers's theory of sexual selection in Bateman's *Drosophila* experiments of 1948 and summarizes the primatological evidence for highly variable and often active roles of females in managing sexual consortships. Feminism can help us identify stultifying habits of thought bound up with cultural stereotypes that put the quest for completeness on the wrong track (McGill, Dewsbury, and Sachs 1978; Bleier 1984, 1986; Fausto-Sterling 1985).

The following view of the way a science develops makes sense of the changes that have taken place in sociobiology as illustrated by the foregoing examples. Standards for plausibility are raised as sociobiology develops in its quest for completeness. In a sexist society, sexist explanations are judged more plausible than nonsexist ones in dealing with basic ideas, e.g., each sex tries to control the reproduction of the other sex. During initial phases of the emerging field, ideological presuppositions generate explanatory questions and answers. How else could effort at explanation begin, when extending a science into a new domain? As the field develops, it reacts more and more to its own body of results than to preconceptions in its own society. Explanations are constructed, evaluated, and revised according to evaluations of previous explanations. Barash's explanation is no longer plausible, relative to the set of currently available explanations. As the field develops, it generates internal controls in conjunction with growing sophistication in results and evaluative procedures, enabling it to maintain an increasing degree of autonomy from the ideologies that rule its own society. These internal controls initially concern criteria of acceptability bound up with theory, gradually encompass criteria involving research programs, and eventuate in criteria pertinent to conceptual frameworks.

## Implications

Our previous discussion contains some implications for assessing science that indicate the range of elements found in the structure of explanatory research.

A virtue of Quine's criteria of plausibility is that they make sense of scientific debate in terms of the structure and procedures of scientific thought. Everyone has been socialized with mythical, stylized views of "the scientific method" which imply that if we just carry out that method, we will find the truth and everyone will agree on what that truth is. But if scientific method leads us to look for potentially conflicting features of explanatory theories and hypotheses, the potential for debate is inherent in scientific method. This fact was already pointed out in the trade-off between derivability and truth implicit in Hempel's views on confirmation and Popper's views on disconfirmation. Judgements of plausibility—involving multiple criteria, controversial presuppositions and inferences, scientific and cultural ideologies—are objects of legitimate debate.

In emerging sciences like sociobiology, each explanation confronts many points of evaluation that involve plausibility judgements, and so controversy is to be expected. When scientists in the field begin to agree on the plausibility judgements, the controversy wanes. At that point we have a good indication that the field's status changes from being an emerging, prevalidated science to being an established, validated science. The transition occurs when its results are validated primarily by reference to previous results rather than being continually undermined by evaluations in terms of preconceptions induced by the general intellectual and common-sense milieu of ideas. This transition is not yet on the horizon for human sociobiology because guiding ideas are so challenging to our preconceptions. One such guiding idea is that even though behaviors are not in our genes, the course of cultural evolution is grounded in the effects of the cumulative result of genetic evolution to the extent that the bearers of culture are organisms whose motives reflect evolved fitness-maximizing strategies.

Despite the rhetoric and associated polemics, sociobiology is an ordinary science like any other science, one full of rival explanatory strategies and hard decisions about what to give up when criteria for acceptability conflict. Sociobiology is a heterogeneous field in which no one knows what a completed set of evolutionary theories and data on social evolution data would be like, not a monolithic perspective with a single explanatory strategy. Hence, it cannot be evaluated once and for all in one fell swoop, but must be evaluated so as to take account of subtle relations among interacting research components. It must probe validity in terms of the interplay of assertions, concepts, aims, methods, and results in ways that reflect a representative plurality of ideological orientations.

To sum up our discussion in this section, although plausibilism is false, plausibility is a necessary condition for acceptability. If an explanatory hypothesis is to unify antecedently held theories and facts, then it should be plausible in Quine's sense: conservative, modest, simple, general, and refutable. Criteria of plausibility are criteria for deciding which explanations are worth constructing, assessing, and improving. They are not criteria of truth, as are conditions of confirmation and disconfirmation. The criterion of conservatism functions as a particularly important entry point by which ideologies, both cultural and scientific, make their impact on the construction and evaluation of explanations in sociobiology, considered even in terms of their scientific status. Ideological influences can never be purged from science and so cannot be regarded as biases (which assumes they can be eliminated). Instead, proper evaluation employs standards sensitive to ideologies. We can learn how to live with them, hoping that, in the conscious battle between rival programmatic orientations, the truth has a better chance of being revealed than if we deny or ignore them as "unscientific."

## 2.3 Progress and Reductionism

### Progressivism

Typically, traditional empiricist philosophy of science (e.g., Hempel, Popper, Quine) focused on the products of science, whereas recent historicist philosophy of science (e.g., Kuhn, Lakatos, Laudan) focused on the process of scientific development. Logical empiricism took logically perspicuous reconstructions of theories as its basic unit of analysis, designing its list of validity-making properties as unchanging logical and empirical conditions. Recent historical philosophy of science takes research programs for generating a sequence of observations and theories as its basic unit of analysis, designing its list of validity-making properties as changing presuppositional conditions. This difference in focus has fostered the false impression that older and recent images of science are always incompatible. Yes, there are incompatibilies, e.g., over whether there can be a normative logic of scientific method universal for all science over the entire history of science (Holcomb 1987b). We are not concerned here with the "stability thesis," but with the methodology of sociobiology now.

However, if we focus simultaneously on the products and process of science, then some formerly conflicting opinions can be reconciled. Logical empiricist norms have implications for science-in-process. Discoveries about guiding presuppositions can be incorporated into norms of method. Our use of Hempel's revised empiricist conception of sufficient confirmation (1.4) led us to supplement atemporal logical and empirical criteria (1.3) with the changing aim-oriented standards of sociobiology's conceptual framework (1.2). We have used Quine's empiricist conception of plausibility (2.2) to supplement fixed criteria of plausibility involving observation-theory match with changing plausibility standards according to sociobiology's programmatic presuppositions (2.1). Judgements of how to and how not to adjust auxiliary assumptions (1.3), so crucial in matters of theory application (1.2), also lead assessment in terms of theories into assessment in terms of programs.

Once we bring the process of science into focus, we need to treat a given formulation of a sociobiological explanation as part of a sequence of formulations. Is the explanation the right kind of explanation, one that makes progress? That depends on whether it is guided by the right sort of theoretical assumptions and whether its specific versions are revised so as to protect those assumptions while handling previously anomalous facts and new facts as well. The direction of the revisions is controlled by an underlying research program. If you evaluate the scientific status of sociobiology in terms of progressive research programs, and only in terms of them, then you are adopting a "progressivist methodology." So let us examine "progressivism": A sociobiological explanation is acceptable just in case it is guided by and contributes to a progressive research program.

Lakatos clarified progressivism. Four aspects of Lakatos's theory of validity in the context of scientific change are significant for sociobiology: the question of the sense in which an explanation is falsifiable, the role of novel explananda in yielding progress, the identification of explananda as familiar or novel and its import for reductionism, and deviations from impartiality in keeping the record of successes and failures that determine whether work is progressive. Consider each in turn.

## Falsifiable Units

Lakatos devised his theory to come to grips with misgivings over Popper's theory of falsification. Lakatos (1970) recounts Popper's falsifiability condition: "A theory is "scientific" if one is prepared to specify in advance a crucial experiment (or observation) which can falsify it, and it is pseudo-scientific if one refuses to specify such a "potential falsifier." By "theory," Lakatos and Popper mean a systematized set of generalizations, e.g., the wave and particle theories, classical and quantum mechanics, and relativity theory in physics.

Hence, their talk of falsifiability is immediately applicable to sociobiology only as a criterion for judging the validity of evolutionary theory as a whole. The sociobiology debate is not over that judgement, but over whether explanations in sociobiology misapply evolutionary theory. In evolutionary biology, as compared to some areas of physics, explanations are much more the focus of acceptability judgements than whole theories. The route from general theory to actual cases is far more complex than in mechanics, in the sense of requiring far more case-specific intervening assumptions or auxiliary hypotheses. The scientific status of such theories turns on whether the theories issue disconfirmable explanations/predictions, not on whether the theories are falsifiable. Very general biological theories (and models) are disconfirmable only indirectly in virtue of their disconfirmable explanations or predictions. For any explanandum, there is never just one explanation logically derivable from evolutionary theory, but many possible explanations suggested by it according to sets of different evolutionary scenarios. Since evolutionary theory is already established, it would be fallacious to infer its falsity from the falsity of various problematic explanations/predictions about sociality issuing from it.

Compare explanations generated from evolutionary theory and from Newton's theory. Suppose we apply Newtonian mechanics to our solar system (Putnam 1974, 65). An explanans may consist of just four generalizations—Newton's three laws of motion plus his law of universal gravitation—and a few auxiliary simplifying assumptions describing initial conditions and boundary conditions— no bodies exist except the sun and earth, the sun and earth exist in a hard vacuum, and the sun and earth are subject to no forces except mutually induced gravitational forces. Approximations to Kepler's laws of the earth's orbit are logically derivable from this explanans. These few sentences yield what we normally count as a "realistic" explanation or prediction; it states a "fact" despite the idealizations in the explanans.

Similarly, Barash's explanation of the double standard consists of a few evolutionary generalizations and quite a few simplifying assumptions (1.3). The result is normally regarded as an unrealistic explanation or prediction; it states a falsehood due to idealizations in the explanans. Due to the differential import of the idealizations made in the simplifying assumptions, Newton's explanation seems to us a full-blooded explanation, whereas Barash's explanation seems to us merely an explanation-sketch.

Popper's falsificationism was motivated by contrasting Einstein's gravitational theory with the theories of astrology, Marx, and Freud (Popper 1963). He regarded Einstein's theory as incompatible with certain possible results of observation (recall the eclipse experiment), whereas every human behavior can be interpreted as compatible with those theories. Popper once thought that evolutionary theory is unfalsifiable but later changed his mind. Suppose it is unfalsifiable, say, because we cannot justifiably regard all its auxiliary assumptions as fixed and so cannot definitively point the arrow of falsification at the theory rather than the auxiliary assumptions. That would discredit falsifiability as a demarcation criterion, not evolutionary theory. Even physical theories are normally unfalsifiable:

> Is, then, Popper's falsifiability criterion the solution to the problem of demarcating science from pseudo-science. No. For Popper's criterion ignores the remarkable tenacity of scientific theories. Scientists have thick skins. They do not abandon a theory merely because facts contradict it. They normally either invent some rescue hypothesis to explain what they then call a mere anomaly, or, if they cannot explain the anomaly, they ignore it, and direct their attention to other problems. Note that scientists talk about anomalies, recalcitrant instances, not refutations. History of science, of course, is full of accounts of how crucial experiments allegedly killed theories. But such accounts are fabricated long after the theory had been abandoned. (Lakatos 1970)

Lakatos decided that Popper's falsificationism is based on ignorance of how science does and should work. Sexual selection theory is unfalsifiable and properly so, because of its great scope and generality and complexity. Explanations of reproductive behavior are unfalsifiable and properly so, because the sorts of flaws critics point out can always be viewed as anomalies to be explained away or ignored. We can reconcile both Popper's and Lakatos's insights by noting that, strictly speaking, the most which could possibly be regarded as provably false is a specific formulation of a specific version of an explanation of reproductive behavior. The initial version given by Barash can be modified in various ways, some retaining allegiance to its seeming adaptationist character and male bias, others more and more closely resembling the rival explanation by Lancaster, with its seeming explanatory pluralism and female bias. We should assess explanations in terms of research programs manifested as a series of changes in initial, purposely oversimplified and unrealistic, explanation-sketches.


## Judging Progress


Taking the idea of a novel fact to be intuitively clear, Lakatos derived from his condition of novelty a criterion of science and pseudoscience. A research program is theoretically progressive if and only if theoretical advance precedes empirical advance. Otherwise, the research program is theoretically degenerative. If, on balance, the program tends to generate explanations of novel facts through theoretical refinement, theory anticipates data, and so the explanatory program is progressive. But if, on balance, the program tends to rationalize facts given by prior beliefs by testing the ingenuity of its practitioners, data anticipates theory, and so the explanatory program is degenerative. So far, so good. He goes on to claim that programs that are continually theoretically progressive count as valid science, whereas hopelessly degenerative research programs count as invalid or pseudo-science. However, all strict demarcation criteria have failed. Instead, we simply note that it is more rational to accept explanations issuing from programs on balance progressive rather than degenerative.

The rub comes with the phrase "on balance." It could never be a purely quantitative notion, since the relative importance of theoretical lag and theoretical anticipation must obviously be taken into account. Further, a research program may be theoretically progressive for some time, then be theoretically degenerative ever after. Or, it may start out theoretically degenerative and turn theoretically progressive, as human sociobiology might be proceeding. Or, it may flip flop from one state into the other in ways that its advocates and critics could not foresee. Lakatos's theory implies that research programs cannot be instantly or finally refuted or validated. ". . . while it is a matter of intellectual honesty to keep the record public, it is not dishonest to stick to a degenerating program and try to turn it into a progressive one" (Lakatos 1970). Our use of scientific method is incapable of deciding whether we should abandon human sociobiology, fearing that its anomalies will never be resolved, or remain working on it, hoping that we can find some way to resolve its anomalies.

Lakatos's critique of Popper's falsificationism combines with his own identification of the existence of research programs in science to have immediate implications for the usual critiques of sociobiology. For example, a rationale behind the critique of adaptationism is that "we would not object so strenuously to the adaptationist program if its invocation, in any particular case, could lead in principle to its rejection for want of evidence" (Gould and Lewontin 1979, 587). This rationale misconstrues the unit said to be falsifiable. First, particular explanations, i.e., particular formulations of the explanans and explanandum in a version of an explanation of a certain kind are potentially rejectable or acceptable. Second, explanatory programs are not the sorts of items in principle rejectable in a way quickly decidable by reference to cases taken one at a time. Research programs sanction certain kinds of explanation that bridge underlying theory and particular cases. Research programs cannot be assessed directly from single cases. Instead, they are judged by complex inferences from the overall record of successes and failures in numerous cases, judgements of the form "Does the record show that the kind of explanation is worthwhile or hopeless for attaining completeness?"

In such judgements, the prospects for the kind of explanation need to be informed by an accurate understanding of its historical context. In this vein, Ruse (1989) stresses the fact that even though human sociobiology is new, it is not a new paradigm (or: research program), and that this historical fact helps orient the range of expectations we might have about what sociobiology can and should do. Sociologically, human sociobiology is new, with its own journals, organizations, name, supporters, and detracters. Epistemologically, human sociobiology is not a new paradigm, not something existing in isolation that can earn praise and blame all by itself. Ruse (1989 168–169) draws the implications of some points made in 1.2:

> But, epistemologically, human sociobiology must be seen as part of the overall Darwinian synthesis (Ruse, 1987a). It is a branch of basic evolutionary theory, no less than is paleontology, or biogeography, or systematics. Furthermore, our understanding of the particular contingencies of our own species cannot and should not be divorced from what other biologists tell us about ourselves, for instance from what those who study our recent past (the paleoanthropologists) have to say. What does this mean, in effect? It means that human sociobiologists have an obligation to speculate and a certain credit to draw on. We know that natural selection was crucially important in the development of life. We know (at least, we have strong evidence that) natural selection was important in the development of human life. . . . We know . . . , that animal sociobiology strikes new successes, almost daily. Moreover, some of the greatest successes have been with primate species, close to ourselves. Overall, therefore, the presumption is that sociobiology might throw some light on us humans. To do this, they must (and may) speculate and expect to be taken seriously (at least, genuinely tolerated).

In effect, Ruse is taking the Duhem-Quine point that hypotheses are not tested in isolation and is applying it to evaluation, stressing the time dimension. Sociobiological hypotheses are not to be thought of as being constructed, revised, or tested in isolation from their historical, programmatic context. Ruse has argued that excessively critical evaluations have taken the hypotheses of human sociobiology out of their programmatic context, ignoring clear ties to past successes in evolutionary biology and animal sociobiology and ignoring the way those ties guide the meaning, presuppositions, and implications of its hypotheses. The criticisms to which we will naturally be inclined without attention to such matters are, in general, irrelevant to the project being attempted. This has been shown by analyzing the criticisms, showing them to be unjustifiable (Ruse 1979).

Of course, an argument for taking "the Darwinian paradigm" in human sociobiology seriously is no substitute for a plausibility argument or an evidential argument. If it were, we would be "trapped in a circle, where speculation is taken as fact, which is then taken as support for further speculation" (Ruse 1989, 169). Even a legitimate research program may yield uniformly implausible results: "Human sociobiologists had better come up with some findings and some predictions and some connections, or we shall start relegating them to the status of parapsychologists—dreadfully sincere but dreadfully implausible" (1989, 169). What, then, would count as a body of a successful findings, successful predictions, successful connections between evolutionary theory and human social data, where success makes human sociobiology legitimate in a sense that parapsychology is not? Here is where the appeal to novel results, as emphasized by Lakatos, comes into play. Successful results in this sense mean successful novel results.

To place the role of criticism directed against human sociobiology into historical perspective, Ruse (1989, 160) reminds us that

> The theory of Darwin's *Origin* was nigh overwhelmed with problems, internal and external, and there was no shortage of voices happy to proclaim this fact loud and clear. One thinks, for instance, of Darwin's lack of an adequate theory of heredity, and of his troubles with the age-of-the-earth question. . . . But Darwin succeeded because (in Thomas Kuhn's language) he gave biologists a good, working paradigm, within which they could study life's problems. Without the *Origin*, H. W. Bates and A. R. Wallace could not have worked on butterflies, nor could J. D. Hooker have made his brilliant findings about plant distributions (Ruse 1979a). Likewise, I believe that human sociobiology will succeed or fail on its successes, or lack thereof. Does the study of human thought and social behavior, from a Darwinian perspective, lead to new insights and findings, or not? If it does, then criticism (however well-taken) will be secondary. If it does not, then criticism is not needed.

Of course, if human sociobiology turns out to be a dead end, then this historical perspective is quite misleading in its implicit call for advocacy. Lots of new developments in science looked promising in principle at first, from phrenology to phlogiston. Being unable to evaluate human sociobiology with the hindsight of the future historian, we are left with deciding whether it is currently leading to new insights and new findings. Novelty, by itself, is no test of success. Whether some new explanatory idea provides genuine insight and leads to respectable findings depends on strong evidential and plausibility arguments directed toward the novel explanatory idea and novel explanatory findings themselves. And that is the point of many of the criticisms, namely, that the findings do not meet properly high standards of criticism. So novelty concerns which successes are significant and is no substitute for success via the criteria of evidence and plausibility.

## Novel Facts

Buss and Barnes (1986) provide evidence indicating that men and women do have the different mate preferences initially suggested. Men prefer physically attractive and youthful females (signs of fertility) whereas women prefer male mates who are ambitious and good financial prospects (signs of resources for offspring). This pattern is a robust result of applying standard psychological questionnaires to ninety-two married American couples. Their recent work (Cowley 1989) finds the same result in 36 of 37 groups in 33 different societies. They emphasize that even though their work provides rigorously developed confirming data, the data offers no grounds for choosing between explanations in human sociobiology (differential preferences are cues to male and female strategies of reproductive investment) and in social science (differential preferences are the results of structural powerlessness and gender role socialization). Nevertheless, it is argued that if culture were the total explanation, cultures would vary randomly with respect to evolved predispositions, but they do not. Hence, such cross-cultural patterns confirm sexual selection theory in relation to "nothing but culture" theory.

However, this appeal to confirmation alone fails to deal with the difficulty posed by imaginative ingenuity. Given a theory as general and complex as evolutionary theory, and the ability to manipulate intervening assumptions and hypotheses in order to bridge theory and data (emphasized by Duhem 1954 and Quine and Ullian 1978), and some imaginative ingenuity, we can usually devise explanations apparently consistent with the facts. Explanations of known facts degenerate into tests of our ingenuity. Lakatos's (1970) solution is not to appeal to confirmation or disconfirmation per se, but to a property of the facts to be explained or predicted: ". . . all the research programs I admire have one characteristic in common. They all predict novel facts, facts which had been either undreamt of, or have indeed been contradicted by previous or rival programs." If evolutionary theories of human behavior tell us something new, something we would not have learned without those theories, it would be unlikely that they are entirely invalid. Has sexual selection theory in human sociobiology predicted a stunning novel fact or explained an anomalous research finding?

At first, sociobiologists merely took alleged facts from prior beliefs, whether from everyday life or social science, and imbued them with evolutionary significance in order to show that evolutionary theory, far from being irrelevant to or contradicted by human sociality, can illuminate human nature. So advocates like Wilson, Barash, and Alexander found illustrations everywhere. Critics like Gould, Lewontin, and Kitcher emphasized the charlatanism in having us jump to politically dangerous conclusions because we do not survey alternatives. As disputes proceeded over the validity of human sociobiology's incursion into territory formerly reserved for social science, the issue became whether evolutionary explanations could reveal facts unknown from or anomalous to social science.

For instance, Hawkes and Hill (Hawkes et al. 1985; Hill et al. 1987) applied ideas about fitness maximization to explain social structure in a hunter-gatherer culture in Paraguay, the Ache. They found out a number of new facts about differences in foraging patterns of men and women, using an optimal foraging theory standard in evolutionary ecology. Their work appears to conform to high standards of rigorous science (Kitcher 1985, chap. 5). It: (a) formulates precise mathematical models to explain the phenomenon; (b) uses experiment or observation to determine the quantitative values of crucial variables and parameters for applying the general theory to the specific phenomenon; (c) makes detailed observation of the behavior to be explained; (d) is wary of stopping explanatory work too soon, so that research is open ended; (e) investigates discrepancy or reasonable error in the match of explanatory hypothesis to data; (f) is part of an ongoing effort at the marriage of precise theoretical analysis and detailed field research; (g) announces explanatory conclusions with caution; (h) structures our ignorance by identifying precise explanatory questions to be answered if the analysis is to be taken one step further; (i) attempts to overcome difficulties in explanation, not to trumpet hasty, final, grand conclusions.

Although many of the facts uncovered were not known before, it could easily be argued that they could have been learned without the use of sociobiology. However, the form of the facts may be novel. Anthropologists normally explain the fact that hunter-gatherers do not work more than a few hours a day at foraging by postulating that they have limited needs and by hypothesizing that foraging is stopped when these limited needs are fulfilled. Hawkes and Hill counter that there is no principled reason why "fixed food requirements" are set at one level or another and how or why they vary over cultures. Their hypothesis is that there is a direct, positive relation between foraging time and fitness. Whereas anthropological theory predicts that behavioral patterns fit a "limited-needs hypothesis," sociobiological theory predicts that behavioral patterns fit a "fitness maximization hypothesis." Hawkes et al. (1985, 3) conclude from their empirical work that "foragers do not behave consistently in the manner predicted by the postulate of limited needs," but do conform to the postulate of fitness maximization. Their work is designed to explain both new and familiar facts about sexual division of labor by recasting their form.

These explanations are unlike Lakatos's favorite examples, namely, the novel predictions about the eclipse used in testing Einstein's theory of gravitation and about Halley's comet used in testing Newton's theory of gravitation. There, it was obvious that other rival theories could not generate those expectations. Smith (1987, 74) has argued that the data is consistent with the limited-needs hypothesis, properly construed, and that "The limited needs view need not be—and, for many anthropologists, probably is not—conceived of in a way that makes it so contradictory to the theory of natural selection or optimal foraging."

Hawkes (1987) replies that even Smith acknowledges subtle differences in explanations from human sociobiology and from social science that appear similar. She maintains that in principle there is no way to reconcile the two kinds of explanation. The optimization approach of human sociobiology conflicts with the nonoptimization approach of the limited-needs hypothesis. In the nonoptimization approach, resource use varies as a function of different ways to achieving one or another fixed culturally induced goals unrelated to reproductive success. In the optimization approach, resource use varies as a function of different ways of achieving various culturally induced goals that themselves vary as means to the fixed overall goal of the greatest possible reproductive success. The optimization approach demands what the nonoptimization approach denies, namely, that division of labor between the sexes results in part from competition among rival ways for maximizing reproductive success by maximizing foraging returns.

So the issue of whether human sociobiology explains any novel facts turns on the issue of the logical relation between explanation in sociobiology and in social science. The Hawkes-Smith debate shows that it is far from clear that explanations in human sociobiology rival those from social science. The sociobiological journals are full of surprising facts, but these are not novel facts in the sense Lakatos found crucial for progressive programs.

## Reductionism and Completeness

What counts as an acceptable explanation is relative to the set of available rival explanations. The progressiveness of human sociobiology's programs for producing acceptable explanations turns on whether (a) the class of rivals resides exclusively within human sociobiology; or (b) the class includes rivals within social science as well as within its own field. How do we tell which is the case? Determination of the proper class of rivals depends on the aims of human sociobiology. Is reductionism implicated in the requirement of completeness on either sociobiology's observational language (that its observational language is adequate for the expression of any evolutionarily significant social fact) or on its body of theory (that all such facts can be explained by its theories)?

Suppose sociobiology's aim were to uphold reductionism, broadly read as the thesis that all valid explanations in social science are ultimately equivalent to, special cases of, or replaced by valid biological explanations. If social science reduces to biology, then no explanations in an autonomous social science are valid. It follows that explanations in human sociobiology and autonomous social science must be rivals, i.e., (b) holds.

Advocates like Barash (1982, 146) often claim to have refuted this view by saying that "proximate and ultimate explanations are complementary." They identify explanations in social science as in-

voking temporally proximate causal factors. They identify sociobiological explanations as explanations in terms of temporally
distal ("ultimate") causal factors. Why do the proximate mechanisms of behavior that exist, in fact exist rather than others? Because they are ways of surviving and reproducing. Whereas social
science explains human behavior in terms of its proximate causes,
sociobiology describes the proximate effects of those behaviors so
caused on reproduction and goes on to explain the relation between
behavior and reproduction in terms of the cumulative results of
evolution by selection.

However compelling this argument may be on its own terms, it
does not speak to a crucial issue. Must the explanatory theories in
social science that explain behavior in terms of its proximate causes
be tied to evolutionary theory in the right way in order to be validated? If social scientists are free to describe and explain behavior
in ways that need not take into account biological evolution, then it
is likely that their descriptions and explanations of human behavior
will often be irrelevant to or inconsistent with evolutionary theory.
Would evolutionists tell them to go back to the drawing board, to
describe and explain those facts in ways that could be hooked up
properly to evolutionary theory? If so, then the nice connection between proximate and ultimate explanations Barash envisages
serves as a constraint on the validity of social science. To satisfy that
constraint, the theoretical foundations of valid social science would
lie in sociobiology. That's reductionism. Thus, the argument from a
nice proximate-ultimate hookup to the principled denial that social
science and sociobiology are rivals is a logically trivial result of the
reductionist assumption that proper social science is based on sociobiology.

This critique shows that the complementarity argument turns
on assumptions about reductionism. If human sociobiology is reductionist, explanations in a social science whose theoretical foundations lie in biology would complement those in human sociobiology,
but explanations in an autonomous social science would rival those
in human sociobiology. Since social science is currently autonomous
in practice, its explanations are rivals to a reductionist sociobiology
unless a miracle occurs and they fit together by chance or by pre-
established harmony. If human sociobiology is not reductionist, explanations in a social science that are valid autonomously from sociobiology need not rival explanations in sociobiology. Indeed, they
may have little or nothing to do with each other.

This critique of the complementarity argument is vindicated

by noting that it would be a miracle if a social science unguided by evolutionary considerations would on its own describe and explain human behavior in a way directly subsumable under evolutionary theory. This conceptual point is borne out by inspection of the state of sociobiology and social science. In practice, the various social sciences describe and explain human behavior in ways bearing no automatic relation to the theoretical orientation of sociobiology. They are not trying to construct laws of the human species but arrive at their own levels of generality (*pace* Rosenberg 1980). If we try to impose sociobiology on the results of the social sciences without further ado, the conclusions arrived at are implausible and conceptually vexed.

Because our understanding of human behavior is informed by the social sciences operating autonomously from evolutionary biology, the problem of incompleteness is not one of routine extension. Human social behavior, viewed through the lenses of social scientific concepts and theory, seems utterly irrelevant to the expectations induced by evolutionary theory. That basic intuition is a source of why sociobiology seems so wrongheaded to its critics. To take as sociobiology's phenomena the way we understand human social behavior through the lenses of social scientific concepts and theory is a formula for failure. If sociobiology is to show that human behavior, despite appearances, really is relevant to and consistent with evolutionary theory, it cannot add a reproductive interpretation to a nonreproductive description of human phenomena. Success requires that we dissolve the conceptual source of incompleteness, namely, the nonevolutionary conceptualization of human social phenomena in place prior to sociobiology.

The alternative is to reconceptualize human social behavior on its own terms, without the interpretations imposed by a currently autonomous social science, and develop its descriptions and explanations accordingly. Thus, sociobiology must produce its own conceptual frameworks, its own frames of reference by which we conceive of the aspects of human social behavior that are evolutionarily significant. Sociobiology can describe human behavior in a way that abstracts from proximate description and proximate causation in a way that bypasses the theoretical orientation of the social sciences. Sociobiology constructs observation which conforms to its own theory (see chap. 4) and theory which conforms to its own general kinds of explanation for answering evolutionary questions (see chap. 5).

Now suppose that the aim of human sociobiology were completeness. We shall argue that the issue over reductionism and antireductionism is irrelevant to the completeness of evolutionary theory. The sense of completeness used here is analogous to the sense of completeness used in metalogic (recall 1.2). We shall argue by analogy that if the metalogic concept satisfies a certain relevantly similar condition, then so does the metascientific concept. Truth-functional logic is semantically complete in the sense that every tautology of its formal language is a theorem of its deductive system (Hunter 1971, 103). Completeness is a property of a single formal logic having both syntactic and semantic components (P and PS in Hunter's book). It is an internal relation, not a relation between two formal logics. Hence, there is no sense in using a relation between two or more formal logics as a criterion for the completeness of a given formal logic. Evolutionary biology would be complete only if every observed fact of social evolution language can be explained by evolutionary theory. Our analogy makes completeness in science a property of a single science, not a relation between sciences. So it makes no sense to use the reducibility or irreducibility of theoretical systems in social science to the theoretical system in evolutionary biology as a criterion for its internal completeness.

An additional specific argument underscores this presumption that since completeness is an aim internal to evolutionary biology, it is not logically committed to reductionism. Since the degree of completeness is the degree to which evolutionary theory, the theory for the field, successfully covers its own domain. Reductionism is insufficient for achieving completeness because social science does not explain evolutionary aspects of the human condition, and these evolutionary aspects are within the domain of evolutionary theory. Reductionism is unnecessary for achieving completeness because evolutionary science does not explain nonevolutionary aspects of the human condition, these nonevolutionary aspects are not within the domain of evolutionary theory, and such aspects need not be explained by an evolutionary theory that completely covers its domain. So the aim of reductionism is logically independent of the aim of completeness. Since human sociobiology is committed to completeness, it is not committed to reductionism. Therefore, explanations in human sociobiology and in an automonous social science are never rivals as such. The set of rivals resides exclusively within human sociobiology.

Of course, related factual claims in sociobiology and social science may contradict each other, but that is not because they are rivals as such. Barkow (1989c) offers a gene-culture theory of how human organisms receive cultural information, process it, and use it to adopt behavioral plans that achieve evolved goals. He proposes that, with this theory, sociobiology does not replace social science, but renders evolutionary biology compatible with social science.

The same behavior has potentially many aspects or facets (Dretske 1988, 28). Not every fact about behavior needs evolutionary explanation. The issue is which behavioral facts need evolutionary explanation and how do we decide? To show that a behavioral fact is in need of evolutionary explanation, one should show that it has evolutionary significance, not that nonevolutionary explanations are flawed (see chap. 4). This insight reveals that the sociobiology debate has been vexed since both sides have accepted the incorrect assumption that the need for a sociobiological explanation of a human social behavior is directly related to whether or not the usual explanations of that behavior in social science are flawed.

We can expose this incorrect assumption at work. Human sociobiologists want to exhibit their field as a valid science. They construct a set of rival evolutionary explanations and argue that at least one member of the set is a superior explanation to those in social science. Then they argue that social science cannot explain some human behavior and that human sociobiology can explain it. The purpose of doing so is that they believe that, by finding flaws in the explanation from social science, they thereby show that the behavior needs explanation, and by arguing that human sociobiology can explain such behaviors, they show that their field is valid science.

Critical social scientists want to protect social science from biological reductionism. So they stand the argument on its head. They argue that human sociobiology cannot explain the phenomenon and that social science can explain it. The purpose of doing so is that they believe that, by finding flaws in the explanation from human sociobiology, they show that it cannot explain the behavior, and by arguing on that basis that it is invalid science, they show that the behavior needs social scientific explanation. By realizing that sociobiology has the full responsibility for determining what aspects of behavior are evolutionarily significant, we can extricate ourselves from this fruitless rivalry where each side denigrates the work of the other in order to legitimize and validate its own work.

Of course, matters are muddied by the fact that boundaries between evolutionary biology and social science are now routinely crossed in research. How so? We combine the variables typically found in evolutionary biology and social science (Shubert 1989, 31). A traditional social science model of political behavior identifies social statuses and social environment as causative structure, cognitive processes as intervening processes, and political behavior as dependent behavior. A traditional biological model of political behavior identifies biological characteristics, natural and social environment, and basic needs as causative structure, psychophysiological processes as intervening process, and appetitive behavior as dependent behavior. By including both sets of variables in a single theoretical outlook, research identifies novel relations between all such variables. Advances in research cross traditional boundaries between disciplines and create new boundaries inherent in new outlooks.

Instead of reductionism (Rosenberg 1980) versus antireductionism (Smith 1984), we have interdisciplinary or multidisciplinary explanatory theories and programs. Instead of logical ties between theories of reducing and reduced fields, we have new theoretical and factual ties between neighboring fields. Given the changing array of cross-disciplinary outlooks and the changing array of arguments over the relation between sociobiology and social science, identifying what counts as a fact that cannot be explained without sociobiology will remain problematic. Rather than view this issue in terms of reductionism, it is more realistic to treat it in terms of the continual rearrangement of disciplinary resources and the consequent rearrangement of disciplinary relationships.

## Judging Progress Impartially

Lakatos may have underestimated the difficulty of giving an "honest presentation" of the record of successes and failures. It should not need further argument that debate over a number of "isms" functions as an obstacle to impartial presentations of the record: biological reductionism, genetic determinism, sexism and neo-Social Darwinism, and vulgar adaptationism. As long as this situation lasts, consensus over whether sociobiological explanation is progressive or degenerating is virtually precluded.

At the root of many such debates are assumptions about the import of evolutionary explanation for mind and culture as distinctive qualities of human nature. Such metaphysical postulates as "mind and culture free humans from biology" versus "mind and culture constitute the way we adapt to nature" operate as presuppositions of opposing verdicts about progress. These general presuppositions force rejection or acceptance of explanations in human sociobiology relatively independent of their specific content. Those adopting postulates more similar to the former than to the latter will always regard the specific content as either irrelevant to or contradictory to the facts about human social behavior. The point of view inherent in the quest for completeness forces a "Copernican revolution": we should reverse the issue and seek to understand the import of mind and culture as distinctive human qualities for the completeness of evolutionary explanation.

Conservatism (the criterion of plausibility) brings such background information into play in assessing the quality of the kind of explanation and the kind of evidence. We gain control over the kind of explanation by devising research programs for studying the relation of variables involved in mind and culture to evolutionary variables. Now, judgements of evidence are predicated on and thus relative to background information. To give some confirmation to an explanation is to raise its chance of being correct as compared to its chance without that (confirmatory) information. To give some disconfirmation to an explanation is to lower its chance of being correct as compared to its chance without that (disconfirmatory) information. Prior probabilities arise from background information. The ability of a set of data to raise or lower a prior probability depends on whether it tells us anything significantly new, which itself is relative to background information (Rosenkrantz 1977; Good 1967). Since different evaluators have conflicting sets of background information, including stances on "isms" and programs and standards, a consensus about evidential success is not to be expected. Hence, this aspect of the sociobiology debate is irresolvable.

Let us see how this works out, with respect to standards. As a case in point, Ruse uses two examples of explanations in human sociobiology to argue that it has led to new insights and new findings. One is the explanation of sibling incest barriers. He (1989, 178) concludes that

> strengths and weaknesses of the sociobiological position on incest have now been laid out. I suggest that it is reasonable to conclude that, essentially, the sociobiological position on incest is true and enlightening. Since, as noted, the treatment of incest is central to the sociobiological approach, this constitutes a strong reason for regarding the general approach with favour.

The currently favored sociobiological position, in outline, goes as follows. Offspring of siblings are at risk for genetic abnormality. Such abnormality decreases chances for success at survival and reproduction. So sibling incest avoidance is highly adaptive. It has originated and is being maintained by natural selection through some proximate mechanism for disinclination toward choosing siblings as mates. Ruse notes as strengths the fact that incest barriers occur with few exceptions as a robust cross-cultural regularity, that incest barriers and other barriers to extreme inbreeding occur in other species, and that there is some evidence that a proximate mechanism in humans is that we do not desire as mates in adult life those with whom we spend our childhood. Ruse notes as weaknesses the fact that human incest barriers involve cultural taboos, that the explanation should be rooted in theory which explains related phenomena such as parent-offspring incest taboos, that proximate mechanisms for sibling incest barriers will not work for other incest barriers, and that cultural taboos still seem to make biological disinclinations unnecessary.

Now, would critics agree with Ruse in calling the inbreeding prevention explanation of sibling incest true and enlightening? Consider, first, those who find the whole idea of human sociobiology implausible. The fact that incest is a cross-cultural regularity could reflect "laws of culture," not laws of evolution. The fact that incest barriers occur in other species is not telling unless they can be shown to be homologous. The evidence of the proximate mechanism only shows, if true, a positive correlation between those with whom we grow up and those with whom we don't mate, but not why this correlation exists. Suppose there were a positive correlation between those spouses who are Catholic and those spouses who have more children. Would that be strong evidence that Catholics have a biological, genetic inclination to have more children? Certainly not.

Consider, second, those who require high standards of rigor for acceptability. Only qualitative explanation and qualitative evidence is offered. Perhaps we have evolved to find a middle ground between excessive inbreeding and excessive outbreeding, by choosing mates a bit different but not too different from close relations. Where are the mathematical models that give numbers to the measures of an optimal inbreeding/outbreeding prevention balance? Where are the numbers in the empirical work substantiating the models, explaining discrepancies wherever they occur in a justifiable fashion? Where is the underlying mathematical model of gene-culture relations, telling us how genetic transmission of sibling inbreeding avoidance mechanisms interact with the social transmission of sibling incest taboos to give quantifiable predictions about the extent to which mating behavior toward siblings is supposed to be biologically adaptive and culturally adaptive? Where are the case-specific antecedent conditions that permit us to infer the exact form of sibling mating behavior in each cultural context? How do we know that when the details are worked out, the essentials of the explanation won't change?

When we take such misgivings seriously, we see that if one were to view the sociobiological explanation at hand as implausible to begin with, the kind of evidence and reasons Ruse adduces would not change our opinion significantly. Those who found the core idea not insightful before would find it not insightful afterward. Those who found the core idea insightful before, but maintain that identifying a causal source of a behavior is not the same thing as providing a correct explanation of it, would find no correct explanation in it before or after. Sibling incest avoidance is no novel fact, although the form of the fact is expressed differently in sociobiological and in social scientific theory. This is supposed to be human sociobiology's best example? Ruse is only arguing that "it is reasonable to conclude that, essentially, the sociobiological position on incest is true and enlightening," not that "it is true and enlightening." If that conclusion is compatible with "it is reasonable to conclude that the explanation is not true or enlightening," and Ruse has not ruled that out, then his advocacy is based on low standards for acceptance. Since that has been the point of many critics all along, Ruse hasn't shown sociobiology to be progressive. The explanation adduced might be the best one among sociobiological rivals, and acceptable in that sense, but that does not make sociobiology progressive.

The other example of good work in sociobiology cited by Ruse is Borgerhoff Mulder's explanation of bridewealth payments among the Kipsigis in Kenya. That quantitative work falls into the sort of work we identified earlier in Betzig's anthology and so won't be reviewed here. Ruse acknowledges that it involves precise, detailed fieldwork but with little theoretical underpinning. So we have theory in search of data and data in search of theory, hardly testimony to impressive progressiveness by any standard other than that the work is better than what there was before. As Ruse acknowledges, if we are already sympathetic to human sociobiology, then his defense is unnecessary and if we are already unsympathetic to human sociobiology, then his defense is ineffectual. Is the improvement sufficiently significant to make human sociobiology progressive? That is another judgement of the form, "sufficient to satisfy criterion C," the sort for which scientific method gives no answer yielding an evaluative consensus.

However, the fact that we do make judgements of progressiveness, and rightly so, motivates us to recognizes a third set of standards in evaluating sociobiology. First, we need absolute standards for correct sociobiological explanations. We used Hempel's adequacy conditions on sound explanatory reasoning to provide standards for the ideal explanation, an ideal that regulates work and evaluation both in the present and in the future. Second, we need relative standards for actual sociobiological explanations. We used the idea of the best of available explanations for promoting completeness, where completeness required the achievement of ideal explanations in the first sense, a practical concept that tells us not to reject everything we have just because it fails to live up to our ideals. Third, we now introduce a relative standard for progress-inducing actual explanations. We do make judgements about whether sociobiology has progressed that take into acccount positive evidence, negative evidence, plausibility, and worthiness of being taken seriously. To say that today's rival is better than yesterday's is not to say much if neither is impressive or if the change is insignificant. In this situation, we need the idea of a standard for what counts as sufficiently significant change in the state of acceptable explanations at one time and at a later time to justify the judgement that the research program regulating those explanations is progressive. We need to jointly employ standards governing where we are going (absolute standards), where we are now (relative standards) and whether we are getting anywhere (progressive standards).

This third sort of standard is neither an absolute ideal, which may be too difficult to be attained, nor an expression of the standards of the research program itself, which may be too easily attained. It is a standard that relates work in the research program to legitimate expectations about what it should be expected to accomplish. We just used some of those expectations in simulating what critics would say about Ruse's recent advocacy of human sociobiology. These are standards that speak to the specific content of the explanations. They can be expressed as obstacles to be overcome (e.g., What evidence would make the sibling incest avoidance explanation plausible in the face of the variation of incest behavior with variation in cultural taboo?). Or they can be expressed as conditions to be achieved (e.g., What combination of theoretical refinement, empiricial refinement, and connection between the two would make us view the explanation as respectable?). To justify such standards, we need to show that they are neither ideally attainable nor always attained, but feasibly attainable given the research situation with a reasonable amount of expertise and work.

To close, let us back up and put our results in this section into perspective. We have already argued that a basic thesis of logical empiricism is true: acceptable explanations meet appropriate logical and empirical standards. We now can see that a basic thesis of historicism is true: acceptable explanations meet appropriate historically changing standards relative to background information. The critical attitude leads us to control relevant components of background information, transforming tacit rival "metaphysical" presuppositions about the nature of animals and humans into explicit rival research programs. In any case, progressivism is unjustifiable because assessment in terms of progressive research programs is to be combined with assessment in terms of theories. Hence, programmatic progress is necessary but insufficient for acceptability. In addition, since the standards internal to a research program may be too high, or more often, too low, we need standards external to it in order to evaluate its ability to guide research, that is, its progressiveness or regressiveness. Plausibility acts as a bridge between assessment in terms of theories and assessment in terms of research programs. Novel explananda also act as a bridge insofar as research programs contain theoretical cores that must explain novel facts in order to be progressive.

Explanations in sociobiology are acceptable only if generated by a research program that explains familiar facts in new forms and new facts not otherwise accounted for. Due to difficulties in clarifying the relation of sociobiology to social science proper, determination of novelty and what count as rival explanations or programs is more subtle than Lakatos let on. Yet insofar as the practice of sociobiology is directed to the aim of completeness internal to evolutionary theory, it is not committed to biological reductionism. The critical attitude leads us to control the very formulation of the facts to be explained, a procedure inherent in sociobiology's conceptual frameworks. Our previous discussion indicates that issues over whether research programs in human sociobiology are progressive or degenerating are exacerbated by the politicized debate over its relation to various "isms." The intrusion of variations in ideological viewpoint and in standards for finding work respectable makes impartial assessment more difficult than Lakatos let on, resulting in many irresolvable decisions crucial for assessing sociobiology's validity.

Assessments of progress toward completeness cannot be done independently of research programs. They should be carried out by means of impartial judgement of the record of success and failure in explanation. In a situation where everyone has some stance about ideology, whether pro or con or neutral, impartiality cannot mean "unbiased by ideology," since we cannot help but be biased in that sense. Ideology is dangerous to objectivity when it lurks behind the scenes as an unseen determinant of evaluative conclusions, not when it is brought into the light of critical examination for all to see.

## 2.4 Gene-Culture Programs

### Regulative Holism

Sociobiological research attempts to improve our understanding of why we do what we do by generating sequences of revised sets of rival explanations. The direction of modifications in human sociobiology is oriented by presuppositions about the interaction of cultural and biological evolution. These presuppositions function as standards for regulating the direction of research. If you assess the scientific status of human sociobiology in terms of a "sociobiological paradigm" or some other holistic (pronounced, and meaning, "whole-istic") guiding perspective, then you are adopting a "holistic methodology." So let us examine 'regulative holism': an explanation in sociobiology is acceptable if and only if it is acceptable according to the standards of its research program, where a holistic research program is presupposed both in its construction and in its assessment.

Kuhn (1962) advanced this view, provided we interpret the concept of research programs liberally enough to encompass Kuhn's concept of paradigms. Kuhn holds that explanations are not externally validated by some neutral arbiter of scientific method, but internally validated according to their own implicit standards. Kuhn proposed his theory of scientific development built around the paradigm concept in opposition to popularized empiricism's emphasis on observation and theory. The two approaches need not be incompatible, provided both are appropriately reinterpreted, realizing that both approaches pointed to facets of science that are real and that we can dispense with the opposition due to taking each to be the sole truth.

Logical empiricism treated scientific decisions, such as decisions about acceptability, as objective judgements. The opposition between empiricism's objectivism and Kuhn's seeming subjectivism can be reconciled, provided we interpret Kuhn's insights in a way that reveals paradigm-choice as objective value judgement (Holcomb 1989a). The opposition between empiricism's objectivism and Kuhn's seeming relativism can be reconciled, provided we give up Kuhn's temptation to treat facts and truth as relative to a paradigm and retain his insight that the strength of reasons is relative to a paradigm or theory which orients basic scientific decisions (Holcomb 1987c).

Kuhn's study of the history of physics showed that different research traditions have different basic views about explanatory standards for success which are in conflict (Holcomb 1987d). Scientists of historically successive traditions differ about what phenomena are properly included in specialized studies, what aspects of the phenomena are problematic, what the nature of the phenomena really is, what statements are observational as opposed to theoretical, what observational facts are relevant to theory, what meanings the observational and theoretical terms possess, what counts as a properly interpreted observation, what counts as a plausible hypothesis, what counts as a good explanation, what counts as a sufficiently confirmed theory, and which scientific conclusions are acceptable or rejectable.

These decisions are not made in isolation from one another. Their systematic relation indicates that rival evaluations are based on integrated sets of presuppositions. No conclusions can be drawn from the abstract appeal to the criteria of logical structure, confirmation, disconfirmation, plausibility, novelty, and impartiality unless the application of these conditions are guided by some set of commitments. Conditions for acceptable scientific explanations in general need to be supplemented by knowledge specific to the science in question in order to yield any evaluation appropriate for that science. Scientific method, then, involves an element universal for science in general, as emphasized by logical empiricism, and an element particular to the science at hand, as emphasized by Kuhn. Impartiality of evaluation requires that one take proper account of the specific research program with which the explanation is affiliated.

One implication of Kuhn's theory of validation for sociobiology is clear. Evolutionists participating in rival explanatory programs differ on what sociobiological explanations would and do count as acceptable scientific explanations. We should expect the conception and application of the conditions of acceptability to vary so dramatically that they yield conflicting conclusions about whether, for example, sociobiological explanations of male-female differences are acceptable. Our previous discussion fulfills this expectation.

Especially striking to Kuhn was the fact that scientists rarely argued explicitly about the basic research decisions previously listed. Scientific theories were popularly viewed as based entirely on inferences from observational evidence. But no amount of testing can, by itself, dictate these decisions because they are logically prior to testing by their nature. What, if not logical inferences from observations, explains the consensus of a community of scientists with the same tradition at a given time? Kuhn boldly conjectured that the scientists must share common commitments, not based on observation or logic alone, in which these matters are implicitly settled. Most scientific practice is a complex mopping-up operation, based on group commitments, which extends the implications of the most recent theoretical breakthrough. Here is the essence of Kuhn's central concept: the concept of normal science taking for granted a research program (initially called a "paradigm" and later called a "disciplinary matrix"), the locus of shared research-guiding commitments.

Of course, human sociobiology has been permeated by contentious debate ever since its inception. Familiarity with Kuhn's image of science suggests that the various camps adhere to different research programs or that human sociobiology remains in a pre-scientific state. Before we can decide whether human sociobiology fits Kuhn's model, we have to identify what would count as rival research programs in the field, as loci of shared commitments acting as presuppositions of both factual claims and evaluative judgements of acceptability. We will argue that it is not correct to identify its research programs as a set of ideological commitments, such as the notorious "isms," but that it is correct to identify them via gene-culture theories.

## Ideologies as Holistic Research Programs

The sociobiology debate, in the hands of advocates like Wilson and critics like Lewontin, is fundamentally a debate over competing world views. A world view (Weltanshauung) has the sort of holistic character Kuhn emphasized. Kuhn's holistic concept of a paradigm was repeatedly chastised as an analytic tool (Masterman 1970;

Suppe 1977), and deservedly so. However, Kuhn was right that scientists and people in general often do think in all-embracing holistic terms, arguing over the uses of the ontology of a theory as a universal cosmology.

Segerstrale (1985) has shown that Wilson and Lewontin bring with them convictions which function as integrated sets of presuppositions of their rival normative definitions and assessments of sociobiology. Here are some evaluative presuppositions that lead to their conflicting verdicts, according to her analysis. For Wilson sociobiology is good science because it employs systematized, testable theoretical models and conceptual schemes. For Lewontin it is bad science or pseudoscience because it is not based on carefully established facts. Wilson aims to advance scientific research by structuring heretofore messy fields and exploring new territory in a creative fashion. Lewontin contributes to scientific progress by exposing weaknesses in ambitious claims and bringing others back to the straight and narrow path of cautious discipline. Wilson's claims linking genes to culture may be motivated by the urge to show that genes hold values on a leash, thereby undermining traditional theology; he is fighting against the religious dogmatism he had once gullibly accepted. Lewontin finds in genetical explanations of mind and culture the expression of a naive, vulgar biological explanation of the world; he is fighting against the false consciousness of scientism in which he was trained before his conversion to Marxism. Wilson takes reductionism to be a good thing, justified ultimately by materialism, and an effective tool to combat irrational religious dogma. Lewontin takes reductionism to be a bad thing, undermined by Marxism, and the source of scientifically incorrect claims and politically oppressive ideology. To understand what is at stake in the debate over sociobiology, one should follow Kuhn's advice and undertake a social psychological study of differences among individual members of evolutionary biology.

In so doing, we should take care not to make the causal link between ideological commitment and holding certain views in, for example, genetics too strong. Couldn't Lewontin have reasons for rejecting reductionism other than his Marxism? Couldn't he have the same reasons others have and yet be a Marxist? It is difficult to know, even from the testimony of personal interview, what causes these beliefs. Normally, we are not permitted more than a "maybe" or a "possibly" in stating such connections. Thus, differences over scientific method, strategies for gaining knowledge, the nature of what exists, and moral preferences—holistic world views—act as presuppositional commitments that may affect Wilson's advocacy and Lewontin's critique of sociobiology. Such hidden causative factors pervade evaluative reasoning about the field. This sad state exemplifies what Kuhn was talking about in stating that proponents of rival paradigms talk through each other, only partially communicate, and hold rationally irreconcilable positions.

Rather than perpetuate the battle between unlimited holistic views of life, we should assess sociobiological explanations by establishing their power and limits. Self-discipline means not to try to do everything at once, whether in science or in philosophy. To identify an alternative to the regulative holism of Wilson and Lewontin, notice the unlimited nature of the domain of explanation that Lewontin, Kamin, and Rose (1985) attribute to sociobiology: (a) "Wilson defines sociobiology as "the systematic study of the biological basis of all social behavior" (234); (b) "The central assertion of sociobiology is that all aspects of human culture and behavior, like the behavior of animals, are coded in the genes and have been molded by natural selection" (236–37); and (c) "Not since Hobbes' *Leviathan* has there been such an ambitious program to explain and prescribe for the entire human condition beginning with a few basic principles" (235).

Intuitively, there is no reason why sociobiology has to endorse such ambitious claims in order for it to be a legitimate, valid science. Indeed, such ambitions seem to hinder its becoming a legitimate, valid science. This unlimited scope pushes us to always go for more, rather than to circumscribe our project to finding feasible solutions to manageable problems. It is hard to see how a science with such an unlimited scope could ever be successful.

The quest for a completed evolutionary theory carries a rationale for doing human sociobiology internal to science. This aim legitimates the field in principle but does not validate it as practiced, which also depends on the quality of its explanatory methods and explanatory results. By distinguishing two kinds of projects according to their scope, we can identify what sort of human sociobiology is illegitimate and what sort of human sociobiology is legitimate.

An effort to explain all human social phenomena through natural selection acting directly on heritable phenotypic variation would involve biological determinism, reductionism, and adaptationism in some sense. Research programs committed to an unlimited domain are illegitimate because their resources for constructing total world views are so meager that they are blind to many behavioral facts. An effort to show that evolutionary theory is complete within its own scope, where the scope is limited to aspects of sociality involving cause-effect relations to survival or reproduction, does not entail an effort to explain all human social phenomena. Research programs committed to a limited domain of this sort are candidates for legitimacy since they do not aspire with "vaulting ambition" to be total world views. Human sociobiology, as disciplined inquiry aimed at completeness, is not a total world view, but an attempt to make evolutionary theory applicable to a part of its limited domain in whatever way is relevant to and consistent with the social data. As a science, it is not in need of a world-view interpretation.

Human sociobiology, assessed in terms of the aim of completeness in its limited domain in the context of inquiry, is identified independently of any particular sociopolitical ideology. Such independence follows from the very concepts of scientific inquiry and sociopolitical ideology. A scientific inquiry is an effort to find out about something, to find out what is true and what is false. Scientists investigate, arrive at findings, and draw conclusions. Inquiry aims to find out the truth; ideology assumes the truth is evident. Even so, the choice and content of explanatory questions and answers are ideologically influenced, as shown previously.

Assessment of sociobiology in the contexts of inquiry, belief, and action produces at the same time confusion. The political consequences of acting on an explanation believed true involve assessments of the current political situation that are neither reasons nor standards for judging its research value. Hence, we should dissolve rather than solve the issue over sociobiology's political significance, understood in terms of whether sociobiology is committed to or uncommitted to a certain political agenda. To try to choose between the two alternatives is to move from one context to the other without realizing it, to try to answer an unanswerable question.

Biological determinism, reductionism, adaptationism, and so forth are far more general than human sociobiology. It follows that they cannot be definitive of what is unique to its research programs, but at most incorporated into them. Hence, those "isms" are not research programs in Kuhn's sense, which were research orientations definitive of specific fields guided by theoretical cores. A reasonable candidate for such theoretical cores in human sociobiology are gene-culture theories.

Barash (1982, 151) identifies three plausible general theories about the relation between biology and culture. All three assume that extreme critics are mistaken in arguing from the assumption that genes and culture are irrelevant. This assumption is refuted by recent primatology and animal sociobiology, which go to show that genetic transmission and at least rudimentary forms of cultural transmission do interact in the production of behavior. And non-cultural organisms fail to have the genes that underlie the capacity for culture. All three assume that extreme advocates are mistaken in arguing from the assumption that for every human behavior there is a distinct array of genes which encode that behavior and that every gene-behavior complex has been optimized by direct nat-ural selection. That assumption is refuted by recent critique of the hardened Modern Synthesis. How should we extend evolutionary theory to make it relevant and consistent with human sociality? Why is culture adaptive to the extent that it is adaptive? We should investigate the middle ground between these two refuted extremes.

Let us consider two sets of rival explanatory programs for doing so, one reported in 1982 by Barash and the other detailed in the 1989 issue of *Ethology and Sociobiology* about evolved con-straints on cultural evolution. The initial set of rival theories of gene-culture interaction include: dual inheritance theory, coevolu-tionary theory, and epigenetic theory. This range of alternatives has been modified, expanded, and reconceptualized as human sociobiol-ogy developed between 1982 and 1989. The point of the present identification is to bring home Kuhn's point that proper evaluation requires that one take proper account of the specific research pro-gram with which the explanation is affiliated. So let us consider what each would say is involved in the simple explanation: "Why is culture adaptive to the extent that it is adaptive? Because human sociality evolved by natural selection."

## Gene-Culture Theories as Research Programs

Consider the situation in 1982. According to dual inheritance theory, (Boyd and Richerson 1985), genes and culture are mechani-cally distinct systems of inheritance, but behavior is the product of both predispositions resulting from genetic inheritance alone and predispositions resulting from cultural inheritance alone. Contrary to Barash (1982, 152), this theory is an advance on and rival to the vague thesis that "culture frees us from biology" or "the transmis-sion of culture short-circuits biological heredity." Instead, both sorts of transmission interact to yield deviations from (a) behavior fulfilling optimal genetic fitness expected in ideal conditions according to the population genetic theory as found in the Modern Synthesis and (b) behavior fulfilling culturally induced goals independent of reproductive success expected in ideal conditions according to traditional social science.

It had been thought that though humans evolved according to the same biological mechanisms as did other species, biological mechanisms only elucidate the "preconditions for human life," not the "conditions required for human survival and development, and for this we must refer to other sciences, beginning with anthropology" (Reed 1978, 47). In other words, once cultural transmission, selection, and evolution began, human behaviors became unrelated or randomly related to genetic transmission, natural selection, and biological evolution. Using mathematical models, it has been shown, on the contrary, that behaviors subject to dual inheritance have a character different from what would be expected from genetic or cultural transmission alone. Richerson and Boyd create a system of models of cultural transmission, selection, and evolution formally comparable to that of genetic transmission, selection, and evolution. This enables us to envisage a culturally optimal phenotype in relation to a genetically optimal phenotype. Different sets of values for relevant variables and parameters lead to different outcomes. The actual phenotype may be culturally and genetically optimal, culturally suboptimal and genetically optimal, genetically optimal and culturally suboptimal, or culturally and genetically suboptimal. Wishing to distance their evolutionary outlook from that of Wilson, Boyd and Richerson take their work to be outside human sociobiology; yet Barash counts their work as within the field. This is an example of Kuhn's point that research programs are central to the normative self-definition of particular fields.

Kitcher finds in the work of Richerson and Boyd two contributions: augmented resources for model-building (augmented explanatory resources) and identification of evolutionarily stable conditions which maintain behavior that does not maximize fitness (thereby refuting adaptationism). He (1987, 94–95) relates this work to completeness: "Neo-Darwinian evolutionary theory must be completed in certain respects if it is to provide the basis for constructing models that apply to species with a system of cultural transmission (most prominently, but not only, *Homo sapiens*)." Richerson and Boyd (1985, 12) understand the significance of their work in terms of completeness and consistency:

> The adherents of one school of thought, which we will call 'human
> sociobiology' have tried to develop a theory of cultural evolution which
> is derived from the Darwinian theory of organic evolution. . . .
> Because human sociobiology represents the only really serious at-
> tempt to date to develop a logically complete theory of human be-
> havior that is consistent with what we know about organic evolution,
> we frequently will compare its results with our own.

Their conception of sociobiology's significance is consonant
with the one proposed here, with important differences. They identify the aims of human sociobiology with both goals expressed in the
sentences quoted above. The present conception identifies the aim of
human sociobiology with the goal expressed in the second sentence
alone. The attempt to develop a theory of cultural evolution derived
from a neo-Darwinian theory of organic evolution is one of many
possible ways of achieving completeness. Their use of 'completeness'
involves the ambiguity just exposed: whether a completed evolutionary theory is one that explains (a) everything about human sociality
or about human nature (unlimited domain) or (b) only limited aspects of human sociality involving cause-effect relations to survival
and reproduction (limited domain). The present conception offers a
variety of arguments for giving up (a) and restricting ourselves to
(b). They correctly emphasize the importance of consistency, lest
completeness of application be achieved at the price of contradiction
between theoretically induced expectations and independently gathered facts. We agree on the significance of arguments concluding
that a given gene-culture theory, such as dual inheritance theory,
can guide successful explanation: sociality in cultural organisms is
neither irrelevant to nor incompatible with evolution.

The Boyd-Richerson program for attaining completeness is intended as a rival to two other programs proposed prior to 1982.
Epigenetic interaction theory (Lumsden and Wilson 1981) captures
the presuppositions grounding the line of advocacy made popular by
E. O. Wilson. Coevolutionary interaction theory (Durham 1979; Alexander 1979a) captures the line of advocacy made popular by Alexander. (Sometimes all gene-culture theories are called "coevolutionary theories"; the label does not matter.) On both theories, humans
evolved according to the same mechanisms as other species, and
those mechanisms govern the preconditions of specific human behaviors, not the specific behaviors themselves. Once cultural transmission, selection, and evolution began, they are maintained and
constrained in form and content by genetic transmission, natural

selection, and natural evolution. Lumsden's and Wilson's epigenetic theory as well as Alexander's coevolutionary theory depict the development of human individuals and the evolutionary trajectory of human populations in ways that make precise the idea that "because people are the products of the evolutionary process, biology enables and constrains culture, making it generally biologically adaptive."

The two theories differ on the role they ascribe to genes. On epigenetic theory, human individuals have a direct genetic propensity to acquire some cultural traits rather than others as part of their developmental (epigenetic) pathways, and these traits are subsequently acted on directly or indirectly by natural selection and other evolutionary processes. On coevolutionary theory, human individuals have no direct genetic basis for any specific cultural trait, but make choices among cultural practices as a partial product of inner motivations, motivations shaped by the course of natural evolution. Both theories recognize a plurality of evolutionary processes that predispose us to act to enhance reproduction. Epigenetic theory posits that selection operates on genetic variation underlying variable cultural traits and explains behavioral differences between cultures. Coevolutionary theory posits that cultural traits are affected by the cumulative results of selection on shared fitness motivators and explains behavioral differences within a culture.

Thus, the two theories imply radically different kinds of evolutionary explanations. For each specific behavior, epigenetic interaction theory requires a hypothesis about its genetic basis, a hypothesis about its adaptive significance, a hypothesis about the role of natural evolution in its evolutionary history, and a hypothesis about its significance with respect to human nature. This theory, being presupposed by Wilson, leads to the sort of explanations the critics expected since the traits are explained using an expansion of the resources found in traditional population genetics.

Coevolutionary interaction theory requires none of this even though it holds that human behaviors both originated and are maintained in order to serve biological needs. Instead it requires a hypothesis about the genetic basis, adaptive significance, selective and evolutionary history of motivators that direct our physical, emotional, and mental activities at doing the things which in the general evolutionary past normally enhanced reproductive success. But this postulate is not developed explicitly into models; it is left as a "black box" that processes our behavioral choices according to reproductive criteria. Like other organisms, we inherit from our ancestors a moti-

vation to adopt behaviors correlated with fitness promoting strategies. Although the black box approach is mysterious, it is justified
by saying that it is a consequence of our ignorance of the actual ways
genes and behavior are linked and that we already make some such
postulate when studying animal behavior.

Actual explanations arising from the outlook of coevolutionary
interaction theory do not spell this out in detail, but leave it as an
undeveloped presupposition. The formulation of the explanans and
explanandum need not fit into any expanded population genetics
model but are to be developed as suited for the particular type of
behavior under study. Specific human behaviors do not evolve by
natural selection on their genetic basis since there is no genetic
basis specific to them. Our behaviors are entirely environmentally
produced in that sense, the sense that many social scientists keep
insisting on their claims against sociobiology.

Their inference that genes and evolution are irrelevant to our
behaviors is misguided inasmuch as it unduly restricts the possibility of relevance to that scenario, one of direct genetic causation and
direct natural selection. Instead, fundamental motivators "to act
reproductively" evolved by natural selection on their genetic basis.
The ensuing explanations explain behavior, not directly, but indirectly in terms of selection on genes. Viewed in a proximate time
frame, specific behaviors are not directly caused by genes at all but
are causally influenced by what is caused in part by genes. Viewed
in an evolutionary time frame, behaviors are explained, not directly
in terms of natural selection, but indirectly in terms of the cumulative effects of natural selection acting on basic motivators caused in
part by genes. For selection to be effective in aiming our nongenetic
behaviors toward reproductive success, neither human nor nonhuman organisms need consciously to intend to reproduce or to be
aware of the basic motivators.

To make these three explanatory outlooks more concrete, suppose that we found that human males and females choose mates
according to preferences (males desire physically attractive females,
females desire males likely to gain wealth, power, and status) which
are not correlated to reproductive success. This seems to be the case
in contemporary societies. How should we evaluate explanations of
mate choice along the lines of Barash, Lancaster, Buss and Barnes,
etc.? Dual inheritance theory might imply that those explanations
had been falsified because culturally induced gender roles in this
particular case have molded our mating patterns semi-
independently of factors including genes, adaptation, natural selec-

tion, and other evolutionary processes. Epigenetic interaction theory might lead us to revise the explanations so as to incorporate another hypothesis. Perhaps genes of males or females code for different strategies of mate choice, but we have not identified them appropriately or have overestimated their selective significance. Coevolutionary theory would lead us to revise the explanations so as to incorporate another hypothesis, too. Perhaps the novel environments we have created using traits that have no specific genetic basis in turn lead to situations which sever the connections between sex-typical strategies of mate choice and reproductive success. Each proposed hypothesis is rational to make, given the appropriate theory of gene-culture interaction.

Thus, evidence for or against particular explanations is intrinsically inconclusive and is given its significance by presuppositions themselves generated by one of the three basic theories. What should we do in the face of negative evidence? Dual inheritance theory suggests that we have one more reason to deny that human behaviors are currently generated by proximate mechanisms aimed at biological fitness alone. Epigenetic interaction theory leads us to revise the explanation-sketch so as to illustrate its affirmation that human behaviors are generated by proximate mechanisms traceable to specific genetic effects. Coevolutionary interaction theory leads us to revise the explanation-sketch so as to illustrate its affirmation that human behaviors are generated by culturally induced proximate mechanisms, mechanisms untraceable to specific genetic effects, according to a system of biological goals, goals traceable to specific genetic effects in principle but not in practice due to our ignorance of the human genome.

By 1989, gene-culture theories and their relations are more complicated. A persistent theme is "complex psychology" (Barkow 1989b). Instead of explaining behaviors as directly subject to selection, autonomous and complex psychological abilities mediate between natural selection for genetic fitness and behavioral outcomes (Lopreato 1984; Barkow 1989c; Kitcher 1988).

Richerson and Boyd (1989) have pursued their dual inheritance theory and its ability to model processes giving rise to both adaptive and maladaptive behavior. They argue for its ability to represent four possible outcomes of evolution: genes keep culture on a leash, promoting biological fitness; culture keeps genes on a leash, promoting cultural fitness; genes and culture evolve according to a host-pathogen analogy; or both genes keep culture on a leash and culture keeps genes on a leash. They speculate that all are common but that the last is the most important. Again they "view the application of population genetical methodology to cultural evolution as a friendly amendment to human sociobiology, but one that is essential to a complete Darwinian theory of human behavior" (196).

Lumsden (1989) pursues his epigenetic theory whereby socially transmitted traits increase or decrease in frequency according to innate learning rules tuned to recognize adaptively advantageous behaviors. For culture to be transmitted and learnable at all, there must be evolved constraints on mental development; otherwise culture would lead to such reductions in fitness that hominids having culture would be selected against, in relation to hominids without culture. (Alexander is not in this journal issue. His (1987) book on moral systems invokes a complex psychology; see chap. 4.)

Other promising approaches differ radically from the previous three gene-culture theories. MacDonald (1989) adopts a behavioral-ecological-contextual gene-culture theory. Economic production, social controls, and personal ideology act as contextual variables that mediate between selection for genetic fitness and behavior. The central tendencies in behaviors expected from selection for genetic fitness underdetermine behavior, which then is either adaptive or maladaptive in a genetic sense according to the specific interactions between contextual variables and psychological proximal mechanisms. Symons (1989) adopts a neo-Darwinian approach allegedly superior to recent Darwinian anthropology. Instead of taking behavior to be designed to maximize fitness, adaptive design is manifested at the psychological level. Hence, measurements of differential reproduction, such as the random correlation between mate preference and reproductive success that provide disconfirming evidence for traditional sociobiological explanations, are virtually irrelevant to their rigorous testing. Barkow (1989a) identifies several reasons why information present in a culture may tend to lead to maladaptive behavior. Natural selection has favored traits in individuals that enable them to revise socially transmitted fitness-reducing information. Such revisions produce modifications in the existing culture. Tooby and Cosmides (1989) regard cultural change as too rapid to produce changes in predispositions laid down in Pleistocene ecological conditions. We are adapted to those conditions, not the present ones. Natural selection favored, not a single all-purpose capacity for learning, but many specific learning capacities used to solve diverse information processing problems of social exchange we faced in Pleistocene conditions. Reciprocal altruism and other modes of selection acted on cognitive programs.

These newer approaches are very interesting and no doubt will give way to new approaches even more interesting. Evaluators cannot afford to overlook the ways that these new approaches transcend their former evaluations. From this brief comparison of gene-culture theories present in 1982 and in 1989, we can see how some of Kuhn's once-shocking claims might make sense of the sociobiology debate. Debate over the scientific acceptability of any explanation in human sociobiology is laden with some research program or other, i.e., laden by commitment to some gene-culture theories and associated patterns of reasoning and concepts. Research interprets the meaning of the facts that lead to the resolution of specific research problems with the aid of gene-culture theories. From the point of view of specific explanations, a gene-culture theory acts as a set of guiding assumptions or presuppositions that connect the workings of evolution by natural selection with the kind of social organisms found in humans and our primate ancestors. As long as critics and advocates presuppose the correctness of different basic gene-culture theories in their conclusions about acceptability, their debate will exhibit the phenomena associated with incommensurability.

These phenomena include: rival standards for judging acceptability, partial communication between adherents of different basic theories, circular reasoning involved in arguing from one's basic theory for a given judgement of acceptability when the basic theories are at issue, and different meanings for such terms and contrasts as "adaptive," "affected by natural selection," "genetically based," "nature versus nurture," "innate versus learned," "proximate versus ultimate causes," and "biological versus cultural." Since the critical attitude directs us to critically examine presuppositions when possible and relevant to unresolved issues, it directs us to develop whatever evidence it takes to decide between rival gene-culture programs, and later between their successor programs, for completing evolutionary explanation.

## Implications

Our discussion of Kuhnian research programs contains implications for adaptationism, biological reductionism, biological determinism, and holistic assessments in general. Consider each in turn.

An implication for adaptationism is that current efforts to explain why culture is adaptive yield a host of new expectations about which aspects of evolved cultural behavior are adaptive or maladaptive. Sociobiology includes many rival research programs, each motivating its own set of rival explanations and standards of evidence. Rival programs lead us to revise previous adaptive explanations in different ways in the face of disconfirming evidence. Hence, evidence is relevant and significant relative to the presuppositions of rival research programs that determine the fact-related standards for correct and faulty reasoning. Whether a flaw repeatedly found in sociobiological explanations is peripheral, important, or devastating depends on whether it concerns the program affiliated with those explanations itself, or just one of its particular articulations. There is a potential for circular reasoning here, one that will be addressed in the next section.

An implication for biological reductionism, which denies the autonomy of the social from the biological sciences, is that gene-culture theories identify a complex psychology which mediates between evolutionary imperatives and behavior, making it hard to draw a line between sociobiology and biologically oriented anthropology (Rhindos 1985), psychology (Tooby 1985; Crawford et al. 1987), or political science (Shubert 1989). Any informed discussion of whether chemistry reduces biology obviously must take proper account of the relation between biochemistry and molecular biology. The usual discussions of whether sociobiology reduces social science are premature and probably misleading since existing boundaries between biology and social science are routinely crossed and an analogous relation between sociobiology and evolutionary social science has not yet been established.

An implication for biological determinism, which exploits biology to identify limits to human behavior that thwart aspirations for radical social change, is that biology not only limits but also enables culture (Barkow 1989a). Criticism of human sociobiology which view it as genetic determinism presumes that the positive view of genes and culture underlying the criticism is better than the view underlying explanations in human sociobiology. This presupposition is often false since gene-culture theories turn such rival presuppositions into detailed theories. The relation between genetic determinism and sociobiology varies for different gene-culture theories.

Because the set of rival gene-culture theories changes as sociobiology develops, the relation between genetic determinism and sociobiology itself changes. As of 1982, Alexander's coevolutionary theory is further from genetic determinism than Wilson's epigenetic theory, with the Boyd-Richerson dual inheritance theory even further removed. As of 1989, the idea that a complex psychology mediates between evolutionary imperatives for genetic fitness and behavior has been incorporated into each of these gene-culture theories and serves as a point of departure for new gene-culture theories and perhaps a different sort of research program altogether. The usual assessment of human sociobiology in terms of genetic determinism is unjustifiable because its simplistic conception of gene-culture relations is insensitive to the fine-grained distinctions that differentiate gene-culture theories. According to typical conceptions of biological determinism, sociobiology is not biologically determinist in practice. This is a strong argument that sociobiology is not committed to genetic or biological determinism.

Debate over the role of ideology in sociobiology furnishes the sort of agreement and disagreement Kuhn wished to explain by postulating the existence of research programs ("paradigms"). The identification of actual research programs targeted in assessing sociobiology should be made relative to a given context of analysis. Relative to the context of inquiry, a research program is an integrated set of disciplinary, conceptual, and methodological commitments attaching to a basic theoretical orientation. Now, physicists not only speak of Newtonian theory, they speak of Newtonian physics, Newtonian concepts, and Newtonian calculative methods. Collectively, they form an integrated research program. We can do the same for evolutionary theories that bridge genes and culture. Theories of gene-culture interaction form theoretical cores of research programs in human sociobiology. Various gene-culture theories carve out of the domain of all human social phenomena various classes of behaviors said to be in need of explanation. Without them, there would be no reliable general decision procedures for taking a class of human social facts and separating the class of facts that have evolutionary import from the class of facts which lack it. Sociobiology would be undecidable in a sense analogous to that in metalogic. The heterogeneity of approaches here refutes the justifiability of the usual holistic method of assessment, namely, to lump sociobiological explanations together under one banner and evaluate them in one fell swoop without regard for decidability.

The justification of assessments of sociobiology that ignore the regulative function of research programs is defeated because the acceptability of an explanation depends on internal standards given by its associated research program. However, assessment according to regulative holism is also defeated because all-embracing holistic programs are not subject to critical control within science, leaving science at the mercy of extrascientific commitments. To extricate the assessment of sociobiology from regulative holism, sociobiology should no longer be conceived as a type of explanation fully revealed in its explanations produced so far. It must be conceived in terms of its process of development toward establishing completeness in its own limited domain, with each result playing a role in the entire sequence, and with each proposed explanation and each ensuing evaluation subject to internal direction-giving controls.

## 2.5 Empirical and Conceptual Problem Solving

### Problemism

Assessed in terms of the context of inquiry, we want our explanations to help solve important explanatory problems. So the specific role of an explanation consists in its problem-solving power and limits. The ultimate principle of success in problem solving is the reduction of incompleteness. The specific explanatory role of an explanation within the framework of explanatory inquiry oriented by the aim of completeness is given by the way it attempts to solve explanatory problems so as to reduce the number, variety, and significance of aspects of animal and human social behavior that stand in need of evolutionary explanation but cannot so far be explained. If you understand the scientific status of sociobiology to rest on its problem-solving aptitude, and only on its problem-solving aptitude, then you are adopting a "problemist methodology." So let us examine 'problemism': an explanation in sociobiology is acceptable if and only if it helps solve explanatory problems, where progress is achieved in solving empirical and conceptual problems at various levels of generality.

Here we have another twist on the idea of completeness. Ruse (1989 175) regards unresolved problems expected in the course of research as indicating that sociobiological explanations are incomplete:

> What can be said against the claim that sibling incest bariers are rooted in biological nature, adaptively preventing close inbreeding?

For a start, there is the fact that we are dealing only with sibling incest. What about parent-child couplings, which ought biologically to be just as disadvantageous? I take it that someone who raised this point would be doing so less as an outright criticism and more as a complaint that the sociobiological attack on incest is incomplete. And I would agree that sociobiology would be seriously incomplete were there no evidence of biological barriers to parent-child incest, or if (far worse) parent-child incest were common.

We have here a set of related inferences. Since the social facts concerning parent-child incest are unexplained by evolutionary theory, the (currently) acceptable sociobiological explanation of incest is incomplete. Given the importance of incest for understanding mating and parenting, sociobiology and evolutionary biology are significantly incomplete.

A preoccupation with problem solving that verges on problemism is found in Laudan's theory of validation. Three aspects of Laudan's (1981) theory are pertinent to the assessment of sociobiology: the classification and identification of empirical and conceptual problems, the inclusion of both retrospective and prospective dimensions of evaluation into the conception of acceptability of explanations, and the conception of progress in terms of advances in solving explanatory problems. We will consider each, then present the implication of multiple levels of generality for identifying the unit of assessment, and finally incorporate problem solving into our cumulative array of criteria for assessing emerging sciences.

## Kinds of Problems

Problems are classified as empirical or as conceptual problems.

At the empirical level, I distinguish between potential problems, solved problems, and anomalous problems. 'Potential problems' constitute what we take to be the case about the world, but for which there is as yet no explanation. 'Solved' or 'actual' problems are that class of putatively germane claims about the world which have been solved by some viable theory or other. 'Anomalous problems' are actual problems which rival theories solve but which are not solved by the theory in question. (Laudan 1981, 146)

We can easily place empirical problems in these classes when we have a consensus about past explanatory success and failure. Before 1962, altruism was a potential problem for selection theory. Hamilton (1964, 1) stated that "if natural selection followed the classical models exclusively, species would not show any behavior more positively social than the coming together of the sexes and parental care." Wynne Edwards (1962) claimed to have solved it by invoking group-selection theory, making it anomalous for individual-selection theory. If we regard cooperation involving some degree of altruism as a defining or typical feature of animal societies, it follows that social behavior in general was a momentous potential problem for selection theory. But no one else was convinced that Wynne Edwards had solved it.

To convert sociality from an anomalous to a solved problem for individual-selection theory, Hamilton modified individual-selection theory through his concept of inclusive fitness: the total proportion of an individual's genome that is passed to the next generation through direct progeny and through individuals with a common ancestry. Hence, cost/benefit analyses of adaptive significance must take account of consequences to both progeny and individuals with common ancestry. E. O. Wilson (1975, 1) introduced sociobiology by identifying its central problem as "how can altruism, which by definition reduces personal fitness, possibly evolve by natural selection?" The problem was "solved by kin selection" (but see Edelman 1981–82, 12). The solution was achieved by progress on several fronts at once: evidence, method, theory, and concepts. The solution was gained through new evidence (calculation of inclusive fitness) obtained through new methods (detailed cost/benefit analysis) in relation to new theory (kin selection) made possible by new concepts (genotypic selfishness despite phenotypic altruism).

However, this scheme is not so easily applied in cases of dissensus or current work. Wynne-Edwards never regarded any amended form of individual selection as capable of solving the problem of altruism, including kin selection. His recent book (1988) claims that the phenomena he originally discussed still need to be explained by group selection. He suggests that D. S. Wilson's (1979) theory of trait-group selection will do the job. Whether the problem of altruism is classified without further ado as "solved" or "anomalous" with respect to individual and group selection can be decided only by begging the question against some rival position.

The same difficulty applies to gene-culture theories. Recall that they each assume that culture does not make evolutionary imperatives for maximizing genetic fitness irrelevant to humans. That position cannot be made into a rival-gene culture theory because it implies that any theory combining traditional evolutionary and traditional cultural variables makes irrelevant variables seem relevant. Sociobiologists initially treated patterns in human social organization as potential problems for evolutionary theory. Extreme critics became committed to an evolutionary approach that admits the validity in principle and in practice of animal sociobiology but regards human sociobiology as invalid both in principle and in practice. Such critics would deny that the problems addressed in human sociobiology are potential problems because they are not problems at all. Why not? The phenomena to be explained remain outside the limited domain of evolutionary theory.

These critics would say that they do not "deny evolution." In the present terms, they favor the quickest path to completeness; they legislate a highly restricted domain for evolutionary theory by fiat, so that human sociality is not a source of explanatory incompleteness in the first place. Unless good arguments for that proposal are given, this is also the laziest path to completeness, for it absolves one of ever having to do any real research on the evolution of human sociality. Proponents of gene-culture programs have conceptual resources for undermining the usual presuppositions that lead to attaining completeness by fiat rather than by research.

Moreover, rival gene-culture theories motivate their own associated classifications. The early formulations of gene-culture theories that try to explain behavior directly regard their adaptive significance as potential, solved, or anomalous problems. Recent gene-culture theories that explain behavior by invoking a complex psychology to mediate between evolutionary imperatives and behavior attach adaptive significance to mediating factors, not to behaviors themselves. The adaptive value of behavior is a problem for the early theories, not the recent ones.

Laudan (1981, 148) states that "in the simplest cases, a theory solves an empirical problem when it entails, along with appropriate initial and boundary conditions, a statement of the problem." That is, he regards solving a problem merely as a relation between statements of theory and data. Suppose we insist that derivability and empirical adequacy must be jointly satisfied. We are unlikely to judge the explanation highly confirmed if we judge it implausible. Each gene-culture theory is associated with different local standards governing when an explanation is plausible in virtue of being the right kind of explanation. So, to say that "gene-culture theory T solves the problem of male-female differences in mating behaviors" reduces to "T solves that problem according to the standards inherent in T"! Kuhn's emphasis on the incommensurability of problem-identifications and problem-solutions rears its ugly head. It seems that there is no objective, external, and decisive standard of correct identifications of explanatory problems and solutions independent of commitment to a given research program.

Situations in which theories are confronted with conceptual problems can also be classified (Laudan 1981, 146):

(1) when T is internally inconsistent or the theoretical mechanisms it postulates are ambiguous;

(2) when T makes assumptions about the world that run counter to other theories or to prevailing metaphysical assumptions, or when T makes claims about the world which cannot be warranted by prevailing epistemic and methodological doctrines;

(3) when T violates principles of the research tradition of which it is a part;

(4) when T fails to utilize concepts from other, more general theories to which it should be logically subordinate.

Ironically, our previous discussion shows that sociobiologists confront all of these kinds of conceptual problems, but that difficulties arise in identifying what theory in human sociobiology is to count as T. Is T Barash's theory of male-female differences in mating and parenting? If so, (1) does not really apply because there is no clear reason why we should call Barash's statements about the double standard a theory rather than an application of theory or a theoretical explanation of data. Is T a theory such as Fisher's (1958) theory of sex ratios, Hamilton's (1964) theory of genetic altruism, Trivers's (1972) theory of parental investment, or Maynard Smith's (1982) theory of evolutionary stable strategies? If so, (2) does not really apply because those theories do not make claims about humans as such, since they do not mention any particular species at all. Is T a theory of gene-culture evolution? If so, (3) does not make sense because there is no research tradition of which it is a part, given that it helps define a research tradition. Is T evolutionary theory? If so, (4) does not make sense because there is no other, more general theory in sociobiology that subsumes it.

## Theories and Research Programs

There is, it seems, no single identification of theory T in sociobiology that encompasses all of these kinds of conceptual problems. Rather than try to find the sort of theory that captures all four qualities, let us think about the root of the difficulty here. Such questions arise from a method of evaluation normally employed in philosophy of science. Philosophers of science wish to study normative judgements in science in general. So, given training in both science and philosophy, they issue edicts about conditions of acceptability for explanations in any science whatsoever. This project entails abstracting away from the details of any one particular science. So their units of analysis—observations, theories, research programs—necessarily ignore the special qualities of scientific studies in each scientific specialty. No wonder scientists find their edicts irrelevant. Philosophical arguments provide reasons to hold that sociobiological explanations, as scientific explanations, are acceptable if and only if . . . (a list of universal conditions for all science is cited).

These conditions of acceptability are predicated on certain assumptions about the properties and relations of observations, theories, and research programs that follow neither from general philosophical considerations about knowledge nor from detailed study of all scientific specialties. It is only an optimistic hope that the assumptions about the properties and relations of the favored units of analysis are satisfied in the special sciences to which they are applied. If the units of analysis appropriate to the science at hand do not fit the assumptions behind the conditions of acceptability, the verdicts may mislead more than inform. Laudan (1981 144) shows awareness of this problem: "There is a range of levels of generality of scientific theories ranging from laws at one end to broad conceptual frameworks at the other." Principles of testing, comparison, and evaluation of theories seem to vary significantly from level to level." This is quite true of human sociobiology, as we have seen.

Noticing this point, oddly enough, does not prevent Laudan from stating normative generalizations about theories and research programs in all sciences. Since he gives clarifying illustrations using scientific examples from physics, chemistry, and geology, we can see how to apply his normative generalizations to fields like them and test them. But is sociobiology relevantly like those fields? A lack of immediate fit between norms and practice may indicate that the actual practice is deficient, that the normative principles are deficient, or both, or that the way they fit together is deficient. The empirical tests that support his norms (Donovan et al. 1988) concern the establishment of new theories, not efforts to extend an established theory so that it is explanatorily complete. Since this distinction is crucial for understanding sociobiology's research situation, that evidence is not immediately relevant.

Laudan evidently thinks of general philosophical theories of science as being tested by case studies of various sciences. All right, is his general distinction between theories and research programs sufficiently relevant to sociobiology to make the crucial distinctions we need to identify what count as research programs in sociobiology?

> There are significant family resemblances between certain theories which mark them off as a group from others. Theories represent exemplifications of more fundamental views about the world, and the manner in which theories are modified and changed only makes sense when seen against the backdrop of those fundamental commitments. I call the cluster of beliefs which constitute such fundamental views 'research traditions'. Generally, these consist of at least two components: (i) a set of beliefs about what sorts of entities and processes make up the domain of inquiry and (ii) a set of epistemic and methodological norms about how the domain is to be investigated, how theories are to be tested, how data are to be collected, and the like. (Laudan 1981, 150–151)

The primary reason for distinguishing research programs from theories is that when observations or theories are modified, these modifications proceed along a direction that makes a selection from all possible pathways, and this selection indicates the existence of higher-order guiding assumptions or commitments. What kinds of commitments?

Philosophers think in terms of metaphysics (study of existence, reality, the kinds of things in the world as a whole), epistemology (study of belief and knowledge and the means for their attainment), and axiology (study of values). For Laudan, a research program is the locus of commitments driving the direction of theory modification and change in the categories of metaphysics (views of the nature of the entities and processes studied), methodology (views of how to conduct proper studies of these entities and processes in order to achieve the aim of knowledge) and axiology (views of the cognitive values whose satisfaction qualifies the work in the field as knowledge).

This broad conception allows ideologies to qualify as scientific research programs. An ideology, broadly conceived, is an integrated set of views about the world (metaphysics or cosmology) which preaches that certain states of affairs ought to be attained and others ought to be avoided (axiology) and delivers an agenda on how to do so (methodology). So biological reductionism, genetic determinism, vulgar adaptationism, and panbiologism can be easily represented as ideologies fitting Laudan's criteria for research programs. Gene-culture theories and their ontological, methodological, and axiological commitments also qualify as scientific research programs. Which of these are proper candidates for research programs— metascientific ideologies or fundamental views associated with gene-culture theories? Until we decide, we cannot extract a verdict for sociobiology's validity from Laudan's theory of validation. This result underscores the point that because of the way philosophies of scientific method are constructed, there is no uniquely determined way to apply them to cases in actual science, and different applications may yield radically different results for the assessment of the science at hand.

## Problem-Solving Success

Suppose we were to properly identify rival sociobiological research programs. How should we evaluate their relative success? Since they dictate procedures and attitudes logically prior to the results of tests, they are in no sense directly testable. On Laudan's problem-solving approach, one theory is more acceptable than its rival if the former is more effective in solving problems. Effectiveness is a complex function of the number and importance of the empirical and conceptual problems confronting each theory. Since closely related theories belong to a research tradition, a research tradition is to be evaluated in terms of the problem-solving effectiveness of its constituent theories. Laudan contrasts judgements of acceptability and promise, interpreted as the contrast between retrospective and prospective timeframes of evaluation. Our concept of acceptability includes promise, containing both retrospective and prospective dimensions of evaluation.

Using retrospective evaluation, one research tradition is more acceptable than its rival if the former has generated theories that have been more effective in the past at solving problems than the theories generated by the rival. Using prospective evaluation, one research tradition (program) is more acceptable than its rival if the former has a greater potential for generating theories that will be more effective in the future at solving problems than the theories generated by the rival. By combining retrospective and prospective dimensions of evaluation, we arrive at a determination of whether a research tradition is progressive or degenerative. At any time in the life history of a research tradition, combine its retrospective and prospective acceptability into a single score. Then compare the scores at any two times. The result is a measure of progressiveness. If the acceptability of a given research tradition is greater as time proceeds, it is progressive; otherwise, it is degenerative. As with Lakatos's measure of progressiveness, a research tradition can flip-flop between states of progressiveness and regressiveness or maintain one of the two states. You can't scientifically predict the future of science.

Judgements of progressiveness are complex because theorizing works at various levels of generality. There are theories of evolutionary processes applicable to all organisms. There are theories of gene-culture interaction applicable to human organisms and sometimes to primates. There are theories of sexual selection applicable to all sexually reproducing organisms, others to certain orders, classes, families, genera, species, populations, or subpopulations. Judgements of progressiveness might involve the following levels: (a) an 'underlying theory', namely, evolutionary theory in general, to be construed as a system of related theories; (b) a 'major theory', namely, an extension of evolutionary theory to cultural organisms via a gene-culture theory; (c) a 'minor theory', namely, an extension of a gene-culture theory to behavior governed by sexual selection; (d) a 'theoretical hypothesis', namely, a core thesis in that extension; and (e) a 'particular explanation', namely, each application of that thesis. Successive formulations of particular explanations are to be evaluated in terms of how clearly and consistently they connect theoretical variables and social data. To evaluate progress in increasing the degree of coherence between theory and data, one must do justice to the relations among such levels.

## Targets and Units of Analysis

How ever we map out relations of generality, we are confronted by questions basic to any method of evaluation. What is the proper target of evaluation? What is the ultimate unit of assessment? Are we to evaluate evolutionary theory by evaluating subsumed major theories, minor theories, theoretical hypotheses, and particular explanations? If so, the target of evaluation is evolutionary theory; other levels of generality are assessed, not just for their own sake, but as a means to the end of assessing evolutionary theory. Or are we to evaluate particular explanations by evaluating each sequence of particular explanations and subsuming theories at each level of generality all the way up to evolutionary theory? If so, the target of evaluation is the particular explanation; other levels of generality are assessed, not just for their own sake, but as a means to the end of assessing particular explanations.

This choice has momentous consequences for understanding what it means to "evaluate sociobiology." Since success and failure is transmitted in both directions, it is a chicken-or-the-egg question. To clarify the structure of evaluation spanning multiple levels of generality, we need to distinguish (a) what it means for an achievement to be made in sociobiology, which involves properly subsuming facts under theory, and (b) what it means for sociobiology to achieve its goal, which involves proper subsumption of facts under a theory that connects all the facts in the domain with the theory.

The research value of evolutionary theory is to explain, predict, or otherwise impart understanding. If evolutionary theory did not apply to actual organisms, it would be useless. The unit of achievement is something that answers questions about why or how such-and-such actual social behavior did evolve or could have evolved: an explanatory hypothesis, explanation-sketch, or explanation about actual particular events, whether explained singly or collectively. Generalizations at any level of generality have their utility in the explanation of facts, and evolutionary facts are facts about what happens at particular times and particular places to evolving populations. Our target of assessment is a specific formulation of an explanation which is validated to the extent that we have reason to think that it subsumes particular events under generalizations so as to satisfy the criteria we have discussed.

Claims at all the relevant levels of generality previously distinguished are invoked in order to adequately decide which sociobiological explanations count as acceptable scientific explanations. Even so, the ultimate criterion for whether an explanation is acceptable is its specific explanatory role in contributing to achievement at the greatest level of generality. The ultimate conclusion of explanatory work in sociobiology as a whole is that evolutionary theory has been shown by successful application to be relevant to and consistent with social behaviors, social roles, social context, and social organization in all species. Our criterion of success for sociobiology as a whole is the extent to which we can establish this conclusion.

It is a short step from recognition of the chicken-or-the-egg character of assessment to a distinction between what is being assessed and the terms in which we are to assess it. It is pointless and misleading to assess sociobiology as such in one fell swoop, since any conclusion about the success of sociobiology as a whole must be made on the basis of the validation of particular explanations. The target of assessment—what is being assessed—is the particular explanation. The units of analysis—that by which we assess what is to be assessed—consist in theories, research programs, and conceptual frameworks. To understand the specific explanatory role of any particular explanation, one must analyze relations between each level of theoretical generality to identify its unique contribution to explanatory relevance and explanatory consistency.

On one hand, one must analyze from the top down: how is the formulation of its explanans and explanandum constrained by higher levels of theoretical generality so as to make evolutionary theory more relevant to social data? On the other hand, one must analyze from the bottom up: How does the evidence for the truth and against the falsity of the statements formulated in its explanans and explanandum filter up to higher levels of theoretical generality so as to make evolutionary theory consistent with social data? Some sort of circularity is at play here. It is better thought of as a type of coherence found in inquiry critically aware of its starting points and structure than as a vicious circularity that commits a logical fallacy.

Every particular explanation is unique. The explanatory role of every explanation, given in terms of its contribution to relevance and consistency, so construed, is unique. Therefore, the conceptual framework built around the aim of completeness is more basic a unit of analysis than theories and research programs. In what sense? The specific explanatory role of a particular explanation captures what is most essential to its being the particular, unique explanation it is. If we are to evaluate small units by subsuming them under big units, we need to distinguish the special relationship each small unit has to the big units. That is the root concept of a specific explanatory role. Each explanation has its own specific explanatory role, given the kind of explanation it is and the kind of evidence by which it is tested.

The specific explanatory role is the particular way the explanation contributes to achieving the completeness of evolutionary theory: the way the explanatory problem it confronts is posed and the aspect of the problem it addresses, the way the attempted solution extends the domain of evolutionary theory to encompass new aspects of social evolution, the way the attempted solution brings the resources of evolutionary theory to bear on the phenomena explained, and the degree of success the explanation has in solving the problem by applying those resources to those phenomena relative to other rival explanations. If we evaluate explanations in biology in terms of whether they are correct scientific explanations while ignoring their role in research given by these underlying decisions, we will miss the point of the explanatory work that created the explanation in the first place. These are decisions about problems, domain, resources, and performance evaluation—the components of a conceptual framework. Since many explanations are guided by the same basic ways of making the decisions involved here, one and the same conceptual framework often characterizes the specific explanatory roles of many explanations. Therefore, when we evaluate the research value of particular sociobiological explanations, we should do so in terms of their specific explanatory roles in contributing to completeness.

Our discussion in chapters 1 and 2 has substantiated the perspective for evaluating sociobiology and has grounded the three-unit model of theory structure in terms of theories, programs, and frameworks, as stated in section 1.1. We will conclude by emphasizing the way our discussion motivates that perspective, summarizing the way we have elaborated the three-unit model, and anticipating the ensuing discussion of conceptual frameworks.

# The Three-Unit Model

As to perspective, a homely analogy may help. Anyone who has served on committees knows what keeps things from getting done and what enables things to get done. For many decisions, especially when breaking new ground, there are basic, conflicting differences in orientation. If we wait for an acceptable decision, in the sense of one arrived at through the resolution of basic differences, we will wait forever and nothing will get done. But if we insist on at least doing something, counting some available alternative as an acceptable decision, then we will bracket basic differences so that we can agree on what it is we are to do and get on with it.

Science is no different. Certain attitudes in assessment prevent explanatory work from being done, whereas other attitudes in assessment enable explanatory work to be done. If we wait for acceptable explanations of human sociality, in the sense that they fulfill our best ideas about relations between science, knowledge, morality, and the good of mankind, we will wait forever, because no such consensus will ever emerge. But if we insist that one of a given set of rival available explanations is the best for pointing the way to future research, and regard acceptability in this pragmatic sense, then we suspend differences of opinion about the ethical, sociopolitical, and philosophical significance of those explanations. Science can stand on its own, without the help of externally imposed interpretations that can never be scientifically established or refuted. Let's do sociobiology for its own sake and evaluate sociobiology for its own sake.

The unlimited objective of trying to explain all of the human condition at once in terms of evolutionary imperatives is mirrored by the unlimited assessment of those explanations in terms of sociobiology's implications for every facet of our view of life. Self-discipline means self-imposed boundaries in which to work in ways we can control; not everything about an explanation in sociobiology is relevant to its scientific status. The only way to extricate ourselves from a debate which threatens to encompass everything is to realize that sociobiology has a self-limited scientific objective which is to be assessed by a self-limited assessment. We assess the scientific (not the ideological or philosophic) status of particular sociobiological explanations (not the field as a whole) within the context of inquiry (not within the contexts of belief or action) by focusing on their specific explanatory roles (not just anything about the explanation) in giving evolutionary theory the ability to cover its own explanatory domain (not the ability to provide a key to human nature).

A systematic perspective must combine at least three units of analysis (theories, research programs, frameworks) into an integrated picture of what is involved in a justifiable evaluation. For instance, although evidence is crucial for evaluating explanations as acceptable or unacceptable, their proper assessment involves many more conditions. It is not good enough to find some evidential flaws in the explanations in order to judge them unacceptable since the significance of these flaws depends on matters of commitment to various research programs and conceptual frameworks for completing evolutionary theory.

We have seen how the completeness project changes our understanding of philosophies of validation by supplying the aim-orienting judgements about results. This supports the main thesis that the framework of inquiry oriented by the aim of completeness is the fundamental unit of analysis. All previous sections came to the conclusion that acceptability is determined by matters of completeness. If completeness is as important for assessing the scientific validity of explanation in sociobiology as it appears to be, we need to identify the structure and procedures of thought associated with it. The fundamental unit of analysis in the sociobiology debate is a framework of commitments regulating the direction of research development having the following interacting components: successions of specifications of problems, domain, disciplinary relations, and performance evaluations.

The cumulative picture that emerges may be summarized as follows, one which elaborates the three-unit model. It summarizes the relationships that refine the use of our evaluative tools by grounding multiple criteria of acceptability in multiple units of theoretical scientific thought.

An explanation in sociobiology is an acceptable scientific explanation in the present knowledge-situation with respect to the context of inquiry if and only if its acceptance possesses greater expectable value for fulfilling the aims of sociobiological research than does the acceptance of any rival available explanation. The expectable value is judged against a background of expectations supplied by sociobiology's conceptual frameworks, each of which consist in successions of basic conceptions of problems, domain, disciplinary relations, and performance evaluations relevant to promoting the aim of completeness.

The resulting structure of cognitive controls represents the system of design inherent in the capacity of sociobiology to produce knowledge through its own principles and procedures of constructing, revising, and evaluating explanations. Through these principles and procedures, the framework of sociobiological research embodies the self-corrective character of scientific knowledge. From the point of view of the framework, scientific method means the production of explanations in order to draw out their conditions of acceptability through continual revision of particular explanations.

Explanations in sociobiology have the following properties that collectively determine whether they are acceptable scientific explanations:

(1) theory-laden properties pertaining to the explanation considered as a finished product of explanatory inquiry:
(a) general logical conditions: consistency, derivability, lawlike-

ness, empirical content, adequate translatability into logical form, etc.

(b) general empirical conditions:

    (b1) conditions of truth-value: confirmation, disconfirmability, record of severity and result of attempts to disconfirm, association with novel explanandum, etc.

    (b2) conditions of plausibility: conservatism, simplicity, modesty, generality, realistic complexity, ideological openness, etc.

(2) program-laden properties pertaining to the explanation considered as an unfinished product in an ongoing process of explanatory inquiry:

    (a) local logical conditions: reasoning about how to conduct inquiry, about how to construct, revise and improve explanations, about standards of plausibility, etc.

    (b) local empirical conditions: guiding multilevel theory, ideas, factual and theoretical background information, etc.

    (c) problematic conditions: conceptual and empirical problem-solving capability, record of failures and successes, progressiveness, problematic presuppositions and implications, etc.

(3) framework-laden properties pertaining to the explanation considered as performing a specific role in extending the underlying established theory:

    (a) problematic conditions: criteria concerning goals and development.

    (b) domain conditions: criteria concerning scope and modality.

    (c) disciplinary conditions: criteria concerning resources and kind.

    (d) performance conditions: criteria concerning power and limits.

This list organizes the key criteria we can profitably take from the theories of scientific validity developed by Hempel, Popper, Quine, Lakatos, Kuhn, and Laudan. Previous chapters elucidated the theoretical and programmatic conditions in terms of completeness; they showed that we should take into account sociobiology's frameworks of explanatory inquiry oriented by the aim of completeness in order to apply the theory-laden and program-laden conditions properly to the field. Remaining chapters elaborate the framework-laden conditions, now taking the aim of completeness for granted.

The status of an explanation as an acceptable scientific explanation, evaluated in the context of inquiry, is properly determined by assessing its specific role in promoting the completeness of evolutionary theory.

That role is precisely understood in relation to an explanatory

framework having the following related components: (a) the formulation of the problem addressed by the explanation in relation to
the explanatory goals of the field and the state of historical development of the field toward those explanatory goals; (b) the formulation
of the facts to be explained (the explanandum) in the explanation
according to the scope and modality of the factors doing the explaining: (c) the formulation of the factors doing the explaining (the explanans) according to the resources and kind of explanation found in
relevant disciplines: (d) the formulation of the performance evaluation of the explanation in promoting completeness according to the
power and limits of the explanation in meeting its specific objectives.

Hence, the distinctive features of the explanatory role of a
given explanation include its associated goals, state of development,
scope, modality, resources, kind, power, and limits. These are the
topics to be investigated in the last four chapters of this book, topics
that in their interconnections have been neglected by mainstream
philosophy of science. The four components of conceptual frameworks (of the sort involved in explanatory work in sociobiology and
relevantly similar sciences) will now be described so as to give an
initial handle on the ways they are related.

Consider the problem component. Our journey through various
philosophies of validation has been oriented by the identification of
the central problem in sociobiology as the problem of how to extend
evolutionary theory so as to minimize sociality as a source of incompleteness. Successful application of a revised neo-Darwinist theory, as inherited from the Modern Synthesis, to both humans and
animals is a necessary condition for attaining completeness. This
fact helps explain the true meaning of the "New Synthesis," why
criticisms of sociobiology have ultimately targeted evolutionary theory in general and its deficiencies in application (e.g., adaptationism) and why some advocates believe that one cannot reject human
sociobiology in principle unless one also rejects evolution and neo-
Darwinism. Both advocates and critics accept the truth of evolutionary theory as an underlying theory, tempered by familiarity with its
recent critiques. Of course, we should not confuse the truth of evolutionary theory with its completeness or the worth of a goal with the
lack of success of results. Just because evolutionary theory is regarded as basically true, we are not justified in thinking a certain
explanation acceptable or in regarding those who judge it unacceptable as being against evolutionary theory.

Now look at the domain component. Because completeness is
completeness within a domain, the solution to the central problem of

sociobiology requires accurate specification of its domain. This intrinsic connection between the problem and domain components of sociobiology's conceptual frameworks contributes to its character as an integrated whole. So it is conceived as neither a mere ordered collection of parts or as a mystifyingly monolithic perspective, but as a system of relations that endure the coming and going of particular specifications of components. The particular relations that obtain at a given time is a matter of history. Advocates sometimes talk as if everything about current human sociality is explainable by evolutionary theory. Critics reply that nothing about current human sociality is explainable by rigorous applications of evolutionary theory. In such situations, advocates act as if sociobiology's domain included all human social phenomena and critics act as if its domain includes only the phenomena of hominid evolution but not of cultural and social history. Recognition of the completeness project points toward reconciliation. At present, the central problem can be solved if sociobiology carves out of the domain of all current human social phenomena the smallest possible domain needed to render the Modern Synthesis complete in practice.

Turn next to the disciplinary relation component. Because of the way sociobiology carves out its domain, it is theory-bound by the disciplines entering into the Modern Synthesis. The Modern Synthesis was much more than population genetics reconciling mutation and selection as significant factors of change. It showed that "nothing makes sense except in the light of evolution," unifying systematics, developmental biology, morphology, physiology, behavioral biology, and so forth. Sociobiology's New Synthesis aims to extend the Modern Synthesis, revised upon critique, to encompass animal and human social behavior. This entails specification of intrabiological disciplinary relations. Animal sociobiology provides the primary resources, involving contributions from evolutionary genetics, evolutionary ecology, and ethology (Barlow 1980). They provide something akin to Lakatos's hard core, the presuppositions most immune from revision in the face of disconfirmation. Even though sociobiology develops a protective belt of defense mechanisms around central insights, the extent to which they are subject to criticism and revision is greater than Lakatos lets on. Criticisms of human sociobiology identified flaws that rebounded against animal sociobiology and evolutionary biology in general, e.g., adaptationism.

Finally, reflect again on the performance component. Given the problem, domain, and disciplinary components of sociobiology's framework of research, which criticisms of sociobiology are of central import for its success? The frameworks of research orients both substantive claims and evaluations. So the developmental course of human sociobiology is steered far more by its central problem and evaluation of performance in solving it than the many miscellaneous criticisms of actual or apparent flaws that may be adduced. That is, many of the debating points won or lost in the sociobiology debate are irrelevant to its success or failure. As Lakatos (1970) noted, alleged "refutations" of specific variants in a research program are irrelevant since their existence is fully expected. Claims about the relevance of various issues to the project of completeness that encompasses many programs can be rationally justified only by properly identifying fundamental categories of criticism.

The biological literature suggests such candidates for the fundamental categories of criticism as issues like the genetic conditioning of human sociality, legitimacy of animal-human comparisons, the limits to natural selection in guiding evolutionary change to create and maintain adaptation, and the intrusion of mind, learning, values, rationality, culture, onto all social traits. The philosophical literature would identify the fundamental categories as the ontology, epistemology, and epistemic axiology of sociobiology. But these biological and philosophical categories cannot be basic categories of criticism. They cannot be basic in the sense that they fail to capture what is specific to sociobiology as such. We have shown that the significance of any flaws in its explanations pertaining to these issues is to be decided by reference to the orientation induced by the quest for completeness. The answer is almost too obvious: the fundamental categories simply are sociobiology's changing specifications of problems, domain, disciplinary relations, and performance evaluations. This answer makes precise the truism that the self-critical attitude is inherent in scientific method. A paramount intellectual value of sociobiology is to evaluate itself and so to revise its normative self-definition by criticizing and revising its orienting framework of research.

Whenever we hear about "conceptual frameworks," we should ask what structure they have that enables them to function in the ways they are supposed to function. How does sociobiology work as a science? As specific studies pursue the completeness problem (central problem) by applying resources from various disciplines (disciplinary relations) to various topics in the domain under study (domain), the resulting explanations are evaluated for their scientific acceptability in order to make appropriate revisions (performance evaluation) designed to promote completeness. Let us, then, turn to the task of elaborating this idea by showing how the distinctive features of explanations are influenced by each component of conceptual frameworks.

# PART II

Conceptual Frameworks as the Unit of Analysis

# CHAPTER
# 3

## PROBLEM CONCEPTUALIZATION

### 3.1 The Modern Synthesis and the New Synthesis

### Explanatory Goals and Development

When we speak of the scientific enterprise, we recognize that science is a systematic purposeful activity. Our evaluations of a science must treat it as such. A well-articulated explanation is one whose reconstruction fulfills the dictates of the critical attitude with which scientists evaluate their own science, both in terms of its products and its process of development toward its unique explanatory goals. A conceptual framework is a system of intellectual controls over the way we conceive the specific explanatory role of an explanation in contributing to the aims of the science at hand.

The most basic component of a conceptual framework is the underlying conception of the explanatory problem addressed. Problems are, roughly, questions raised for inquiry, consideration, or solution. The most important problems, with respect to evaluating sociobiology's success, are those questions concerning obstacles in achieving basic goals involved in the quest for completeness. Disciplined research is oriented at overcoming those obstacles, not sweeping them under the rug in order to trumpet grand speculations and sweeping conclusions.

Judgements of the validity and significance of a particular sociobiological explanation are justified only if they accurately capture the contribution that the acceptance of the explanation is likely to make to furthering the objectives of inquiry. Debate over sociobiology's validity and significance persists, in part, because no consensus on goals has emerged. What are sociobiology's goals? What should its goals be? And how do we justify our answers in a historically sensitive manner? The historical rationale for sociobiology is its goal to extend evolutionary explanations so that they are not just established for a wide range of phenomena—the "Modern Synthesis"—but complete enough to include social phenomena in our overall picture of the evolution of life on earth—the "New Synthesis."

In order to properly judge the degree that explanations are well-tested and well-articulated, they must be reformulated to make explicit their role in achieving explanatory completeness. Sociobiology's central problem is how best to extend the theory and data to achieve completeness. Its subproblems are posed by lack of theory-data fit that prevents explanations of sociality from being well-tested and well-articulated. Lack of clarity about what is involved in the activity of justifying goal attributions to sociobiology renders judgements about sociobiology's goals unjustifiable. Lack of clarity about what is involved in justifying judgement of progress toward those goals renders judgements about sociobiology's development unjustifiable. Now, evolutionists take for granted that Sociobiology's New Synthesis bears a close relation to the Modern Synthesis. We need to clarify the role this relation plays in our assessments.

This chapter clarifies what is involved in understanding sociobiology's goals and development. It elaborates the three-unit model by clarifying the character of a sociobiological synthesis that achieves completeness and by clarifying the manner of development toward that synthesis. The course of the argument is as follows.

In section 3.1, the ground is cleared for identifying sociobiology's scientific goals by exhibiting the limits of the usual attributions of goals to sociobiology viewed as an ideology. Then Mayr's view of the Modern Synthesis is used as a tool for understanding the Modern Synthesis and its relationship to the New Synthesis. It is argued that attributing to sociobiology the goal of completeness is inherent in this relationship, thereby justifying the identification of sociobiology's goal proposed by the three-unit model in a historically sensitive manner. The thesis that sociobiology's New Synthesis has a goal structure based on that of the Modern Synthesis and has a mode of development parallel to that of the Modern Synthesis is documented by comparison of historical and recent events.

In sections 3.2 and 3.3, this chapter goes on to discuss the sort of progress toward a New Synthesis we should expect to find in sociobiology, using two central problems as examples: the problem of altruism and the problem of the units/levels of selection. Four basic rival models of scientific development are now standardly discussed in philosophy of science: cumulative, corrective, revolutionary, and gradual development. It is argued that each of these models is motivated by an affiliated theory of the validation of scientific claims to knowledge. Given the discussion of these theories of validation in the previous chapters, we are able to ground views of the historical development of science in views of the validation of science and ground both in the three-unit model of theory structure.

By showing that the development of work on the problem of altruism has cumulative aspects, corrective aspects, revolutionary aspects, and gradual aspects, we arrive at a more inclusive conception of the way problem solving generates scientific progress. A "challenge-response" model of scientific development is proposed: scientific activity is directed at problem solving so as to achieve the most defensible response to the most severe challenge while revising antecedent basic commitments in the least damaging way. This model makes sense of all four sorts of progress as variant outcomes of a single problem-solving norm.

## Scientific and Ideological Goals

Critics (e.g., Lewontin) dramatize the fact that sociobiology, like any science, reflects its cultural context, by going so far as to define sociobiology in terms of ideologically pernicious goals. As neo-Social Darwinism, sociobiology "is basically a political science," exemplifying the historical regularity that "the most prestigious academics in the most prestigious academic institutions have over and over again tried to legitimize a given social order by the production of ideological tools" (Lewontin 1977a). As reductionism, sociobiology is "that failed attempt to convince us that human history and culture can be understood only when reduced to biology" (Lewontin 1981). As biological determinism, "*Sociobiology: the New Synthesis* is the manifesto of a new, more complex version of biological determinism," that "attempts to show that the present states of human societies are the result of biological forces and the biological 'nature' of the human species" (Lewontin 1977b). As reductionism and determinism, sociobiological methods are devised for reducing social phenomena to reified individual behaviors caused by biochemical brain events changeable by genetic rather than environmental intervention (Lewontin, Kamin, and Rose 1985). As adaptationism, sociobiology is "a program of explanation and exemplification in which the purpose of the investigator is to show how organisms solve problems optimally, not to test if they do," with the result that sociobiology "so vulgarizes natural selection and the theory of adaptation that it does not have a claim to be a serious form of scientific investigation" (Lewontin 1979).

The basic pattern of historical interpretation this critique imposes on sociobiology is simple. Sociobiology is scientifically unfounded, as revealed by ideologically sensitive assessments of its explanatory methods and results. We cannot understand the attraction and persistence of sociobiology without identifying its ideological role in history as a recent form of Social Darwinism, biological determinism, reductionism, and adaptationism. Because sociobiology reflects the false doctrines and reactionary politics of these ideologies, it is unscientific and politically dangerous.

Is it justified to define sociobiology in terms of goals that necessarily make it bad science in service of bad ideology? Sociobiological explanation has in fact reflected these ideological causes and effects, as previously documented. However, the fact that sociobiology has been a certain way does not imply that it necessarily is that way. To define it according to the commitments in Lewontin's definitions implies that those commitments are not accidental to sociobiology but are necessary to it, so that an evolutionary biology of sociality not making those commitments would by definition not be sociobiology. That would make it impossible to meaningfully say such things as, "Sociobiology has changed. It has cut its ties with the notorious 'isms' and now treats them as tangential to its real concerns." The term "sociobiology" does not matter. What matters is that there is a continuity of the sort of work collected by Wilson in *Sociobiology*, collected in such journals as *Ethology and Sociobiology*, and collected in such anthologies as the *Human Reproductive Behavior* volume by Betzig, Borgerhoff Mulder, and Turke. Since we cannot rule out such a future, incorporating those ideological goals into our very conception of sociobiology is epistemologically unjustified even if sociologically informative.

We are justified in being sceptical of the validity of explanations that appear to fit these ideologically motivated goals and methods. But such evaluations tell only half of the story. Such ideological "isms" are far more general than sociobiology itself and so cannot be definitive of what is unique to its goal structure. They capture sociobiology's external appearance, its relation to the social environment, the context of its ideological causes and effects of explanatory acts. They fail to capture sociobiology's internal rationale, its quest for completing the Book of Rigorous Evolutionary Explanations, which had left the chapter on animal and human sociality blank. For example, Lewontin's criticism of some of early sociobiology's practice as adaptationist was well taken, but it fails to capture later practice or sociobiology's goals as a discipline. There will continue to be important scientific disputes over whether the role of adaptation in living organisms envisaged in explanatory programs goes beyond an acceptable limit or does not go far enough, but such problematic matters of emphasis are not definitive of an entire discipline.

If an overarching scientific goal is to be justifiably attributed to sociobiology, insofar as its explanations extend the range of well-articulated and well-tested explanation but are not yet well-articulated and well-tested, justification must operate *sui generis*. Present goals are to be justified by appeal to past goals and intervening changes in the knowledge-situation. Hence, we should locate the goals of the New Synthesis in relation to the goals of the Modern Synthesis, taking into account the way recent advances in research force us to reassess the validity of its goals. A logically complete theory of evolution that includes natural selection as a chief direction-giving force would have to successfully explain macroevolution (the Modern Synthesis) and social evolution (the New Synthesis). Attributing the aim of completeness to sociobiology is justified by showing it to have been a proper aim of evolutionary theory all along. The New Synthesis has the same basic rationale as the Modern Synthesis.

Sociobiology, whether the sociobiology of humans or of nonhumans, should be evaluated as an extension of the Modern Synthesis that attempts to extend the goal structure of the Modern Synthesis into the realm of sociality. If and when these derived goals are achieved to the extent that the Modern Synthesis achieved its goals, there will be a New Synthesis. To clarify this point, we need to answer two questions of paramount importance. The term 'synthesis' can mean a process or a result. What is the New Synthesis, as a result, properly supposed to be? What is the typical character of the process of development toward a New Synthesis?

These questions can be answered satisfactorily only by reference to a picture of the Modern Synthesis. Of course, our understanding of the Modern Synthesis is itself changing, if only because each generation must interpret its relation to the past anew. The usual summary description of the Modern Synthesis as "the fusion of Mendelism and Darwinism" is true but fails to illuminate the relation between the Modern Synthesis and the New Synthesis. Mayr (1980, 1985) has provided an influential, detailed picture of the nature of the Modern Synthesis and of the debate and changes occurring before its completion. Mayr's account is relevant and useful for sharpening our vision of the New Synthesis, the role of the present debate over sociobiology, and the relations between the two syntheses. Sociobiology should be evaluated both as a comparable case, an attempt to produce a synthesis that undergoes development and debate of the sort Mayr described, and as an extension of the Modern Synthesis itself. Sociobiology's goal structure derives from its effort to produce a synthesis. Because conceptual problems occupy the focus of Mayr's model, it is a conceptual model of syntheses. Since it is the only conceptual model of syntheses that will be discussed, by "the conceptual model" we will mean Mayr's model, as generalized here.

## A Conceptual Model of Syntheses

What is the character of the Modern Synthesis, as a result?

The term "evolutionary synthesis" was introduced by Julian Huxley in *Evolution: The Modern Synthesis* (1942) to designate the general acceptance of two conclusions: gradual evolution can be explained in terms of small genetic changes ("mutations") and recombinations, and the ordering of this genetic variation by natural selection; and the observed evolutionary phenomena, particularly macroevolutionary processes and speciation, can be explained in a manner that is consistent with known genetic mechanisms. (Mayr 1980, 1)

This definition captures the conceptual skeleton of the Modern Synthesis, not including reference to the vast body of knowledge given in neo-Darwinist evolutionary biology. It is often said that the Modern Synthesis now encounters many disputes over fundamentals, e.g., selectionism versus neutralism, gradualism versus punctuated equilibria, and individual versus group versus genic selection. However, although such issues encompass the current body of knowledge based on the Modern Synthesis, most do not capture the defining attributes of the 'Modern Synthesis' (Mayr 1985). The reason some evolutionists tell us to give up the theory of the Modern Synthesis is that they conceive it according to additional substantive claims now subject to debate. How best to distinguish the defining attributes of the synthesis itself from its associated body of knowledge is far from clear. However, we do already operate with some such distinction and find it useful even if it is rough, vague, not sharp, and not subject to consensus.

This definition conceives the Modern Synthesis in terms of the achievement of two explanatory goals. The second goal explicitly involves explanatory consistency, which here has been used to analyze what is involved in a completed evolutionary theory, the main aim of sociobiology. So it is reasonable to hypothesize that Mayr has given us resources to define sociobiology's goals, in relation to the Modern Synthesis, as explanatory goals independent of many debates specific to human sociobiology, general sociobiology, and evolutionary biology in general.

What is the character of the Modern Synthesis, as a process?

> For the historian of science, the events during the synthesis illustrate in the most graphical manner certain phenomena and processes that in a similar manner have occurred again and again in the history of science. The resistance to new ideas, the role of terminologies, the failure of communication, the fusing together of disjunct pieces into new theories, the bridging of gaps between hierarchical levels, the role of generalizers, and many other phenomena are important not only for objective historiography but also for an understanding of the actual method of science. (Mayr 1980, 44)

These features of the development of the Modern Synthesis are sufficiently general to apply to other comparable cases. We have the resources to describe the development of sociobiology, in relation to the Modern Synthesis, as the development of a synthesis of a kind found in science in general, not one unique to sociobiology. We will show that these phenomena do seem to characterize the growth of sociobiology and its debate. To do so, we need to reconstruct Mayr's conceptual account of the Modern Synthesis so as to pry apart peculiarities of the Modern Synthesis from a general model of one kind of historically recurring synthesis. The resulting model has a five-part structure, that is, a structure given by five basic postulates.

First, the synthesis is an achievement in which explanatory consistency between theory and data is attained; the recalcitrant data can be explained in a manner consistent with the theory. Second, the state of the area of study before the synthesis is characterized by opposition to the theory used to attain explanatory consistency, different schools of thought on how the domain should be studied, and a widening split between those primarily concerned with the theory used to attain consistency and those primarily concerned with the variety and complexity of the phenomena found in the domain. Third, factors delaying the synthesis include reasonable resistance to new ideas resulting from these divisions, conceptual differences between the two sides, faulty concepts on both sides, and terminological differences between the two sides that reflect these conceptual differences. The result is continual misunderstanding and partial failure of communication that delays the synthesis past the time when the relevant facts are known.

Fourth, factors bringing about the synthesis include exchange of the most viable parts of each side's thought relevant to the explanatory consistency to be achieved, the fusing together of formerly separated ideas into new theories, and the overcoming of misunderstanding and miscommunication by generalizers, who learn how the other side looks at matters, and by bridge builders, who introduce clarifying language and conceptual innovations. Fifth, the nature of the synthesis so attained is primarily conceptual rather than empirical. It hinges on combining diverse basic conceptual orientations into a coherent whole rather than the finding of missing observational or theoretical facts. Newfound facts do contribute to achieving the synthesis, but they would not bring it about by themselves and their contribution is mediated by conceptual progress. The result is rightly called a synthesis, not because it achieves consistency, but because it (a) achieves consistency on the basis of conceptual exchange and coherence, (b) combines diverse conceptions into a coherent whole, retaining their integrity, and (c) puts together elements that seemed disparate, disconnected, or opposed.

In order to apply these five postulates of the conceptual model of syntheses to sociobiology, some simplifying assumptions have to be made. Mayr's model accurately captures, not the Modern Synthesis in all its facets, but some features of the Modern Synthesis important for a possible New Synthesis; this assumption has to be tested against rival views of the Modern Synthesis, where the inadequacies of Mayr's model are shown to be important for capturing the way sociobiology is developing toward its aims. This assumption will be critically discussed after applying the model. Moreover, the New Synthesis counts as a comparable case; this assumption is reasonable because of sociobiology's status and character as a branch of evolutionary biology but must be tempered with the caveat that the development of sociobiology will take into account the collective memory and critique of the Modern Synthesis. Given these assumptions, the relation between the Modern Synthesis and the New Synthesis has two dimensions: a formal similarity, since each satisfies the conceptual model of the character and development of syntheses, and a substantive similarity, since sociobiology takes the Modern Synthesis and its ongoing critique as a point of departure.

The quest for a New Synthesis is based on and parallel to the Modern Synthesis. Our whole perspective on sociobiology changes once we look at it in these terms. Suppose a completed New Synthesis of the 1990s bears a relation to the sociobiology of the 1970s and 1980s analogous to the relation the completed Modern Synthesis of the 1940s bears to the evolutionary biology of the 1920s and 1930s! This statement is a predictive ideal of what sociobiology ought to be; it is not now a completed synthesis. The good news is that, on this supposition, the contentious polemics over sociobiology in the 1970s and 1980s no more prevents a New Synthesis than the heated debates of the 1920s and 1930s precluded the Modern Synthesis.

## Postulate One

The first postulate of the model states that a synthesis is an achievement of explanatory consistency between evolutionary theory and social data. Advocates and critics alike conceive social behavior as just another kind of trait subject to evolution by selection, thereby validating the goal of extending our best version of evolutionary theory to the realm of sociality. Let's adopt Mayr's (1980 1) wording to cast the New Synthesis in the image of the Modern Synthesis, making the parallel exact.

> *Definition.* The term "New Synthesis" was introduced by E. O. Wilson in *Sociobiology: The New Synthesis* (1975) to designate two hypotheses: gradual social evolution can be explained in terms of genetic changes, recombination, and the ordering of this genetic variation by natural selection; and observed evolutionary social phenomena, particularly those involving cultural processes and primate evolution, can be explained in a manner that is consistent with known genetic mechanisms.

The form of this specification of sociobiology's goals has implications for the components of conceptual frameworks in sociobiology. The definition of goals has the form "Gradual social evolution can be explained in terms of specified explanatory factors; and observed social evolutionary phenomena can be explained in a manner consistent with what is known about these factors." A conceptual framework for explanatory work directed toward these goals, according to the three-unit model, consists of conceptualizations of problems, domain, discipline, and performance.

To understand the explanatory problems that sociobiological inquiry pursues, we need to understand its problems as obstacles in arriving at sound arguments for these ultimate explanatory conclusions and we need to conceive of the development of these problems as development toward these conclusions. To understand the explanatory domain that sociobiological inquiry treats as its set of topics of inquiry, we need to understand the scope of what is evolutionarily significant about social change and social phenomena and to understand whether explanation of what is explained thereby shows it to be expected as actual, possible, or necessary. To understand the discipline that constitutes sociobiological inquiry, we need to understand what constitutes the totality of explanatory factors in its set of explanatory resources and the relations among the kinds of explanations they deliver. To understand the explanatory performance of sociobiology, we need to understand what counts as an appropriate evaluation of the specific role of explanations in generating these explanatory conclusions. Chapters 3, 4, 5, and 6 take the first steps in the direction of clarifying these ideas.

The content of this specification of sociobiology's explanatory goals will, no doubt, be problematic. It should be, since the critical attitude directs us not to accept any important statement in research uncritically. Some automatically interpret the sentence "the observed evolutionary phenomena . . . can be explained in a manner that is consistent with known genetic mechanisms" as meaning that no other mechanisms of transmission of traits are to be allowed than those found in orthodox population genetics. It follows that sociobiology in any version cannot allow for partially independent cultural transmission and that a version which does so allow is not an extension of the Modern Synthesis. Hence, the dilemma: if sociobiology allows factors outside orthodox population genetics to be invoked in its explanations, then it is not an extension of the Modern Synthesis; but if sociobiology does not allow other factors, then it will support the notorious "isms," as Lewontin charges.

This reading and consequent objection is not intended here. The intended interpretation is that we should read the meaning of Mayr's statement and its counterpart for sociobiology in the modest sense in which consistency means consistency, that is, the absence of contradiction, not the provision of necessary and sufficient conditions. Eldredge (1985, 119) remarks:

> No, the problem with contemporary evolutionary theory is not that its essential neo-Darwinian paradigm is incorrect. The problem is that the consistency argument of the synthesis (as developed, for example, in Mayr's (1980, p.1) statement; see also Gould, 1980a), is itself troubled. That argument says that the core neo-Darwinian paradigm (the theory that deals with the origin, maintenance, and modification of within-population genetic structure) is consistent with all other known evolutionary phenomena. This credo, innocuous and undeniable as it is, has been expanded to mean that the neo-Darwinian paradigm of selection plus drift are both necessary and sufficient to explain all other known evolutionary phenomena. My position here, and the position of all other doubters of the completeness of the synthesis that I know of, is simply that the neo-Darwinian paradigm is indeed necessary—but is not sufficient—to handle the totality of known evolutionary phenomena. And for some phenomena it may not even be necessary.

Similarly, the analogue of Mayr's statement formulated about the New Synthesis in the modest version is as "innocuous and undeniable" as such a sweeping statement could be. The dilemma presupposes the expanded, unintended claim that orthodox population genetics is both necessary and sufficient to explain all known evolutionary phenomena relevant to sociality. That expanded reading may commit sociobiology to something like the notorious "isms," but such a hardened version of the Modern Synthesis and the New Synthesis does not logically follow from the modest version even Eldredge endorses.

To press the dilemma, the issue is whether, under any available description, variations of culturally important animal or human behaviors within a population are subject to additive genetic variance. If they are not, then there is no way in which cultural evolution of those traits can correlate with genetic evolution in the sense of the Modern Synthesis. Hence, such behaviors remain outside the scope of any extension of the Modern Synthesis into a new Synthesis. If variant cultural behaviors do not correlate with genetically controlled variant traits, then no extension of the Modern Synthesis is necessary or sufficient for their explanation.

This objection would hold on either the (unintended) 'sufficiency' or 'necessity' readings, as if human sociobiology stands or falls with genetic determinism. However, both early and recent practice in human sociobiology violates that presupposition. For instance, Alexander's gene-culture program posits that people within a culture behave differently because different local natural and social environments require different adaptive responses, even if human beings are genetically identical for specific social behaviors. As early as 1979 Irons advanced the principle that "different patterns of culture and social organization are the evolutionary outcome of the propensity of humans to modify their behavior in such a way as to promote most effectively their reproductive interests in any environment" (Ruse 1989, 181). The ability to modify behavior is genetic, but the resulting behavioral variants are not supposed to correlate with genetic variants. In the *Human Reproductive Behavior* anthology, studies examine striving for wealth, prestige, and power as a proximate means for attaining reproductive success. Cultural success correlates with reproductive success for males in nonindustrial (i.e., traditional) societies, as found in 102 societies taken from the Standard Sample of Murdock and White (Barkow 1989c, 204). Behavior variants between cultures are not supposed to correlate with genetic variants.

The form of the objection is important. Unless some feature of the Modern Synthesis distinguishes explanations that do or do not extend it, the conception of the New Synthesis as an extension of the Modern Synthesis is vague. Something is an extension that achieves consistency if and only if it succeeds in showing that data on cultural behaviors do not contradict orthodox population genetics. This means that derivations of data from theory can both incorporate orthodox population genetics and contain all true statements. Such a theory need not be based on orthodox population genetics alone. It might be based on a gene-culture theory with a complex psychology. If so, explanation based on orthodox population genetics alone would be neither necessary nor sufficient for the explanation of cultural data. Even so, consistency would be achieved by combining it with novel extensions.

The following research-guiding argument expresses historically grounded necessary explanatory goals of sociobiology. Premise one: In principal and in practice, gradual evolution in general can be explained in terms of phenotypic variation that corresponds directly or indirectly to genotypic variation and the ordering of phenotypic variation by selection. Premise two: Social behavior is a quality of the phenotype of some organisms. Premise three: Hence, in principle gradual social evolution can be explained in terms of social variation that corresponds directly or indirectly to genotypic variation and the ordering of social variation by selection. However, in practice gradual social evolution cannot be so explained. Premise four: In principle evolutionary theory is complete, i.e., for each true statement about evolutionary phenomena in the domain of animal and human sociality, that statement can be translated into an explanandum inferable from an explanans formulated from evolutionary theory. Premise five: Practice follows principle. Conclusion: Let us extend evolutionary theory and observations of evolutionary phenomena to show that in practice gradual social evolution can be so explained. (A parallel argument holds for the claim about observed evolutionary phenomena.)

## Postulate Two

The second postulate of the conceptual model states that the area of study before the synthesis is characterized by opposition to the relevant theory, different schools of thought on how to study the domain, and a split between those working to extend the theory and those worried about doing justice to the variety and complexity of the phenomena. Mayr notes that the present acceptance of the neo-Darwinian view of evolution makes it hard for us to comprehend how fervently it was opposed in the 1920s and 1930s. Future acceptance of a future New Synthesis (the product, not the process of development) may likewise make the present opposition hard to comprehend.

> The very few books on evolution written by authors who were firm adherents to neo-Darwinism (such as Haldane, 1932) had various shortcomings. None of these was greater than their attempt to explain evolution in terms of changes in gene frequencies. This explanation left most nongeneticists thoroughly dissatisfied because events at the level of the gene did not at all explain the organismic phenomena studied by paleontologists, systematists, ecologists, and students of behavior. (Mayr 1980, 3)

In reading Mayr's comments with the debate over human sociobiology in mind, we get the uncanny feeling of *deja vu*. The character of presynthesis writings of neo-Darwinians in the 1920s and sociobiologists in the 1970s and 1980s like Wilson, Barash, Alexander, and Trivers provoked opposition. Pop sociobiologists give the impression that they were explaining cultural evolution in terms of changes in gene frequencies, leaving others dissatisfied because events at the level of the gene do not explain cultural behavior and cultural evolution. Hence, the criticism is not just "(unreasonable) resistance to new ideas," as the popularizers tell themselves, but a conflict over explanatory reductionism brought on by the style of explaining acts. In response, Barkow's gene-culture theory posits that, "Applying evolutionary theory to culture requires a series of multi-level, mutually compatible explanations that move from genes to neurophysiology to individual motivation to social interaction to sociology" (1989c, 225).

It is a subtle, but momentous slide from a moderate to an extreme version of what an evolutionary synthesis would be. Mayr endorses the moderate doctrine (A): Evolution can be explained in terms of genetic changes and the ordering of genetic variation by natural selection, and evolutionary phenomena can be explained in a manner consistent with known genetic mechanisms. The point of making a statement of the moderate form is that among all the explanatory factors of X is the factor Y, that various obstacles prevented us from seeing how Y could possibly be successfully employed in the explanation of X, and so to show that Y can indeed be used to explain X by discovering how Y can be used to explain X would be a marvelous achievement. To make a statement of the moderate form (A) in this research situation, "X can be explained in terms of Y," does not imply that "X can be explained primarily or solely in terms of Y."

If we forget this problem situation, taking the doctrine (A) out of its historical context, we risk overinterpreting it and substituting for (A) an extreme doctrine (B) which would have that implication. It is a short slide from (A) to an extreme doctrine Mayr rejects (B): Evolution can be explained by reference to genetic changes as the overriding source of phenotypic variation and the ordering of genetic variation by natural selection as the overriding force of evolutionary change, and all phenomena of evolution can be explained in a manner consistent with known genetic mechanisms by appeal to genes and natural selection alone. The moderate doctrine (A), allowing for a wide array of explanatory resources, expresses a genuine explanatory pluralism. The extreme doctrine (B), ignoring the complexity of factors of evolution, tends toward a restrictive explanatory monism.

By misinterpreting sociobiology in terms of variants of (B) rather than variants of (A), practitioners do an injustice to their own field and evaluators cannot help but become critical. In sociobiology they find the very thing they have been arguing against for years:

movements away from the full use of all the explanatory resources of evolutionary theory and toward (B) or some variant of (B). For example, this explanatory method is found in what Gould and others call "the hardening of the Modern Synthesis" in recent years. When the slide from (A) to (B) is made in the context of human sociobiology, the way is open to identify sociobiology's goal structure with the goals of biological reductionism, biological and genetic determinism, and adaptationism.

The way out of the addictive fascination with those "isms" in understanding what sociobiology is all about is to realize that its proper aims should be understood as continuations of the aims of the most moderate version of the revised Modern Synthesis on which evolutionists can justifiably form a consensus. This would involve formulating precise variants of (A) and (B) that take account of the full range of explanatory resources, specifying how they should and should not be combined, and using them to clarify sociobiology's goal structure. Here we see that the conceptualization of sociobiology's explanatory resources is part and parcel of the conceptualization of its explanatory aims and development in a historically sensitive manner.

There was a plurality of competing theories of evolution before the Modern Synthesis that he classifies according to his criteria of population thinking versus typological thinking and hard versus soft inheritance: Geoffroyism, Saltationism, Orthogenesis, Darwinism, and neo-Darwinism (Mayr 1980, 4). That today—before the New Synthesis—there is a plethora of competing theories of social and/or cultural evolution that arise from the biosocial tradition needs no documentation. Even within human sociobiology during the 1970s and 1980s, very different rival theories are being developed at different levels of generality, e.g., as described when discussing Laudan's theory of validation. For example, Boyd and Richerson (1975, 158) classify theories in human sociobiology according to the relative importance of genetic and cultural variation in explaining behavioral variation in humans: pure environment (exemplified by Alexander 1979a), pure genes (exemplified by Darlington 1969 and perhaps Wilson 1975), genes plus culture (exemplified by Lumsden and Wilson 1981), and environment plus culture, (exemplified by Durham 1976a,b).

The gap widened before the Modern Synthesis between the geneticists/theorists, primarily concerned with genetic theory, and the systematists/naturalists, primarily concerned with doing justice to the diversity and complexity of adaptive phenomena. "Each group not only dealt with different subject matters but also asked basically different questions. When it came to the interpretation of evolutionary phenomena, their conclusions were often diametrically opposed." (Mayr 1980, 6). The wide split in subject matter, questions, and methods between sociobiologists and social scientists is well known. Again, an unnecessary adversarial relation has developed between the popularizers primarily concerned with extending selection theory and those critics primarily concerned with doing justice to the diversity and complexity of human cultural and historical phenomena. The same explanation is judged acceptable by some and unacceptable by others because their orientations incorporate a wide split in what they take to be the proper explanatory topics, questions, methods, theories, and concepts that define explanatory problems in studying human sociality.

## Postulates Three, Four, Five

Postulate 3 of Mayr's model identifies factors that delay the synthesis. It is not hard to locate in the sociobiology debate many of the factors that delayed the Modern Synthesis: (1) resistance to new ideas (due to styles of explaining acts, due to the history of waves of evolutionism in social science promising more than was achieved, due to the political character of the evaluation of human sociobiology); (2) conceptual differences between evolutionary and nonevolutionary perspectives on social phenomena (evident in different meanings of contrasts including innate/learned, genetic/environmental, animal/human, biological/cultural, nature/nurture, biological determinism/cultural determinism, social/cultural); (3) conceptual differences in the thought of social scientists and evolutionists (thinking in terms of proximate versus remote causes, thinking in terms of intentions, goals, or reasons versus thinking in terms of results regardless of intention, goal, or reasons, explanation by appeal to lower versus higher organizational levels, thinking in terms of the genotype/phenotype distinction versus persons or agents); and (4) faulty concepts on both sides (failure to clearly distinguish social behavior, social context, and social organization as well as faulty concepts of genetic causation, transmission, development, and function), and terminological differences that reflect these conceptual differences.

Many faulty versions of ideas we now take for granted promoted misunderstanding and delayed the coming of the Modern Synthesis: the genotype/phenotype distinction, the distinction between hard and soft inheritance, the chance/accident distinction, as well as concepts of variation, mutation, recombination, and natural selection. The previous parallel makes it likely that the sociobiology debate is permeated by a related host of faulty concepts that delay the coming of the New Synthesis.

Postulate 4 of the conceptual model identifies factors producing the synthesis. Mayr described in detail what factors contributed to the attainment of the Modern Synthesis. Mayr had access to a completed synthesis, and so could work retrospectively at identifying what contributed to it. But the New Synthesis has not yet been achieved. Indeed, only after a synthesis occurs could one have overwhelming evidence that the present state is a presynthesis stage. For all we know, the present debate may never lead to a New Synthesis and may only lead us down a blind alley. We cannot know beforehand that a New Synthesis is achievable, although once we achieve it (if it is achieved) we can identify the factors of its achievement.

Still, we can now say that if a comparable synthesis occurs, there may be counterparts for the following exchange of concepts between geneticists and naturalists that led to the Modern Synthesis. Geneticists gave naturalists not only a distinction between genotype and phenotype, but also mutation, recombination, gene interaction, hard inheritance only, and natural selection as the only directive force in evolution. Naturalists gave geneticists not only population thinking, but also the multidimensionality of polytypic species, the biological species concept, phyletic evolution, and the role of behavior and change of function in the origin of evolutionary novelties. This exchange was facilitated by bridge builders who introduced new terminologies, enabling researchers to state needed generalizations, clarify faulty concepts, and reconcile conceptual differences. Todey, Barkow (1989c) is one such bridge builder, whose terminology of "goals, plans, and codes" is proposed to help make sociobiology compatible with social science.

Part 5 of the conceptual model describes the character of a synthesis brought about by all the conceptual exchange and clarification:

What was the particular missing piece of information or missing theory that had previously prevented the synthesis, the discovery of which now made it possible? No such missing piece was involved. Nearly all the individual components of the synthesis represent insights that were acquired during the 1910–1930 period (as far as the nature of genetic variation is concerned) or even before (such as the understanding of species and speciation by the naturalists). (Mayr 1980, 39)

If the New Synthesis were to depend on finding elusive facts about the relative roles of genes and natural selection in molding social behavior, or other areas of factual dispute over which advocates and critics have become so exercised, then the unlikelihood of obtaining the missing facts would render the achievement of the New Synthesis unlikely. Yet if the New Synthesis is primarily conceptual rather than empirical, so that conceptual progress guides empirical progress, then we have reason for optimism. As far as we know, sociobiology can produce a unified account of the evolutionary basis of animal and human sociality that counts as a New Synthesis. The present polarization over sociobiology, far from precluding a genuine New Synthesis, may just be typical presynthesis activity.

## Discussion of the Conceptual Model

There are rival views of the Modern Synthesis. Some differences between these rival views may make a difference to our understanding of the New Synthesis, whereas other differences will not. We cannot decide such matters until we first draw out the implications of each in isolation and later in relation to one another. Mayr's model is adopted here as a limited, first approximation, to be scrutinized in relation to the implications of rival views on the way to a more impartial and balanced account. For instance, Mayr does not write a historian's history but uses history to elaborate and vindicate his own special views. Mayr writes biological history the way Russell wrote philosophical history and so his viewpoint is often criticized as "slanted." For instance, his criticism of so-called "bean bag genetics" led him to oppose the standard view that the Modern Synthesis was achieved primarily by the work of population geneticists. This clash of viewpoint is particularly pertinent to sociobiology, e.g., Wilson's gene-culture program is heavily rooted in population genetics and population ecology.

A general model of syntheses cannot itself anticipate ongoing reinterpretation of past achievement in the light of present programs for achievement. The various gene-culture programs discussed previously bear differing relationships to population genetics and population ecology. We cannot now anticipate which one, if any, will win out since we cannot now anticipate how the range of gene-culture programs will change or will give way to a different sort of research program. To develop the general model from Mayr's view of the Modern Synthesis is not to say that Mayr accurately captured all aspects of the Modern Synthesis. The task is to extract certain general elements about its character and the way it was achieved that are relatively independent of specific, substantive issues about past and present research. What is endorsed here about Mayr's view of the Modern Synthesis is no more than the general model as structured into five postulates. It is endorsed, not as the correct model, but as one of the models to be drawn from in constructing a feasibly adequate model.

Recall that we used Hempel's model of explanation in a way that does not endorse the inferential conception of explanation. It was regarded as a model of the inferential structure of explanatory reasoning, whatever the nature of explanation may be. Here, we are using Mayr's ideas to form a model of evolutionary syntheses. Similarly, rather then endorse the present model as capturing the nature of syntheses, it is regarded as a useful model of the conceptual dimension of syntheses. We need to develop a better model of syntheses that illuminates the relations between the Modern and the Sociobiological Syntheses. This task is crucial to the quality of sociobiology's normative self-definition. The present use of Mayr's model both illustrates and motivates this main point.

The best views of the Modern Synthesis agree that its conceptual dimension was absolutely crucial. According to the conventional view

> the synthesis is the product of three phases of development: (1) resolution of early difficulties raised in the early days of genetics, largely through the work of Fisher, Haldane, and Wright; (2) the publication of Dobzhansky's *Genetics and the Origin of Species* (1937), which fused concepts of the genetics of populations with the mainstream of Darwinian thought; and (3) the demonstration by systematists (e.g., Mayr 1942), paleontologists (e.g., Simpson 1944), and practitioners of various other biological disciplines that the data of their respective fields are consistent with genetic principles. (Eldredge 1985, 43)

The conventional view thus acknowledges that a conceptual phase (phase 2) preceded and guided an empirical phase (phase 3). Mayr's model challenges the separation of phases 2 and 3. He argues that

the conceptual phase included contributions by geneticists (Dobzhansky), systematists (Mayr himself), paleontologists (Simpson),
and perhaps others. He makes this case by showing that his own
contribution, as found in the main argument of his *Systematics and
the Origin of Species* (1942) was to fuse genetical and Darwinian
concepts using a systematist's conceptual perspective. It included:

> population thinking, the immense variability of populations, the grad-
> ualness of evolution, the genetic nature of gradual evolution, geo-
> graphic speciation, the adaptive nature of observed variation, belief in
> the importance of natural selection, and the gradual nature of macro-
> evolution (Eldredge 1985, 59)

Since Mayr's motivation is to argue that the conventional view dis-
counted much of his own contribution, we should expect it not to be
impartial or balanced. Our use of Mayr's model treats it as a resource, not a last word.

Eldredge's critique of the Modern Synthesis has several important implications for sociobiology's New Synthesis. First, in critically analyzing the influential works of Dobzhansky, Mayr, and
Simpson, he presents the body of thought that supplies the context
of Mayr's two conclusions of the Modern Synthesis. Just as those two
conclusions cannot be understood apart from that context, so the
projected analogous hypotheses of the New Synthesis cannot be understood in isolation from the present body of neosynthetic thought.
Second, in using this critical analysis to capture the structure and
content of the Modern Synthesis, he justifies the accuracy of Mayr's
two conclusions as correctly capturing the essentials of the Modern
Synthesis and notes that it is even more accurate when applied to
later developments (Eldredge 1985, 100, 114–15). His work justifies
taking Mayr's two conclusions as our point of departure for formulating the essential theses as goals of the New Synthesis. Third,
in describing where the Modern Synthesis went wrong and suggesting how to fix it or go beyond it, he provides an example of how
our best version of evolutionary theory is not found in the Modern
Synthesis itself, but in an updated revision of it or successor to it.

If we were to revise Mayr's two conclusions in the light of Eldredge's proposals, we would end up with something like the following. Mayr's two theses hold for social microevolution and are necessary but insufficient to capture social macroevolution. We must
reconceptualize the ontological commitments of those theses so that
evolutionary phenomena consist of the evolution of genealogical

hierarchies (genes, chromosomes, organisms, demes, species, and monophyletic taxa) and ecological hierarchies (molecules, cells, organisms, populations, communities, and regional biotas). Eldredge's arguments for explicitly incorporating all the items subject to evolution into evolutionary theory (not just genes, organisms, and populations) have counterparts for sociobiology. We need to reconceptualize the ontology of sociobiological theory so that it not only is hierarchical in this sense, but also so that it captures relations between organismic behavioral interactions, social roles, social groups, social organization, and any social hierarchies. Although Eldredge's views are quite critical of the Modern Synthesis, they provide further grounds for using models of syntheses that emphasize conceptual change for conceiving the New Synthesis.

Hierarchy theory's ability to capture holistic patterns has not been accompanied by a specification of causal processes acting on hierarchies as triumphant as those of populations genetics. For Eldredge, the problem of understanding genealogical hierarchies is to reconcile the facts that variation is continuous and that taxa are discontinuous. Human sociobiology confronts this problem: if social variation is continuous, how could the discontinuity between nonhuman and human sociality evolve? Eldredge proposes that speciation is a result of changes in species mate-recognition systems, involving reproductive adaptations—an alternative to isolating mechanisms, but neo-Darwinian nevertheless. Note that some sociobiologists explain the initial evolution of culture as a result of autopredation and sexual selection. Hominids with high cultural capacity more successfully attacked each other or resisted attack on each other. Mate selection for autopredatory success increased cultural capacity (Barkow 1989c, 154), a factor of speciation for *Homo Sapiens*.

## Implications of the Conceptual Model

The conceptual model of syntheses connects interestingly to the views of Laudan, Lakatos, Popper, and Hattiangadi.

Note how well Mayr's model fits Laudan's emphasis on conceptual, not just empirical, problems in science. The empirical phase of the Modern Synthesis could not have occurred without its conceptual phase, but not conversely. This fact is the kernel of truth in Mayr's view that the Modern Synthesis was primarily conceptual rather than empirical, even though Mayr underestimated the contribution of Dobzhansky's empirical work (Bechtel 1986). Sociobiologists need to clarify their visions of the way the goals of the New Synthesis involve both conceptual and empirical phases of research. Goal clarification should be as normal in research as hypothesis testing.

The conclusion reached is that, "On the basis of the conceptual and empirical work done, unsolved problems in explaining macroevolutionary change could be overcome." The Modern Synthesis is not a claim to have a correct or empirically adequate account of all evolutionary change. If it were, it would claim to have finished basic research, which would be hubris in the extreme. Evolutionists often argue against this or that doctrine they associate with the Modern Synthesis and claim that we need to get beyond the Modern Synthesis. That attack often reads into it a more ambitious result than what it involves, an overinflated caricature.

The conclusion of the Modern Synthesis, as stated in Mayr's reading of Huxley's *Evolution: The Modern Synthesis*, was stated in the form "evolution can be explained in such-and-such a manner." Conspicuous by its absence is any specification of what the implicit validation of this explanatory approach amounts to. He didn't say "adequately explained," "correctly explained," or use any other term of validation. What sort of validity, then, should we expect of it? We should not regard it as an absolute, a timeless conclusion about having achieved adequacy or any other sort of finished validation. In this sense, to speak of an "unfinished synthesis" is a category mistake. The conclusion is historical. To endorse the Modern Synthesis is to endorse the claim that its architects found a conceptual, theoretical, methodological, and empirical basis for guiding future research far superior to what there had been before.

To acknowledge the historical fact that evolutionists after the Modern Synthesis knew what they were doing in a way that evolutionists before it did not is not to endorse the theses of the Modern Synthesis. Gould (1982, 382) interprets Mayr's first conclusion of the Modern Synthesis as a gradualist thesis and Mayr's second conclusion as a reductionist thesis, both cogently argued (on those readings) to be inferior to punctuated equilibrium theory.

Reconsider the first conclusion that "gradual evolution can be explained in terms of small genetic changes and recombination, and the ordering of this genetic variation by natural selection." Gould interprets it as implying that gradual allelic substitution is a model for all evolutionary change, that rates of evolutionary change are so uniform that they do not allow for periods of rapid change during speciation and periods of stasis after speciation, that the importance of nonhistorical constraints of form on the design of organisms is ruled out by the selectionist emphasis on function, and so forth. Reconsider the second conclusion that "the observed evolutionary phenomena, particularly macro-evolutionary processes and speciation can be explained in a manner that is consistent with the known genetic mechanisms." Gould interprets it as implying that speciation is always an extension of gradual, adaptive allelic substitution to greater effect, that adaptive advantage is so pervasive that large amounts of neutral or maladaptive variation are not found during or after speciation, that individual selection is the only effective form of selection and that species selection is absent or unimportant in macroevolution, and so forth.

Now, it is undeniable that the neo-Darwinist theory of evolution as found in the 1940s is false on many points of detail in application to many areas of evolutionary study. Paleontology is a case in point. Why expect a theory to last sixty or so years in the first place? We would be surprised if the theory had not broken down. Whether or not we read all these implications into Mayr's statement of the Modern Synthesis, no one today accepts the theory used in the Modern Synthesis in its entirety. To anticipate the results of 3.1 and 3.2, it will be shown that even within the relatively short span of sociobiology, the theory used in sociobiology has undergone or is undergoing cumulative change, corrective change, revolutionary change, and gradual change. If so, it is a short step to recognize all four sorts of change in the theory inherited from the Modern Synthesis. In identifying corrective change, it will be argued that the theory of inclusive fitness actually contradicts the theory of individual selection inherited from the Modern Synthesis. So the sense in which sociobiology is based on the Modern Synthesis is not that the theory of the Modern Synthesis is as fine now as it was in its own day. Rather, in various revised versions it orients problem solving in sociobiology in a way that rivals in its own day do not.

Gould (1982, 382) describes what is happening to Darwinism:

Current critics of Darwinism and the modern synthesis are proposing a good deal more than a comfortable extension of the theory, but much less than a revolution. In my partisan view, neither of Darwinism's two central themes will survive in their strict formulation; in that sense, "the modern synthesis, as an exclusive proposition, has broken down on both of its fundamental claims." However, I believe that a restructured evolutionary theory will embody the essence of the Darwinian argument in a more abstract, and hierarchically extended form. The modern synthesis is incomplete, not incorrect.

As punctuated equilibrium theory develops, so does the conception of Darwinism and the modern synthesis with which we try to understand its relation to the past theory (see Ruse 1989). Punctuated equilibrium theory is a revised version of the neo-Darwinian theory of the Modern Synthesis in a historical sense. However much it departs, it takes its cue from the Modern Synthesis, not something else. The Modern Synthesis is still incomplete with respect to both macroevolution and social evolution.

The research-oriented character of the conclusion helps us see that many critics of the Modern Synthesis are criticizing it as finished research, not as a historical achievement. Even they don't want to go back to a stage of research conceptualized according to typological thinking and soft inheritance. They don't want to go back to Geoffroyism, Saltationism, Orthogenesis, or Darwinism in the forms they were advocated before the Modern Synthesis. For instance, although Gould's punctuated equilibrium theory was given a Saltationist interpretation, he disavowed the Saltationist thesis that speciation occurred regularly in a few generations and instead regarded speciation covering fifty thousand years as a geologically instantaneous jump. Such critics don't want to go back to the ways of thought whereby we could not incorporate mutation and selection into a single theoretical scheme compatible with the data of macroevolution. Gould wants to combine the functionalist ideas of selection, the stochastic ideas of new variation, and the structuralist ideas of the inner architecture of organisms into a scheme relating microevolution and microevolution. Such a scheme could not be dreamt of before the Modern Synthesis. Since no one wants to go back to the views of evolution before the Modern Synthesis, even those who rightly claim that we need to get beyond it are tacitly endorsing it in the historical sense.

A test of the cumulative retention of the Modern Synthesis is this: given that our present opinions differ from those found in the Modern Synthesis, if they differ more radically from what Mayr called neo-Darwinism than from the competing schools of thought, then the Modern Synthesis has not been cumulatively retained. We may not want to call ourselves "neo-Darwinists" in order to stress progress in research since the Modern Synthesis, but the critics of the Modern Synthesis most respected today (e.g., Gould, Eldredge) are squarely in the tradition of the neo-Darwinists as compared to the other competing schools of thought at the time of the Modern Synthesis. The neo-Darwinist approach of the Modern Synthesis was the best available approach at the time, even considered now. This is the sense in which a sociobiology's New Synthesis is based on the Modern Synthesis and the sense in which sociobiology is antecedently committed to the Modern Synthesis. There is no point in advocating a stronger sense of cumulative retention since it would be immediately refuted.

Familiarity with gene-culture theories suggests a parallel that motivates the conceptual model of the New Synthesis. In the 1970s sociobiologists and antisociobiologists debated about whether genetic transmission or social transmission drove evolutionary change in cultural species, as if one could not consistently incorporate genetic and social transmission into a single theoretical scheme. Thus, "genes versus culture" plays the role in recent debate that "mutation versus selection" did in the early debate. In the 1980s a variety of gene-culture programs aimed to reconceptualize the problem and prove the lack of contradiction with theories. As Lakatos emphasized, these theories could also guide development of a body of novel results.

Our metalogical definition of completeness reveals what these gene-culture programs have achieved and have yet to achieve. What has been achieved is that novel facts are expressible in a theoretical system. The observation language expresses what counts as evolutionarily significant behavior in cultural organisms. The theoretical language that explains how the behaviors subject to both social transmission and genetic transmission evolve. This is a large step toward completeness. When we show that the observation language can represent all the behaviors we count as evolutionarily significant behaviors and that the theoretical language allows us to explain all the kinds of evolutionarily significant social facts available to us, then we will have a new synthesis that achieves completeness. But the Modern Synthesis did not even achieve completeness in that sense. It furnished a theoretical system that formed the basis for future problem solving. If some gene-culture program or its successor goes through both the conceptual and empirical phases of research that the Modern Synthesis did, and thereby showed us that it contains the basis for future problem solving, then it will meet the standard of success set by the Modern Synthesis. Thus, real achievement is best measured, not by some ahistorical standard like adequacy or correctness, but by a historical standard like fertility.

Mayr's insight also underscores the emphasis of Popper on contradictions. Popper treated all intellectual problems as contradictions and treated solutions as resolutions of contradictions (Berkson 1987, 87). Popper emphasized contradictions between theory and data. Similarly, we have treated the problem of an incomplete evolutionary theory as a contradiction between expectations produced by Darwinian selection theory and social data, e.g., it would lead us to think that widespread altruism cannot evolve but we observe that widespread altruism is a fact. We have also treated a solution as a resolution of the contradiction, where a full resolution would make evolutionary theory relevant to and consistent with social data.

Recall that 'consistency' includes both (a) the semantic concept of the truth of all the statements used in the inferential structure of the explanation (via Hempel's model of explanation, chap. 1) and (b) the epistemic concept of resistance to falsification despite severe efforts at falsification (via Popper's view of evidence, chap. 2). The role of the semantic concept is to insure that the contradiction itself disappears, whereas the role of the epistemic concept is to insure that we have good reason for thinking that the contradiction is gone. To conceive of what sort of sociobiological synthesis would achieve consistency in both senses, use the Modern Synthesis as a model for the New Synthesis.

The general lesson is this: To attain consistency and, between theory and data, reconceptualize. In the case of the Modern Synthesis, natural selection theory was incomplete until it was reconceptualized so that the genetic basis of selection was consistent with data on macroevolution. In the case of the New Synthesis, evolutionary theory remains incomplete until it can be reconceptualized so that the genetic basis of selection can be rendered consistent with data on social evolution. This has already been partly accomplished with respect to the data on altruism, as found in the conceptual work differentiating various types of altruism to be discussed in the remainder of this chapter.

Moreover, Mayr's insight calls for an analysis of problems that also recognizes contradictions between different metaphysical world views, as found in Hattiangadi's analysis (Berkson 1987). In the case of the Modern Synthesis, the geneticist-experimentalist view of evolution as gradual change in relative frequency among genetically controlled traits from one generation to the next seemed to contradict the naturalist-taxonomist view of evolution as the formation of new species and their adaptive radiation to new niches. No resolution occurred by debating between world views as such, but by creating a theoretical scheme that transformed world-view presuppositions into a scientific theory subject to scientific controls.

In the case of a New Synthesis, the sociobiological view of cultural evolution as an environment-tracking device for changes on a time scale of individual lifetimes seems to contradict the anti-sociobiological view of cultural evolution as the cooperative organization for producing means to satisfy needs, producing new needs, and renewing itself. The preceding discussion of the conflict between world views (e.g., Wilson and Lewontin) suggests that resolution at the level of world view is unlikely. Instead, transformation of metaphysical presuppositions into gene-culture theories subject to the usual scientific controls narrows the field of controversy addressed so that resolution becomes a real possibility. Synthetic gene-culture theories bear a role in the New Synthesis similar to the synthetic mutation-selection theory in Modern Synthesis.

## 3.2 The Altruism Problem

## Arguments for Cumulative Development

What sort of development should we expect to find in sociobiology, ignoring the accidental contingencies of research that affect its development on the scale of particular explanations? This question is best construed as a question about the character of sociobiology's extension of the Modern Synthesis into a New Synthesis. That is, what sort of development would count as explanatory progress, as progress toward the ultimate explanatory conclusions which constitute the goals of the New Synthesis? If we can't understand what would count as explanatory progress, then we are unable to adequately evaluate the success or failure of sociobiology.

To make the issue manageable, we shall focus on the problem of explaining altruism as it is addressed in animal sociobiology, as if we were writing a simple history of attempts at progress. Four basic rival models of scientific development are preeminent (Kourany 1985): cumulative, corrective, revolutionary, and gradual development. We will consider each in turn in the remainder of this chapter, showing how the altruism problem was pushed through successive refinements of evolutionary thought into the units/levels of selection problem.

According to the cumulative model, explanations promoting the extension of the Modern Synthesis into a New Synthesis that produce progress are additions to previous ones. This is the standard view inherent in the highly stylized view of scientific method in which we are trained. It will later be argued that the theory needed to explain altruism, which stands as sociobiology's most impressive achievement, actually contradicts the theory of the Modern Synthesis. Hence, the cumulative model is false about details in theory structure. Because the development of physics has this character (e.g., that quantum mechanics and relativity theory reveal the falsity of Newtonian mechanics), many have rejected the cumulative model altogether. That's going too far. To show that the hypothesis "transitions in details of theory structure are cumulative" is false does not show that the hypothesis "there are other aspects of science that are cumulative" is false.

In response to that fallacious inference, it will be shown that the cumulative model is inherent in basic research orientations assumed in explanations of altruism. Four arguments will be supplied for thinking that the cumulative model does capture important aspects of development: the argument from accumulation, the argument from problem identification, and the argument from special cases, and the argument from completeness. Consider each in turn.

First, the argument for cumulative development from accumulation asserts that progress occurs as explanations accumulate. This view is suggested by Hempel's method of assessment, insofar as it envisages progress as the accumulation of correct explanations. The difficulty is that we need a good reason to think that we have correct explanations in the first place. Cumulativity is inherent in confirmationist methodologies. One group of confirmationists boldly claim that we have sufficient confirmation to regard our best explanations as true. Since the standards for correctness—derivability, lawhood, empirical import, truth—are difficult to achieve, others say that the cumulative model leads to scepticism. Few scientists claim that all the statements used in their explanations are true. In reaction, another group of confirmationists advance the cautious claim that, even if we don't have such decisive confirmation, the well-confirmed explanations accumulate. However, our discussion in chapters 1 and 2 against confirmationism recognizes many more criteria of success than confirmational success in evaluating explanations. The items said to accumulate should be judged in terms of the totality of these criteria.

Moreover, we have advocated the joint use of two sorts of standards: absolute standards of correctness and relative standards of acceptability. There is progress in sociobiology in the form of the accumulation of acceptable explanations, where the standards satisfied rise significantly. An explanation is judged acceptable when it is the best of available rival explanations. This holds even if we have insufficient reason to regard it as correct, having evaluated it on the basis of the totality of criteria of validation discussed in chapters 1 and 2. Since the standards satisfied by the set of rivals normally get higher as work on the set of rivals continues, the accumulation of acceptable explanations is normally the accumulation of what we judge to be better and better explanations.

Second, the argument for cumulative development from problem identification asserts that problems are chosen according to their importance as obstacles to completeness and that their importance is decided on the assumption of cumulative development. The reason why the problem of explaining altruism has loomed so large in the development of sociobiology is that sociality cannot be explained unless altruism is explained. Since stable social interactions, social roles, and social organization require behaviors toward others that do not immediately benefit oneself, altruism was regarded as the greatest obstacle preventing evolutionary theory from being complete.

We are accustomed to answering questions of the form "Why does that animal behave the way it does?" by saying, "Because that behavior is good for the group or the species." A variety of social phenomena were interpreted in this manner (Wynne-Edwards 1962). For instance, ritualized male-male contests for access to females often lead to lack of reproduction by the losing male. It was postulated that animals adopt social conventions which lead them to curtail their own reproduction when they become aware of rising population density. Such population control mechanisms are explained as being "good for the species." This explanation requires self-imposed restrained breeding by individuals, a form of altruism. Provided we regard cooperation involving some degree of altruism as a defining or typical feature of animal societies, to explain animal sociality we must explain altruism. An explanation of altruism is a precondition for an explanation of sociality.

Explanations of behavior in ecology must be consistent with theories in population biology about how natural selection works. Wynne-Edwards drove home the point that explanations of the evolution of a trait "because it is good for the species" require selection among groups, not just among individual organisms. If Darwinian individual selection were the only cause of evolutionary change at work, altruism would be selected against because it hurts the individual's relative chance of reproductive success in its population. If group selection were the only cause of evolutionary change at work, altruism would be selected for because it helps the chances of the population as a whole avoid extinction. In our example, populations of restrained breeders are less likely to go extinct than populations of maximally breeding individuals, which would overexploit their food resources due to overpopulation. Thus, the observed frequency of altruistic traits would reflect the relative strength of Darwinian individual selection against them and group selection for them.

Extensive use of group-selection hypotheses went against the grain of neo-Darwinian theory as inherited from the Modern Synthesis. Recall Mayr's description of the achieved synthesis as involving general acceptance of two conclusions. First, gradual evolution can be explained in terms of small genetic changes and the ordering of this genetic variation by natural selection. Second, the observed evolutionary phenomena can be explained in a manner consistent with known genetic mechanisms. Now, the form of selection used to generate these two conclusions was individual selection. So the orthodox view in population biology was that most or all significant evolutionary change is due to individual selection (Gould 1980).

The body of knowledge used to generate the Modern Synthesis has an irreducible emphasis on individual selection. If we deny that emphasis, then the very idea of the body of knowledge found in the Modern Synthesis becomes vacuous. The model of cumulative development cannot be saved by interpreting past explanatory achievements so liberally that they lose their doctrinal content. Adherence to the Modern Synthesis led evolutionists to follow the rule that we should accept group-selection explanations only when efforts at explanation by individual selection are exhausted. This methodological rule obviously is predicated on the cumulative model of development, since it implies, positively, that new explanations are additions to old ones, or negatively, that old explanations are not lost as new ones are gained.

Wynne-Edwards's group-selection explanation of social conventions held great significance for the adequacy of the Modern Synthesis. If social behavior typically involves altruism and altruism cannot be explained without appeal to group selection, then the Modern Synthesis is incomplete. Social behavior would form a class of observed evolutionary phenomena that cannot be explained consistently with known genetic mechanisms and the ordering of genetic variation by individual natural selection.

One strategy to reduce the incompleteness of the Modern Synthesis is to argue that the observed social behaviors are not cases of genuine altruism or, if altruistic, did not evolve because of their benefit to the group. Williams (1966) adopted this strategy of argument from the Darwinian pole of the Modern Synthesis to debunk most of the usual group-selection explanations (he allowed for group selection in the case of the house mouse t-allele). He emphasized the need for a precise vocabulary to study adaptation.

To decide whether a behavior is selfish or altruistic in terms of natural selection, one must engage in extensive cost/benefit analysis, assessing the overall balance of all the costs and all the benefits found in the results of the trait on its possessor's survival and reproduction. Many cases of altruism could be exposed as merely apparent and not genuine, once hidden costs of altruism or hidden benefits of selfishness had been uncovered. An influential example is Lack's (1954a,b) work on birds. Contrary to Wynne-Edwards's assumption, Lack showed that maximal breeding is not always favored by individual selection. Some birds project more offspring into the next generation of their evolving population by producing fewer eggs than physiologically possible. Reduced clutch size is not necessarily altruistic.

Moreover, a behavior good for its possessor may also be good for its group or for its species, but evolve solely because of the benefit to its possessor. According to the preceding expanded cost/benefit analysis, most cases of genuine altruism thought to require group selection could be explained in principle by individual selection as well. Given the methodological rule predicated on cumulative development, the most parsimonious or most conservative attitude is not to reject explanations in terms of individual selection when the benefit to the group could be viewed as an incidental or fortuitous effect. Using such arguments, Williams both raised the critical standards for explaining adaptation and convinced ecologists that group-selection hypotheses should be viewed with suspicion.

Third, the argument for cumulative development from special cases asserts that social behavior is a special case of phenotypic traits, that social relations count as a special case of selection pressures, and that the new selection processes which explain altruism are special cases of individual selection. Hence, the basic explanatory perspective of the Modern Synthesis is retained.

Consider sociobiology's theoretical resources, as we might describe them to an audience qualitatively, without going into the population genetics formalism. Basic methods include the comparative method for naturalistic field studies, breeding and hybridization experiments for controlled laboratory studies, and so forth. Basic concepts include those about different facets of evolution (the fact of evolution, the chronological course of evolution, and the causes of evolutionary change), concepts about different kinds of causes (proximate versus ultimate causes), concepts about the nature of the organismic self (organisms have two layers of self, namely, genotype and phenotype), and concepts about the causal factors of evolutionary change in populations (mutation, recombination, selection, drift, migration), and so forth.

Given these theoretical resources, various special case arguments are compelling. If the organismic self consists in a phenotype developed from an inherited genotype in relation to the environment, and if the phenotype includes organismic morphology, physiology, and behavior, it follows that social behavior is a special case of the phenotype. If selection is a cause of evolutionary change, then all selection must either be group selection or individual selection, further subdivided according to the relation between selection and the genotype and the relation between selection and the phenotype. Any contribution to studying the levels and units of selection obviously counts as another addition to prior studies of selection.

A selection pressure is anything that can reduce, increase, or otherwise bias the organism's ability, with respect to the genotype, to perpetuate copies of its genes, and with respect to the phenotype, to produce viable offspring of itself or others in the evolving population. Before sociobiology, the kinds of selection pressures studied included climate, weather, food shortages, predation, parasites, and disease. Social relations and mate shortages are obviously additional selection pressures, and so are studied in sociobiology. The idea of cumulative development here is obvious since explanations of organismic survival and reproduction in terms of social relations and mate shortages are to be added to those in terms of the other selection pressures. Indeed, the fact that social relations count as an additional selection pressure is strong reason to regard the domain of social phenomena as within the scope of evolutionary biology. That is why a complete evolutionary theory would have to explain sociality.

A number of new selection processes were constructed to deal with social relations and mate shortages regarded as selection pressures. Those involving individual selection, and perhaps group selection as a last resort, include sexual selection, parental investment, parental manipulation, sex-ratios, reciprocal altruism, and r- versus K- selection. These selection processes are special cases of how selection works in general, and so explanations whose explanatory factors include them are to be added to previous explanations in terms of natural selection.

These relatively simple and undeniable statements about sociobiology's theoretical resources provide compelling arguments in principle that the cumulative model of development is presupposed in (a) its rationale as a new field within evolutionary biology, (b) the methodological maxims taken from the Modern Synthesis which guide the identification of important problems and the paths of research in problem solving, and (c) the very conception of sociobiology's explanatory situation.

Fourth, the argument from completeness asserts that the idea of cumulative development is inherent in the idea of completeness. The fact that sociobiology confronts problems conceived and weighted in significance according to their contribution to completeness itself involves the cumulative model since the very idea of completing an established theory implies cumulative retention of the theory itself and its past explanatory successes. Even Gould (1980, 105) holds that "the modern synthesis is incomplete, not incorrect." To deny that model would be to deprive sociobiology of both the theoretical base from which it operates and the Modern Synthesis it takes as its point of departure. Put bluntly, to go somewhere, you have to start from somewhere.

It is hard to see how any discussion of details in particular sociobiological explanations could overturn such a common-sense view of scientific development. We should conclude that the role of sociobiological explanations in promoting completeness depends on its role in solving explanatory problems, problems identified and initially pursued on the model of cumulative development as special cases of problems in evolutionary biology in general.

## An Argument for Corrective Development

Our conclusion in favor of the cumulative model was drawn from arguments concerning sociobiology's explanatory problems, viewed from afar. Logically, it is possible that the cumulative model breaks down when we examine the theory for the field, viewed closely enough to make details in the structure of the theory significant. The corrective model of development is suggested by Popper's method of assessment insofar as it envisages progress as the elimination of disconfirmed explanations. According to the corrective model, explanations promoting the extension of the Modern Synthesis into a New Synthesis are corrections of previous ones, with the previous ones being discarded, strictly speaking, as false. Kourany calls this the "evolutionary model," since Popper has likened it to mortality selection, the elimination of organisms unfit for survival by natural selection. To avoid terminological confusion, let us call it the "corrective model."

> . . . according to the evolutionary model of scientific development, the new theories in a field are replacements of, rather than additions to, older theories in the field. In this sense the development of the field is not cumulative. But in another sense, we are told, that development is cumulative, for the new theories in a field typically yield results at least as good as those of their predecessors in all those areas in which the predecessors were successful, while yielding different and better results in other areas as well. Thus, the new theories typically preserve the successes of their predecessors while adding to them, allowing a closer adaptation to nature. Indeed, according to the evolutionary model, this preservation of old successes and addition of new successes is the mark of scientific progress, allowing rational assessment of scientific change. (Kourany 1987, 230)

The argument for the corrective model from theory structure asserts that explanatory theories are generalized to cover broader domains at the price of being restructured in ways that reveal their earlier formulation, strictly speaking, as false. This argument presumes that generality is a validity-making factor of theories, which is incorporated into Quine's method of assessment as a factor of plausibility. Barash (1979) treats sociobiology as an effort to generalize evolutionary theory so that its domain is extended to encompass sociality in prefacing his popularization of the field with Einstein's motto: "The ground aim of all science is to cover the greatest number of empirical facts by logical deductions from the smallest possible number of hypotheses." To jointly achieve generality and modesty, sociobiology could not extend the domain of evolutionary theory by retaining past evolutionary theory for nonsocial facts and constructing a wholly new theory for social facts. Instead, it generalizes past evolutionary theory so that the unification of the domains of nonsocial facts and social facts takes place in a natural way.

To make the unification natural rather than artificial in terms of theory structure, often essential concepts in the theory have to be reworked. This happened when Hamilton generalized the concept of fitness so that it explicitly recognizes social relations as an additional selection pressure, yielding the concept of inclusive fitness. Let us continue our history of sociobiology by viewing Hamilton's theoretical achievement according to the corrective model. Recall Wynne-Edwards's role of triggering debate over individual versus group selection, which motivated adherents of the Modern Synthesis to try to handle selection involving social relations with the theory of individual selection as far as possible. Recall the second goal of the New Synthesis, namely, that the observed evolutionary phenomena can be explained in a manner consistent with known genetic mechanisms. This aim required that Williams's arguments about how to and how not to explain adaptation be supplemented with a theoretical demonstration that explanations in terms of individual selection were consistent with known genetic mechanisms.

Another strategy to reduce the incompleteness of the Modern Synthesis is to expand the concept of individual selection to encompass selection processes different in their genetic mechanism from Darwinian individual selection (Holcomb 1986–87). Hamilton (1964, 1971a, 1971b, 1972) adopted this strategy from the Mendelian pole of the Modern Synthesis to increase the scope of explanations of behavior in terms of individual selection theory.

Given the orthodox population genetic outlook on evolution, the organism's "goal" is to maximize its genetic contribution to its evolving population. Which body happens to carry a given gene involved in that genetic contribution is a subsidiary matter. This view is not new, but is a basic evolutionary perspective shared by such architects of the Modern Synthesis as Fisher and Haldane. Fisher (1958, 27) set the stage for sociobiology in stating why reproductive value includes the present value of future offspring:

> To what extent will persons of this age, on the average, contribute to the ancestry of future generations? The question is one of some interest, since the direct action of Natural Selection must be proportional to this contribution. There will also, no doubt, be indirect effects in cases in which an animal favors or impedes the survival or reproduction of its relatives; as a suckling mother assists the survival of her child, as in mankind a mother past bearing may greatly promote the reproduction of her children, as a fetus and in less measure a sucking child inhibits conception, and most strikingly of all as in the services of neuter insects to their queen. Nevertheless such indirect effects will in very many cases be unimportant compared to the effects of personal reproduction.

Haldane was supposed to have answered the question "Would you ever be prepared, on evolutionary grounds, to sacrifice your life for another?" by declaring that "I would willingly lay down my life if I could save more than two brothers, four cousins, and so forth" (Kitcher 1985, 79). Hamilton (1964, 42) repeats this now oft-quoted remark, and Williams (Williams and Williams 1957) had similar ideas. Yet Darwinian individual selection was based on a concept of fitness that counted only the genes passed to the next generation through direct progeny. Hamilton (1964, 1) wrote, "If natural selection followed the classical models exclusively, species would not show any behavior more positively social than the coming together of the sexes and parental care." In other words, if the classical models exhausted the content of evolutionary theory, the only social behavior explainable consistently with known genetic mechanisms would be mating and parenting. Classical evolutionary theory would be incomplete since it could not explain any other social behavior consistently with known genetic mechanisms.

Inclusive fitness is defined, roughly, as the total proportion of an individual's genome passed to the next generation through direct progeny and through individuals with a common ancestry. This definition of inclusive fitness generalizes the Darwinian concept of fitness. Sociobiology seems (falsely, it will be argued) to adopt the cumulative model, as a generalization of classical theory.

Hence, cost/benefit analyses of adaptive significance must take account of consequences to individuals with common ancestry as well as progeny. Hamilton's theorem is that (genes for) altruistic behavior will evolve by individual selection when $K1/r$, where K is the ratio of recipient's gain to altruist's cost and r is the fraction of genes identical by descent in the altruist and recipient. Even the toughest cases of altruistic social behavior suddenly became understandable using inclusive fitness. Facts about social behavior that had been counterexamples to the completeness of evolutionary theory were turned victoriously into shining examples of its successful application to social behavior. For instance, kin selection seemed able to explain why female sterile casts evolved in the social insects. Because the female worker is related more closely to her sisters ($r=3/4$) than her offspring ($r=1/2$) in haplodiploid mating systems, it may be more adaptive for her to be sterile and rear her sisters than bear her own progeny.

Now, this way of expressing Hamilton's insight readily conforms to the cumulative model. The concept of Darwinian fitness was described as tracing genetic contribution through direct progeny alone. The concept of inclusive fitness was described as tracing genetic contribution through individuals with common ancestry in addition to direct progeny. These descriptions make it seem that Darwinian fitness is a special case of inclusive fitness. Hence, the concept of Darwinian fitness is retained because it is included in the concept of inclusive fitness. Similarly, descriptions of new cases which could be explained by inclusive fitness theory make it seem that the new explanations of social behavior are simply to be added to the old explanations of nonsocial behavior. But these appearances are deceptive.

Strictly speaking, the individual-selection theory containing the inclusive fitness concept is logically inconsistent with the classical individual-selection theory. Inclusive fitness is not defined in terms of classical (personal) fitness, e.g., not in terms of Ego's offspring plus the offspring of Ego's relatives devalued by their coefficient of relatedness. Classical fitness does not even appear in inclusive-fitness theory. Instead, classical theory is eliminated as false and Darwinian fitness is eliminated as conceptually inadequate. Why? Inclusive-fitness theory contains an analogue to classical fitness. In the mathematics, personal fitness is "stripped" by discounting aid from relatives and then "augmented" by an inclusive-fitness effect (Kitcher 1985, 81). Classical theory counted all of Ego's offspring, failing to distinguish whether or not offspring exist because of aid from relatives. It thereby allowed that personal fitness is affected by aid from relatives. Inclusive fitness includes offspring of Ego's relatives only if Ego's help is responsible for their existence and excludes Ego's offspring that exist because of help received from relatives. Classical theory affirms what the new theory denies, a contradiction. An analogue to Darwinian theory can be derived as a special case of inclusive theory, but not Darwinian theory itself as found in the Modern Synthesis. Old explanations are falsified and corrected by new ones.

The contradiction implies that talk of kin selection in sociobiology is conceptually confused when it adopts the view that classical theory explains some cases whereas inclusive-fitness theory explains other cases. If inclusive-fitness theory is true, there is no such thing as kin selection. Inclusive-fitness theory shows how there can be kin selfishness without group selection. Kin selection cannot be a form of group selection, where the groups are families, because the calculation of genetic relationship is based on the fact that r is a continuous quantity. The values of the variable r vary continuously from self, to siblings and parents, to first cousins, to second cousins, to third cousins, and so forth. Continuous variation implies that there are no discrete breaks between family and nonfamily, but group selection requires discrete breaks between groups. Nor is kin selection a selection process in addition to classical individual selection since from the point of view of inclusive-fitness theory, there is no process of classical individual selection operative in nature.

This result does not mean that the classical selection models have no methodological utility. In many cases evolution "may be treated as if it were dependent on the relations among the classical fitnesses" (Kitcher 1985, 83–84). Often, inclusive fitness is either identical to or only trivially different from classical fitness, considered as numbers. If so, we may use classical fitness when aid among relatives is hard to calculate. A similar situation exists in physics. Popper emphasized that Newtonian theory is false according to relativity theory (Kourany 1985, 230), due to differences in conceiving reference frames. Even so, analogues to Newton's laws are derivable from relativity theory that are predictively equivalent for middle-range objects.

## Multiple Forms of Development

Evaluations of sociobiology need to take account of the fact that research into selection processes not only has a history, but also develops in ways guided by preconceptions about its relation to the past. Assessment of sociobiology requires that we take account of its historical role, both the role it presupposes in anticipating its future and the role we can attribute to it with hindsight after it has undergone significant development. This fact creates further need for both retrospective and prospective assessment of sociobiology, which Laudan emphasized.

However, tension is created by the combination of (a) the anticipation of future research according to the cumulative model inherent in problem solving and (b) the analysis of past research according to the corrective model inherent in developing established theory so that it extends to new phenomena. On the cumulative model, acceptable explanations extend past successes by assuming the truth of some claims in the body of knowledge associated with the Modern Synthesis, claims used in establishing its explanatory conclusions. On the corrective model, acceptable explanations extend past successes by reworking theory structure where the price of successful extension is that past individual-selection explanations are at the most good approximations but conceptually inadequate and false.

The tension in combining the cumulative and corrective models together with the tension of using both the Modern Synthesis and its critiques as the point of departure heighten the critical attitude. Research in sociobiology cannot afford to incorporate past explanatory successes as beliefs since the development of inquiry into the evolution of sociality necessarily involves practical uncertainty about how much of past explanatory perspectives we can retain and how much we must relinquish to complete evolutionary theory. Progress, then, need not be construed merely as the accumulation of past explanations, on the assumption that they are true justified beliefs. Progress is progress toward an overarching aim. Successful explanations of sociality that constitute advances toward that aim are by definition progressive, where progress consists in the refinement of theoretical explanation, even if they reveal the falsity or unacceptability of past explanations.

The cumulative model of development is adopted in research insofar as it identifies and pursues problems posed by obstacles to completeness. The corrective model of development is adopted in research insofar as it restructures existing theory to handle problems posed by obstacles to completeness. The corrective model is explicitly focused on theoretical claims, but our example of Hamilton's explanation of altruism through inclusive-fitness theory showed that the source of theoretical restructuring is the reinterpretation of the basic concept of fitness. Reconceptualization contains the potential for radical change, not just in theory structure, but in the very terms we use to understand nature. Hence, it is possible that the reconceptualization necessary to handle the problem of explaining altruism has the unintended consequence of producing radical change in world views. On the revolutionary model of scientific development, the new theories that replace old theories give scientists new ways of thinking about, describing, explaining, and even seeing the world. The revolutionary model of development is suggested by Kuhn's method of assessment insofar as it envisages progress as a radical break in research traditions whereby new research programs induce revolutionary change.

We will continue our emphasis on reconceptualization by discussing arguments for the revolutionary model from holistic change and from conceptual change and shall then draw implications from that discussion for the gradual model. In so doing, we will push the altruism problem into the fascinating and subtle problem of the units and levels of selection.

## An Argument For Revolutionary Development

The argument for the revolutionary model from holistic change asserts that cumulative and corrective development occurs when basic presuppositions and commitments are shared but that new research programs embody conflicting sets of presuppositions and commitments, and therefore the shift of allegiance from one research program to another may be so holistic that it induces a revolution. Popularized empiricism presumes that scientific theories are rationally chosen by logical inference on observation (whether through confirmation or disconfirmation) and that science progresses cumulatively through the accretion of observed facts and theoretical explanations. But this view is inadequate because the structures and procedures of science are far richer than it recognizes. By treating science in terms of observations and theories as its units of analysis, it fails to recognize the procedures and structures of science that come into focus only in terms of research programs as an additional, more basic, unit of analysis:

> . . . the impression is that, after perhaps, an initial period of groping toward the right questions and the right methods, the history of a scientific field has consisted in a series of individual discoveries and inventions—namely, the ones reported in the field's texts; that, one by one, in a process like the addition of bricks to a building, scientists—working with the same methods, aims, and problems as their modern counterparts, and observing the same world—have added another fact, concept, law, or theory to the modern body of technical knowledge. (Kourany 1985, 229)

Kuhn's study of the history of physics revealed that practitioners of a scientific field working with different theories in fact work with different methods, aims, and problems. The cumulative and corrective models fail to recognize the way rival theories are associated with rival sets of methods, aims, and problems. If we study scientific development, we will see that the transition from acceptance of one theory to another, if the theories are basic to the field, is a holistic transition from one rival set of theory-laden methods, aims, and problems to another. The omission of concepts from this list of changeable tools of research matters because radical conceptual change supplies new concepts with which to formulate radically new sets of theories, methods, aims, and problems.

Let us continue on with our history of work on the problem of altruism according to the revolutionary model. Conceptual change deserves emphasis since it figures prominently in the conceptual model of syntheses. Kuhn's view suggests that we can rewrite the impact of Williams's and Hamilton's work in holistic terms.

The notorious metaphor of "the selfish gene" considers organisms as vehicles constructed by genes to perpetuate themselves (Dawkins 1976). Using the metaphor to popularize the new theory, Dawkins explained adaptive social behavior in ways that combined the ecological viewpoint of Williams (it evolves due to individual rather than group selection) with the genetic viewpoint of Hamilton (it evolves according to the criterion of gene perpetuation regardless of which body transmits the genes to the next generation). The combination contains revolutionary potential.

Some critics misread Dawkins as literally applying human ethical terms to genes. Expressed as another charge of anthropomorphism, it typically fails to distinguish altruism/selfishness of the genotype and of the phenotype. The Modern Synthesis viewed organisms as having two layers of self, namely, an inherited genotype and a developing phenotype. The moral concept of an altruistic act requires an intention to act in a manner designed with regard for the interests of other persons. The contrast between altruism and selfishness within evolutionary theory classifies evolutionary processes according to causal concepts, involving no such concepts as intent, regard, and persons. Misinterpreted as claims about psychological states ("scratch an altruist and watch a hypocrite bleed"), the charge conflates proximate and ultimate concepts of altruism and selfishness, i.e., psychological states and selection processes. The operation of selection as a process is the same for all phenotypic traits, whether involving intentionality or not.

It is vital to distinguish selfishness and altruism as relations between individuals and as categories for classifying behavior (Voorzanger 1984). Phenotypically selfish behavior (the relation) falls into the class of behaviors that increase the organism's own relative chances for reproductive success. Phenotypically altruistic behaviors (the relation) fall into the class of behaviors that increase the relative chances for reproductive success of other members of the group. Dawkins's point, implicit in Hamilton's theory of inclusive fitness, is that behavior in either class, whether phenotypically altruistic or phenotypically selfish behavior, can evolve by individual selection, provided the behavior is genotypically selfish (the class). Genotypically selfish behavior (the class) is defined, roughly, as increasing the relative chances that copies of the genes of its organismic possessor are perpetuated in the evolving population. Using the insights about rigorous functional explanation of adaptation found in Williams's critique of group selection explanations, Dawkins showed how to interpret mating choice, parental care, family relations, aggression, cooperation, and so forth as genotypically selfish. He thereby revealed how the new evolutionary theory could apply to the main social behaviors in nonhuman species, thereby vindicating the presumption that evolutionary explanation is incomplete without sociobiology. Presumably, if nonhuman or human cultural behavior turns out to be genotypically altruistic in general, then it either contradicts or is irrelevant to present theory.

Dawkins did not address actual social behaviors in all their detail and complexity, but only showed how some kinds of behavior could be explained in a manner relevant to and consistent with evolutionary theory. Thus, there are two ways to reduce incompleteness: to achieve relevance and consistency with respect to general kinds or particular cases of sociality. It is one thing to understand how a general kind of behavior is possible, that is, how it could be included in the repertoire of behaviors in a species given evolutionary processes and historical trends. It is another to explain why organisms in a particular population behave the way they do at a particular time and place and in particular circumstances. Criticism of pop sociobiology on the grounds that the explanations were not backed up by sufficient evidence is unjustified when it fails to distinguish these two strategies for reducing incompleteness. The sort of evidence demanded is normally suitable for explaining why people do certain things at a particular place and time, in all their detail and complexity, not general kinds of sociality. Often, the specific role of such explanations in the framework oriented by completeness is to explain kinds of sociality in general. So such evaluations are defeated by ignoring explanatory roles.

Evidence relevant to testing explanations of particular instances or of kinds of sociality should therefore take into account the genotype/phenotype distinction. The data which seemed to render evolutionary theory incomplete could then be reconceptualized so that it supported evolutionary theory. The demand to reconcile social data and evolutionary theory in regard to altruism is a problem both empirical and conceptual in character. Wilson (1975, 1) formulated the demand as "How can altruism, which by definition reduces personal fitness possibly evolve by natural selection?" Wilson simplified the generally accepted conclusion, accepted after the work of Williams, Hamilton, and Dawkins, that the problem was "solved by kin selection." This solution supports the utility of the conceptual models of syntheses for capturing the "How-possibly?" explanations needed to achieve a New Synthesis.

We have seen that the solution was gained through new evidence (e.g., calculation of inclusive fitness), obtained through new methods (extensive cost/benefit analysis) applied in relation to new theory (inclusive-fitness theory), all of which is made possible by new concepts (e.g., genotypic versus phenotypic selfishness). It would be unreasonable to deny that a full solution would involve such holistic progress in scientific evidence, method, theory, and concepts. Hence, we expect work on fundamental theory that furthers the objectives of the New Synthesis to embody the conception of holistic progress demanded in the argument from holism for the revolutionary model.

## 3.3 The Units/Levels of Selection Problem

### Conceptual Change in Selection Theory

The argument for revolutionary aspects of development in sociobiology from conceptual change asserts that work on solving the problems of altruism and the units/levels of selection is producing such dramatic conceptual refinement that a revolution is occurring in the way evolutionists understand the way evolutionary processes involve genes, organisms, and groups of organisms in their operation and effects. This argument will be developed at length, not by focusing on what does and does not count as a revolutionary change, but by focusing on the present state of conceptual debate.

Some read Dawkins as attempting to reduce all selection to the lowest level of organization, single genes. That is a form of reductionism, not the reduction of the social to the biological sciences, but reductionism within evolutionary biology itself. Recall that the theoretical resources of the Modern Synthesis embody the distinction that all selection must either be group selection or individual selection, so as to reflect the difference in the relation between selection and genotype and the relation between selection and phenotype. Dawkins's combination of the insights of Williams and Hamilton required him to clarify these matters. So he (1982a,b) contrasted vehicle selection, the way selection acts on phenotypes, with replicator selection, the way selection acts on genotypes. His thesis (Holcomb 1986–87) is that whatever biological objects are vehicles (following Williams, usually individuals and rarely groups), only single genes are replicating entities that survive through evolutionary time (following Hamilton, the unit of selection is the ultimate criterion of fitness). We can speak equivalently of individuals or groups (vehicles) maximizing their inclusive fitness or of genes (replicators) maximizing their evolutionary survival.

Now, the problem of the units and levels of selection is far from being solved (Holcomb 1988–89). One of the most difficult problems in evolutionary biology, it is so central that the character of work toward a solution has challenged commitments about evidence, methods, theory, concepts, and aims. Its solution may reveal the falsity or inadequacy of large parts of the body of knowledge associated with the Modern Synthesis. There is no consensus on what terms to use to express the way various entities enter into various aspects of processes by which organisms evolve by selection.

Thus, we are forced to use problematic terminology. Perhaps the theory requires a hierarchical expansion on which many levels of effective selection occur, none of which is privileged, contrary to earlier emphasis on individual selection. Call this the "levels of selection" approach. Perhaps genes form a level so unlike the others and so privileged in terms of the effects of selection, that it is a unit of selection in a sense different from other levels of selection. Call that the "selfish-gene" approach (see Brandon and Burian 1984).

This general meaning can be made more specific in numerous ways. Let us use the term 'level of selection' to designate levels of causal transaction involved as determinants of reproductive success: the entities at various levels of biological organization whose traits have effects that eventuate in various degrees of reproductive success. Let the term 'unit of selection' designate biological entities involved as determinants of the evolutionary effects by which reproductive success is calculated: the entities transmitted from generation to generation that control the evolutionary effects of reproductive success. The "levels of selection" approach claims that what counts as a unit of selection is given by the 'level of selection' concept, and that the 'unit of selection' concept just defined is a misnomer and concerns something else. The "selfish-gene approach" claims that the idea of a unit of selection is ambiguous and that both the 'level of selection' and 'unit of selection' concepts are needed to clarify it. At stake is whether proximate concepts, such as 'level of selection', are sufficient for describing how selection operates, or whether in conceiving selection, proximate concepts must be oriented by ultimate concepts, such as 'unit of selection'.

A basic argument for the levels of selection approach is that the selfish-gene approach combines an important explanatory claim with a trivial nonexplanatory claim. Identifying a gene, organism, or group as an entity whose traits affect reproductive success is crucial to the kind of causal explanation found in selection theory. Genes are crucial for the way selection pressures are effective or ineffective in producing evolutionary change. Of course levels of selection other than genetic units are not units of transmission. Of course in every case of evolution by selection there is selection of genes in the sense of differential transmission. Since these truisms hold regardless of what level is the level of selection, they cannot possibly illuminate the dispute over the levels of selection.

A basic argument for the selfish gene approach is that the levels of selection approach prevents us from accounting for why fitness is correctly identified in inclusive-fitness theory. Without genes as the ultimate criterion of fitness, they have no reason not to identify fitness with something else. On a causal analysis in which causes are the key, possible effects do not count for much. Traits entering into a selection process have many kinds of effects. Why not identify organismic fitness with effects on health? Why not identify it in terms of survival alone, with no reference to reproduction, or as reproduction through direct progeny alone? Differential reproduction is the only way to contribute to the ancestry of future generations. What counts as a level of selection depends on the way fitness is identified in ultimate terms, not merely in proximate terms.

Moreover, inclusive-fitness theory was designed to come to grips with the relation between the case of direct contributions of genes through one's own offspring and indirect contributions of genes through the offspring of others. For example, the same numerical contribution of genes can be made by perpetuating genes in multiple bodies or in one's own body. The mathematics of inclusive-fitness theory calculates the relative influence of direct and indirect reproductive success in a variety of circumstances. The concept underlying the mathematics identifies the evolutionary self-interest of every individual organism as the maximal representation of its own genes in future generations. Thus, the gene is the ultimate criterion of fitness. To give up this concept is to renounce the insights of the last twenty-five years.

A basic rebuttal by proponents of the levels of selection approach is that the selfish-gene approach turns on a confused concept, namely, evolutionary self-interest. This concept has nothing to do with the debate over altruism initiated by Wynne-Edwards. It conflates concepts relating to organisms, which can have altruistic or selfish traits, and concepts relating to genes, which cannot have altruistic or selfish traits. By passing back and forth between a level of selection and a unit of transmission in the same breath, it creates a bad analogy that causes confusion.

A basic rebuttal by proponents of the selfish-gene approach is that the selfish-gene concept is essential for bridging two perspectives. When we take the organismic perspective, we describe the way organisms compete to be maximally reproductively successful by behaving in ways that enable them to perpetuate copies of genes identical by descent to their own through their own reproduction or through the reproduction of others. When we take the genetic perspective, we describe the way genes compete to maximally increase in frequency in future generations by helping to construct bodies which behave in ways that perpetuate them. The selfish-gene concept is essential for devising translation manuals that enable us to use mathematical proofs about the way genes change in frequency in various circumstances to generate explanatory insights about fitness and levels of causal transaction.

The argument from conceptual change for the revolutionary model asserts that whichever approach, including other potential rivals, is eventually accepted, evolutionary theory will be so fully reconceptualized that a revolution will have occurred. The previous discussion reveals that there are radical conceptual differences which make a choice between either approach radical, as compared to each other and to classical theory. Kuhn located revolutions by revealing episodes in which adherents to rival programs argue from their own program for their own program and against rival programs (Holcomb 1987c). To supply some raw materials for the revolutionary model, we will exhibit this sort of episode by showing that Sober and Williams cannot agree on a common set of concepts or the logic of the reasoning that biologists pursue (a point generalizable to other parties to this debate). We will delve into their preanalytic choices, first, in regard to the relation between individual and group selection, and second, in regard to the relation between individual and genic ("gene-ic") selection.

## Individual Selection and Group Selection

Dawkins is well known for advocating the selfish-gene approach. Sober (1984) advances a number of arguments against that approach, holding that it obscures the conceptual core of evolutionary theory. Sober used one of Williams's insights as an important tool in constructing these arguments, but Williams (1986) replied that he disagreed with most of what Sober said on the issue. Sober (1986, 122) responds to Williams's critique:

> In his comments on my book, Williams seems to draw back from what I think is the main conceptual insight of his book, *Adaptation and Natural Selection*. This is the distinction between group adaptation and fortuitous group benefit. He there gives the example of a deer population in which individual selection for being fast (this being advantageous for evading predators) leads the average speed in the herd to increase. A consequence is that the population is less likely to go extinct. This is good for the group, but it is not a group adaptation, since group selection was not the cause.

Given the quality of Williams's conceptual work, Sober's charge that Williams renounced his own main conceptual insight is implausible. Instead, we should suspect that Sober has misinterpreted Williams, where partial miscommunication signals rival controlling presuppositions. One is Sober's decision not to distinguish levels of adaptation from levels of selection in portraying Williams's view, a contrast made by Williams here and Sober elsewhere. Another is Sober's adherence to the "levels of selection" approach, and Williams's advocacy of the "selfish-gene" approach. Sober (personal communication) holds that the Dawkins/Williams view is ambiguous between the trivial, true claim that evolution is describable as changes in gene frequency and the substantive, false claim that no selection occurs at anything but the genic level.

Sober and many others (e.g., Mayo and Gilinski 1987) hold that in cases where differences in mean reproductive rates among groups are merely summative results of fitnesses of group members, group selection is not genuine and reduces to individual selection. They thought they learned this from Williams. Instead, Williams holds that in such cases there is group selection, if groups thereby exhibit heritable variation in fitness, but not necessarily group adaptation, since the traits promoting differential mean reproductive rates show no signs of being fashioned as they are because they were good for the group in the past. The main point of Williams's (1966) book is that group selection exists but has not been effective in fashioning traits selected for or against at the group level into group adaptations. Since group adaptation is rare and group selection should be invoked to explain adaptation only when there is group adaptation, group selection rarely explains adaptation. His reductionism concerns evolutionary effects of selection, not a reduction of group to individual selection as processes. This reading will be so surprising to some that they will demand plenty of evidence. Here is enough evidence to make us rethink the whole issue.

First, the preceding quote from Sober correctly notes that Williams's book emphasizes a distinction between a trait fashioned by selection for a goal at a level and a trait that confers an incidental beneficial effect at a level. This contrasts adaptation with mere advantage. Adaptation occurs when selection is effective in establishing advantageous traits. This version of the deer example is not a case of group selection since it concerns a single herd and so heritable variation in fitness among deer herds is not represented in the case. Because there is no group selection, there is a fortuitous group benefit, but no group adaptation. Since the example can be interpreted according to Williams's distinction, it does not show that Williams has renounced his own distinction. Suppose we add to this case several other herds undergoing the same process. By chance alone, there might be heritable variation in fitness among the several deer herds. This would be group selection. Nevertheless, the traits that evolve will be those that maximize the fitness of individuals and not the herds. To know which traits will evolve, we would have to find the trait that maximized individual, not group, fitness. That simple point is the sense in which statistical summation involves group selection but not to group adaptation. This is not to say that individual selection plus statistical summation is group selection. For any level X, X is a level of selection if and only if there is heritable variation in fitness among Xs. Both individuals and groups are levels of selection in this sense but genes are not; heritability does not apply in the same sense to genes.

Second, Williams often writes that adaptation should be attributed at no higher level of organization than is demanded by the evidence. Yet he never says that the level of objects whose traits are selected for or against should always be attributed to the lowest level. His parsimony argument concerns levels of adaptation, not levels of selection. The selfish-gene approach is a form of reductionism in the vague sense of emphasis on lower-level processes. It does not readily fit standard ontological accounts of the reduction relation (or linguistic accounts). Ontological accounts are typically variations on two themes: reduction-as-replacement by something more basic (higher-level processes are to be eliminated and replaced by lower-level processes) and reduction-as-equivalence to something more basic (higher-level processes are equivalent to special cases of the operative lower-level processes). Since the selfish-gene approach does not deny that selection acts on levels higher than that of single genes, it is not a form of reduction-as-replacement. Since it does not treat group selection as a special case of individual selection and reduce group selection to genic selection via transitivity, it is not a form of reduction-as-equivalence.

Instead, the selfish-gene approach acknowledges that selection acts on both organisms and groups but maintains that selection is most effective at genetic levels. Alexander (1987) cites work (including Williams's) leading to this conclusion, claiming that it has already induced a revolution:

> It is part of the recent revolution in evolutionary theory that we know that natural selection is generally more powerful at lower levels in the hierarchy of organization of life, such as genes, chromosomes, and genomes (e.g., Fisher, 1958; Williams, 1966; Lewontin, 1970, Dawkins, 1976, 1982[a]; Alexander and Borgia, 1978; Alexander, 1979a, Leigh, 1977). We know this, first, because effectiveness of selection depends on the amount of difference between the involved entities, the heritability of differences, and generation time (Fisher 1958; Lewontin, 1970). All of these features are more conducive to selection being potent at levels approaching the gene and less potent at group and population levels. (Alexander 1979a)

Williams's book (1966) is primarily about the effectiveness of selection. It does not deny the existence of group selection, just its effectiveness:

> Natural selection can be effective only where there are certain quantitative relationships among sampling errors, selection coefficients, and rates of random change. The selection of alternative alleles in Mendelian populations meets the requirements. Other conceivable kinds of selection do not. . . . Reasons are advanced for doubting, a priori, the effectiveness of group selection. (Williams 1966, vii, viii)

Third, in another passage contrasting a population of adapted insects and an adapted population of insects, Williams's focus (1966, 108–109) is on the level of adaptation, not the level of selection. Immediately thereafter he states that "like the theory of genic selection, the theory of group selection is logically a tautology and there can be no sane doubt about the reality of the process. Rational criticism must center on the importance of the process and on its adequacy in explaining the phenomena attributed to it." So Williams regards selection among groups as units as just as real a process as selection among individuals as units. This is inconsistent with Sober's treatment of Williams's view as denying the existence of group selection in a sense autonomous from the selection of alternative alleles of individuals. No inconsistency arises if Williams's reductionism concerns the effects of selection on adaptation, not the existence of a selection process.

Fourth, a key argument for the usual view is figure 1 (Williams 1966, 97): it seems to mean that if group selection exists, then group adaptation exists. But this reading falsely presumes that the arrow from group selection to group adaptation symbolizes an "if . . . then . . ." conditional. Williams's headings of "evolutionary process" and "evolutionary outcome" require that his are arrows of causation. Reading from bottom to top, we have: (1) the only process of selection that can causally account for group evolution with group ("biotic") adaptation is group selection; (2) fortuitous benefits to groups arise from individual selection or from chance processes or from both; they needn't be explained as group adaptations arising from group selection; (3) where group benefits arise as statistical summations and selection operates on their hereditary basis, the only form of selection that must exist is genic selection, i.e., selection on alleles of individuals.

Fifth, on Sober's interpretation Williams's book would be permeated by confusion in his own purposes. If cases of statistical summation are not cases of group selection, by intuition alone, there is no reason for Williams to discuss them in detail in relation to mathematical models and design features. Yet he does so. Except for rare cases such as the house mouse t-allele and the myxoma virus in rabbits, Williams chides group selection explanations of traits thought to be adaptations "for the good of the group" as unacceptable because (a) mathematical models show that group selection can counteract the effects of individual selection only in boundary conditions rare in nature and unsatisfied in the kinds of sociality given group selectionist explanations, (b) the genetic, morphological, physiological, and behavioral machinery associated with prevalent traits show good evidence of design by individual selection but not group selection, (c) a principle of parsimony or conservatism dictates that group adaptation should not be admitted when the facts are reconcilable with individual selection alone.

Sixth, other key evolutionists regard Williams as objecting to "group selection" as an explainer of adaptation and not as an existing process:

> Evolution by natural selection requires that there be entities with the properties of multiplication, variation, and heredity. Given these properties, entities will evolve characteristics ensuring their survival and reproduction ("adaptations"). Individual organisms have these properties. Wynne-Edwards proposed that groups of organisms might also have them, and hence might acquire adaptations ensuring group survival (for example, epideictic displays). It was this meaning of group selection—a phrase describing a whole evolutionary mechanism, not just a selective process—which was criticized, I think rightly, by G. C. Williams and myself, among others. My own objection was quantitative: there is usually too much intrademic selection for the process to be effective. (Maynard Smith 1984, 238)

Seventh, Williams (1985, 8–9) explicitly admits the existence of group selection but not its importance for adaptation:

> My assessment is that selection at any level above the family (group selection in a broad sense) is unimportant for the origin and maintenance of adaptation. I reach this conclusion by simple inspection. An organism appears to me to be trying to maximize its genetic contribution to future generations of the population to which it belongs. I see little to suggest that it is playing any subordinate role in the interest of that population. It participates in the game of life as an individual contestant, not as a member of a team. . . . The unimportance of group selection for adaptation need not imply that it is unimportant in other ways. As Leigh (1977) has pointed out and Wilson (1980) argued in detail, the total selfishness of every individual in a community need not mean that group selection is without effect in the evolution of that community. [e.g., for speciation]

Potential counterevidence from Williams's earlier language loses its force in the face of this contrast. For instance, one might object that he (1966, 103) states "unless there are such things as biotic adaptations there is no need for the theory of group selection." But the context is obviously explaining adaptation. So the sentence should be understood as meaning " . . . for the theory of group selection (to explain adaptation)."

Eighth, Williams (1986) comments on Sober's book that he (Williams) "would find it confusing to use adaptive group properties as an axiom of group-selection theory, rather than a measure of its importance." In other words, Sober confuses levels of selection with levels of adaptation.

These eight pieces of evidence supply strong reason to think that Sober and Williams have made preanalytic choices which have prevented them from agreeing on a common set of concepts or a common logic with which to express the relations between individual selection and group selection. Intuitively, their positions are incommensurable. On the correct supposition that other theorists involved in the debate over individual and group selection confront similar sorts of incommensurability, such episodes provide raw materials for the kinds of incommensurability arguments used to argue for the revolutionary model of scientific change.

## Individual Selection and Genic Selection

How does genic selection fit here? Sober (1984, 5) states:

> Williams saw the importance of distinguishing a herd of adapted deer from an adapted herd of deer. When a fast herd survives and a slow one goes extinct, one can describe the former as fitter than the latter. But the fact that this process can be "represented" by assigning fitness values to groups hardly shows that it is driven by group selection. Yet, while avoiding the mirage of group selection, Williams is, I think, taken in by the mirage of genic selection. He argues that since a selection process that issues in evolution can always be "represented" in terms of fitness values that attach to single genes, it is correct to think of the single gene as the unit of selection. The idea that the fitness value of a gene may be a mirage—a reflection of selection processes that occur at higher levels of organization—is swept aside. The crucial distinction first drawn with respect to the question of group selection is obliterated when a lower level of organization is considered.

In the last sentence, Sober has misconstrued Williams's distinction with respect to group versus individual selection. Being "driven by group selection" is ambiguous between whether group selection fails to produce group adaptation (a) because group selection does not exist or (b) because group selection exists but is ineffective in producing group adaptation. We now need to show that Williams has not obliterated his distinction when turning to individual and genic selection. Again, rather than attribute Williams a basic inconsistency, we should look for conflicting presuppositions that lead Sober to misinterpret Williams on genic selection. Sober takes the issues of individual versus group selection and individual versus genic selection to be the same sort of issues. This presupposition is inherent in the "levels of selection" approach. Williams takes them to be crucially different sorts of issues. That presupposition is inherent in the "selfish-gene" approach.

Contrary to Sober, Williams does not think that the single gene (better: allele) is always the level of selection; rather, the allele is always the unit of selection, no matter what the level of selection may be. His representation argument has been misconstrued. Some common currency is needed in which to record the cumulative results of heritable variations in fitness that occur at multiple levels. Williams likens this to bookkeeping, in which the results of causal transactions are recorded in ledgers using money as a currency. Just as the smallest unit of currency is the penny, the smallest unit for recording the results of selection is the allele. The fact that the results of selection can always be represented in terms of genic fitnesses is strong reason to identify genetic units as units of selection in a bookkeeping sense. Attacks on genic selectionism by Wimsatt (1984) and Sober and Lewontin (1984) point out limitations on this approach, but are misguided because Williams did not claim the explanatory power they denied. It just looks that way to those who conflate levels and units of selection and assimilate explanation here to citations of causal efficacy.

This reading is borne out in Williams's (1985) article that presents a table summarizing his approach. He states, "This approach (Table 1) emphasizes the distinction between selection and response to selection (Arnold and Wade 1984) or Hull's (1980) replication and interaction. I think Hull's interactor is more clearly descriptive than Dawkins' (1982a) vehicle." The distinction here, obscured by variations in terminology, is between levels of selection (levels of cause-effect transaction) and units of selection (results of levels of cause-effect transaction). Williams's table plots the hierarchy of levels of organization against two questions. Are objects at a level involved in natural selection as a history of biological success and failure? This is a question about levels of selection. He answers that the gene is not but that individuals, families, trait-groups, populations, and taxa are levels of causal transaction. Are objects at a level involved in selection as a record of that history? This is a question about units of selection. He answers that the single gene is, that sometimes genotypes are, that phenotypes, families, trait-groups are not, and that gene pools of populations and taxa are units of selection.

Sober's mistake exerts a pervasive influence on his discussion of genic selectionism. Sober (1984, 278) writes, "In every case of evolution by natural selection, regardless of the level at which the process occurs, there will be selection of genes. What is distinctive about genic selection is that there must be selection for a gene."

First, Sober argues that the selfish-gene approach yields unacceptable explanations because it rests solely on the 'selection of' concept. Sober shows that this concept is inadequate for causal explanation since it concerns effects, not causes. He recognizes that the selfish-gene approach emphasizes results of selection but fails to recognize its purpose for doing so, namely, bookkeeping. It is irrelevant to criticize accountants for keeping the books in monetary terms on the grounds that profits and losses are the result of causal transactions among people. It is irrelevant to criticize the selfish-gene approach for keeping the evolutionary books in genetic terms on the grounds that differential transmission of genes is the result of causal transactions between organisms and environments. The point of bookkeeping is to track the results of causal transactions, not to record causes. The transmission argument is about bookkeeping. But this does not mean that Williams has renounced the idea that the selfish-gene approach is explanatory. It is explanatory regardless of the level of selection, in the sense that genetic contribution to later generations provides the basis for the concept of fitness used in all evolutionary explanations.

Second, Sober (1984, 313) argues that what is distinctive about genic selectionism is that although the concept 'selection for properties' applies to genes, the causal conditions required for its application are rarely satisfied in nature due to polygeny. When many genes cause the same trait, no one of them has a univocal causal role, a requirement for causal explanation. This is intended to refute the selfish-gene approach, but this criticism is irrelevant since Williams thinks of genes as units of selection common to all selection processes, no matter at what level of cause-effect transaction they occur. Whenever the gene is a unit of selection, there must be some other level of cause-effect transaction involved. We should identify the appropriate level of causal transaction (i.e., the individual or the group), and, if we employ a univocal causal role analysis of causal explanation, decide whether its properties have the relevant univocal causal role. The selfish-gene approach, then, can accommodate Sober's causal analysis of selection. Williams's phrase "selection of alternative alleles" of individuals (1966, 8., 96–97) is as much a way of talking about individual selection as is Sober's phrase "selection for properties" of individuals. Sober conceives the selfish-gene approach as denying that individual or group selection occurs. Yet in his remarks on evolution and ethics (1989, 182–3), Williams states flatly that "to argue about whether selection is more important at the level of the individual or the gene . . . makes no sense."

Sober does not have philosophical objections to Williams's claims that group selection is too weak to routinely cause group adaptations or that genes are useful for bookkeeping. Sober objects to what he considers independent arguments of parsimony, representability, causation, and transmission. However, this analysis suggests that Williams does not take such arguments to be conceptually independent of these two claims. The key issue is over what to connect and what to separate, over what to distinguish, and over the import of various distinctions. There is enough material to reexamine here to potentially induce radical conceptual change. We have here a dispute similar in conceptual penetration to that found by Mayr in evolutionary biology before the Modern Synthesis and to that found by Kuhn and Laudan in other areas of science. Interestingly, Kuhn used these disputes to argue for the revolutionary model, whereas Laudan used them to argue against it and for the gradual model. We now turn to that issue.

## An Argument for Gradual Change

Just as the corrective model arose as a critique of the cumulative model, so the gradual model arises as a critique of the revolutionary model. The former two models focus on truth and falsity. The latter two models focus on the rate and the extent of change. In this sense, it is false that all four models must be rivals. The revolutionary model is adopted in research insofar as conceptual change guides a holistic change in world view. By attacking the argument from holistic change, one arrives at the gradual model. On the gradual model the various elements of research programs operate semiautonomously as partially independent elements, so that one element can change without requiring all elements to change, making change gradual and partial. Recall that the cumulative model focuses on the big picture of problem solving, restricted in scope by the corrective model's focus on details of theory structure. Similarly, the revolutionary model focuses on the big picture of radical transitions from one monolithic world view to another, restricted in scope by the gradual model's focus on the details of change on a smaller time scale. On a macro time scale we look at initial and final situations and find radical change. On a micro time scale we look at successions of intervening events and find piecemeal change. The dispute between the gradual model and the revolutionary model obscures the fact that the same situations fits both models when appropriate time scales are chosen.

The gradual model is suggested by Laudan's theory of validity, which analyzes research programs as commitments about ontology, methodology, and aims built around a theoretical core.

> ... scientific theories, methods, and goals have tended to function as independent elements in the history of science. Sometimes the theories of a scientific field have changed, sometimes its methods, and sometimes its goals. Occasionally two of the elements have changed simultaneously. But rarely have all three changed at once. ... Like the revolutionary model (and unlike the cumulative model) the gradualist model allows no progress toward one complete set of truths about the world, and like the revolutionary model (and unlike the evolutionary model) it allows no progress toward ever more successful accounts of the world. ... In short, the gradualist model, unlike the revolutionary model, allows the sort of progress that occurs when a change of one component of a scientific field (for example, its methods) occurs, and is rationally justified, given the character of its other components (theories and goals). (Kourany 1987, 233)

Laudan's (1985) critique of the holistic argument is directed against Kuhn's (1970) chapter entitled "The Nature and Necessity of Scientific Revolutions." This target is important, for it enables us to pry apart aspects of Laudan's critique that were unnecessarily intertwined.

First, his critique is successful in showing that revolutionary change is not inevitable, but is misleading since Kuhn's own "Postscript" (1970) also implies that it is not inevitable. As long as Kuhn treated research programs as unanalyzable wholes, their very conception required that transitions from one program to another be holistic. In his "Postscript," he backed off from his earlier claim that there is necessarily one paradigm for any successful scientific field, unless the field's anomalies are so great that it is undergoing crisis or revolution. This caveat implies that transition in programs do not necessitate the replacement of one field by another field. In the "Postscript," Kuhn also abandoned or clarified his earlier talk of programs as "paradigms," treating them instead as disciplinary matrices induced by exemplars. Exemplars are exemplary achievements, typically cited in texts used to train scientists on how to solve problems in their field, thereby setting the standard for future work in the field. As scientists model their work on exemplars, concrete guides showing how research should and should not be done, a disciplinary matrix of associated symbolic generalizations, models, concepts, and methods emerges. The source of unity in perspective is just a past theoretical breakthrough used in science education. Once programs are analyzed into related elements, elements whose relations are not fixed by identity with a monolithic whole, it is possible for elements to change simultaneously or gradually, and which sort of change occurs will be a matter of fact about the history of science. So Kuhn's revised conception of programs itself leads to Laudan's result.

The major difference lies with exemplars. Kuhn's "disciplinary matrices," like his "paradigms," must contain exemplars. Laudan's "research traditions," being combinations of aims, theories, and methods, do not necessarily contain exemplars. The exemplars, interpreted not just as successful applications but as successful applications that set the standard and approach of work in the field, give research programs an internal degree of cohesiveness not necessarily found without them. Due to Kuhn's emphasis on exemplars and Laudan's deemphasis on exemplars, one and the same situation may change in ways that look revolutionary to Kuhn and gradual to Laudan. Unless a gene-culture program included exemplars in Kuhn's sense, then they would not count as Kuhnian paradigms or disciplinary matrices. In the absence of those types of research programs, Kuhn's model of scientific change implies that human sociobiology remains in a prescientific state, an implication which treats prevalidated science as a form of nonscience.

Second, the historical question of to what extent actual change in science is holistic or gradual depends on which approaches in the field are identified as research programs. Rival world view programs (e.g., those of Wilson and Lewontin) enter into debate as rival integrated sets of background philosophical commitments supplying the rationale for evaluative decisions. A choice between them would be a radically holistic change, embodying Kuhn's views of revolutionary change with a vengeance. Rival gene-culture programs yield rival approaches in studying genes, natural selection, relations between biological and cultural evolution, and adaptation. A choice between them would lead to quite different sets of explanatory aims, methods, and concepts, embodying Kuhn's emphasis on the integrity of disciplinary matrices as a whole involving significant holism.

Rival units/levels programs (selfish-gene and levels of selection approaches) present different ontologies for evolutionary theory in general, ontologies fairly independent of specific evolutionary aims and methods. Almost any explanation can be interpreted by either approach. A choice between them could leave other elements of the research situation in place, embodying Laudan's emphasis on the partial independence of elements within programs. But the significance of those other elements would be transformed.

In sum, various identifications of sociobiological research programs lead to a variety of types of change: radical holistic change, significant holistic change, significant gradual change, or extensive gradual change. There is no reason, a priori, to think that science must conform to any one of these patterns. Which type of change occurs varies according to the historical contingencies of the situation. So, rather than try to choose between them, we need to construct a view of change that is more bound up with the structure of explanatory inquiry itself.

## The Challenge-Response Model

What, then, would constitute progress in sociobiology? Let us adopt the common-sense notion of progress as an orderly change of state in a direction with a value. In sociobiology, the overarching value is to do its part in completing evolutionary explanation. Progress occurs when the best response at a later time is better than the best response at an earlier time, with respect to the incompleteness posed by animal and human sociality. We are already committed to the Modern Synthesis. Progress is progress toward a state whereby the complete range of evolved phenomena can be comprehended, with the revised Modern Synthesis forming the basis for problem solving with respect to macroevolution and the New Synthesis forming the basis for problem solving with respect to social evolution. If so, our task is to defend the best version of evolutionary theory we have, modifying the theory of the Modern Synthesis to take account of critiques from other areas of evolutionary biology. We defend it against the most severe challenges to completeness we find posed by our study of animal and human sociality.

The best response meets the challenge posed by manifest incompleteness in the most defensible manner, maximizing the severity of the challenge and minimizing revisions in the updated Modern Synthesis. The three questions we need to answer to decide whether something counts as the best response are: (1) Does the response treat the challenge in its most severe form? (2) Does the response minimize revision of what is being challenged? and (3) Does the response meet the challenge in the most defensible way? These questions spell out in more precise terms the general intellectual method of trying to defend a position against its most severe objections (Holcomb 1989b).

The best response is the cognitively most desirable response among available responses. As in optimality models, each response tries to optimize something, given the constraints. The best response meets the perceived challenge, as constrained by specification of the particular explanatory problem posed by sociality and specification of the particular tension between social data and evolutionary theory at hand. The best response is defensible against welltaken, significant criticisms, thereby maximizing the adequacy of the response itself. The best response understands the challenge in its strongest plausible form, as a challenge constituted by seeming irrelevance and inconsistency between social data and evolutionary theory, thereby maximizing the severity of the challenge with respect to the explanatory problem addressed. The best response revises the antecedently adopted version of the Modern Synthesis as little as possible, thereby minimizing change in the challenged explanatory scheme.

As happens in optimality models generally, there will be tradeoffs in optimizing a response. It may be easy to provide a defensible response to an explanatory challenge formulated in a very mild way but hard to provide a defensible response to an explanatory challenge formulated to undermine central basic tenets of the Modern Synthesis itself. Such trade-offs offer a variety of reasonable possibilities in reacting to the challenge of incompleteness. In the effort to provide a defensible response, one may not treat the challenge in its most severe form. In the effort to treat the challenge in its most potentially damaging form, one may not be able to come up with a defensible response. In the effort to both recognize the severity of the challenge and construct a defensible response, one may end up producing radical changes in the views antecedently held.

This conception of progress provides a key for making sense of the fact that we can find elements in sociobiology that conform to each of the canonical models of scientific change. Let us, first, review our results, and next, state the derivation of all the elements from efforts to satisfy the criteria of progress pertinent to the challenge-defense model.

The justification of assessment presupposing any one of the main models of development, to the exclusion of others, has been defeated. The issue "Which model of scientific development is correct?" is ill posed. It should be stated as "Which aspects of scientific development are cumulative, which are corrective, which are revolutionary, and which are gradual?" In sociobiology, the cumulative model captures the big picture of theoretical problem solving, the corrective model captures details of transitions in theory structure, the revolutionary model captures the big picture of orienting presuppositions, and the gradualist model captures the details of transitions in orienting presuppositions. Use of confirmational or disconfirmational criteria of validity (motivating the cumulative and corrective models, respectively) takes theories as the basic unit of assessment. Use of holistic or atomistic presuppositional criteria of validity (motivating the revolutionary and gradualist models, respectively) takes research programs as the basic unit of assessment.

Our hybrid model naturally derives basic aspects of all four models from the idea of achieving the most defensible response to the most severe challenge while revising antecedent basic commitments in the least damaging way. Those basic commitments lie in the goals of the New Synthesis given by the legacy of the Modern Synthesis. The criterion of minimizing change in the challenged explanatory scheme is a conservative force whereby scientists try to do work that fits the cumulative model but in the process end up doing work that fits the corrective model. We saw that the general orientation of work on altruism aimed at making cumulative progress but the development of inclusive-fitness theory to explain altruism yielded corrective progress.

The criterion of maximizing the severity of the challenge is a revolutionary force whereby the most severe criticism of past work affects many parts of the antecedent orientation at once, and so scientists try to do work which creates a holistic alternative to that failed orientation. We saw that work on the units of selection aiming to come to grips with altruism ended in holistic change in theory, significant data, concepts, and methods that yielded revolutionary progress, but along the way each component was revised individually and so gradual progress occurred.

The criterion of constructing a maximally defensible response is a force of conceptual clarification whereby scientists try to make conceptual sense of the fundamental theory underlying these changes. We saw that work on conceiving the levels and units of selection has resulted in a debate between such rival conceptual schemes as the levels of selection approach and the selfish-gene approach. The difficulties of agreeing on a common set of terms and assumptions have made this one of the great unsolved problems in biology.

Although both animal and human sociobiology confront the quest for completeness and have made progress toward completeness according to this conception of progress, their research situations have been quite different. There have been three phases in the development of sociobiology, each designed to address an obstacle to completeness. The first phase is the effort beginning in the 1960s to account for the very possibility of altruism. The result is a sophisticated array of mathematical models of various selection processes, marking the emergence of sociobiology as a theoretical science. Since the theory is about organisms generally, it is equally applicable to human and nonhuman organisms. The second phase is the effort beginning in the 1970s to use this theoretical breakthrough to account for the diversity of behavior across the social species. The result is the systematization of a host of studies of animal social behavior, marking the emergence of animal sociobiology as an observational and theoretical science. The third phase is the effort beginning in the late 1970s through the 1980s to account for the very possibility and diversity of human social behavior. The result is a host of controversial claims about human sociality, marking the ongoing debate about the scientific, ideological, and philosophical status of the extension to our own species.

Mathematical and qualitative models of gene-culture processes bear a role in research similar to the role of mathematical models of selection processes constructed to explain altruism. The question "How is culture possible?" is translated "How do genetic and cultural transmission interact?" just as "How is altruism possible?" was translated "How does natural selection operate on multiple levels of organization?" In the 1950s and 1960s, animal sociobiology tried to explain animal sociality in vain. The source of failure was that it did not have a sufficient base in selection theory and genetical theory to construct explanations fitting the Modern Synthesis. These explanations were far from rigorous because they tried to explain the diversity of animal sociality before answers about how animal sociality is possible. Altruism could be described but its explanation was a mystery prior to the advent of inclusive-fitness theory.

Human sociobiology in the 1970s and 1980s was in a position similar to that of animal sociobiology in the 1950s and 1960s. Human sociobiology has tried to explain the diversity of human sociality in the absence of prior answers about how human culture is possible. Without gene-culture theories as well constructed and deserving of acceptance as the new theories of altruism, human sociobiology lacks a sufficient base in selection theory, genetical theory, and psychological theory to construct rigorous explanations. A New Synthesis may be well on its way in animal sociobiology but remains a promise and a hope in human sociobiology. Thus, human sociobiology faces a task far more difficult than that faced now by animal sociobiology. For these reasons, animal sociobiology now is far more rigorous than human sociobiology, as is evident from Kitcher's assessment.

This assessment of the state of progress has implications for how to evaluate sociobiology. For instance, the differential difficulty of doing rigorous work in the present research situation should be taken into account in assessment. It is unfair for Kitcher (1987a) to judge the validity of human sociobiology today by how well it measures up to animal sociobiology today. That comparison is bound to make human sociobiology look bad. Of course, Kitcher wanted to get the result that no study in human sociobiology is rigorous as part of his plan for protecting society from dangerous views about the biological basis of human nature. The appropriate comparison is between human sociobiology today and animal sociobiology before the development of inclusive-fitness theory, game theory, evolutionary stable strategy theory, and so forth. Then, the research situations of animal and human sociology would be candidates for comparable research situations in that regard.

There is, however, a difference that prevents a comparison between human sociobiology today and animal sociobiology then. Although they would be comparable with regard to the state of development of explanatory resources, they would not be comparable with regard to the state of development of explanatory domain. When evolutionists applied the new explanatory theory to their chosen species of study, no one cried "Foul." When sociobiologists apply those same resources to humans, almost everyone else cried

"Foul." We find it hard to accept ourselves as being subject to evolutionary processes in the ways required by the very idea of applying inclusive-fitness theory, game theory, and optimality models to ourselves. Unless human sociobiology is in a similar research situation with animal sociobiology or with another science trying to extend established theory into a new domain, both with respect to the explaining factors and the phenomena explained, comparisons using the same standards for success are unfair.

Is human sociobiology an actual, legitimate science? Apart from the difficulty of seeing that and how human sociality is evolutionarily significant, whatever answer we give would also apply to animal sociobiology in the 1950s and 1960s. Before consensus on how altruism is possible, Kitcher's method of assessment yields the result that animal sociobiology was not then a science. The sense in which animal sociobiology then and human sociobiology now are not sciences is that they are not established sciences. Established science is rigorous science involving significant consensus on fundamentals and evidential success—the sort of science that has a paradigm in Kuhn's sense, the sort of science he called "normal science." To evaluate a science whose research situation is not one of an established science with the criteria and standards pertinent to established science is unjustifiable. Normative expectations are appropriate only if they take into account the state of development, goal structure, and research situation of the science evaluated.

All the models of development discussed so far are models involving established science: the accumulation of truths, the correction of past approximations to the truth by current theory, the revolutionary transition from normal science under one paradigm to normal science under a different paradigm, and the gradual change of a research program where we can rely on some elements in successful research to justify changing other elements in research that confront anomalies. All four models presuppose that current research involves significant consensus on fundamentals and evidential success. All four conceptualize scientific development according to rival preferred criteria for valid science. None of them do justice to scientific development of the sort faced by animal sociobiology in the 1950s and 1960s and faced by human sociobiology in the 1970s and 1980s, namely, transition from unestablished to established extensions of an established science.

These models are not only used by historians to record scientific history, but are adopted in scientific research itself insofar as it makes decisions about its own development to assess past explanations, revise current explanations, and construct new explanations. The history of sociobiology can be written using each of the models in a way that makes the aim of completeness the overall aim of sociobiology and rationale for its direction of research. Hence, the goals and development of explanation in sociobiology should be assessed in terms of the explanatory problems posed by the aim of completeness. The quest to arrive at a New Synthesis oriented by explanatory completeness is better served by a conception of progress-as-refinement that subsumes and integrates the ways these models capture various aspects of research development. Refinement can take many forms, some involving cumulative progress, others involving corrective progress, others involving revolutionary progress, others involving gradual progress, and most likely other forms of progress as well.

# CHAPTER
# 4

## DOMAIN CONCEPTUALIZATION

### 4.1 Expanding the Evolutionary Domain

### Explanatory Scope and Explanatory Modality

Given that explanatory completeness is the degree to which a theory adequately covers its intended domain, a conceptual precondition for solving explanatory problems is the accurate specification of sociobiology's domain. One has to know what evolutionary theory's proper domain is—what behavioral facts should or should not be given evolutionary explanation—before deciding whether it is complete. Once we clarify the explanatory problem addressed by the explanation, we must decide how to reformulate the data so that its evolutionary significance is explicit, a precondition for bringing it within the scope of evolutionary theory. What, exactly, about sociality are we trying to explain? Some critics think that sociobiology can explain only why humans are cultural organisms that have a capacity to interact with each other, whereas advocates have far more specific explananda in mind.

Sociobiologists keep meeting resistance when they explain this or that human behavior or social institution. We often hear objections of the form "That's not biological" (and hence not within the scope of evolutionary theory) or "That's not biologically determined (and hence not explained by evolutionary theory as a necessary part of the human condition). Note that necessity is a modal concept. It involves a grammatical form or category characteristically indicating predication of an action or state in some manner other than as a simple fact. According to our challenge-response model of scientific development, sociobiology requires a conceptual framework which represents evolved human attributes in a way that responds to challenges involving scope and modality. This chapter identifies what is involved in conceiving human sociality in order to respond successfully to these challenges. Think of issues involving the conceptualization of sociobiology's domain using the scheme 'input—explanation—output'. Matters of conceptualizing the phenomena to be explained in order to bring them within the scope of theory pertain to the processing of the input. Matters of conceptualizing the phenomena upon being explained to express what makes them actual, possible, or necessary pertain to the output.

Human reproductive behavior is a good candidate for something specific that seems essential for completeness. Once mating and parenting are explained, other behaviors can be explained within the context of mating and parenting, and so the number and variety of kinds of behavior explained will radiate outward from a firm basis. Domain specification procedures are needed to answer the question "To achieve relevance and consistency, how should we reformulate sentences stating the behavioral facts in need of explanation?"

The history of attempts to apply evolutionary theory to the human species has been rife with debates in which critics charge that they illicitly amplify the scope of biological and evolutionary factors and in which advocates maintain that the preconceptions of the critics illicitly restrict their scope. The concept of human nature attributes to us a single nature, a conception that does not first recognize various aspects and then interrelates them as a whole, but rather tries to talk about the entire human condition in one fell swoop. The debate over whether sociobiology illuminates or obscures human nature starts from the unanalyzed presumption that true propositions about how this or that fact makes evolutionary sense would have an immediate implication for human nature. On that basis, advocates assert the truth of such propositions and critics assert their falsity. This presumption, and the debate based on it, is vexed because it fails to realize that the domains of the various sciences are limited, and so only certain aspects of humans can be conceived according to the conceptual apparatus of the science at hand. Sociobiology potentially illuminates the aspects of humans that its conceptual apparatus is designed to detect, but the big picture of all basic aspects of humans is forever beyond its grasp.

A principled way to transcend this sort of debate, then, is to recognize that the import of the explanations is limited by their narrowed focus on certain aspects of behaviors to the exclusion of others. One can't have it both ways, drawing automatic inferences between evolutionary altruism—a comparative, nonpsychological, reproductive concept—and vernacular altruism—a noncomparative, psychological, nonreproductive concept (Sober 1988). We can't both bypass nonevolutionary aspects of behaviors in order to expose their evolutionary significance and claim that the new explanation corrects prior views about those aspects (e.g., Alexander 1987, who mistranslates philosophical claims about morality into evolutionary terms). Nor do we need to criticize explanations of evolutionary aspects of behaviors in order to retain our prior conceptions of the aspects of behaviors usually theorized about. Since only certain aspects of human sociality are evolutionarily significant, evolutionary theory has a limited scope. It can illuminate only what comes under its scope. So it needs a framework that regulates both the processing of social facts acting as input in order to bring them under its scope and the processing of evolutionary conclusions acting as output in order to draw implications for prior views of sociality. This chapter argues that disciplined science can control domain specification through procedures in specifying the conceptual commitments of an augmented domain: description, classification, expansion, and limitation.

## Embedding and Projecting

Let us begin this course of reasoning by placing in philosophical context our question, "To achieve the kind of coherence between evolutionary theory and social data needed to bring about a New Synthesis that achieves explanatory completeness, how should we reformulate sentences stating the behavioral facts in need of evolutionary explanation?" Standard views of explanation are of little help since they sidestep the issue. Logical empiricists took theories as their unit of analysis. For instance, we have used Hempel's account to clarify the logical and empirical aspects of finished explanations as they are based on theories (1.2, 1.3). Historical presuppositionists took research programs as a more basic unit of analysis. For instance, we have used Kuhn's account to clarify how a good explanation conforms to the rules of construction and validation of its affiliated research program (2.4).

Hempel portrayed an ideal of explanation attainable only after an initial period of groping toward the right questions and the right methods. Such logical empiricist models leave us unable to evaluate science in the process of exploratory research, the sort of groping found in animal sociobiology in the past and human sociobiology in the present. Kuhn portrayed an actual practice of explanation in which dogmatic scientists take for granted the most recent theoretical breakthrough, where an end to such groping is declared by fiat and consensus. Such historical presuppositionist models leave us unable to evaluate exploratory research that is critical about its own basic commitments. To clarify the evaluation of explanations that extend established science into a new part of its intended domain according to the critical attitude, we adopt a conceptual framework as an even more basic unit of analysis.

Problem specification leads to domain specification. Some problems in sociobiology concern the clarification of its domain, raising such questions as:

(1) What considerations (or, better, types of considerations, if such types can be found) lead scientists to regard a certain body of information as a body of information—that is, as constituting a unified subject matter or domain to be examined or dealt with?

(2) How is description of the items of the domain achieved and modified at sophisticated stages of scientific development?

(3) What sorts of inadequacies, leading to the need for further work, are found in such bodies of information, and what are the grounds for considering these to be inadequacies or problems requiring further research?

(4) What considerations lead to the generation of specific lines of research, and what are the reasons (or types of reasons) for considering some lines of research to be more promising than others in the attempt to resolve problems about the domain?

(5) What are the reasons for expecting (sometimes to the extent of demanding) that answers of certain sorts, having certain characteristics, be sought for those problems? (Shapere 1977, 80)

Traditional accounts of the inferential structure of explanation conceived explanation as subsumption under generalizations with the aid of antecedent conditions. Subsumption was then treated as a purely logical exercise of subsuming data under theory, as if conceptual problems of inconsistency and irrelevance had already been solved. Suppose we are given a theory seemingly inconsistent with data, as altruism had seemed inconsistent with natural selection theory. Suppose further that we are given data seemingly irrelevant to theory, as human culture seemed to render human sociality beyond the evolutionary domain. In this situation, domains are conceptualized through two kinds of procedures: embedding, leading to how-possibly explanations, and projection, leading to how-actually explanations.

In a correct scientific explanation, the facts to be explained are first (a) embedded in the possibility space created by the theoretical factors doing the explaining and then (b) projected from it with the aid of empirical data as the only rival possibility actualized (mathematically, the space is given by sets of possible values of variables). Embedding activities in sociobiology are successful when they reveal the evolutionary significance of the behaviors explained, according to appropriate standards of plausibility for how-possibly explanations. Projecting activities in sociobiology are successful when the how-actually explanations adduced for those evolutionarily significant behaviors satisfy the sound-argument model of explanatory reasoning and the symmetry thesis, according to appropriate standards of evidence. The demand to reveal the behavior as the only rival possibility actualized does not rule out probabilistic explanation. The rival possibilities are entire evolutionary scenarios, each with its own array of probability distributions. An explanation's scope (the phenomena in the domain to which it applies) and modality (the phenomena explained are thereby shown to be possible, actual, or necessary) are conceptualized according to various ways embedding and projection procedures are carried out.

The concepts of embedding and projecting may be hard to comprehend, but they are crucial for capturing the explanatory ability of causal theories:

> Evolutionary theory aims not only to describe the patterns that may be found in the history of life on earth but also to characterize the processes that produced them. Its strategy for identifying the actual causes that have shaped the tree of life is the usual scientific one: scientists try to characterize a range of possible causes of evolution, and then to determine which of the possibilities actually obtained. The actual is understood by first embedding it in the possible. (Sober 1984, 14)

Given social data, how should we make it relevant to evolutionary theory? We reformulate the data so as to reveal it as possible given the theory. That is, we embed the data in the possibility space of theoretical variables. As Sober notes, Fisher said that if we wish to understand why the sexes are, in fact, always two, then we need to consider the consequences experienced by organisms of two, three, or more sexes. Evolutionary theory describes the possible causes and outcomes of evolution in its source laws and consequence laws. Laws about the sources of evolutionary change include those concerning conditions that generate heritable variation in fitness, mutation, migration, immigration, and genetic drift. Laws about the consequences of evolutionary change include conditions arising from the mutual interaction of those forces of evolutionary change.

Given evolutionary theory, how should we make it consistent with social data? We reformulate the theoretical generalizations exhibiting relations between variables and combine them with statements about the actual course or outcome of evolution to project the facts from the theory. Projection requires singular claims about evolutionary patterns ("such and such kinds of events do commonly happen or do rarely happen as evolution proceeds") and general claims about evolutionary processes ("such and such kinds of events can happen as evolution proceeds"). For instance, issues over group adaptation concern whether, given that group selection can produce group adaptation, group selection has been sufficiently effective to make group adaptations more than a rarity. Embedding and projection combine to identify why the particular theoretical possibility we find in nature, rather than some rival theoretical possibility, is actual. For instance, if some feature is good for the group, we do not understand why it evolved unless we can say why it evolved rather than some feature that is not good for the group. Scientific explanation yields understanding by embedding the actual into the possible and then by projecting the actual from the possible as the only rival possibility actualized.

In Newtonian celestial mechanics, for instance, planets are embedded in the mathematical space of theoretical variables by treating them as particles obeying Newtonian laws. Relative to that theory, that is what it means to reveal the actual as theoretically possible. We are justified in regarding the data on planets as relevant to the theory. Inferences from effects to causes are risky since all but one rival possible set of causes is not the actual set. So successful embedding does not justify us in singling out one theoretical scenario rather than others as the cause of its observed state of motion. Hence, embedding is only a first step, to be followed by projection. It turns how-possibly explanations into how-actually explanations.

The difference is already built into our intuitive distinction between a plausible explanation, which states why the event might have happened, and a correct explanation, which states why the event actually did happen. The difference makes sense of why human sociobiology is charged with being long on theory and short on evidence, creating plausible but not correct explanations. It has devoted more attention to the prior procedures of embedding (speculating about adaptive significance, identifying the space of possibilities for gene-culture coevolution) than the ensuing procedures of projection (incorporating sufficient empirical detail and complexity into those hypotheses to explain why we do what we actually do).

The first task is to embed the actual world into a set of theoretically possible worlds. There are many possible evolutionary scenarios for the evolution of human sexuality (e.g., Lovejoy's and Parker's scenarios for the origin of concealed ovulation; see Barkow 1989c). Hypotheses can be tested only against actualities, not possibilities. The scenarios are at best internally consistent and loosely consistent with other data and theories.

The second task is to project the actual world from that set of theoretically possible worlds. For a given explanation, projection is finished when we justifiably regard the actual behavior, not just as theoretically possible, but also as the only rival possibility actualized. Here empirical testing eliminates rival possibilities, as contradicted by pertinent actual facts. The most rigorous form of hypotheses to be tested are those asserting that the only rival theoretically possible scenario which is actualized in the real world is the one used in the derivation of the facts. Hence, the comparative character of the explanatory hypothesis requires that proper testing involves both confirmational and disconfirmational work. Here we have another reason for adopting the view of acceptance proposed in 1.5, namely, that the acceptability of a hypothesis is constituted by whether it is the best among rival available hypotheses.

Causal explanations reduce incompleteness in their embedding phase by showing that in principle the facts are relevant to and need not contradict the theory, and in their projective phase, by showing that the facts actually confirm and do not contradict the theory. We are justified in regarding the theory as relevant to and consistent with the data since our causal explanation satisfies both the criteria of derivability and truth. What counts as the array of rival causal scenarios taken into account by the empirical tests is given by the research program at hand, as proposed in chapter 2.

To grasp the character of explanation in sciences like sociobiology, explanations should be evaluated for their acceptability in a manner that integrates all three units of analysis into a single scheme. We can now state how embedding and projection procedures involve all three units—the underlying theory, the conceptual framework, and the research programs—and four distinctive features of explanations—their scope, modality, resources, and kinds. Given the underlying theory (evolutionary theory), effort to form a rational scheme of its completeness (conceptual framework) is articulated through the perspectives of rival research programs (e.g., dual inheritance, epigenetic, coevolutionary) according to embedding and projection decisions about scope (limits on the range of social behaviors in need of evolutionary explanation and/or explainable by the kind of explanation at hand), modality (explained behaviors are shown to be theoretically possible and/or actual rather than necessary), resources (total array of potential explanatory factors) and kind (type of explanation given by the character of the specific explanatory factors utilized). This scheme shows how the three-unit model makes sense of the overall picture of the research situation in sociobiology.

## Domain Extension and Sociopolitical Questions

It may seem that the present view of sociobiology overlooks the question of whether the completion of the Modern Synthesis by sociobiology is an unproblematic goal. Is it not simply assumed at the outset that as long as sociobiology can complete the Modern Synthesis by extending its domain to encompass animal and human sociality (whatever this might turn out to mean), then sociobiology will be acceptable? Is this simplistic view not blind to social and political questions related to issues sociobiologists discuss? By noting the ways in which this reading is a misinterpretation, we can see better how our results fit together and place problems in clarifying sociobiology's domain in proper perspective.

First, social and political questions have been shown to be crucial to the explanations sociobiologists propose. Evidence has been supplied for social and political influence on the content of explanations (recall the subsection of 2.2, Ideology and the Content of Explanations). Evidence has been supplied for social and political influences on the aims of explanation (recall the subsection of 2.3, Ideologies as Holistic Research Programs). Evidence has been supplied for social and political influences on the public presentation, interpretation, and evaluation of explanations (recall the subsection of 1.3, The Politics of Accepting Explanations). The character of sociobiology as ideology has been emphasized by boldly claiming that each of these explanations has an ideological status as well as a scientific status (recall the same subsection). With respect to the description, explanation, and improvement of what happens in sociobiology in the name of science, the present analysis is ready to stress these and further ways in which social and political questions go to the heart of sociobiological research.

Second, it has been maintained that the social and political questions do not exhaust the scientific status of sociobiology. The false dichotomy "science or ideology" has led advocates to deny the ideological character of sociobiology in order to assert its scientific character and has led critics to deny its scientific character in order to assert its ideological character. Through the concept of "science and ideology," the debate predicated on this false dichotomy has been transcended and a more balanced view of sociobiology has been advocated.

Because science is a form of inquiry, and form does not guarantee content, one cannot justifiably defend the content of any scientific explanation by saying "we arrived at it through the scientific method." The content of explanatory hypotheses, theories, programs, and frameworks reflect ideas of knowing, inquiring, acting, believing, valuing subjects. Decisions at every stage in the use of scientific methods reflect both epistemic and nonepistemic values. So the fact that sociobiology, in virtue of its status as a science, aims to complete the range of evolutionary explanation by pushing the Modern Synthesis into the realm of sociality does not at all subvert any of the above facts about its ideological character.

The explanatory conclusions a science arrives at can never be validated independently of the belief systems of its practitioners and audience. One can never justifiably attack the validity of those explanations on the naive expectation that they are supposed to be independently validated and on the realistic realization that they are not so validated. So the fact that sociobiology, in virtue of its status as ideology, is a reflection and projection of the social and political commitments of its practitioners and audience does not at all subvert any of the epistemic relationships between sociobiology's New Synthesis and the Modern Synthesis.

Third, since social and political questions do not exhaust the scientific status of sociobiology, we need social and political evaluations of sociobiology that take into account its scientific aspects. Reasons have been given to think that any interpretation of sociobiology which draws its implications for human nature should realize that those implications are not inherent in its ontology (recall the subsection of 1.2, Completeness and Human Nature). Reasons have been given to think that the concept of acceptance pertinent to scientific research is not a function of social and political reasons or standards, but rather an explanation's contribution to aims internal to research (recall the subsections of 1.2, Refutation of Politically Based Standards, Use-Specific Acceptance, and Hypotheses and Theories). Even acts of identifying aims internal to research have a socio-political dimension.

Fourth, the phrase "sociobiology will be acceptable" has never been used here because it is symptomatic of the sort of thinking that obscures the scientific status of sociobiology through a failure to make important distinctions. We have talked throughout this book about the acceptability of particular explanations (or explanation-sketches or explanatory hypotheses—recall the subsection of 2.5, Targets and Units of Analysis). We have distinguished the acceptability of particular explanations from the legitimacy and validation of sociobiology. The legitimacy of sociobiology as a scientific enterprise depends on its goals (recall the subsection of 3.1, Ideological and Scientific Goals). The validation of sociobiology as a scientific enterprise depends on its ability to generate results that promote the achievement of its most basic research goals, judged according to joint use of standards of correctness (1.3), acceptability (1.4), and progressiveness (2.3). Thus, the notion of validation proposed here is far more fine grained than is recognized in the objection.

Fifth, sociobiology's research goal structure has been identified as being oriented by the goal of achieving explanatory completeness. The proposal that sociobiology should be evaluated as an extension of the Modern Synthesis which attempts to extend the goal structure of the updated Modern Synthesis into the realm of sociality has been argued in detail (3.1). The degree of advance toward the goals induced by the quest for explanatory completeness is to be measured in terms of how well or poorly the resulting explanations satisfy the totality of criteria for acceptability that relate to its theories, research programs, and conceptual frameworks (recall the summary in the subsection of 2.5, The Three-Unit Model). So the assumption of the reading that sociobiology is here viewed as acceptable merely because it has the goal of completeness is the opposite of the present project to adapt our use of demanding evaluative criteria to the exigencies of aim-oriented science.

Sixth, what it means to complete the Modern Synthesis has been stated. To complete the Modern Synthesis is to do the research necessary to transform the hypotheses that were constructed in parallel to the conclusions of the Modern Synthesis into substantiated conclusions (recall the subsection of 3.1, Postulate One). The model by which this construction was guided has been described in general and in concrete detail, critically discussed, and its implications have been drawn in ways that clarify the meaning and import of achieving completeness (in the remainder of 3.1). What it means to complete evolutionary explanation has been explicated in a historical sense, an intuitive sense, and a metalogical sense (1.1). To complete evolutionary explanation by means of a synthesis is to produce a synthesis that fulfills the historical, intuitive, and metalogical analyses of completeness so as to satisfy the array of evaluative criteria well enough to provide a basis for problem solving in a way comparable to that of the Modern Synthesis.

Seventh, of course the completion of the Modern Synthesis is a problematic goal. Any goal attribution to sociobiology is problematic, given the controversy now surrounding it. However, if there is to be a sociobiology at all, it is relatively unproblematic to attribute to it the goal of attempting to complete evolutionary explanation. To work at subsuming sociality under evolutionary processes is, in effect, to work at completing evolutionary explanation. At least, that goal is unproblematic relative to the obviously problematic goals of illuminating the nature of animals and the nature of humans (as the advocates propose) or else relative to the goals of the notorious "isms" (as the critics propose). Of course, it is problematic how research should proceed to achieve that goal; but that is the case with any prevalidated science. The problems facing sociobiologists are being discussed in as comprehensive and organized a manner as possible by locating the way they relate to various criteria attaching to theories, research programs, and conceptual frameworks.

Eighth, the conception of sociobiology as an extension of the Modern Synthesis seems to accept more than just the aims stated in Mayr's version of the conclusions of the Modern Synthesis. It would be naive to uncritically accept the body of research knowledge associated with the Modern Synthesis. After all, we want to complete evolutionary explanation with the best combination of data, methods, theory, programs, and conceptual frameworks available. The Modern Synthesis, viewed as results and not just aims, is out of date. In that sense, we would not want to complete the Modern Synthesis. So the misinterpretation cleared up here does have a kernel of truth. The conception of sociobiology as an extension of the Modern Synthesis is indeed problematic. Let us now examine this conception.

## Strategies of Domain Specification

Our interest here lies in raising questions about whether any extension of the neo-Darwinist theory of the Modern Synthesis will work in dealing with cultural organisms. In the "worst" scenario, in order to get an evolutionary theory that provides the basis for posing and solving problems of social evolution in cultural organisms, a revolution in evolutionary biology would have to occur. Kuhn was often asked, "Is such-and-such an episode normal science or revolutionary science?" He would answer, in effect, "That depends. Normal or revolutionary for whom?" This answer fits his sociological approach to science, where science is viewed in terms of the subculture of scientists. One and the same episode can be revolutionary with respect to the preconceptions of one group of researchers and normal with respect to the preconceptions of a different group. In order to develop this issue of extension-versus-revolution, we can draw some implications from what might be a comparable case in physics, for all we know now.

The Modern Synthesis and the New Synthesis have both similarities and differences. One important difference is that evolutionary biology was not what we would consider now to be an established science before the Modern Synthesis. Evolutionary biology is established before a possible New Synthesis, largely by the success of the Modern Synthesis. The proper comparison with sociobiology would be a case of a theory, regarded as a long-established and nearly complete theory of its intended domain, confronted in a corner of its domain resistant to successful treatment.

For example, the synthetic evolutionary theory in much of the 1900s has been almost as dominant as was Newton's theory in much of the 1800s. Newton's mechanics is a paradigm middle-range theory in physics; it applies quite successfully to physical objects at normal ranges of spatiotemporal variation. Even so, efforts to extend its application to micro-objects failed dismally; it predicted that electrons would spiral into the atomic nucleus in a fraction of second, thereby being unable to account for the stability of the atom, creating inconsistency between theory and data. Efforts to extend its application to objects moving at speeds approaching the speed of light also failed dismally, also creating explanatory inconsistency. The drive for a complete physics, one able to handle the totality of basic physical phenomena, became successful by giving up efforts to extend Newtonian mechanics. Instead, the radically different theories of quantum mechanics and relativity theory were constructed.

For all we know, the neo-Darwinian synthetic theory, which deals with microevolution (the origin, maintenance, and modification of genetic structure within populations) may be successful only for organisms at normal ranges of genotypic-phenotypic variation. It seems that the "higher" social organisms having traditions (e.g., primates) and cultures (humans) exhibit little within-population genetic variation in social behavior despite large amounts of within-population phenotypic variation in social behavior. If so, such social phenomena lie outside the normal ranges of genotypic-phenotypic variation. The analogue to Newtonian theory suggests that the drive for a completed evolutionary biology, one able to handle the totality of basic evolutionary phenomena, would require the construction of radically different theories to handle cultural evolution (social transmission and the origin, maintenance, and modification of cultural behavior).

Our current evolutionary theory is unable to explain social behavior in cultural organisms. There are three main strategies of domain choices: restriction, extension, and transformation. One can restrict the domain of evolutionarily significant behavior by agreeing with extreme critics of human sociobiology that social behavior involving cultural evolution does not fall within the scope of any version of evolutionary biology; incompleteness is an illusion since cultural behavior is not in need of biological, evolutionary explanation. Or, one can extend the domain of evolutionary phenomena by agreeing with advocates of human sociobiology that cultural behavior is within the scope of current evolutionary theory; incompleteness is genuine since cultural behavior needs biological, evolutionary explanation but can be explained by adding new theories to traditional evolutionary theory, as proposed by gene-culture programs involving a complex psychology. Or, one can transform the domain of evolutionary phenomena on the analogue of the fate of Newtonian mechanics. One can hold that cultural behavior does fall within the scope of current evolutionary theory; current evolutionary theory (like Newton's) is, strictly speaking, false and no extension of it via gene-culture programs or any other programs will successfully handle the recalcitrant cultural data, data that can be accounted for successfully only by a radically different evolutionary theory.

On the strategy of domain restriction, we deny the relevance of the sorts of sociality found in cultural organisms to evolutionary theory in any form. Sociobiology of noncultural organisms is legitimate, but sociobiology of cultural organisms is illegitimate whether it extends current neo-Darwinian theory or adopts a radically different theory. This strategy confronts a line-drawing problem. There is abundant ethological data on traditions, and not just in the higher primates, e.g., otters who teach offspring to break open sea anemones with rocks, and their offspring in turn teach it to their offspring. If the behavior of organisms having traditions is evolutionarily significant but the behavior of organisms not having traditions is not, then how can we draw a meaningful line of domain demarcation between them, given that the former are the ancestors of the latter? Again, if we put organisms having traditions and organisms having cultures on the same side, a similar line-drawing problem arises.

On the strategy of domain extension, we uphold the relevance of the sorts of sociality found in cultural organisms to evolutionary theory. In addition, we try to extend the neo-Darwinian theory we have to make it consistent with the data. Sociobiology of noncultural and of cultural organisms is legitimate. This is the strategy followed by most practitioners who support both animal and human sociobiology. This strategy confronts a unification problem. Given the radical difference between the richness, complexity, and diversity of human cultural behavior and the simple traditions we find in nonhumans, how can one and the same theory apply successfully to all organismic species as diverse as the social organisms, from the social invertebrates to humans?

On the strategy of domain transformation, we also uphold the relevance of the sorts of sociality found in cultural organisms. However, we maintain that any extension of the neo-Darwinian theory we now have will turn out to be inconsistent with the data. So the domain is split into a part where neo-Darwinian theory (like Newtonian mechanics) can apply as empirically adequate for practical purposes, whereas the domain of sociality as a whole requires a radically different theory (like quantum mechanics). This strategy confronts a meaning problem. Remember that Bohr and others tried to construct a quantum mechanics as a rational generalization of Newtonian mechanics. They were successful in doing so only at the price of creating a quantum mechanical formalism whose meaning they did not understand and one whose interpretation remains one of the enigmas of physics. It will be hard enough for sociobiologists to come up with sufficient ingenuity to create a radically new theory of sociality (a) from which they can calculate fitnesses and so forth for social behaviors and (b) that can be used to account for sociality in both noncultural and cultural organisms. But once they find a predictively successful global theory of sociality, will they have the right concepts with which to understand the basic terms and principles of the new formalism?

Although sociobiology is traditionally understood in terms of the strategy of domain extension, there is no reason why sociobiologists should not pursue all three strategies. All three strategies of domain specification are strategies for achieving completeness since all three are ways of making evolutionary theory relevant to and consistent with the social data that is properly part of the domain of evolutionary biology. The strategy of domain restriction does this in the fastest way possible, namely, by restricting the domain so that sociality in cultural organisms is outside of the proper domain. We will look at the sorts of arguments for doing so, posed as objections to Alexander's explanation of monogamy on the strategy of domain extension.

Before recounting the procedures used in extending the domain, note that principled argument can be given against restricting the domain. The fact that human behavioral interactions and human social institutions can be embedded into the space of evolutionary possibilities is considered to be the most persuasive sort of argument for doing human sociobiology. Sociobiologists have repeatedly argued as follows in order to show that the sort of sociality found in human cultural organisms has evolutionary significance, and so is in need of evolutionary explanation:

> Human beings, like other animals, are products of the evolutionary process. Human behavior is simply one aspect of the human phenotype. Hence patterns of human behavior have evolutionary explanations. Human societies are constituted by individual human beings and by their individual forms of behavior. Hence there are evolutionary explanations of human social institutions. Since natural selection is the dominant force in the evolutionary process, both the individual patterns of behavior of individual human beings and human social institutions are shaped by natural selection. We can thus explain the way in which people behave and the kinds of social institutions that we find in human societies by identifying selective advantages that those forms of behavior and those social institutions have conferred on the people who engage or participate in them. (Kitcher 1988, 295)

This argument concerns general reasons for expanding the domain currently covered and does not speak to the issue of whether current theory or a radically different theory should be used to cover the augmented domain. Therefore, it is neutral between the strategies of domain extension and domain transformation. Kitcher goes on to defend a sophisticated form of this argument that takes into account standard criticisms about confusing evolution and history, atomizing phenotypes into discrete isolatable behaviors, and identifying social institutions with individual behaviors. On that basis he constructs a sophisticated way of embedding human sociality into evolutionary scenarios. His proposed program for completing evolutionary explanation basically adds on new theoretical variables to old ones, thereby adopting the strategy of domain extension rather than domain transformation.

Kitcher describes the kinds of theoretical variables that can be expected to operate in a single generation in relation to a life cycle schema. He develops hypotheses about incest avoidance from an array of theoretical variables that treat behavior and social institutions in relation to underlying psychological mechanisms, development, genetics, and forces of cultural change. The research strategy is to start from simple models that incorporate the important kinds of factors and gradually assemble all and only relevant factors. In intervening steps, conclusions from simple models are not to be subverted by the later, more complex models.

Here we have another variant of the sort of gene-culture research programs discussed in chapter 2. It seems as if sociobiology has undergone change of the sort that mirrors the development of psychology. Very roughly, when behaviorism was the dominant approach, behaviors were explained using stimulus-response theory as responses directly induced by proximate stimuli. This sort of theory may have been all right for pigeons and mice, but it failed to take account of the sort of cognitive processing found in higher primates and especially humans. So cognitive psychology developed, where the path from stimulus to response is mediated by all sorts of intervening cognitive processes. Stimuli do not cause responses. Instead, stimuli are activating events that are then processed according to variable cognitions, whether identified as views, beliefs, opinions, values, meanings, attitudes, ideas, expectations, philosophies, etc. These are the cognitions that lead to the observable behavioral responses and that humans can control and change, cognitions posited by such therapies as rational emotive therapy.

However we wish to tell the story, the point is that sociobiology seemed at first to make genetic causation the overriding proximate causal factor, just as behaviorism seemed to make environmental stimuli the overriding proximate factor. Now it has incorporated the conceptual resources of psychology and anthropology to combine genetic factors with environmental factors and cognitive factors. Gene-culture programs that emphasize a complex psychology and use cognitive psychology to do so are not subject to the charge of biological determinism in the form normally directed against sociobiology.

We will examine Alexander's implicit decisions in extending sociobiological theory to the human domain in order to answer the question "Why is it thought in large societies that monogamy is morally right?"

The very idea of explaining human monogamy in the way that Alexander does is conceptually shocking. As we might expect from our discussion of altruism, behavior according to the sentiment that monogamy is morally right is a product of evolved predispositions to act altruistically in the phenotypic sense but selfishly in the genotypic sense. Our preconceptions yield two standard objections. Isn't such an obviously culturally influenced trait properly explained by social science, not by sociobiology? Given the way the observed monogamy is connected to sexual-selection theory that males have evolved to be "promiscuous" and females have evolved to be "faithful," is monogamy now revealed to be a biologically determined part of human nature? On the challenge-response model, sociobiology needs to take on the challenges posed by such objections in order to defend its basic neo-Darwinian commitments.

Section 4.2 addresses the first objection. It shows how the usual objections to possibility of such explanations of uniquely human attributes are easily rebutted by appealing to the sorts of decisions found in these strategies and procedures of domain specification. It argues that when debate over human sociobiology, social science, and human nature ignores these conceptual procedures, it is inadequately grounded. These arguments lead us to conclude that the debate over biological reductionism, insofar as it involves relations between domains of human sociobiology and social science, is reoriented by taking account of these domain specification procedures.

Section 4.3 addresses the second objection. It shows how such uniquely human attributes can be explained by sociobiology without involving biological determinism. "Biological determinism," in the usage of such influential critics as the Sociobiology Study Group, is analyzed as an umbrella term for a variety of distinct modes of explanation: cosmological explanation, ideological explanation, fatalist explanation, essentialist explanation, and determinist explanation. It is argued that if we pursue the implications of disciplined evolutionary inquiry for human nature, we see why a sociobiology aimed at explanatory completeness transcends biological determinism in all of these forms. It does not generate the sort of biological necessity found in any of these versions of biological determinism, the source of fear that sociobiological explanations make the phenomena explained biologically inevitable. These arguments show that the debate over biological determinism and human nature, insofar as it involves the modality of necessity, is reoriented by taking account of these domain specification procedures.

## 4.2 Morality as an Evolved Phenomenon

### Theory-laden Behavioral Description

Having presented the main general argument for extending the domain of evolutionary theory to include human social behavior and human social institutions, we are in a position to examine the procedures of domain specification used to execute the strategy of domain extension. These procedures presuppose that such human social phenomena are within the intended domain of evolutionary biology. We will now identify what is involved in representing human morality in such a way that it is an evolved phenomenon, and thus in need of evolutionary explanation.

Recall our definition of completeness from section 1.2:

Definition. A theoretical system T in evolutionary biology that contains an observation language O is complete with respect to the class of all evolutionarily significant social facts if and only if (1a) O is adequate for the expression of any evolutionarily significant social fact and (2a) every available fact expressed in O is or can be explained by T.

Clause (1a) of this definition is indispensable for understanding human sociobiology. The function of each of the three strategies of domain specification is to tell us in general terms whether social behavior in cultural organisms counts as an evolutionarily significant social fact. The function of the procedures of domain extension is to tell us how to adequately represent those social facts deemed evolutionarily significant, given the strategy of domain extension. The observational language of T is the language in which those facts are represented. The observational language O is contained in the theoretical system T. So we should not be surprised if the language in which evolutionarily significant social facts about human morality are described is itself laden by evolutionary theory.

Scientific theories explain facts, not expressed in any old form, but expressed in a form relevant to the theory. Kuhn brought attention to this point in a way that does not require us to distinguish theories, programs, and frameworks. They are all 'theoretical' in contrast to 'observational' in the sense of involving systematic interpretations of observations. We have just motivated this insight by simple inspection of our definition of completeness. As Kuhn showed, theories explain observations reformulated so as to be relevant to theory, e.g., in his comparison of Newtonian and Aristotelian mechanics. After recounting the example, this insight will be refined by locating ways in which behavioral description is laden by three units of a theoretical system T: theory, program, and framework.

Consider three levels of scientific claims in the clash between Aristotelian and Newtonian explanation: an upper level of theory, a lower level of theory-laden observation (observable facts), and a still lower level of theory-neutral observation. At the lowest level, suppose we have the observation to be explained, for example, that Newton's apple drops to the ground when it falls. The fact that the distance between the apple and the earth decreases is a theory-neutral fact. That is, the fact can be understood and treated as an observable fact without recourse to either Aristotle's or Newton's theory. Even this fact involves some degree of interpretation and expectation, and hence some implicit theory, and so is not a theory-free fact. Whether or not there are any theory-free facts, theories do not directly explain theory-neutral facts, but only theory-laden facts.

Newton's theory involves the law that gravitation involves forces whose effect is proportional to mass times acceleration. Hence Newton's theory explains the movement of the apple toward the ground in the form "the earth and the apple are being pulled together." Aristotle's theory involves the idea that all material objects strive to return to their natural place. Hence Aristotle's theory explains the movement of the apple toward the ground in the form "the apple is seeking its natural place."

The two explanations differ dramatically. Newtonian theory does not even conceive material objects as having a natural place, certainly not one obstructed by the earth. Aristotelian theory does not even formulate quantitative laws as found in modern science, much less one like Newton's third law (Toulmin 1961). Neither Aristotle's nor Newton's theory directly explains why the distance between the earth and apple decreases. Newton explains why the earth and the apple are being pulled together by subsuming it under generalizations about attractive forces between material objects. Aristotle explains why the apple is seeking its natural place by subsuming it under generalizations about natural states and interfering factors. Sociobiology is not unlike physics and other sciences when it explains facts, not directly in the terms in which we commonly express them, but in the special terms it uses to reinterpret them. The meaning of sociobiological explanations turns on how explained facts are reconceptualized to express their evolutionary significance.

This kind of reconceptualization, and the embedding procedures used to yield framework-laden descriptions, is found in Alexander's book, *The Biology of Moral Systems*, 1987, in his thoughtful construction of an explanation (33–70) of how moral behavior and institutions of morality evolved. The explanation is grounded in the context of sexual-selection theory and parental-investment theory, the theory of fitness strategies by which parents distribute resources to offspring. The problem of the bearing of evolutionary theory upon the interpretation of moral behavior is too broad and complex for more than passing mention here, but Alexander's treatise contains some excellent examples of embedding procedures at work. Choosing some of these examples for the purpose at hand, and not as a way of describing or endorsing or evaluating his book, we shall use extensive quotation followed by some brief comments.

First, there are procedures of framework-laden description. *Explanatory Goal Procedures.* "Ultimately, how can we develop an appropriate set of subtheories from general evolutionary theory that will predict and account for variations in ethical and moral behavior?" (35); this question functions to posit the explanatory task of extending evolutionary theory to explain diversity within the human species, just as animal sociobiology explains diversity among species. Alexander concludes that "evolved human nature and morality are compatible" and that "morality as generally conceived is neither contrary to nor independent of selection" (p.xv). In our terms, his conclusion is that the facts about morality are neither inconsistent with nor irrelevant to selection theory, an explicit conclusion about completeness. The goal is to extend the theory of evolution by natural selection to explain moral behavior and its diversity among human beings, thus eliminating a longstanding source of incompleteness.

*Point of Departure Procedures.* Evolutionary theory "explains our underlying nature" (3). Recent developments in evolutionary biology which show that "natural selection has been maximizing the survival by reproduction of genes, so that we are evolved to maximize our genetic contribution to future generations by creating and aiding both descendent and nondescendent relatives" (2–3). Inclusive-fitness theory represents recent theoretical advances that are all we need as our point of departure in eliminating morality as a source of incompleteness by explaining its natural history. This functions to take the strategy of domain extension as the guiding strategy of domain specification.

Second, there are some procedures of program-laden description.

*Presupposition Procedures.* Moral traits are learned traits in the sense that variations in moral behavior are "determined by environmental not genetic variations" (7); this claim functions to adopt the genetic approach of the coevolutionary program. Morality is to be "understood only if societies are seen as collections of individuals seeking their own self-interests" (3); this claim functions to reconceptualize societies as evolving populations in order to embed facts about human societies in the theoretical world of population genetics. "We must distinguish two effects of natural selection, namely, the sorting among existing genetic variations that produce different phenotypic effects or traits and the accumulation of genetic units that in particular environments lead to particular phenotypic effects or traits" (21); this claim functions to divide rival gene-culture programs. Both effects must be significant for explanations affiliated with the epigenetic program to work, whereas only the latter effect must be significant for the coevolutionary research program to work.

The coevolutionary program renders evolutionary theory relevant to morality even if culture changes massively and quickly as compared to genetic change and even if there is no genetic variation underlying significant moral variations in the domain. ". . . it is always true that the cumulative history of natural selection continues to influence our actions by the set of genes it has provided humanity" (23); this claim functions to assert that the latter effect is significant, and hence that in principle acceptable explanations can be constructed if guided by the coevolutionary program. "Moral systems are societies with rules" (1); this claim functions to define societies as evolving populations bound by (especially moral) rules. The new explananda include social organization, explained as the collective outcome of rule-governed behaviors selected for maximal inclusive fitness.

Third, there are procedures of theory-laden description.

*Levels of Description Procedures.* Alexander (15–16) gives an example of the way "proximate" and "ultimate" levels of description are related, showing how his explanations do not invoke "genetic mechanisms as privileged proximate causes." Start from everyday observations interpreted by the language of common sense so as to be relatively neutral between various scientific theories (e.g., a man walks to the restaurant). Transform that description into a description in the language laden by proximate causes (e.g., the man is hungry, which caused him to seek food). Omit any analysis or explanation in terms of proximate causes (e.g., omit any reference to actions of nerves, muscles, hormones, sense organs, thought processes in producing the behavior or the role of genes and learning in individual development). This functions to adopt a neutral position on the relative priority and influence of genes and other proximate causes on behavior.

Next, transform the description from the language of proximate causes to the language of ultimate causes (e.g., effort to assuage hunger is part of a lifelong effort to build and maintain a phenotype). Reclassify the trait as a particular sort of effort to build and maintain a phenotype (e.g., effort to assuage hunger is a form of direct somatic effort with immediate payback). Explain why the behavior so classified evolved (direct somatic effort with immediate payback is expected to arise in situations of hunger as a cumulative result of natural selection). These procedures apply both nonsocial traits (e.g., food-gathering behavior) and social traits (e.g., behavior according to moral rules). Here it is obvious that the "facts" are not directly explained, but are raw materials to be processed into a form expressed in terms which render them relevant to evolutionary theory.

*Intradomain Relevance Procedures.* Within the domain of morality, we need to sort out which aspects of moral behavior and organization are relevant. "Human interests" are crucial to understanding the existence of morality (33); this functions to limit the explananda to those aspects of behavior that involve goals, goals explainable as effects of the history of efforts to do things which enable organisms to survive and reproduce. "The most general principle of human behavior is that people are in general following what they perceive to be their own interests" (34); this functions to identify the behavioral pattern that underlies all behavior having both moral and evolutionary significance.

*Problem Identification Procedures.* We need to identify the specific explanatory problems the explanation of morality is suppose to address. (Given the previous decisions, Alexander conceives problems in terms of explaining the goal-oriented aspects of morality by showing how those goals came about as ways of accomplishing ends promoted by natural selection.) The conclusion from recent advances in theory and data is that "the ultimate interest of organisms is to maximize the likelihood of survival of their genes" (37–38); this functions to identify the ultimate end promoted by natural selection. "Moral and ethical problems and questions exist solely because of conflicts of interest; moral systems exist because confluences of interest at lower levels of social organization are used to deal with conflicts of interest at higher levels" (33); this functions to set the stage for explaining both cooperation and conflict in terms of goals beneficial ultimately to individuals, not to groups, so that morality can be explained by appeal to individual selection, not group selection.

"The theory of lifetimes most widely accepted among biologists is that individuals have evolved to maximize the likelihood of survival of not themselves, but their genes, and that they do this by reproducing and tending in various ways offspring and other carriers of their own genes—descendent and nondescendent relatives" (38); this functions to conceive the problems in terms of embedding the goals involved in morality into the realm of possibilities given by the inclusive-fitness theory of individual selection.

*Theory Extension Procedures.* In order to connect behavior and evolutionary imperatives, we need to extend selection theory to encompass all phases of the life cycle. "Reproductive effort" is distributed in various proportions over one's lifetime as effort put into one's body (somatic effort), the body of genetically related individuals (extraparental nepotistic effort), mating (mating effort), and one's offspring (parental effort) (39–41). This functions as a ground for making distinctions in the effect of moral judgements on the life course. Aging (senescence) begins very early on, immediately after help or resources are given to siblings, because the expense of reproductive effort reduces residual reproductive value (37–42); this claim functions to discredit the presumption that aging occurs in humans merely at the end of life, based on survival as the ultimate end.

*Theory Combining Procedures.* Once a part of evolutionary theory has been suitably extended, we need to combine it with other parts of evolutionary theory to generate cumulative extensions in explanatory success. Alexander combines his theory of lifetimes (which adds senescence to previous life-history theory) with Williams's (1957b) theory of how senescence relates to natural selection. The combined theory is proposed to explain such things as "Why do we and they (other organisms) become increasingly fragile, susceptible to disease, incapacitated, senile, and dead?" (43). Again, the usual answers—wearing out, accumulation of toxins, death mechanisms—cite proximate rather than ultimate causes, and so are not even candidates for explanations, since what is to be explained is why these rather than other possible proximate causes exist. Williams posits that selection opposes these effects of aging but has not prevented them because the same genes which have good effects on the phenotype favorable in early life are deleterious later.

*Explananda Identification Procedures.* Upon combining new and old theories, the behaviors now encompassed by the revised total theory need to be identified. "Senescence theory, together with sexual selection and parental investment theory, therefore predicts (or explains) a large number of differences between human males and females, including their relative body sizes, mortality and senescence rates, relative frequencies in the population (i.e. sex ratios), relative amounts of parental care, relative times to maturity, relative rates of lawbreaking, etc." (63). These claims function to produce continuity in domain between previous explanations of male/female differences not involving morality and the present explanation of male/female differences involving morality. Previous explanations enlarged the domain through animal-human comparisons. But only humans have morality. So other procedures for establishing continuity in domain must be and are used.

*Explanation Revision Procedures.* Given the subsumption of new items to be explained under the extended theory, some older explanations are to be revised, now revealed as partly true and partly false. "Because males typically gain more by increasing numbers of offspring via multiple matings, while females typically gain more by giving more parental care to fewer offspring, even the human male competes sexually a little more intensely" (55); this functions to show that the restructuring of evolutionary theory induced by the present extension affirms the truth of the standard selection hypothesis (e.g., Barash's). "On average, he (the male) takes more risks than the female, and is more likely either to fail completely in reproduction or to outreproduce the average female. As a result, he has a higher rate of mortality and, correspondingly, has evolved to senesce sooner, a fact reflected in the relatively large number of widows around the world" (55); these claims function to show that the restructured extended theory fits the evidence for the behavior pattern that human males are more sexually competitive than human females, drawing the new implication that sex-specific mate strategies lead to differential morality rates and life histories.

"To the extent that males and females (of any species) commit themselves to lifetime monogamy, the interests of two individuals in a pair approach being identical"; this functions to falsify previous hypotheses that mate selection on male choice favors polygyny and on female choice favors monogamy. (Coevolutionary theory permits culturally induced human choice a decisive role in creating behavioral variation.) ". . . to the extent that (1) philandering is unlikely or too expensive to be profitable, (2) the relatives of one or the other are not significantly more available for nepotistic diversions of resources, each member of the pair will profit from complete cooperation with the other to produce and rear their joint offspring" (70); these claims function to state conditions in which monogamy is favored by selection, conditions presumed to regularly occur.

Why is it thought in large societies that monogamy is morally right? Alexander is now ready to propose an explanation. Socially imposed monogamy, bathed in moral rules, uses confluences of interest at the level of the mating pair to minimize competitiveness within the society and maximize the ability of the society to deal with conflicts with other societies. Monogamy is a confluence of interests at the lowest level of social organization, the pair bond. Young men at the age of maximal sexual competition are the most divisive class of individuals in a given society, i.e., they are the warriors. Socially imposed monogamy not only reduces male-female conflict, but also reduces male-male conflict, because it is a way of leveling the reproductive opportunities for men. The foregoing conceptual moves supply a context that imposes a tacit content to Alexander's explanations of moral judgements about sexual behavior. Articulating the coevolutionary program oriented by the aim of completeness, such explanations appeal to antecedent conditions involving socioculturally induced variations, variations taken as a given and not "reduced to biology" as critics assume. Thus, what is "environmental" is just as "biological" as what is "innate." Isolated from these conceptual decisions, the meaning of his explanations will be misinterpreted, and ensuing evaluations will miss their target.

These examples drawn from Alexander's explanatory work collectively indicate the complexity of embedding procedures. Surely the justification is defeated for any assessment that fails to do justice to the way the description of the explananda is laden with conceptual frameworks, research programs, and theories. A host of related procedures involving all three units are needed to embed social phenomena properly into the world as described by evolutionary theory. Whether Alexander's claims are true or false, they express the sorts of decisions that must be made in order to describe human behaviors so as to reveal their evolutionary import. Evaluation of a particular sociobiological explanation has or lacks critical force according to how accurately it captures the role that explanation plays in promoting completeness. That role is created by the set of explanatory commitments the explanation gains as a result of the way the explanation is laden with a theory, a research program, and a conceptual framework. This result argues strongly in favor of the three-unit model.

## Unjustified Domain Restrictions

Once social behavior has been described in terms making it accessible to evolutionary theory, it has to be reclassified to ensure continuity from the old domain to the new augmented domain. The old domain and new domain are restructured to maintain a unified total domain. Alexander's (1987), chapter two, makes claims that function to structure the domain of human morality as it explains how societies with moral rules might have evolved and as it classifies the kinds of morally significant behaviors in the terms provided by his theory of lifetimes, a theory of the organismic life cycle. The explanation and classification in turn provide background for conceptual, rather than empirical, arguments for the resulting explanations. Conceptual arguments supply reasons to think that abandonment of explanations guided by the coevolutionary research program would arbitrarily restrict the domain of evolutionary biology.

There can be good reasons for choosing a radically challenging or revolutionary research program independently of that program's production of theoretical and factual discoveries (Kleiner 1985). The generation of explanations affiliated with novel research programs can be justified independently of evidential success. Such reasons apply to the embedding phase (independently of the projection phase) of explanation construction and validation. Judgement that an explanation is acceptable—the best among rivals—presupposes the legitimacy of the kind of explanation of which it is an instance. The research program presupposed in the explanation helps make it the kind of explanation it is. It is a short step to realize that defense of the superiority of an explanatory program should precede its use in arguments to the best explanation among rivals.

Kleiner's example, the emergence of the Darwin-Wallace research program in opposition to Lyell's for explaining the origin of species, has two sorts of important implications. It is useful for seeing that sociobiology is not just a completion of the Modern Synthesis, but also a completion of the Darwinian revolution. And it shows how programs in sociobiology can be rationally supported by direct arguments. Research programs can be supported indirectly by attention to the theories that articulate them and the facts that provide evidence for the theories, or directly, by conceptual arguments, some of which focus on domain specification. Argument that an explanation is acceptable involves empirical elements, i.e., arguments that its factual and theoretical claims are true, and conceptual elements, i.e., arguments that it offers a kind of explanation superior to its rivals. One can rationally support the superiority of a given kind to rival kinds by referring to desirable features of that kind: factual, methodological, conceptual, and epistemic coherence (Kleiner 1985). Let us attend to the general form of the conceptual arguments found in Kleiner's example, so that we may later construct logically similar arguments about sociobiology.

Our explanatory schemes should be substantively (factually) coherent. Lyell's research program of natural theology viewed all life as ordered according to God's plan of creation. The scheme explains one kind of phenomena with radically different claims, making it factually incoherent:

> In sum, Darwin's reflections indicate that the natural theological programme offers mutually incoherent hypotheses. On one hand certain fossils and biogeographical phenomena can be explained by natural causes, respectively migration and fossilisation of remains of dead organisms. Yet the same kind of phenomena are, in other circum-

stances, explained differently, namely by a supernatural hypothesis involving the placement of organisms in certain locales and the supernatural creation of fossils." (Kleiner 1985, 377)

Our explanatory schemes should be methodologically coherent. Lyell's explanatory scheme postulated natural causes for the extinction of species, whereas it postulated supernatural causes for the origin of species. On one hand, the extinction of species is explainable by causes acting now, causes that are knowable, causes knowable through their effects. On the other hand, the origin of species is explainable by causes not acting now, causes unknowable, or if knowable, knowable by something other than ordinary human observation, experiment, and inference (i.e., authority of the Bible, revelation, faith). This scheme is methodologically incoherent since it explains the time, location, and form of species extinctions with radically different methods than the time, location, and form of species origins.

Our explanatory schemes should be conceptually coherent. Lyell's scheme strongly contrasted species with varieties within a given species. Once classified as a "variety" or a "species," it distinguishes permanent varieties from transitory species only by differences of degree in internal variation. To account for selective breeding of domesticated animals, it is thought conceptually possible for one variety to transform into another as a result of the accumulation of heritable variations. To maintain belief in the eternity of species, it is deemed conceptually impossible for one species to transform into another as a result of the accumulation of heritable variations. This scheme is conceptually incoherent since it treats the same item both as a slight difference in degree and a radical difference in kind.

Our explanatory schemes should make distinctions that are epistemically coherent. Yet the points at which Lyell divided phenomena into those mutable or immutable, those caused naturally or supernaturally, and those whose causes are knowable or unknowable, are given no defensible reason. Such arbitrary divisions in specifying the domain render Lyell's program less preferable than a rival program on which different basic divisions are well argued. Since explanations have a unifying character, the fewer the basic divisions of phenomena in specifying the domain, the more desirable the explanatory program and the higher the preferability of its explanations.

Consider how these criteria might apply to sociobiology. Alexander's chapter two (1987) explains morally relevant behavioral in-

teractions and social organization in terms of conflicts and confluences of interests.

> So we are provided with the general hypothesis that tendencies to-
> ward moral behavior, and the establishment of moral systems, are
> vehicles for promoting the goals of society as a whole: that they devel-
> op because all of the individuals of society often share the same goals;
> that, ultimately, these goals involve competition with and defense
> against other human groups; that, except in times of severe external
> threats recognized by everyone as requiring extreme cooperativeness,
> the ideal of universal indiscriminate beneficence is not met within
> groups; that the ideal morality has never even been approached be-
> tween societies or nations; and that, because some degree of within-
> society competition probably occurs nearly all of the time, every indi-
> vidual may be expected to use the impetus toward realizing the goals
> of everyone to his own advantage by promoting a slightly greater
> degree of "morality" in his neighbor than in himself . . ." (Alexander
> 1987, 104)

There are good and bad criticisms that focus on the details of
such explanations. Consider the common, underlying presumption
that there must be something wrong with the details since it is
wrong to expand the evolutionary domain to include morality, which
is "uniquely human." In our terms, this generic criticism simply
assumes that the rival strategy of domain specification, the strategy
of domain restriction, is the only proper strategy for attaining completeness. The criticism is reminiscent of Kuhn's insight that arguments over research programs ("paradigms") are circular since the
disputants argue from their own approach for their own approach
and against the rival approach. The criticism takes various forms:
(a) extreme version: once cultural evolution began, all human social
behaviors are explainable by social science and hence no human
social behavior is explainable in terms of biological evolution; (b)
moderate version: expansion in principle is legitimate for some specific features of human sociality (e.g., reproductive behavior) but not
others (e.g., morality). The grounds for rebuttal are that either version presupposes an epistemically incoherent division in domain
between evolutionary biology and social science. That is, the generic
criticism reasons from one or another arbitrary restriction on domain. We will show that Alexander's explanation here is constructed
in such a way as to try to anticipate and escape the generic criticism.
We will also show that the Kuhnian circularity here does not beg the
question in the logical sense of assuming what must be proven since

the generic form of criticism is given a variety of independently arguable contents: the objections from adequate explanation, from human uniqueness, from culture, from complexity, from biological needs, from meanings, from parsimony, and from origins.

*The Objection from Adequate Explanation.* A standard demand is that particular events be adequately explained if we are to accept any expansion of the evolutionary domain beyond the fact that we do behave in such a way that we survive and reproduce. The obvious rebuttal is that the phenomenon explained here is not the sum total of actual morally relevant individual behaviors in all their particularity (which involves projection), but how it is possible for the kind of behavior involved in morality to evolve (which involves embedding). How is it possible for moral tendencies of individuals and for societies bound by moral rules to evolve, since selection seems to make impossible the existence of rules and behaviors promoting the greatest good for the greatest number? Alexander's explanation gives part of an answer based on inclusive-fitness theory. Social reciprocity should evolve when, on average, donated benefits yield less fitness costs to the donor than returned benefits yield fitness benefits to the donor. Fitness benefits and costs apply to reproductive effects due to cooperation or conflict based on perceptions of wealth, power, and rank.

*The Objection from Human Uniqueness.* A standard challenge is that humans are so unique among species that their sociality must be explained by social science, not sociobiology. In what way are they "so unique"? Critics often cite the fact that humans respond cooperatively and competitively to others in their group, a social context which must be treated by social science alone. In response, Alexander's theory explains why we live in groups at all. It extends the list of the main kinds of selective forces in nature from nonsocial forces alone (climate, weather, food shortages, predators, parasites, diseases, mate shortages) to include social forces (competition and cooperation, whether between-group or within-group). The difference between human and nonhuman sociality in this regard is that only in humans are organisms of the same species the most potent selective force! The same causes of group living operative in other species, such as cooperation against predators or external threat, also operate in the evolution of human group living. The criticism from uniqueness is factually incoherent in explaining the same kind of (evolutionary) phenomenon—behavior influenced by social forces—one way in animals, another in humans.

*The Objection from Culture.* It is often objected that only humans have culture and the cognitive and moral capacities that underlie culture. Critics think that culturally influenced social behavior must be explained by social science alone; biological methods are blind to matters of human mind and culture. In response, whereas earlier proposals viewed culture as a device for tracking changes in the natural environment, the previous explanations motivate the view of culture-and-personality as a device for tracking changes in the social environment: "special attributes of the human psyche (form) a system for prediction and manipulation of the future—especially the social future—when the main actors will be other humans" (Alexander 1987, 78). To ask "Which came first, human psychological capacities or human social organization?" is a chicken-or-the-egg question. A postulated end (conflicts and confluences of reproductive interest among individuals), a postulated selective pressure (the fact that we are our own most hostile force of nature), and a postulated proximate mechanism (direct and indirect reciprocity) combine to form key explanatory factors for the origin of cognitive capacities involved in morally relevant behavior (self-awareness, consciousness, purpose, conscience, rules enacting restraints on methods of seeking self-interests). Criticism from cognition is methodologically incoherent in explaining the same kind of phenomenon—the development of bodies and brains that track environmental changes to achieve reproductive goals—according to different methods in animals and humans.

   *The Objection from Complexity.* Another challenge is that human sociality is far more complex than animal sociality, and that its complexity makes it different in kind, so that it must be explained only by social science. In response, Alexander extends the standard sociological concept of reciprocity in conjunction with his theory of lifetimes to classify human behavior as selfish or altruistic in evolutionary terms. Since human interests are reproductive interests, providing they are described on an evolutionary time scale, and since natural selection is the chief guiding force of evolutionary change, the only behaviors having large effects on reproduction expected to evolve in normal circumstances are genotypically selfish, whether phenotypically selfish or altruistic. Here, the theory of altruism is at work, guided by the assumption that when individual interests and group interests coincide, the only level of selection that need be postulated is individual selection.

   Explanations of human behavior integrate ultimate causes (division of effort aimed at genetic success) and proximate causes (mechanisms by which this effort is directed at genetic success). The challenge from complexity ignores the fact that reproductive effort of any type may occur through the proximate mechanism of reciprocity, whether direct (the return for the investment goes directly from the recipient to the donor) or indirect (the return for the investment either goes to the donor from someone other than the recipient or goes to someone other than the donor). Explanation of morality encompasses the diversity of social behaviors via a classification of the kinds of reproductive effort according to various proximate mechanisms into sixteen "atoms of sociality" that may be genotypically selfish, whether or not they are phenotypically selfish or altruistic (Alexander 1987, 83). The explanation encompasses diversity in morally relevant behaviors via a classification of the interaction of motivations and outcomes in determining whether the behavior is theoretically expected to be judged moral or immoral (Alexander 1987, 98–99). Criticism from complexity is methodologically incoherent since it would explain the same phenomenon—proximate causes—through different methods of study in animals and humans.

The Objection from Nongenetic Behavior. Typically, critics oppose sociobiology because of its genetic orientation. For example, Bleier (1984, 41) attacks sociobiology, that is, Wilsonian sociobiology:

> . . . the fundamental scientific issue is the role of genes and biology in determining characteristics and behaviors. This is an issue of central importance for the validity of Sociobiology, since this theory asserts that our behaviors and social relationships, our culture itself, have evolved through natural selection involving gene transmission of behavioral "traits". An opposed view is that our behaviors and culture represent evolutionary adaptations that have been transmitted through teaching and learning; that what has evolved biologically and culturally is the brain and its increasing capacity for innovation and learning; that culture has its own nongenetic evolutionary history.

Alexander's explanation of the evolution of morality includes social transmission and genetic transmission. In the sense of Mayr's view of the Modern Synthesis, Alexander's approach reconciles the view attributed to sociobiology with the view alleged to oppose it. Instead of asserting that our behaviors, social relationships, and cultures evolve by natural selection, it proposes that all three are influenced by what has evolved by natural selection. It does not envisage significant amounts of genetic variation correlated to variation in behaviors, social relationships, and cultures. It allows for their transmission through teaching and learning but maintains that we use our behaviors, social relationships, and cultures to maximize our reproductive success as far as possible given local conditions. It allows that what has evolved biologically and culturally is the brain and its increasing capacity for innovation and learning but maintains that the nongenetic evolutionary history of culture reflects the way we use our brain to instantiate strategies of fitness maximization. It insists that we employ both the fitness maximization strategies given by the legacy of our genetic evolutionary past as governed by natural selection and as well as new fitness maximization strategies appropriate to our cultural way of life. Criticism from the independence of behavior from natural selection on genes is conceptually incoherent since it opposes basic conceptions of social phenomena and evolutionary processes that should be synthesized.

*The Objection from Biological Needs.* A common preconception is that human social behavior is not undertaken to meet biological needs but contains its own rationale, and hence is explainable only by social science. Alexander uses his classification scheme to extend what are rightly counted as biological needs far beyond the usual list. On the theory of lifetimes, every behavior of an organism is categorized as somatic effort or reproductive effort, with the latter dividing into mating effort, parental effort, and extraparental effort. All behaviors of human organisms so classified are candidates for explanation by evolutionary theory. The idea that biology explains nothing more than the fact that we have to eat, drink, urinate and defecate, seek shelter, and avoid danger illicitly restricts behaviors which fulfill biological needs to those of direct somatic effort.

There is also indirect (socially mediated) somatic effort. It may operate via direct reciprocity (purchases of goods to be used by oneself to fulfill bodily nonreproductive needs involving exchange of resources between buyer and seller). It may also operate via indirect reciprocity (cooperation with relatives or nonrelatives involving returns that fulfill bodily needs, where the social investment come from someone other than the recipient or else goes to someone other than the original investor). Reproductive effort of any type may occur through the mechanism of direct nepotism (the return from social behavior of the investor accrues to a relative of the original investor through the investor's own assistance) or through indirect nepotism (the return for social behavior accrues to the investor's relative through third parties). Criticism from biological needs is conceptually incoherent since it explains the same phenomenon— biological needs—differently in humans than in animals.

*The Objection From Meanings.* A widespread preconception is that human behavior involves meanings, not genes. The presumed absence of genes for specific human behavior is interpreted as freeing behavioral differences from proximate mechanisms that count as biological causes. We attribute meanings to the acts of ourselves and others, meanings having "no biological basis." However, "indirect reciprocity involves reputation and status, and results in everyone in a social group continually being assessed and reassessed by interactants, past and potential, on the basis of their interactions with others" (Alexander 1987, 85). True, these assessments involve meanings and acts of attributing one meaning rather another are not the products of genetic programming. We conceptualize what we do in three ways: (a) in ignoring our subjective reasons, intentions, and meanings, we discuss 'behavior'; (b) in including the agent's subjective reasons, we discuss 'action'; and (c) in including how it is intended to look to others and how others interpret it, we discuss 'acts' (Reynolds 1980, xxiii, xxiv). Reproductive effort via indirect reciprocity spans any behavior, action, or act bearing cause-effect relations to survival and/or reproduction. This is so, no matter what the complexity of indirect reciprocity as a proximate mechanism and regardless of the character of the psychological and social interactions involved. Criticism from 'meaning-not-genes' is conceptually incoherent in conceiving biology—the study of organisms—so narrowly that it includes animals at the price of excluding humans.

*The Objection From Parsimony.* Many criticisms can be given a principled basis in Newton's Rule of Reasoning I, namely, admit no more causes than are true and sufficient to account for the phenomena, together with Newton's Rule of Reasoning II, namely, as far as possible assign only the same causes to the same effects. Such criticisms take the sorts of causes treated by social science to be true and sufficient to account for the phenomena. It is a short step to think that evolutionary explanations of human sociality must be wrong or unnecessary in principle. However, the contrast between proximate and ultimate levels of description reveals that it is false to presume that the phenomena explained in social science proper and human sociobiology are identical. The very act of regarding a behavior as an effect, in the context of a given science, subsumes that behavior under the theoretical orientation of the science. So the objection from causal principles is conceptually incoherent when it ignores theory-laden description.

To capture the difference in explananda, various phrases are helpful: "they explain different behaviors," "they explain the same behaviors differently conceived," "they explain different aspects of the same behavior," or "they explain on different time scales," or "they explain behaviors described in theory-neutral terms, but do so only indirectly, directly explaining only behaviors described in theory-laden terms."

*The Objection from Origins.* A presumption of the general public is that humans, like other primates, evolved biologically, but once culture originated and cultural transmission of information became crucial for the transmission of variation from generation to generation, human behavior was transformed, thereafter lying outside the domain of evolutionary biology. It may be acknowledged that rudimentary forms of some human behaviors originated in biological evolution, but it is insisted that those behaviors are not now maintained by natural selection. In response, the distinction between two effects of natural selection, the sorting or accumulation of genetics units that lead to different phenotypic effects in different environments is pertinent here. It is arbitrary to hold that the gene-and-learning complexes that predispose behavior in the ways oriented by prior evolution suddenly cease to function just because mind and culture appeared on the scene. Their functions may be transformed, just as the results of the activity of the reptilian brain are transformed by the development of the (paleo- and neo-) mammalian brain. To discover the exact character of the transformation is the immensely difficult task to be solved in making human sociobiology an established science.

To sum up, efforts to extend sociobiology's domain are usually subjected to criticisms that drive a wedge between human behavioral variation and evolutionary processes. Variations in human behavior are said to be peculiarly "social," "environmental," "socially complex," "nongenetic," "not concerned with biological needs," "due to cognitive or moral capacities," and so forth. Such criticisms generally infer from facts about the proximate causal origin of human behavioral variation to its exclusion from the domain of evolutionary biology. Such criticisms fail to take proper account of inclusive-fitness theory's roots in Mayr's two-step model of evolution, on which the developmental origin of variation occurs independently of the later sorting among that variation by natural selection. To cite a new source of variation in humans does not exclude the operation of natural selection. However, if the transmission of that variation is nongenetic, the behavioral variation might escape explanation by the theory of the Modern Synthesis. That is why nongenetic modes of transmission are now explicitly taken into account by the new gene-culture theories. Behavioral variation transmitted socially rather than genetically does not exclude the operation of natural selection in a more subtle way. The usual objections are theoretically uninformed, objecting to a caricature of the explanatory theory.

Rhindos (1985) created quite a stir in anthropology by suggesting that "the mode of transmission of cultural characteristics ("the inheritance of acquired traits") is irrelevant to the applicability of a selectionist model for evolutionary change." He goes on to argue that the symbolic aspects of culture form the sort of undirected, heritable variation Darwinist selectionism requires. Although he takes himself to work outside sociobiology, his theory that "the capacity for a nongenetic determination of specific cultural acts was probably one of the causes of the evolution of the genetic capacity for culture itself" counts as a gene-culture theory. Its rivalry to the others qualifies it as sociobiological, or as belonging to the interface where disciplinary affiliation does not matter.

When comparing innovative, nontraditional theories in human sociobiology and other fields, disciplinary lines are blurred or routinely crossed. Such events make it unrealistic, unimportant, and misleading to demand strict demarcations between human sociobiology, evolutionary anthropology, or evolutionary psychology. The dichotomy inherent in the presumption that all human social behaviors are explainable in social science and hence no human social behavior is explainable by human sociobiology is itself vexed.

We have seen how Alexander's work is designed to meet the usual objections against human sociobiology, which is not to say that it does not succumb to more sophisticated objections. Given the challenge-response model of development, it makes significant progress. It takes on one of the most severe challenges to the completeness of evolutionary theory as developed on the strategy of domain extension, namely, human morality. It utilizes a number of procedures for expanding the domain while extending the theory so as to retain basic evolutionary commitments, procedures whose conceptualization is implicit in the resultant explanations. The extension is constructed in such a way that it responds with prima facie success to the usual challenges to any such extension.

Criteria for a well-articulated sociobiological explanation have been shown to include the following: (1) clear indication of its role in embedding and/or projection, (2) clear affiliation with a strategy of domain specification, (3) clear indication of the way its explanandum is described, classified, and conceptualized so that it is evolutionarily significant, and (4) clear presentation of commitments that guide a natural response to objections. In addition, we can argue about whether such moves are proper moves to take and use these as criteria for acceptable explanations.

## 4.3 Biological Determinism and Human Nature

### Domain Expansion and Limitation

Domain specification procedures are needed not only to construct justifiable expansions of the evolutionary domain, but also to create justifiable limits on the newly expanded domain. There is no once-and-for-all, informative, all-purpose, definitive delimitation of human sociobiology's domain. To describe its domain as "human social behavior" is as vague as it is true. For example, sociobiology has been defined as "the systematic study of the biological basis of all social behavior" (Wilson 1975, 2). Again, the sociobiology of moral systems has been defined as the study of "everything about the life and natural history of moral systems, as seen through the eyes of a biologist" (Alexander 1987, title page).

Such definitions mislead by implying that sociobiology reduces to a field, which ignores its theories, research programs, and conceptual frameworks. One reading of such definitions is maximally expansive: human sociobiology's domain includes all facets of all human behaviors that involve sociality. This reading legislates by fiat that there is nothing about human sociality which is not biologically explainable. Another reading is maximally restrictive: since human sociality has no biological basis or contains no biological phenomena, human sociobiology's domain is empty. With such ambiguity, preconceptions wreak havoc, feeding the metascientific debate over total world views. If the domain is empty, the field does not exist. If the domain includes everything, then it is hard to see why human sociobiology would not be committed to a panbiological cosmology.

Instead, we have seen that one can argue about the explanandum directly; all the domain decisions previously identified can be subjected to critical scrutiny. The truth lies in between the extremes of explaining nothing versus everything about human sociality. Judgements about the upper bounds of exclusion and lower bounds of inclusion are undecidable except with recourse to a purpose that orients selection of the domain, a scientific purpose. We recommend the following orientation: What is the smallest possible domain within the domain of all human social phenomena needed to achieve completeness? This way of stating the issue is grounded in a counterpart to Newton's Rule of Reasoning I, namely, admit no more effects than are needed to be explained in order for the theory to be complete within its scope. 'Complete within its own scope' is a very different idea from that of complete, which suggests 'complete within an unlimited scope'.

Advocates of human sociobiology typically explain new phenomena without stating the limits to what can be explained or to what can be illuminated by such explanations. That omission plays into the hands of extremists who make evolutionary biology a total world view. Critics typically point out weaknesses of the new explanations without stating what new explananda are potentially explainable. They play into the hands of extremists who deny that anything about human sociality has evolutionary significance. Advocates and critics are then logically forced to debate about what sociobiology can do for total world views, for human nature, or for other disciplines—items external to sociobiology as a science. We should be debating about what counts as evolutionarily significant variation in human sociality—items internal to sociobiology as a science. If we insist on debating the utility of sociobiology for enhancing or distorting total world views, human nature, or other disciplines, then we should do so only upon taking into account sociobiology's own limited domain within which it strives to be complete.

There are precedents. Dispute over evolutionary significance was crucial for the emergence of modern evolutionary genetics (Van Balen 1987, 437):

> The Mendelian research program should be seen as a continuation of Bateson's own program, which he presented in his Materials for the Study of Variations (1894). Here Bateson, quite explicitly, formulated several constraints ("limitations") on the study of variation, heredity and evolution. The most important constraint concerned the size of the variations: "The first limitation thus introduced concerns the magnitude of Variations" (Bateson 1894, p.18). Bateson's aim in starting the program in the first place was to give support to his conviction that only large variations or "sports" were evolutionarily significant. These variations could be constitutive of new species and were stable enough to avoid the swamping effect of blending inheritance. The second constraint formulated by Bateson was a corollary of the first one: being large, evolutionarily relevant variations had to be discontinuous too.

Van Balen goes on to show how factual discoveries that led to increasing support for the chromosomal theory of heredity eventually led to the rejection of these constraints. Although the chromosomal theory was initially used to articulate the Mendelian program, the theory led to discoveries involving small discontinuous variations, a tension resolved by changing the programmatic constraints. Conceptual innovations used to make sense of these discoveries removed obstacles to understanding the genetic causation of continuous variations. By reconciling the discontinuity on the level of the hereditary factors (genotype) with continuity on the level of inherited properties (phenotype), a foundation was laid for the ensuing Modern Synthesis of the Mendelian theory of heredity and the Darwinian theory of evolution. Conceptual arguments about what counts as evolutionarily significant variations in humans may likewise help induce a New Synthesis.

Decisions about what variations would count as evolutionarily significant are smuggled as preconceptions into the battle over total world views in the sociobiology debate. For example, critics make what is considered to be an important distinction between biological potential and biological determinism. They hold that biology gives us a potential to behave the way we do but does not determine our behavior. And they charge that sociobiology is a form of biological determinism, which is supposed to be factually false and politically dangerous. Let us examine whether this distinction holds up to scrutiny in the light of gene-culture theories.

"Humans are animals, and everything we do is constrained, in some sense, by our biology" (Gould 1981, 328). In what sense is all human sociality biologically explainable? In going on to cite only those constraints involving our morphology (narrow range of adult size among species), physiology (we do not photosynthesize but instead eat meat and plants), ecology (we live in the gravitational world of large organisms), and development (we age and die), Gould conspicuously omits social behavior. The omission implies that human sociality cannot be explained directly in evolutionary terms, only indirectly in terms of nonsocial evolutionary constraints. In effect, this citation of constraints follows the strategy of domain restriction without justifying it. That strategy needs to be justified, not assumed, as is evident from the rebuttals to other attempts at line drawing we surveyed. The coevolutionary program makes rival conceptual commitments. It rejects Gould's identification of "biology" with "the results of our genetic construction" as overly restrictive. It implies that appeal to social directly explainable explananda is implicated in explanations of nonsocial directly explainable explananda. For example, to explain the evolution of concealed ovulation and enlarged breasts in hominid females, Alexander cites the behavioral selective advantage females gain from deceiving males about ovulatory status and nutritional reserve (see Barkow 1989c, 340).

Rival criteria for deciding what is evolutionarily significant about human sociality typically reflect such rival preconceptions. Let us examine criteria involving genes. Critics often equate "biological" with "genetic." Without clarification, that idea would make somatic mutations in nonhuman organisms nonbiological just because they are not inherited. It would make the sex of social insects like bees nonbiological. Which larvae become males or females is triggered by the food given them, an environmental as opposed to genetic sex-determination mechanism. Let us see whether "genetic" works as a criterion for domain demarcation when it is elaborated.

A persistent move is to use specificity as a criterion of evolutionary significance: no specific behavior has evolutionary significance since human genes do not code for specific behaviors.

> In one sense, the debate between sociobiologists and their critics is an argument about the breadth of ranges. For sociobiologists, ranges are narrow enough to program a specific behavior as the predictable result of possessing certain genes. Critics argue that the ranges permitted by these genetic factors are wide enough to include all behaviors that sociobiologists atomize into distinct traits coded by separate genes. (Gould 1980, 329)

On the coevolutionary program, explanations do not require that human behavioral variation explained directly correlates with genetic variation. For example, natural selection ideally eliminates all but the fittest gene-trait complex. Ideal natural selection leaves lots of phenotypic variation uncorrelated with genetic variation, a situation the coevolutionary program posits to be common. The presence of social behavioral variation not corresponding to genetic variation is compatible both with ideally strong selection and with no operative selection at all, making testing difficult. Sociobiology is not unique here. The fossil record does not supply the data about gene frequencies needed to test population-genetics theory either.

Let the term 'trait' be general enough to encompass phenotypes, behaviors, proximate psychological or physiological mechanisms leading to behaviors, or other behavioral preconditions. Evolutionists distinguish between (A) whether a particular behavioral variant characterizes a particular genotypic variant—an "innate" trait such that gene 1 correlates with trait 1, gene 2 correlates with trait 2, and so forth in a given environment; and (B) whether a particular set of behaviors characterizes a particular genotypic variant—"learned" traits such that gene 1 correlates with traits 1, 2, 3 and gene 2 correlates with traits 4, 5, 6, and so forth in a given environment (Alexander 1979b, 66). Current theory can handle more subtle distinctions in gene-environment-trait relationships.

Both sorts of traits have evolutionary significance, according to traditional theory. Selection sorts between the average social effects of gene 1 and gene 2 in both cases. Variants of type (B) ranges of genetic influence envisaged by sociobiologists are compatible with the specificity criterion. Most rival gene-culture theories based on a complex psychology that mediates between genes and behavior envisage wide ranges of genetic influence. Many critics just criticize, using unsubstantiated assumptions about gene-environment-trait relationships of their own. They do not go on to do the research that tells us what the genetic basis of human sociality is. Such criticisms are poor criticisms on two grounds: they do not advance research and they beg the question.

Many gene-culture researchers find it absurd to think that there is just one gene for culture. Instead, a capacity for culture itself requires many cognitive skills, with many underlying genes related in indirect, complex ways to these skills. The question arises of how narrow are the ranges of influence of these genes:

> If ranges are narrow, then genes do code for specific traits and natural selection can create and maintain individual items of behavior separately. If ranges are characteristically broad, then selection may set some deeply recessed generating rules; but specific behaviors are epiphenomena of the rules, not objects of Darwinian attention in their own right. I believe that human sociobiologists have made a fundamental mistake in categories. They are seeking the genetic basis of human behavior at the wrong level. They are searching among the specific products of generating rules—Joe's homosexuality, Martha's fear of strangers—while the rules themselves are the genetic deep structure of human behavior. (Gould 1981, 329)

Again, talk of "deeply recessed generating rules" is compatible with gene-culture theories involving a complex psychology. They don't try to explain Joe's homosexuality or Martha's fear of strangers as direct effects of genetic rules. Those are caricatures of what is hypothesized to be evolutionarily significant explananda. What counts as "deeply recessed" anyway? Many advocates and critics alike accept some picture of a hierarchical organization of rules, with the lowest levels generating extremely variable specific behaviors and the highest levels generating extremely fixed general behaviors or behavioral goals (Wenegrat 1984, Barkow 1989c).

In these and other ways too poorly thought out to mention, initial debate on what is "biological" has exhibited all-or-none thinking, vague criteria of evolutionary significance, discipline bashing and glorification, and psychologically manipulative sloganeering. All this is symptomatic of our ignorance of what role genes really have in human social behavior. The debate evolved to focus on issues of domain expansion and limitation behind the rhetoric: rule structure, identification of rules specific to various preconditions of behavior, genetic and environmental determinants of the rules, and criteria such as universality and evolutionary stability for distinguishing environmentally and genetically transmitted strategic rules.

Even so, some gene-culture theories have tried to remain within the essential conceptual paradigm of the Modern Synthesis where possible.

> Material, ecologic, and historical forces produce cultural possibilities, which are then selectively retained by individuals pursuing genetically determined personal motives appropriate to their environment (see Alexander, 1979a; Durham, 1979). All new cultural features, according to this view, are eventually screened for concordance with evolved social motives. Thus, cultural evolution may be driven by processes that are Lamarkian, nongenetic, and reversible (Medawar, 1976), but it is nonetheless constrained by Darwinian, genetic, and irreversibly established individual preferences. (Wenegrat 1984, 24–25)

Wenegrat's statement makes explicit the way coevolutionary theory satisfies Mayr's "two-step" model of natural selection as involving the origin of variation independent of its possible selective value. Culturally produced variations count as the undirected variations (in Rhindos's 1985 sense) of the first stage, which in turn are filtered through the selective criteria inherited from our evolutionary past at the second stage.

Human sociobiology, as in Mendelian genetics, seems to be changing programmatic constraints on what counts as evolutionarily significant variation. Critics have their preferred history: human sociobiology first tried to explain specific behaviors that are universal among all humans, necessarily part of human nature, and fixed by genes; then, under the influence of criticism, it gave up such biological determinism, adopting Gould's counterthesis of biological potential. Yet this may be just another case where critics first regard radically new views as "absurd," then "reasonable but wrong," then "true and we knew it all along." Advocates have their preferred history: human sociobiology has all along tried to explain human behaviors similar in evolutionary significance to those explained in animals, leaving precise hypotheses about fitness, selection, adaptation, genes, evolution, and culture open as rival theories and programs develop. Yet this may be just another case where advocates reinterpret previous claims too loosely in order to make it seem that they were never wrong. Historians will have to decide whether such ideas as specificity and universality have changed their status as criteria for domain limitation.

## Transcending Biological Determinism

Biological determinism makes biology the key to human nature, thereby merging with panbiologism. Explanations interpreted according to biological determinism yield a picture of human nature dominated by biology. They do not yield the minimum picture of human nature required for attaining completeness. It is important to transcend the typical interpretation of explanations in human sociobiology as biological determinist explanations while sharing the repugnance of the critics at the biologization of human nature. The classic Sociobiology Study Group (hereafter SSG) article, "Sociobiology—A New Biological Determinism" (SSG, 1978a—a revised form of their 1976), will be used as an example (Lewontin is a primary author of these articles). Consider just the first paragraph in detail, on the supposition that if a line-by-line analysis shows it to be full of sleights of hand, then an analysis of the whole article would be even more damaging (see Wilson 1976; Ruse 1979).

> Biological determinism attempts to show that the present states of human societies are the result of biological forces and the biological 'nature' of the human species. Deterministic theories differ in detail, but all have a similar form. They begin by describing the particular model of society that corresponds to the author's socioeconomic prejudices. It is then asserted that the characteristics of that society are a necessary consequence of the biological nature of the human species.

> Therefore, present human social arrangements are either unchange-
> able or, when altered, will demand continued conscious social control
> because the changed conditions will be "unnatural".

Consider the SSG's first sentence. Given the article title, the audience reads this definition with the thought that sociobiology is
biological determinism. If so, the structure of explanation would be
this: the explanatory factors are biological forces and the biological
nature of the species and the explained phenomena are all states of
human societies. But the structure of explanation aimed at completeness, following Hempel, is not timeless: the explanatory factors
are forces guiding evolutionary change and past states of human
societies (including local cultural conditions and complex psychology) and the explained phenomena are subsequent states of human
societies (including present states) insofar as they involve cause-
effect relations to survival and reproduction. Biological determinism,
but not human sociobiology aimed at completeness, requires an unchanging set of traits that constitute human nature (including traits
we would like to change, hence the political danger). Because the two
structures of explanation are radically different, a human sociobiology aimed at completeness transcends biological determinism.

This sentence also sweeps under the rug the crucial issue of
whether determinism is meant in an exclusionary or compatibilistic
sense. A truism of science is that causal explanation embodies determinism in the sense of presupposing that no events are uncaused.
Physical determinism states that all physical events have physical
causes. Biological determinism states that all biological events have
biological causes. Evolutionary determinism states that all evolutionary events have evolutionary causes. If human sociality involves
events that have evolutionary significance, then those events have
evolutionary causes. If the first sentence read, "Evolutionary determinism attempts to show that the present states of human societies
which have evolutionary significance are the result of evolutionary
forces and the past evolutionary states of human societies," no one
should be against it. This innocuous form of determinism is implicit
in a completed evolutionary theory. It is compatible with the causal
and lawful explanation of human sociality in the physical, biological,
and social sciences to which we are accustomed.

By ignoring the procedures of description, conceptualization,
classification, expansion, and limitation, the actual sentence delivers a different implication. Rather than giving the impression that
sociobiology, like any science, engages in causal explanation, it gives

the impression that sociobiology recognizes no causes other than biological causes. This impression is explicitly stated in the preface to the Sociobiology Study Group's book (1978a). It states that "biological determinism attempts to explain much of the present human condition as a natural outgrowth of biological phenomena. Human nature is explained solely in terms of Darwinian evolution, gene expression, hormonal reality, or other purely biological processes." In this sense, biological determinism and biological reductionism come to the same conclusion (Lewontin, Rose, and Kamin 1985). To cite how biological causes condition human sociality would be to exclude the causes invoked in the social sciences. Human sociobiology would destroy the social sciences as we know them, replacing them with biology. No wonder readers think that sociobiology is dangerous and should be resisted. Exclusionary determinism is undermined by sociobiology aimed at completeness, in principle because it ignores the embedding procedures needed to attain completeness, and in practice because gene-culture programs combine explanatory variables found in the biological and the social sciences.

"Deterministic theories differ in detail, but all have a similar form" (SSG 1978b). There is a difference between whether we are thinking about the determination of specific behaviors of individuals by genes and environment or the determination of the course of evolution by evolutionary processes. Evolutionary explanations explain the course of evolution, a course that is independently given. There are all sorts of ways to conceptualize causality—in terms of necessary and/or sufficient conditions, natural necessity, constant conjunction, triggering versus standing causes, predisposing versus determining causes, etc. Such differences are crucial to make precise what "biological determinism" means. By lumping all sorts of different views under the label of biological determinism, readers who already have gene-phobia (fear that genes are super-causes that overwhelm the effects of other causes) and identify "our biology" with "our genetic makeup" become wary of human sociobiology. The SSG accuses sociobiology of misdescribing human behavior by using categories formerly applied to animal behavior. They do the very thing they criticize, namely, use overly general categories to ignore crucial distinctions.

"They begin by describing the particular model of society that corresponds to the author's socioeconomic prejudices (SSG 1978b)." Any causal explanation must begin with a description of the phenomena to be explained. The SSG load the idea emotionally by talking about "prejudices." Since the word "prejudice" connotes a claim that is false and politically dangerous, readers get the impression that human sociobiology is false and politically dangerous. An entirely different impression would have been created by saying that human sociobiology begins with "an objective description of society."

Since all descriptions in a new science begin under the influence of views common in the society of the practitioners, it is perverse to infer a lack of objectivity from the fact that descriptions of society involve socioeconomic preconceptions. To note that each person's assertions, including that of scientists, have certain causes in no way casts doubt on the truth of those assertions. The SSG's reasoning has socioeconomic causes and adopts a certain model of society. Lewontin's commitment to a Marxist conception of society and its notion of false consciousness is at work in their view of sociobiology as a social weapon for the status quo. By parity of reasoning, if the reasoning in human sociobiology is not objective because ideologically caused, neither is their own. This result illustrates the futility of confusing justification and causation, a familiar point. The critical attitude inherent in the quest for completeness could never support biological determinism, which merely rationalizes the status quo. As controlled by the critical attitude, it regards all aspects of explanations as subject to criticism, including inputs from and outputs to society.

"It is then asserted that the characteristics of that society are a necessary consequence of the biological nature of the human species" (SSG 1978b). In any causal explanation the phenomena explained are given the status of effects of the explanatory factors. By saying that the features explained are a "necessary consequence," the SSG ignores the character of the explanatory factors and the modality of the explained phenomena. On Hempel's model of an ideal explanation, the explananda are deduced from premises about explanatory factors. The kind of consequence involved is a logical inference, that is, a relation between sentences. The idea that human sociality is a necessary consequence of the nature of the species mistakes logical inference for a mysterious relation in nature. It makes present states of human societies seem mysteriously created by the order of nature. That sort of necessity is irrelevant to attempts to satisfy the sound-argument model of explanation, involving a necessary relation between conclusion and premises.

"Therefore, present human social arrangements are either unchangeable or, when altered, will demand continued conscious social control because the changed conditions will be "unnatural" (SSG

1978b). What justifies the SSG in inferring this conclusion from the preceding premises? They don't say, using "therefore" to mask the need for argument. Since they give no reason, we don't know why they didn't draw some other conclusion. The hidden premises to get a logical deduction here would capture two views of human nature, namely, "If something is part of human nature, it is unchangeable" and "If something is part of human nature and changed, it would revert back to its original form without continued conscious social control." The SSG never tries to show that any part of the view it labels "biological determinism" makes sense or is plausible since their point is that biological determinism is based on false claims and shoddy concepts. Strangely, they use the very patterns of thought they find intellectually and politically despicable to critique it.

This method of critique itself puts sociobiology on the defensive. Biological determinism so conceived is not something any scientist would want to endorse. So all sociobiologists can do is to deny that their explanations are biological determinist. This method removes the focus from the truth or falsity of reasonable claims about causation or human nature, the subject of serious debate. Instead, it focuses on whether scientists are guilty of an intellectual crime. The bottom line, in even seemingly nonpolitical criticisms about evidence (e.g., adaptationism), is the behavior of scientists and its public power. Here we see that the method is designed for evaluating the ideological status of explanatory acts and reports of explanatory acts, not the scientific status of the explanations.

The bad political implications attributed to sociobiology by the SSG follow from the SSG's concept of human nature, not that of even the popularizers. Wilson (1976, 295) used "human nature" as a mere label for "the most widespread, distinctive qualities of human behavior," which is consistent with the falsity of biological determinism in the sense of SSG. Barash (1979, 242) said that "if sociobiology has any validity, our human nature will doubtless change, just as it has changed during our evolutionary history so far." His pattern of explanation is to treat as universal the general fitness-enhancing character of behavior itself, not specific behaviors as presupposed in the charge (Barash 1982, 152). Alexander (1987, 8–9) denies that "biology will be principally useful in locating a core of "basic" or essentially unalterable behaviors that will tell us how far we realistically can go in adjusting human social behavior." He asserts instead that "biological information (is), rather, a means of altering human social behavior—of rerouting it so as to avoid such things as devastating wars or pathological conditions that develop because of faulty self-images."

The SSG's (1978b) answer is that these theorists merely "dissociate themselves from the consequences of their arguments." This answer is unpersuasive because the theorists' arguments don't have the consequences found in biological determinism, since their arguments deny the premises needed to generate those consequences. The charge has stuck because the method of accusation makes it unfalsifiable. The SSG presents no way of testing claims about sociobiology's social function; what would count as a good argument against the charge? Heaven only knows. Experience has shown that no sort of reply is ever deemed adequate, but is always treated as a cover-up for the biological determinism overlaid as an interpretation amenable to any content. By positing that sociobiologists' intentions are irrelevant to sociobiology's social function, whatever they say against biological determinism and whatever meaning they give their explanations become irrelevant.

Of course sociobiology risks explaining behavioral evolution with concepts and claims that merely project ideas of our society. Of course our starting points are provincial and not sufficiently general for identifying animal-human similarities and differences in ways that fit naive ideals of objectivity divorced from social context. Such risks are inherent in any evolutionary biology of behavior, any primatology, any anthropology, and so on. It happens all the time in all these fields. The ideologies that we dispute are the ones we can subject to critical control. So these facts do not uniquely disqualify sociobiology, provided that it subjects its ideological inputs and outputs to critical control, contrary to the impression given.

The logic of a criticism often has a scope that outruns its specific target; by using the "by parity of reasoning" mode of rebuttal, we often find that the criticism proves too much to be damaging. Since these facts don't justify abandoning other fields, by parity of reasoning, they don't justify abandoning sociobiology. Its critical attitude disciplines those starting points of which we can become aware, e.g., the idea that men gain more from increasing offspring number via multiple mates and women gain more from giving more parental care to fewer offspring. The SSG's views of on such matters project its own social ideas no less than the views of the sociobiologists. Since such a projection does not disqualify its own views, it does not disqualify the views of the sociobiologists, if they adopt a critically self-reflective methodology for evaluating their own views.

## Varieties of Biological Determinism

There are principled reasons for thinking that explanations promoting biological determinism do not promote completeness, and conversely. Embedding procedures reveal what makes human sociality possible without thereby endowing the phenomena explained with a politically pernicious necessity. To show this, we need to distinguish various kinds of explanation involving necessity that came to the surface in analyzing the SSG's conception of biological determinism, using male/female differences as an example.

These include: (1) cosmological explanation (sociobiology shows that male/female differences belong to institutions which mirror the order of nature); (2) ideological explanation (sociobiology shows male/female differences in past, present, and future societies to be justified); (3) fatalist explanation (sociobiology shows male/female differences to be fated or predetermined); (4) essentialist explanation (sociobiology shows male-female differences to belong to the essence of being a human organism); (5) determinist explanation (sociobiology shows male-female differences to be causally or lawfully necessary).

Cosmological explanation requires that the explanans contains claims about the order of nature as a whole and the role of male-female differences among organisms in the order of nature. The explanatory relation is a correspondence between the institutional order and the natural order: the institutional order inheres in the natural order. Such an explanation reveals that the social order is what it is because it is part of the natural order. The necessity involved a necessity due to identity, i.e., a part is necessarily part of the whole by which it is identified as a part.

Cosmological explanation does not promote completeness because it fails to recognize the theory-laden nature of explanation. Acceptable scientific explanations explain the facts, not in any old form, but in a form permitted by the underlying theory. Hence, the phrase "social order" is equivocal.

Suppose "the social order" means "the order inherent in facts after they are rephrased in the language of evolutionary theory," i.e., theory-laden facts. Then what would it mean to assert that "the human social order reflects the order of nature"? Nothing. By substitution of equivalent terms, it reads "the social order, insofar as it is conceptualized in the terms of natural science, reflects the order of nature, insofar as it is conceptualized in the terms of natural science."

Suppose "the social order" means "the order inherent in facts as known by common sense and potentially studied by both natural and social science," i.e., theory-neutral facts. By hypothesis, these theory-neutral facts are facts that remain unordered in a relevant theoretical way. Hence, they do not constitute an order of nature, which is a theoretical order.

Finally, if it means "the order inherent in facts as conceptualized by social science," then these theory-laden facts are not facts explained by evolutionary theory at all since the systems of description, classification, expansion, and limitation used in social science and in evolutionary biology are radically different.

The root fallacy lies in misreading the phrase "present institutions arise from the natural order of things" as if it is about facts expressed in the same form to common sense, explained by biological science, and explained by social science. It is a short step to arrive at the politically conservative conclusion that the present social order is biologically inevitable.

Ideological explanation requires that the explanans contains sentences about what should or should not be the case as well as what is, was, and/or will be the case. Otherwise, the fallacy of inferring "ought" from "is" (norm from fact) would hold; we could never in the same breath explain and justify human male/female differences without some normative content to the explanans. The normative content associated with the facts then justifies the normative judgement inherent in the ideology. The norms are typically morally relevant, as in ideologies about social oppression. Since moral norms are norms of obligation, they involve a sense of "must," and hence necessity.

Ideological explanation does not promote completeness because we cannot derive normative judgements from the facts of nature unless we have first imposed normative judgements on the facts of nature. Now, this very project is outside the scope of explanation in natural science. There is no way the methods of natural science can be used to study norms so as to determine the truth values of normative judgements. Causal explanations of male/female differences are justified by reasons indicating the truth of the causal claims. An ideology integrates fact and norm, as in the classic definition as "an integrated set of assertions, theories, and aims which constitute a sociopolitical program." Ideological explanation combines factual claims with norms to justify human practice, i.e., it justifies our own efforts to think and act in certain ways.

When an ideological explanation uses causal facts from sociobiology, the scientific explanation in sociobiology does not justify the ideological explanation, but is merely incorporated into it. Of course the particular judgements scientists make are ideologically influenced. To realize this presupposes that scientific and ideological explanations are to be distinguished conceptually. Otherwise, we would have self-causation, i.e., to say "scientific explanations are ideologically influenced" would be to say "ideological explanations are ideologically influenced," which is absurd.

From time immemorial, each society combines cosmological and ideological explanations in order to legitimate itself (Rifkin 1983, 35). We are born into a society in which the social order is experienced as a "given." But how do the members of a society know that the way that they go about their daily routine is the right way and that the "given" order is the right one? Of course a society's view of what the whole world is about is heavily influenced by the way it organizes itself and its environment—its immediate world. Since that's all we have to go on, we are justified in making inductive inferences (here the problem of induction arises). So the culture's members conclude that the economic, political, and social reality they experience are not just real for them, but indicate a greater reality.

It is only a short step to fashioning a model of nature that is strikingly similar to the world being fashioned by the society. Not surprisingly, people "find out" that their behavior does correspond to the order of nature and for that reason regard their existing social order as legitimate. This is an inherently conservative way of thought. The obvious corollary is that to resist, violate, or try to change the existing social order is to challenge the natural order, which is self-defeating.

Cosmological and ideological explanations are not intrinsic to sociobiology, but arise as extrascientific interpretations of its explanations, i.e., independent of their scientific status. Yet we can make sense of the charge that sociobiological explanations of male-female differences support status-quo sexism. Just apply Rifkin's interpretation to each explanation, disregarding its scientific status. The result legitimates the social relations explained. It's so easy. It's too easy to be intellectually stimulating. People do it anyway. We're not surprised.

Fatalist explanation requires that the explanans contains assertions about a universal plan that comprehends the past, present, and future and subsumes male/female differences. The plan may be generated by a personal being, as in the idea that God generates the world according to his divine plan, or an impersonal process, and may or may not be teleological. Natural selection has taken the place of God in explaining the marvelous variety of adaptation in nature, and so can serve where God has served before to generate a fatalistic view of the human condition. Again, fate or destiny involves the modality of necessity; given the universal plan, whatever is within its scope occurs necessarily if it occurs at all.

Fatalist explanation does not promote completeness because it fails to recognize that a universal or statistical regularity by itself provides no explanation of particular events or patterns. On the sound-argument model, logically general statements about relations between variables together with logically singular statements about initial conditions or boundary conditions, and auxiliary assumptions are needed to explain facts expressed in singular statements. Evolutionary theory must capture the actual historical trajectory of appropriate environments, genes, developmental pathways, and so forth in order to use its general theories to explain particular events or patterns of events. Whether this historical trajectory is part of a universal plan is not relevant to fulfilling the model.

Because embedding procedures do not require extensive identification of particular conditions, sociobiological explanations are mistaken for immediate explanations of particulars by invoking generalizations about male-female differences. The result is a mythic explanation of why males and females behave differently from generalizations, say, about how males and females would maximize their fitness, which falsely makes current behaviors seem destined. But the ahistorical stance of fatalism would hinder satisfaction of the condition of derivability found in the sound-argument model, an adequacy condition crucial to the attainment of a completed evolutionary theory.

Cosmological, ideological, and fatalist explanation are often combined in the presumption that what is genetic is somehow fixed, unchangeable, and beyond our control. An unconscious slide from the fact that we are not in a technological position to change the human genome in ways where we can control the outcomes for social behavior makes it falsely seem that whatever is genetically caused is genetically destined (Midgely 1978). The result is fear that we cannot exercise free will to change behaviors under genetic control or are not morally responsible for social injustices involving traits under genetic control. This result in turn induces worries over the costs of "fooling Mother Nature" or by challenging the inequalities, domination, and oppression witnessed in the current social order. In these and other views of human nature, the moral and factual realms coincide. Given the ultimate political dream of legitimizing the present social order without taking responsibility for doing so, we sanctify our way of life with a concept of nature in which natural laws must be obeyed lest we destroy our relationship with nature and harm ourselves or disappear. But such hopes and worries are fallacious extrapolations from facts about what is under our control in a technological sense to a metaphysical necessity.

Essentialist explanation requires that the explanans contains premises about what counts as the nature of humans in general, about what is essential to being human. The explanatory relation is one connecting the nature of humans in general to the traits involved in human male-female differences. Aristotle's essentialism regarded natural kinds as essential properties in the sense that they constitute part of the identity conditions of individuals. So essential properties involve the necessity of identity, e.g., each thing is necessarily identical with itself. Popularized versions often consider it impossible or horribly detrimental to "try to be something you are not." The moral and factual realms converge in the warning that to try to eliminate the male-female differences of sexist societies is the self-defeating attempt to deny one's own nature.

Essentialist explanation does not promote completeness because to confirm such an explanation we must confirm claims about human nature in general. But claims about human nature in general are not scientific claims. They either bypass the procedures of science altogether, as when they bypass domain specification procedures, or they are philosophical claims in which the fundamental lessons of all fields of inquiry and all types of human experience are related. Since claims made in sociobiology that have no bearing on human nature may qualify as acceptable scientific explanations, acceptability is independent of essentialist explanation. Advocates and critics simply legislate by fiat or subterfuge that certain biological facts are or are not part of human nature, form the core or the periphery of human nature, are essential or accidental to being human, and so forth. Arguments are needed for and against such claims. But the distinctions, claims, and arguments involved are not scientific in character (recall several pertinent points made in chapters 1 and 2). The debate over human nature in this science is not really interested in science, but exploits science in its interest in something else.

There is a legitimate desire to show that explanations of human male/female differences contribute to our understanding of human organisms. But nothing is gained in the self-congratulatory attitude of amplifying "our understanding of human organisms" to read "our understanding of the nature of human organisms." This attitude, together with unexamined inferences from "reveals the nature of the human organism" to "reveals human nature" or to "reveals the true nature of people," yields nothing worthwhile. Scientific methods alone could never justify the needed conceptual connections between 'the human organism', 'human nature', and 'the human person'. The impression Wilson, Barash, Alexander generate is that sociobiology functions as our intellectual savior and will tell us the most profound truths about who we are. Such bold claims are neither legitimate science nor legitimate philosophy, but so much entertainment and advertising. The desire to show that sociobiology serves a need, namely, to tell us something significant about ourselves we did not know before, is best served in a different way.

We should distinguish views about humans adequate for sociobiological research alone, judged in terms of whether they promote the aim of completeness, from the views about humans adequate for integrating such intradisciplinary perspectives into a multidisciplinary perspective. There is no reason why sociobiology is the only discipline to tell us about human nature. If numerous disciplines were assigned that task, and the limitations of their special conceptual frameworks were ignored, no unified picture of human nature could emerge without incommensurability, contradiction, irrelevance, or some lack of coherence. The fact that every discipline has actually produced pictures of human nature that we cannot seem to put together in a satisfying way, try as we may, is testimony to this fact. Each partial perspective must be modified to transcend the embedding decisions that both enable and limit its intradisciplinary use. Those spouting views which assert or deny that some feature is inherent in human nature normally have neither the conceptual skills nor the inclination to do the tremendous amount of conceptual work to fashion even a plausible integrated account.

Sociobiology, as an attempt to extend the Modern Syntheses, is committed to a conception of 'the human organism' which provides no support for the idea that social arrangements are manifestations of the inner or intrinsic nature of human beings and are therefore unchangeable or only changeable at a cost. Consider just three of many reasons. One reason is its conception of the nature of a species; the human species is not defined typologically in terms of a typical type or an essence definable by a list of necessary and sufficient conditions. The human species is defined as an interbreeding, reproductively isolated local population of organisms that exhibits congeries of varying traits, either eventually transforming into another species or going extinct. (The species concept is still much debated.)

Another reason is its conception of the nature of an individual organism. The individual organism is not defined in terms of an inner genetic constitution that gives it innate capacities or natural tendencies to be acted on by accidental environmental factors. Instead the roles of genotype and environment in producing developed phenotype are ontologically on a par and as yet epistemologically inextricable. Since the effects of a genotype are conceptualized via its norm of reaction, a table of correspondences for that genotype between an array of developmental environments and developmental outcomes, there is no particular phenotype which is more "natural" or "typical" or "innate" than any other phenotype.

A final reason lies in the fact that any limits to how social arrangements are modifiable would have to be determined empirically. We would have to breed large numbers of genetically identical individuals, place them in a relevant array of social and individual environments, and study the resulting variation in phenotypes. Since doing so would be technologically infeasible and morally unthinkable, empirical limits to change among genetically based traits cannot be foretold with any assurance. Moreover, in principle any phenotype is open to change to an arbitrarily large degree by either changing the environments or the genotypes. So there is no general logical or empirical relation between the plasticity of a social trait and the presence or absence of genetic differences among individuals.

Determinist explanation requires that the explanans contains claims about the causes or laws governing processes of evolutionary change as well as claims about antecedent conditions relevant to the operation of these causes or laws. Given the antecedent conditions, social behaviors are explained as necessary outcomes of these causes or laws. The modality of necessity here is supposed to be either a necessary connection between cause and effect or a necessary connection of elements in a lawful relation. The two sorts of necessity coincide in the case of causal laws. The necessary connection between antecedent conditions (the cause) and male-female differences (the effect) is guaranteed by the lawful necessity that connects the kinds instantiated in the antecedent conditions with the kinds instantiated in male-female differences.

Determinist explanation requires that past evolutionary events bring about current evolutionary events as a matter of natural necessity. Determinist and fatalist explanation verge on one another in Laplace's conception of a single universal mathematical formula embracing the structure of all events. Given the values of all variables for the state of the universe at any one time, the values of all state variables of the universe at all times present, past, and future are also completely determined. One difference is that determinist explanation requires an antecedent condition to generate the explanation of a particular under a universal plan, whereas fatalist explanation yields explanation from the universal scheme alone.

Fatalism is unsupported by the consequence laws of population genetics models, which make essential reference to antecedent conditions to specify trajectories of populational change as joint effects of heredity, selection, immigration, migration, genetic drift, and meiotic drive. Determinism is unsupported by the character of the relevant causal laws themselves. A given evolutionary change is never necessitated but only probabilistic in two ways. First, ecological source laws render it a product of many independent causal chains creating actual outcomes that are accidental, relative to any single source of fitness difference. There is no single set of formulas that combine all factors creating fitness costs and benefits into a single scheme. Fitness can be specified for traits and suites of traits, but there is no general formula for computing the fitness of any particular organism.

Second, even though population genetic consequence laws provide a single scheme for uniting the effects of all causes of evolutionary change, both the ecological laws stating the source of fitness differences and the population genetic laws stating the consequences of fitness differences are probabilistic laws. To say that a certain mating strategy optimizes fitness is to say that it gives its bearers the best chance of reproductive success. To say that selection caused a certain mating strategy to spread throughout the evolving population is to say that the prevalence of the trait is a probable consequence of the interaction of the forces of evolutionary change. Hence, evolutionary theory provides probabilistic connections among events rather than the necessary connections required for determinist explanation.

The political danger in interpreting sociobiological explanations according to cosmological, fatalist, essentialist, and determinist explanation is the result that the specific behaviors explained are thereby made to seem universal and inevitable. Applicability of evolutionary theory to all organisms consists in process continuity, not a continuity of specific traits, and so does not have this political danger. Those who regard animal sociobiology as legitimate but regard human sociobiology as illegitimate because they find faults in animal-human comparisons have not faced the following problem. If we could not show that our social behaviors have a process continuity with those of other species, we would have no basis for regarding evolutionary processes as applicable to all species.

What is the minimum amount of similarity between (nonhuman) animals and humans needed to include humans in the domain of evolutionary explanation? Our behaviors have facets which can be subsumed under the same processes that subsume the behaviors of all other species. This answer does not mean that our behaviors don't have facets which can be subsumed under other processes as well. Anthropomorphism, the tendency to describe human and animal behaviors in the same terms regardless of whether we are doing the same thing, results from a failure to distinguish process continuity (how evolutionary change occurs) from product continuity (particular features of each species). Logically, it would be sufficient for completeness that no human behavior is describable in the same terms as animal behavior except for those terms which characterize the way behaviors are "produced" by evolutionary processes. That is, completeness requires no more similarity between animals and humans than that needed to subsume facts about their respective behaviors under the concepts of survival and reproduction and under principles which govern processes involving survival and reproduction. Scientific knowledge is, first and foremost, process knowledge.

In conclusion, assessments of sociobiology are unjustifiable when they fail to examine the implications of a completed evolutionary theory for relations between fields of knowledge and for human nature. Real underlying issues in method involve decisions about behavioral description, conceptualization, classification, expansion, and limitation of the domain of evolutionary theory. The public is suspicious of sociobiology due to a misplaced biophobia, where finding out that something we do is "biological" induces fear that we are stuck with it whether we like it or not. The public misinterprets the meaning of sociobiological explanations according to the modality of necessity found in cosmological, ideological, fatalist, essentialist, or determinist interpretations. Explanatory completeness is served by causal or lawful explanations that show what makes human sociality possible and actual, as chapter 5 will demonstrate.

# CHAPTER
# 5

## DISCIPLINE CONCEPTUALIZATION

## 5.1 Ideals of Evolutionary Explanation

### Explanatory Resources and Kinds of Explanation

In our metalogical definition of completeness (1.2), we emphasized that the observational language used to express the facts of the explanandum is actually contained in a theoretical system used to supply the explanatory factors. Upon emphasizing that the formulation of the facts to be explained is laden by that theoretical system, we identified numerous procedures whereby theories, programs, and frameworks guide the formulation of an observation language designed to be adequate for the expression of evolutionarily significant social facts concerning the morality of monogamy (4.2). Given this result, it is reasonable to assume that the theoretical resources and the general kinds of theoretical explanation found in evolutionary biology also guide judgements of which social facts are evolutionarily significant.

The effective design of our explanations is guided by an understanding of the way science explains. We have said that science typically explains by embedding the actual into the possible and projecting the actual from the possible (4.1). Sociobiology both embeds the social facts to be explained in a theoretical system of possible evolutionary scenarios and projects those social facts as the only actualized rival evolutionary scenario. More than a modicum of conceptual skill is needed in jointly using both embedding procedures and projection procedures to fashion an explanation whose explanandum and explanans maximally cohere.

Chapter 4 addressed the question "How should we formulate the explanandum so that it is well-articulated?" It examined embedding procedures for conceptualizing the phenomena to be explained that handle matters of explanatory scope and modality. They refine domain specification by regulating how to formulate the explanandum of an explanation, extending and reformulating social data so that it is relevant to the theory. This chapter addresses the question "How should we properly formulate the explanans so that it is well-articulated?" This chapter examines projection procedures for conceptualizing the factors doing the explaining that speak to matters of explanatory resources and kinds. They refine specification of relative roles of relevant subfields of evolutionary biology by regulating how to identify and formulate the explanans of an explanation, extending and reformulating evolutionary theory's internal structure so that it is consistent with social data. The joint attainment of relevance and consistency yield the sort of synthesis found in an evolutionary biology complete with respect to the class of evolutionarily significant social facts.

A completed evolutionary biology of sociality would explain only those aspects of sociality that are evolutionarily significant (recall 4.3). Further, it would explain all evolutionarily significant aspects of sociality. Decisions about what constitute the totality of evolutionarily significant aspects of sociality are theoryladen, laden by the kinds of theoretical resources and kinds of theoretical explanation used in explaining evolutionary facts. To identify projection procedures, note that each explanation implicitly contains a choice of particular resources among all available resources used as explanatory factors and instantiates a kind of explanation among all the general kinds of explanation found in science.

Suppose that we can formulate social facts as explananda so as to uphold arguments that social behaviors in all species are effects of causal processes on the course of evolution. The next task is to explain why social behaviors in all species actualize the evolutionary possibilities they do rather than theoretically alternative possibilities. That task requires a clear concept of what counts as the range of possibilities, which is given by relations among explanatory factors. So one projection procedure is a resource-choice procedure, a procedure for choosing which explanatory resources are being invoked to do the explaining. The conceptualization of an explanation's explanans reflects a choice of explanatory resources among those that would combine to yield a full explanation of all those aspects of the phenomenon being explained.

Evolutionary explanation uses the main kind of explanation found in science, namely, causal explanation (1.2, 4.3). To understand what is involved in projecting actual social situations from theoretically possible evolutionary scenarios (with the help of empirical facts), we need to understand how all the general kinds of scientific explanation involved in evolutionary explanation relate to its causal character. So another projection procedure is a resource-kind procedure, a procedure for choosing which kind of explanation is being invoked to do the explaining. The conceptualization of an explanation's explanans reflects a choice of kinds of explanation among those that would combine to yield a full explanation of all those aspects of the phenomenon being explained.

Because the explanatory resources and kinds of explanation vary among the subfields of evolutionary biology, an understanding of disciplinary structure is paramount for an informed use of these two projection procedures. Individual explanations, then, each bear some relation to a conception of the totality of explanatory resources and the totality of kinds of explanation found in an ideally full explanation of all the aspects of an evolutionarily significant social phenomenon. We need to understand how the character of the explanatory information found in the subfields would be combined in an ideal evolutionary explanation. In this way we arrive at the notion of an ideal of evolutionary explanation. The procedures of explanatory resource specification and explanatory kind specification used to formulate an explanation's explanans impose on it some relation to an ideal of the general outlines of a total evolutionary explanation. This ideal acts as a regulative norm for governing our conception of what an evolutionary biology that is explanatorily complete with respect to sociality would be like.

To generate ideals of completed evolutionary explanation, there are several ideal specification procedures. First, we specify the general kinds of explanation that each play a role in an ideal total evolutionary explanation of sociality in all species. Second, we specify the essential theoretical variables and resources that play a role in an ideal total evolutionary explanation. Third, we specify the various ways of combining those resources as found in our best theories and research programs. Fourth, we specify the manner in which this constellation of resources is used to successfully handle various problems of explanatory incompleteness posed by various explananda among the ideal set of explananda. Thus, the findings about research-guiding controls related to theories (chapter 1), research programs (chapter 2), problems (chapter 3), and domain (chapter 4) are all to be combined in fully elaborating our regulative ideal.

To fully elaborate this ideal is beyond the scope of the present project. Rather, the point is to show that some such ideal is implicated in practice. Sections 5.2 and 5.3 will address the first of these ideal specification procedures. They identify some issues involved in clarifying relations among the general kinds of explanation found in evolutionary explanation. In so doing, it is argued that there are more kinds than are generally recognized: transitional, compositional, developmental, variational, functional, and normative explanations.

We will now address the second of these ideal specification procedures, using Wilson's seminal (1975) *Sociobiology* as an example. We will uncover an explanatory ideal of essential theoretical resources. It will be argued that, in effect, this ideal expressed Wilson's conception at that time of the main components of a total evolutionary explanation found in a completed evolutionary biology with respect to sociality. Such ideals make the aim of explanatory completeness concrete, providing another avenue by which completeness regulates the specifics of theoretical research.

## An Ideal of Sociobiological Explanation

It is no accident that Wilson wrote his *Sociobiology* in three parts: part 1 on processes of social evolution, part 2 on social mechanisms, and part 3 on the social species. Wilson organized the field of sociobiology in a way that reflects the basic structure of explanation in evolutionary biology. Evolutionary explanations ideally explain (a) past and present distributions of characters in local populations of organisms of various species in terms of (b) the effects of evolutionary processes, given (c) relevant parameters, (d) on mechanisms for survival and/or reproduction operative in the course of the evolutionary past. It is this structure which enabled Wilson to achieve his main task in *Sociobiology*, namely, to "codify sociobiology into a branch of evolutionary biology and particularly of modern population biology," that is, into "the Modern Synthesis" (1975, 4).

In explanatory research, decisions are made about the information in each of these categories. Which characters? Which populations? Which evolutionary processes? Which parameters? Which mechanisms? Each explanation reflects such resource choice decisions, but the procedures for making justifiable choices are not yet well understood. Wilson's figure 1–1 (1975, 5) describes connections between phylogenetic studies, ecology, and sociobiology so as to answer these questions. It specifies the information found in category

(a) of the explanandum and categories (b), (c), and (d) of the explanans. It specifies how (a) the particular behavior patterns we observe today in local populations of social species are to be explained in terms of (b) the effects of interacting evolutionary processes, given (c) parameters of evolution, ecology, behavior, and population, on the (d) course of social mechanisms in the evolutionary past.

The behavior patterns include: group size, age composition, mode of organization, forms of communication, division of labor, time and energy budgets of groups and members. The social species include: colonial invertebrates, social insects, coldblooded vertebrates, birds, mammals in general, nonhuman primates, and humans. The interacting evolutionary processes include: natural selection, mutation, recombination, genetic drift, migration, immigration, and reproductive isolation. The parameters include: ancestral properties (studied in phylogenetic biology), environmental factors and fluctuations (studied in ecology), character development and modifiability (studied in developmental biology), as well as individual birth and death schedules, equilibrial population densities, gene flow between populations, and coefficients of genetic relationship (studied in population biology). The social mechanisms include: group size adjustment, environmental tracking, communication, aggression, cooperation and competition, social spacing and territoriality, dominance systems, social roles and castes, mating and parenting.

This specification of an ideal total explanation functions to put into proper perspective the research choice of explanatory work. For example, it reveals the place of social mechanisms of mating and parenting, the example of sociobiological explanation examined here, in the total scheme of sociobiological research. It provides a scheme into which various particular explanations in sociobiology are to be fitted in order to see their specific explanatory role in eliminating manifest explanatory incompleteness. Only by reference to the completeness of evolutionary theory does the significance of Wilson's detailed ideal come into focus. We will substantiate this point with three arguments: the argument from field formation, the argument from disciplinary identity, and the argument from evaluation.

The argument from field formation asserts that assumptions about the completeness of evolutionary explanation are at work in the formation of sociobiology as a new field. Suppose, contrary to Wilson's vision, that the particular behavior patterns we observe today in populations of the social species cannot be explained, even in principle, in terms of the effects of interacting evolutionary processes on the course of evolutionary history in social mechanisms, given parameters of evolution, ecology, behavior, and population. What would that mean for the adequacy of evolutionary theory? Evolutionary theory would be incomplete in the sense of being false, if it produced wrong explanatory answers to legitimate explanatory questions, or incomplete in the sense of being inapplicable, if it provided none at all. Before the advent of sociobiology in the sense of the work systematized by Wilson, evolutionary theory was radically incomplete because it lacked the explanatory resources to handle the evolution of social behaviors. As committed evolutionists, how should we respond to this situation?

A strategy of domain restriction applied to the evolution of all social behavior in all species, and not just cultural organisms, is out of the question since social mechanisms and particular behavior patterns do enter into cause-effect relations with survival and reproduction. If the addition of new explanatory resources and modification of the existing ones always gave the wrong explanatory answers, then our present evolutionary theory would be false. Our critical attitude demands that we find out if it is false on any extension, as asserted by a strategy of domain transformation applied to all sociality, or just in need of the right extension, as asserted by a strategy of domain extension applied to all sociality (recall 4.1).

This research situation produces a challenge to which the formation of sociobiology is the obvious response, expressed in terms of the challenge-response model of development. The challenge is to develop evolutionary theory and social data to the point that the data will no longer seem irrelevant to or inconsistent with the theory. Hence, a subfield of evolutionary biology must be created in order to meet the challenge to uphold completeness and decide whether the theory is true or false. Call that subfield "sociobiology." In this way one sees that the concept of completeness is the research-guiding aim behind the construction of Wilson's ideal.

The argument from disciplinary identity asserts that Wilson's ideal is the product of a resource specification procedure that enters into the conception of what is and what is not sociobiology. There is a chicken-or-the-egg relation between the priority of completeness and disciplinary identity. Since lack of completeness is why sociobiology exists at all, completeness seems to hold relative priority. Since an established field already had to exist in order for completeness to have any motivating force, disciplinary identity has priority. Completeness requires integration of fields including ethological, populational, ecological, genetical, and developmental biology. Why not incorporate further and further fields? Why not include the social sciences? After all, sociobiology and the social sciences enter into relations by which they share resources.

For instance, the use of optimal design models for studying adaptive significance historically derived from optimization theory in economics. An organism that acted as if it were a rational decision maker for maximizing its evolutionary genetic self-interest would forage for food and find mates efficiently, maximizing fitness benefits and minimizing fitness costs. And anthropology has much to teach sociobiology about methods for the objective description of human culture, so that it develops a discipline which prevents it from merely reading the attitudes of our culture into nature. The criterion for including some fields and ruling out others is that no resource of a field need be integrated into sociobiology unless it is pertinent for understanding explanatory variables in categories (b), (c), (d), or other categories found in an ideal of evolutionary explanation. The explanatory ideal controls the conception of the disciplinary "synthesis."

The idea of completeness makes a difference to the way Wilson's ideal is interpreted in relation to the social sciences. Wilson (1975, 4) provoked much opposition in interpreting this ideal with the words:

> It may not be too much to say that sociology and the other social sciences, as well as the humanities, are the last branches of biology waiting to be included in the Modern Synthesis. One of the functions of sociobiology, then, is to reformulate the foundations of the social sciences in a way that draws these subjects into the Modern Synthesis. Whether the social sciences can be truly biologicized in this fashion remains to be seen.

Recall our previous arguments against this sort of reductionism. We distinguished a sociobiology aimed at completeness within its own intended domain, which is not reductionist, from a sociobiology aimed at covering everything about sociality, which is reductionist (2.3). We insisted that its own intended domain is limited to evolutionary aspects of sociality and showed that its conceptual apparatus is limited in applicability to these aspects, which is not reductionist (4.2, 4.3). So whereas Wilson sees sociobiological theory reformulating the foundations of social scientific theory, we see sociobiology and social science each as sciences with unpredictably shifting conceptual frameworks. The presumption of both reductionism and antireductionism that a completed social science either would or would not be reducible to a completed evolutionary biology violates the natural ontological and methodological attitude. Such "isms" are externally imposed onto science and are unnecessary, unwarranted, and in the end, probably incoherent (1.4).

At present there obviously is no such reduction. But since conceptual frameworks shift in unpredictable ways, we cannot isolate an essence of social science known once-and-for-all either to be autonomous in relation to sociobiology or to be reducible to sociobiology. This attitude does not rule out a mutual exchange of resources. The borrowing of optimality models from economics has occurred and has benefited sociobiological research. But optimality models have been reconceptualized in the process (see the end of 5.3). Given this reconceptualization, there is no reason to think that optimization in economics is theoretically founded on optimization in sociobiology. In general, such resources have to be reconceptualized in order to be integrated into each discipline's conceptual frameworks so as to be made applicable to each discipline's own special explanatory domain.

The argument from evaluation asserts that many criticisms of sociobiology are not good criticisms because they point out something already assumed in research, namely, that evolutionary biology is incomplete. Given the argument from formation, the formation of sociobiology involves awareness of a tremendous discrepancy between the ideal explanation of social behavior we would like to have and the actual explanations we do have. Wilson's ideal functions not only to draw connections between phylogenetic studies, ecology, and sociobiology, but also to articulate what a completed evolutionary theory would be like. It would supply a total explanation for every behavior pattern having evolutionary significance. Evolutionary theory would be complete if everything in category (a) could be derived as expected from exhaustive specifications of explanatory factors in categories (b), (c), and (d), in the sense of the sound-argument model and symmetry thesis (1.2, 1.3). Of course, no behavior pattern has yet been given a total explanation, one supplying qualitative relations between all known factors in categories (b), (c), and (d), let alone quantitative values for all variables and parameters cited as explanatory factors.

Progress toward completeness demands that the best available explanation today meets higher standards than the best available explanations yesterday (2.3). Real explanations, if not discarded, are always in the process of revision in the light of controlling explanatory ideals that themselves change. Critics often ignore this fact in charging that sociobiological explanations are unrigorous applications of evolutionary theory because they do not take into account relevant explanatory factors. The expectation of total, final, correct explanations by the public is a myth of science. The charge of lack of rigor is true, but insignificant as a criticism; it merely expresses the fact that there is a quest for completeness in sociobiology induced by discrepancies between ideally completed and actually incomplete explanations. Thus, the charge is properly directed at sociobiology's presentation, not at its substance.

Two sorts of legitimate criticism are that a sequence of revisions fails to reduce the gap between past versions and a valid explanatory ideal and that an explanatory ideal is invalid. The sociobiological literature gives the impression that most sequences of explanations of a behavior pattern either incorporate more information about a given explanatory factor, more explanatory factors, or apply a given explanatory factor to more behavior patterns than was done in the past. If so, new explanations meet higher standards for attaining completeness, and progress is being made. The mere fact that the actual explanations do not satisfy the explanatory ideal is by itself no criticism at all, but is entirely to be expected since the ideal gains a regulative function precisely by being unsatisfied. Progress comes in two ways: progress at satisfying a given ideal and progress at creating better ideals. Criticisms would best advance the issue by making clear which ideal they operate from. Commitment guides criticism and criticism guides commitment, an uneasy marriage needed to make progress.

In sum, the arguments from field formation, disciplinary identity, and evaluation show that specifications of explanatory resources are rooted in ideals of evolutionary explanation aimed at completeness. The way to clarify the conceptualization of sociobiology as a discipline is by reference to these ideals. An ideal of a total evolutionary explanation of all the evolutionarily significant aspects of sociality also includes a specification of the totality of basic units of sociality. We now move to that topic.

## The Units of Sociality

As sociobiology develops, changes in definitions of sociobiology reflect changes in views on what terms for basic units of sociality are needed to adequately express evolutionarily significant social facts. We will identify some research problems here.

Wilson initially defined sociobiology (1975, 2) as "the systematic study of the biological basis of all social behavior." He later (1980) defined sociobiology as "the systematic study of the biological basis of social behaviors and the organization of societies in all kinds of organisms." The transfer of position in the quantifier "all" both withdraws the appearance of extreme reductionist ambitions and reaffirms the quest for completeness through its implicit reference to humans as another species.

The latter definition affirms an intradisciplinary division of labor in sociobiology, with individualistic studies of behavioral interactions and holistic studies of the forms of social organization among groups. This division of labor, in turn, is easily connected to a more specific delineation of resources. Resources for studying behavioral interactions deal with mate choice, parental investment, parent/offspring relations, member/stranger tolerance, kin/nonkin favoritism, time and energy budgets of individual organisms, and so on. Resources for studying social order deal with group size, age composition, communication, division of labor, time and energy budgets of groups, gregariousness, territoriality, resource acquisition, age- and sex-specific dispersal, family or kin population structure, and so on.

These resource specifications in turn are rooted in basic theoretical resources of various types. Some of these types have been given philosophical analysis. There are concepts fundamental to evolutionary theory in general, such as epigenesis, within-group variation, between-group variation, and hierarchy (Masters; in Fetzer 1985). There are conjectures about fundamental relationships that act as guiding assumptions or play key roles in various research programs, such as phenotype-genotype relations, relations of epigenetic rules to phenotypic and genotypic variation, and relationships between culturgens and social order (Fetzer 1985). There are favored techniques or types of theoretical analysis, such as optimality models, game-theoretic analysis in terms of evolutionarily stable strategies, and inclusive-fitness analysis (Kitcher 1985). There are essential general methods that assume various forms, such as the comparative method and the experimental method (Barash 1982). There are foundational orientations about the ways in which genes, organisms, and groups enter into processes of evolutionary change, as reflected in disputes over the units and levels of selection and adaptation and evolution (Sober 1984).

In addition, we need to recognize basic general conceptions of the units of sociality adopted as the basic terms in which we understand sociality. A completed sociobiology would conceptualize what organisms do in at least three ways—as behaviors, as actions, and as acts (4.2). Programs for reconciling genes, minds, and culture adopt various perspectives on the bearing of evolution on behavior, on action, and on acts. A completed sociobiology would not only make reference to social behavior and social organization, but also to social context.

> [The social group] functions as an environmental context within which they must survive and to which they must adapt. There are, therefore, social forces or social processes that condition the social behavior of individuals. For example, in many territorial avian species, some portion of the population—usually the weaker, subordinate individuals—is forced to peripheral, sub-optimal zones of the habitat. Here individuals suffer increased mortality while continuing to compete with breeding individuals for food and nest sites . . . (Horan 1989, 134)

This reasoning illustrates the point that there are good biological reasons for recognizing additional social units. The interaction of individuals with their social group is distinct from the dyadic, reciprocal interaction of members of the same species and distinct from social organization. Social context is an important determinant of survival and reproduction.

When a new social unit, such as social context, is differentiated from traditional categories, changes are induced in disciplinary structure as explanations are reevaluated and revised according to conceptual changes. Although Kitcher (1985) severely criticizes Barash's work, it is interesting to note that they share similar views on several issues involving basic social units. Because of the common impression that there is no common ground held by sociobiologists who popularize the field and their archcritics, let us document a few points of agreement: dominance hierarchies, relations between groups and members, mating systems.

Early popularized presentations gave the impression that power relations in various animal societies are governed by rigid dominance hierarchies. Examination of the idea of rigid dominance hierarchies has led to a more fluid conception of social roles. Kitcher (1985, 200) criticized Kummer's remarks on dominance on the grounds of vicious circularity. Dominant animals win dyadic behavioral contests because they are dominant and they are dominant

because they win the contexts. Kitcher advises "sensitive researchers" that 'dominant' be given a precise, contextually localized,
operational specification. In a similar vein, Barash notes a need for
concepts involving flexible behavior in relation to group contexts
and to identify roles in relation to situations such as group movements. "Recently, however, there has been increasing recognition
that dominance may have been overvalued as an organizing principle and that it should be replaced by the concept of social role," so
that "individuals may assume different roles for each situation
rather than be typecast into a unitary framework of dominance
ranking" (Barash 1982, 362).

Early popularized presentations also gave the impression that
because individual males are selected to be promiscuous, a polygynous mating system will evolve on the level of social organization.
Kitcher (1985, 195) undermines the implicit vulgar reductionism
here, emphasizing that "the behavior of a group of animals will not
necessarily reflect the predispositions of any of the members of the
group." That fact is implicit in Barash's (1982) distinction between
individual and group properties. Barash devoted his chapter 10 for
sexual selection involving predispositions of male and female individuals and reserved a different chapter, chapter 12, for the ecology
of social systems of groups.

Again, early popularizations gave the impression that a mating
system found in our primate ancestors is thereby shown to be "natural" for humans. But that conclusion is arbitrary, given definitional
looseness. Barash (1982, 274) classifies mating systems according to
time scale, e.g., whether a male-female bond is formed each year, for
one breeding season, or for life. On the basis of a similar classification, Kitcher (1985, 193) notes that if we use the chimpanzee as a
referential model for humans in their natural state, the existing
concepts are so loose that we could describe them as promiscuous,
polygynous, polyandrous, or monogamous at the level of social organization. One way sociobiology has advanced primatology is that we
don't have to rely on referential models since we have strategic models (Tooby and DeVore, 1987). Strategies of fitness maximization can
be stated in general theoretical terms and can be used without requiring that we are similar in specifics, specifics that vary as evolution proceeds, to our ancestors or their relatives. Kitcher uses the
point about arbitrariness to attack sociobiology for claiming that
certain sexist social arrangements are natural and biologically determined, whereas Barash uses the point to dissolve the significance
of dispute over what is "natural."

The actual designation of mating-system type is sometimes arbitrary. For example, among many small mammals the male occupies a home range or territory that overlaps that of several females (see Chapter 16). The females apparently mate with this male, but it is unclear whether a lasting bond is formed. Such a system may therefore be termed either promiscuous or simultaneously polygynous, depending on how one chooses to define the pair bond. What is important is that each species tends to show a characteristic mating system. (Barash 1982, 273)

These three points of overlap raise questions about the fairness of Kitcher's evaluation of sociobiology. What does the fact that many of the substantive, biological points Kitcher makes are found somewhere in the sociobiological literature imply about the fairness of Kitcher's critique? The more important point is that it takes time for relations among social units to be sorted out in order to keep from confusing different sorts of explanations, e.g., of individual behavior, of interactions of two or three or more individuals, of social context, of social roles, and of social organization. Particular explanations are conceptualized according to some implicit theoretical ("theory-laden") conception of the unit of sociality being explained. Such conceptions need clarification if sociobiology is to progress toward a complete explanation of all the units of sociality that bear evolutionary significance.

# External Disciplinary Relations

Instead of appealing to disciplinary ideals to clarify disciplinary structure within sociobiology and disciplinary relations between sociobiology and other disciplines, participants in the sociobiology debate seem to have some a priori conception of disciplines that are smuggled into assessments of disciplines as unargued conflicting premises. By 'a priori', it is meant that the conception of disciplinary identity is made relatively independently of the actual course and aims of research in the discipline. We argued against a priori commitments to reductionism or antireductionism in discussing Wilson's resource ideal. We will now show how this works out in evaluating particular explanations, referring to previous results.

The conceptualization of the disciplinary affiliation of particular explanations is impeded by the common presumption that disciplines have sharp or unchanging boundaries. For each social phenomenon, there are arguments that it is biological and arguments that it is not biological, as if we could know what does or does not count as biological in advance of the research development of sociobiology itself. Take, for example, the politically contentious case of rape. Barash (1979, 53–54) begins his discussion of so-called "duck rape" as follows:

> In her book *Against Our Will*, Susan Brownmiller claimed that only human beings engage in rape. The facts are otherwise. Rape is common among the birds and bees, and is epidemic among the mallard ducks. In fact, large groups of drakes sometimes descend on an unsuspecting female and rape her repeatedly, often causing death, as the victim's head may be held under water for a long period of time. What is going on here? When mallards pair up for the breeding, there often remain a number of unmated males, since there are more males than females in most such species (probably owing to the risks involved in defending eggs against predators). These bachelors have been excluded from normal reproduction, and so they engage in what is apparently the next best strategy: raping someone else's female.

Bleier, like most readers, finds such passages very offensive. This application of the term "rape" to nonhumans uses a term full of human connotations without carefully stripping them away. Barash goes on to say, "Perhaps human rapists, in their own criminally misguided way, are doing the best they can to maximize their fitness. If so, they are not that different from the sexually excluded bachelor mallards." This is a real shocker, and purposely so. With such animal-human comparisons, Barash hopes to show that sociobiology speaks to the gamut of current sociopolitical issues.

The plausibility of Barash's explanations depends on unargued preconceptions with which critics like Bleier take issue. One is whether estrus is defined so that in organisms with estrus cycles it makes no sense to say that any forced copulation of a female coming into heat occurs against her will, making rape impossible. And the assumption that it even makes sense to say that ducks have a will is quite problematic. The misapplication of a human term to nonhumans is then followed by the pseudoderivation of human rape as a special case of the same behavior found in nonhumans, namely, forced copulation. On one hand, it seems that sociobiology employs a value-laden observation language which obscures animal-human differences. On the other, we need not let anthropomorphic concepts blind us to the real phenomena seen (see Burns, Cheng, and McKinney 1980). When we look out of a dirty window, some emphasize the dirt and others the figures seen. Whatever the fate of specific issues over concepts, we don't have to use the same behavioral categories to unify the biology of nonhumans and humans (4.3). Subsuming even radically disparate behaviors under the same evolutionary processes suffices to unify the biology of nonhuman and human sociality.

In terms of completeness, what matters is not whether the behavior expressed as "rape" or "forced copulation" in ducks is similar to the behavior expressed as "rape" or "forced copulation" in humans. What matters is whether the relation of the behavior in ducks to evolutionary processes is similar to the relation of the behavior in humans to evolutionary processes. An observation language adequate to represent evolutionarily significant social facts need not use the same behavioral terms to describe humans and nonhumans. If the point is to subsume the behaviors under the same fitness maximization strategies, then only the terms for expressing and applying the fitness maximization strategies need be the same.

Another unargued preconception is whether the explanation focuses unjustifiably on some cases, the cases of apparent conformity to the adaptive hypothesis, to the exclusion of others, the cases of apparent violation of the hypothesis. Are rape of old women and children counterexamples to adaptive explanations or are both adaptive and maladaptive sexual responses to be explained by the same theory? Expectations about such matters turn on the way the explanations are based on a gene-culture program (2.4, 4.3).

The plausibility of Bleier's criticisms also depends on rival but unargued preconceptions that prejudge a number of issues. For Bleier and many readers, Barash's explanation is implausible and conceptually incoherent because "rape is cultural, not biological," "rape is violence," "ducks don't rape," and "rapists are not trying to reproduce." This response begs the question of whether the cultural character of human rape deprives it of evolutionary import, whether human rape and forced copulation among ducks are evolutionarily similar with respect to processes despite the behavioral differences, of whether the violence in human rape prevents it from being a mating strategy, and whether the intent in rape is a means for producing fitness-enhancing effects. Shields and Shields (Barkow 1989c, 366) combine feminist and sociobiological views of rape. Proximate psychological mechanisms for added conceptions involve hostility to women and assessment of their vulnerability, the sort of point Barash repeatedly made. Data supports added conception and the choice of normally sexually inaccessible women of high reproductive value. Such issues are contoured by gene-culture programs for connecting proximate mechanisms and ultimate ends (2.4, 4.2).

A general reaction is that Barash is excusing male rapists and that he is using sociobiology as a social weapon to hurt women, no matter how hard he denies it. The import of this reaction depends on additional unargued preconceptions about the relation between science and ideology. Bleier charges that explaining rape biologically defuses the political issue. This response begs the question of whether statements of evolutionary causes rationalize political preconceptions or ground political thought in more accurate facts. What we are willing to regard as social facts is shot through with politics. Since Bleier realizes that she is as much implicated as Barash, she boldly claims that she adopts better politics and does better science. In this sense, she shares the view that it is pointless to think in terms of sociobiology-as-science versus sociobiology-as-ideology since its explanations each have a scientific and an ideological status (1.3, 4.1).

An interesting issue is whether sociobiology is politically dangerous and scientifically illegitimate in ways that the social sciences are not. That depends on the particular scientific statements made in each science and on the relevant political context. To be fair, sociobiology would have to be compared to social sciences in a similar research situation and given a similar prestige by the public. However, there probably aren't any such social sciences. No social sciences enjoys the reputation as being as established as evolutionary biology and no social science is viewed by the general public as having the authority of the best natural sciences. Since sociobiology has to meet higher standards in order to be considered as established as the rest of evolutionary biology, it is less scientifically legitimate. Since sociobiology is attributed greater authority, its unsubstantiated results and visions of life are more politically dangerous. Yet even this evaluation of the scientific quality and political danger of sociobiology may be overturned by its future course of research.

Bleier charges that explaining rape biologically makes it falsely appear natural, universal, innate, inevitable, and justified. This response begs the question of whether evolutionary explanations must be given cosmological, essentialist, determinist, fatalist, or ideological meanings. Of course, Barash's denials of the political import of his explanatory acts also beg the same questions. The argument goes on and on, with neither side ever being satisfied with the other side's response. A sociobiology aimed at completeness does not carry these meanings as part of its scientific status (4.3). That normative point holds whether or not it actually carries them as part of its social, political, or ideological status. Since it continues to carry them, it is useful to expose the difference.

When people speak of "our biology" and mean "our genes," there is often more than a trival terminological point at work. It is a category mistake to treat disciplinary distinctions as having ontological significance. Dispute over whether we transcend or are constrained by "our biology" treats "our biology" as something in the world rather than being a study of life. To oppose or reconcile "biology" and "culture" incorrectly treats a field of inquiry about the world as the same in kind with something in the world. The same behavioral pattern can be studied in the physical, chemical, biological, and social sciences. Assumed boundaries about what explanatory factors are "biological" or "social" are routinely crossed in sociobiology and multidisciplinary studies. We set limits in order to both work within them and go beyond them. Disciplinary limits are transient, and intradisciplinary heterogeneity is pervasive. It is pointless to try to decide what is biological and what is cultural in any ultimate sense since any answer would need to be reevaluated whenever a novel field, theory, research program, or conceptual framework involving biology and culture is proposed.

Thus, dispute over whether human rape is "biological" versus "social" is a pseudo-issue that should be dissolved, not solved. There is no such thing as the "nature of the behavior" or the "nature of the disciplines" by which we could decide whether rape is biological or social/cultural or both. Phenomena, as they are in the experienced world, do not have preformed or natural disciplinary labels. Relations among fields are artificial and conventional, not natural kinds. Expectation of deeply revealing answers to questions about disciplinary relations is rooted in the naive realism that what exists is divided up in the same way in which we organize our thought.

How, then, can we elucidate relations between fields? One way is to clarify relations among kinds of explanans typically found in the fields being discussed. Which kinds of explanation are inherent in sociobiology's explanatory ideals and how are they related? Kourany (1987, 28) identifies and differentiates four kinds of explanation:

In a compositional explanation, the properties of objects are explained in terms of the properties of their parts. In an evolutionary explanation, the properties of objects are explained in terms of the temporal development of those objects. In a functional explanation, relatively sophisticated capacities of objects are explained in terms of the sophisticated organization of relative simple capacities of those objects or their components. And in a transitional explanation, a change of state in an object is explained in terms of a disturbance in the object and the state of the object at the time of the disturbance.

Using Kourany's (1987) classification of scientific explanations as a guide, it will be argued that various fields involved in sociobiology typically invoke various kinds of explanation. Our intuition tells us to assume that rival explanations must be of the same general kind, at least, in the absence of further analysis. Hence, explanations of sociality in social science do not rival those in sociobiology unless both explain the same aspects of sociality, as conceptualized according to procedures of domain specification, with the same general kind of explanation, as conceptualized according to procedures of kind of explanation specification. Suppose sociobiologists propose to explain items we think are explainable only by the social sciences, such as the proposed explanations of fellatio and cunnilingus among middle-class Americans that some find ridiculous in principle. The way to argue against them is to argue that there are no good grounds for thinking that the aspects of sociality allegedly explained need to be explained by the kind of explanation invoked.

Inspection of sociobiological and social scientific explanations gives the general result that they normally do not appeal to the very same kind of explanation to explain the very same thing. There may be rivals in the grey area of interdisciplinary work, but that sort of research does not permit us to clearly say what counts as sociobiology and what counts as social science, a precondition for deciding whether sociobiology reduces or rivals or unifies social science. So the usual terms of the dispute over the viability of sociobiology in terms of a presupposed rivalry between sociobiological social scientific explanations is itself vexed. We may conclude that sociobiology does not need to compete with, reduce, integrate, or synthesize the social sciences in order to achieve explanatory completeness. This conclusion is not based on an a priori distinction between disciplines, not some externally imposed a priori idea that stands over research without being grounded in research. It is based on a review of the actual explanations proposed in the course of research so far, and so expresses the natural ontological and methodological attitude. Our views of scientific disciplines and science itself are open to change as the course of scientific research changes, not to be determined independently of the course of research.

## Internal Disciplinary Structure

It has been thought that Wilson's book unifies biology. What is the evolutionary or sociobiological unification of biology properly supposed to be? Our examination of the kinds of explanation used in evolutionary explanation goes to show that sociobiology does not even synthesize biological fields. Rather, sociobiology is or requires the integration or unification of biological fields through study on an evolutionary time scale. The distinction between broad and narrow sociobiology (Kitcher 1985, 114–15) is significant in this regard. Sociobiology in the broad sense includes all the biological disciplines that can be brought to bear on sociality. Sociobiology in the narrow sense includes all the evolutionary subfields that can be brought to bear on sociality.

Narrow sociobiology, first and foremost, is a subset of broad sociobiology since evolutionary biology is one among many biological disciplines. In that sense, what we have called "sociobiology" is better termed "evolutionary sociobiology." Evolutionary sociobiology is aimed at producing a new synthesis that helps to achieve explanation of the complete range of evolutionary phenomena by making social data rationally cohere with evolutionary theory. The nonevolutionary fields of sociobiology need not have that aim, but, rather, have their own nonevolutionary aims.

In employing the inferential model of explanation, we allowed for an indispensable role of the question-answer model (1.2). The basic theoretical resources of sociobiology previously identified are pertinent in different ways to asking and answering different basic kinds of biological questions about organisms. There are questions about immediate causation, questions about development, questions about function, and questions about evolution. Basic kinds of questions that act as requests for explanatory information are closely related to general kinds of explanation as portrayed in Kourany's classification. One and the same kind of explanation can be characterized by describing the explanatory resources of the explanans, as found in Kourany's scheme, or by describing the aspect of the phenomenon being explained, as found in our list of explanatory questions. Broad sociobiology answers these questions, respectively, using causal explanation (explanation of the mechanisms of behavior), developmental explanation (explanation of the development of behavior), functional explanation (explanation of the function of behavior), and evolutionary explanation (explanation of the evolution of behavior). Ideals of what count as a proper explanandum, as revealed by basic kinds of explanatory questions, ought to cohere with ideals of what counts as proper explanans, as revealed by the informational resources associated with general kinds of explanatory answers.

The idea of a sociobiological unification of biology can mean various things, once we distinguish broad and narrow sociobiology. If it means that evolutionary biology unifies biology, then we must consider the fact that biology contains two fundamental theories: molecular biology and evolutionary biology. To decide whether evolutionary biology unifies biology, we need to take account of the relations between molecular biology and evolutionary biology since each has a role in unifying biology (Rosenberg 1985). The question of whether evolutionary sociobiology unifies biology would depend on that decision, one not treated here. If the sociobiological unification of biology means that evolutionary sociobiology unifies broad sociobiology, then we are considering the idea that the evolutionary biology of sociality is the unifying field among all the biological fields that study sociality. Again, that large question turns on whether evolutionary biology unifies biology in general. And it raises another parallel with the Modern Synthesis. Just as the Modern Synthesis brought about rearrangements of the various biological sciences (see the Mayr and Provine volume, 1981), a New Synthesis might also induce new relations among various biological sciences. If a New Synthesis occurs, that would be a matter for future historians to decide.

We are left, then, with the idea that evolutionary sociobiology unifies narrow sociobiology. That is a tautology, for it means only that evolutionary sociobiology unifies all the evolutionary subfields that can be brought to bear on sociality. The real questions are, "What sort of unity in explanatory resources and kinds of explanation does evolutionary sociobiology strive for?" and "To what extent has evolutionary sociobiology achieved an internal unification of its explanatory resources and kinds of explanation?"

These questions are important for understanding the aims and results of a sociobiology aimed at completeness. Our intuitive characterization of completeness spoke of a rational unification between evolutionary theory and social data. Our metalogical definition of completeness required that all available evolutionarily significant social facts can be explained by evolutionary theory. In either sense, the completion of evolutionary explanation by covering all the facts to be explained might take two forms. An atomistic completion would cover all the facts with the theory merely as a set of particular explanations, but no overall unified explanatory picture of the evolution of sociality would emerge. A holistic completion would cover all the facts, not as a summation over a set of particular explanations, but as a general overall unified explanatory picture of the evolution of sociality. Ideals of explanation, such as Wilson's, could be viewed either as tools for atomistic completion or holistic completion.

It is logically possible for a single completion to be both atomistic and holistic, namely, by both providing a complete set of particular explanations and a general overall unified explanatory scheme. A particular sociobiological explanation is one that answers questions about what happens at particular places and particular times to particular organisms. If evolutionary theory could not do that, then it would not explain what makes sociality actual. Consider just the explanations of sexual selection in the social species. They would encompass a number of distinct explanations applicable to somewhere between thousands and millions of species. The number of explanations would be enormously large. That would make the goal of reaching an atomistic completion infeasible. Instead, we try to provide acceptable particular explanations for those particular places, times, and organisms that interest us in each social phylum. Then we generalize, regarding that explanatory scheme as acceptable for evolutionarily significant social facts in general. So a modest holistic completion would be feasible.

To arrive at explanatory completeness, then, the sort of unity within evolutionary theory sociobiologists are trying to achieve is a unity among its general explanatory resources and general kinds of explanation. Their holy grail is an adequate general view of the social evolution of life on earth. In the next section we will lay the conceptual groundwork for this effort. We will clarify the form of the explanans by examining the character of kinds of explanation used in (evolutionary) sociobiology and by identifying relationships among those kinds of explanation.

To anticipate how this task fits into our present results about the procedures of embedding and projection, about explanatory ideals, and about explanatory resources, a few broad points are in order. Assessment of sociobiology is unjustified when it fails to take proper account of the role of its explanatory ideals and related internal standards. Reference to various ideals of evolutionary explanation control the range of evolutionary possibilities. So we cannot explain why the behaviors we witness have evolved rather than others theoretically possible—and thus project the actual from the possible—except by reference to the explanatory resources of those ideals. Those ideals give concreteness to the conception of how a completed evolutionary theory would explain the diversity of sociality across and within species. Standards of progress should focus on improving the fit between actual explanations and the current ideal explanans.

In practice, we do not have total explanations. We cannot yet apply every relevant resource and every relevant kind of explanation found in those ideals. Instead, we make resource choices among evolved characters, evolutionary processes, pertinent parameters, and so forth. We understand these choices in relation to ideals of explanation that, like Wilson's, offer a vision of a completed evolutionary biology. There are resource choices among developmental laws, laws of mortality selection, laws of fertility selection, and laws of genetic transmission, and so forth. We understand those choices in relation to ideals for integrating the organismic life cycle into processes of evolutionary change. A completed evolutionary biology would encompass all these laws. The same goes for each substantive ideal pertaining to knowledge of natural processes. A total explanation of an episode of social evolution would combine the qualities of all the kinds of explanation in evolutionary sociobiology pertinent to evolutionary processes. These include transitional, compositional, developmental, variational, functional, and normative explanation.

In the absence of total explanations, each explanation has a specific explanatory role to play in contributing to achieving the goal of explanatory completeness. That role is given by the way its implicit research decisions about how to connect evolutionary theory with social phenomena so as to make choices from among the resources and kinds of explanation found in those ideals. Each explanation has an implicit task, namely, to connect a given choice of explanatory factors with a given choice of phenomena to be explained according to a given choice of one or more kinds of explanation. Each explanation, then, should be evaluated for the choices it makes and the way it connects theory and data given those choices (see 6.3). To accurately portray the specific way each explanation falls short of the ideals and yet goes beyond previous explanations clarifies its explanatory role in the quest for completeness. These results elaborate the postulates of the three-unit model about the dependency of standards on completeness and about the primacy of specific explanatory roles for proper evaluation.

## 5.2 Evolutionary Change and the Life Cycle

### Transitional Explanation

Sociobiological explanations whose specific role is to bring to bear the explanatory resources of population genetics on sociality typically take the form of transitional explanations. A transitional explanation is defined by Kourany (1987, 29) as one in which a change of state in an object is explained in terms of a disturbance in the object and the state of the object at the time of the disturbance. Hence, explanations purporting to be transitional explanations are not well defined unless they specify what counts as the object, as the state of object, and as a disturbance on the object state. Such decisions about meaning act as presuppositions of particular transitional explanations given by their conceptual framework. Transitional explanations require several procedures of specification: specification of objects, of object states, and of object state disturbance. We will examine each decision in turn, using an example taken from physics.

As a science undergoes historical development, these decisions change as well. For example, consider transitional explanations in physics, as they changed from Aristotle to Newton. They each identify the objects with individual material objects. Aristotelian mechanics focused on earthly objects, whereas Newtonian mechanics treated celestial and terrestrial objects with the same generalizations about point masses. They each identify the state of an object with its state of motion. Aristotelian mechanics distinguished motion from rest, whereas Newtonian mechanics made further distinctions involving momentum. They each identify a disturbance in the object state as one or more forces acting on the object that causes the transition from one state to another. Aristotelian mechanics treated a state totally free from disturbing forces as one of absolute rest, whereas Newtonian mechanics treated it as one of lack of acceleration.

Natural selection is often regarded as a force of evolutionary change since it has a direction (whether it increases or decreases the frequency of a type) and a magnitude (the selective pressure S). Sober (1984) describes the basic structure of evolutionary theory as a theory of forces, regarding evolutionary theory as structurally analogous to Newtonian theory. The analogy enables us to regard processes causing evolutionary change as forces and to focus on what happens to a population when no evolutionary forces are at work, when a given evolutionary force acts alone, and when multiple forces interact to produce evolutionary change. Whatever its faults, the analogy reveals that evolutionary explanation is transitional explanation. Does evolutionary theory deliver transitional explanations because it is structured as a theory of forces? Or is evolutionary theory structured as a theory of forces so that it can deliver transitional explanations? To give a partial answer, evolutionary theory is committed to other kinds of explanation in order for its transitional explanations to be acceptable, and so its structure as a theory of forces is at most primary, not exclusive.

Transitional explanations in sociobiology differ from those in traditional mechanics at the most fundamental level, namely, the conception of the object. In evolutionary biology, the objects undergoing state transitions are populations of individual organisms, not individual material objects. Populations of individual organisms, not individual organisms, evolve. Populations of populations evolve as well. This point clarifies the explananda of transitional explanations in sociobiology. What is to be explained are features of populations and not individual organisms at all. Individual organisms are explained in a derivative sense, considered insofar as they are members of evolvingg populations. Claims about population properties do not entail claims about member properties, except in a statistical sense.

It follows that when human behavior is explained, what is explained is not why I or you have the social properties we do, but why certain behavioral patterns remain within the behavioral repertoire of human populations. We anticipated this point in saying that it is a mistake to regard specific behaviors like "Joe's homosexuality" or "Martha's fear of strangers" as phenomena to be explained by sociobiology. Even if part of the explanation of why you or I have the properties we do is that those properties evolved over a long time, the legitimate content of this point is only that you or I, as members of evolving human populations, have certain properties. Explanations of frequency changes of types A and B do not explain why you have type A rather than type B and I have type B rather than type A. For example, if you act sexually aggressively in situations where I do not, or if you are promiscuous in the ordinary sense and I am not, then the difference in our behaviors remains unexplained because our common membership fails to explain our individual differences (Sober 1984).

The dispute in traditional mechanics over whether the principles of terrestrial mechanics could be extended to apply to celestial mechanics was a dispute in domain specification for transitional explanations. Similarly, the dispute over the relation between the sociobiology of humans and nonhumans is partly about domain specification for transitional explanations. Even "nonsocial" behaviors like the need to eat and sleep have their significance transformed by social context and social organization. To follow our emphasis in section 4.2 on unjustified domain restrictions due to arbitrariness, an a priori line cannot be drawn between social and nonsocial behaviors. If we identify a behavior found in nonsocial species, we cannot assume that it is the very same behavior when found in a social species. So another argument for the importance of recognizing social context as a unit of sociality is that social context of the behavior may be part of the identification of the behavior itself. When, where, why, and with whom we sleep gives sleep its social meaning (Lewontin, Rose, and Kamin 1985).

Once we acknowledge that human "nonsocial" behaviors like sleep are evolutionarily significant, it is arbitrary to deny the evolutionary significance of human social behaviors. There is a slippery slope from recognition of the evolutionary significance of morphology and physiology to that of nonsocial behavior and then to social behavior. Those who endorse animal sociobiology but reject human sociobiology must overcome the arbitrariness of admitting the slippery slope for animals but maintaining a sharp boundary for humans. To do so, their unargued and doubtful assumption of total independence of directions of social change in cultural organisms from genetic change would have to be shown superior to the insights of gene-culture programs.

This slippery-slope dispute hangs on the proper identification of object state and its relation to evolution. An object's state is conceived in population genetics, not surprisingly, as a population's genetic state. A standard population genetic definition of evolution is "a change in gene frequencies." That definition is too narrow since changes in the frequencies of gene combinations or changes in recombination of genes when frequencies are constant also count as evolution. If we conceive genetic states as including genetic conditions of populations other than allele frequencies, evolution occurs when there is a transition from one genetic state to another in a population. State transitions are causally explained as the combined result of forces like mutation, migration, immigration, genetic drift, and natural selection. When is an explanation of state transitions the right kind of transitional explanation? Rival gene-culture research programs give rival answers, according to rival assumptions about the relation between evolutionary significance and genetic states of populations. For example, they differ about the manner in which nonsocial variations in mate selection are screened in accordance with evolved mate-selection strategies having some definite relation to genetic states.

A common assumption is that a behavior has evolutionary significance just in case in the past it made a difference for the population's genetic states in virtue of "its genetic basis." The epigenetic program denies the critic's restrictive construal of this assumption in positing that "to be an evolved constraint is not necessarily to be genetic . . . , and to be genetic is not necessarily to be an evolved constraint on culture" (Lumsden 1989, 26). So critics are unjustified in inferring that human cultural history is not evolutionarily significant from facts that their time scale is normally too short to embody significant genetic change, that there are normally no direct causal links between genes and social phenomena, etc. The epigenetic program readily grants such facts, holding that socially transmitted behaviors become prevalent in populations when favored by learning rules tuned to recognize adaptive behaviors. Evolved constraints increase the probability that some and not other aspects of the cultural environment are used in mental development. The ensuing behaviors have a general genetic basis, which attaches to psychological mechanisms or abilities found in learning.

The concept of a disturbance on a state implies the idea of a possible state in which no disturbances exist. Disturbances are said to interfere with "the natural state" that is undisturbed. Aristotelians and Newtonians disagreed on what counts as a natural state. Given Aristotle's teleological doctrine that all terrestrial objects are "going home," Aristotelians held that if no disturbing forces were present, an object would come to rest. Given Newton's mechanistic doctrine that all material objects are composed of interacting particles, Newtonians held that if no disturbing forces were present, an object at rest would remain at rest and an object in motion would continue in uniform motion. So far, so good. It is said that Aristotelians claimed that rest is natural and "only motion needs explanation," whereas Newtonians retorted that rest and motion are equally natural and "only changes in motion" need explanation. Such phrases embody the common ideas that what is natural needs no explanation and that what counts as an undisturbed state depends on a prior decision about what is natural.

Although the disturbed/undisturbed contrast is inherent in transitional explanation, the natural/unnatural contrast is not. The Hardy-Weinberg principle of population genetics states that neither gene-frequencies nor gene-combination (genotype) frequencies change when no evolutionary forces act on a population's genetic state (given certain assumptions, e.g., random mating). This is not because constant frequencies are more natural than changing frequencies. To be forced to consult views of what is natural/unnatural to make zero-force assertions would be for sociobiology to rely on an independently given metaphysics to guide transitional explanation. That is contrary to the natural ontological attitude, as expressed in section 1.4 about completeness and human nature and developed in section 4.3 on biological determinism.

Instead, what counts as an undisturbed state is given by consulting the facts about how heredity works. The Hardy-Weinberg law is not just a negative statement, one describing the ideal case in which no disturbing factors are present. It assumes a positive statement about a contingent hereditary process: as a matter of fact the hereditary process by itself does not change gene frequencies or genotype frequencies. Heredity could have worked differently, but if so, a different hereditary system would have been just as natural as the present one. Rather than say that evolutionary theory cannot explain the actual hereditary system because it is "natural," we simply note that no theory can explain the facts which act as its own assumptions. Population genetics assumes but does not explain the existence and basic character of heredity, just as anthropology assumes but does not explain the existence and basic character of culture. There is no need to invoke a metaphysics of the natural when a simple fact of logic suffices.

In sum, we have followed the standard view of treating mathematical population genetics as the conceptual core of evolutionary theory (for the mathematics, see Kitcher 1985). It explains in terms of successions of transitions from one genetic state of a population to the next as each new generation comes into being. Transitions in genetic states of populations require the transmission of genes from individuals of one generation to individuals of the next generation. Sociobiological explanations, as transitional explanations, have, at their conceptual core, decisions about what counts as the object undergoing the transition, the state of that object, and a disturbance on object state differ conceptually from those in Aristotelian and Newtonian mechanics.

The organismic self consists in an inherited genotype and a developed phenotype. A total explanation of generational change must do justice to the connection between genotype and phenotypes. The organismic life cycle is pivotal in this regard:

> There is a conceptual gap to be bridged. If the causes of evolution are described in phenotypic terms, and if the effects of evolution are calibrated in the language of gene frequencies, then a "translation manual" must be provided that goes back and forth between these two modes of description. If we look carefully at the connection between the different stages of the life cycle, we can discern the sorts of translation rules that a fully developed theory of forces will provide. (Sober 1984, 37)

Of course, the laws of transformation that connect phenotypes and gene frequencies required in evolutionary theory have been difficult to identify. That does not invalidate the theory since the postulation of such laws constitutes one of the most basic explanatory ideals inherent in the theory.

The regulative ideal according to Sober (adapted from Lewontin 1974a) goes as follows. Recall the basic life cycle of living organisms: we are born, we develop, we either live or we die, we either reproduce or we fail to reproduce. There are laws or generalizations about each phase, which describe evolution using what Mayr called "population thinking." Laws of development concern the joint effects of genes and environment on the development of the organism's phenotype. Laws of mortality selection concern factors of death. Laws of fertility selection concern factors of reproduction. Laws of transmission concern factors of the transmission of genes to the next generation. Ideally, all of these types of causal laws are needed to explain the transition of a population of organisms from one generation to the next. Changes in the frequencies of genetic and phenotypic properties from one generation to the next depend on the cumulative effects of all these factors. This ideal provides a general picture of evolutionary change of the sort we previously identified with a holistic completion since in practice we can surmise the effects of very few of these factors in natural populations.

These laws can be stated so as to clarify genotypic-phenotypic relations. Developmental laws map genotypic properties of the initial population onto their phenotypic properties. They describe how the environment mediates development from a population of zygotes varying in genotype into a population of juvenile organisms varying in phenotype. Two sorts of natural selection laws map these phenotypic properties onto ensuing phenotypic properties within the population in that generation. Mortality selection laws describe the way differential mortality modifies variation in the array of juvenile phenotypes within that same generation. Fertility selection laws describe the way phenotypic differences among adults influence variation in the gamete pool. Transmission laws that map genetic properties of gametes onto genotypic properties of zygotes describe how the genetic composition of the gamete pool affects the array of organismic genotypes.

On this life cycle ideal, transitional evolutionary explanations make the following commitments: a first phase of developmental explanation in developmental genetics, followed by two phases of variational explanation in terms of selection and other forces in population genetics, followed by a fourth phase of compositional explanation in transmission genetics. However, this ideal is now outdated due to recent attempts to apply selection to all phases of the life cycle. Rather than having developmental explanation precede selectionist explanation, selection applies at all points during individual lifetimes (as evident in Alexander's theory of lifetimes). So evolutionary transitional explanations are acceptable only if the relevant developmental, variational, and compositional explanations are acceptable.

As long as either version of this life cycle ideal (or some variant) orients sociobiological research, it follows that a completed evolutionary sociobiology of sociality would be primarily transitional in form but would thereby be committed to developmental, variational, and compositional explanations in order to unify its views of genes and phenotypes.

## Compositional Explanation

Before we go on to discuss developmental explanation as such, we need to show how the distinction in this ideal between compositional and developmental explanation bears on the assessment of sociobiology. Populations have members, whereas individual organisms have parts. In a compositional explanation, according to

Kourany, the properties of objects are explained in terms of the properties of their parts. Transitions in genetic states of populations require the combination of gametes of individuals into zygotes. Hence, transitional explanations have as a precondition some explanation of how the genetic composition of the gamete pool influences the genetic properties of zygotes. Such explanations are constructed in the field of transmission genetics. Hence, transitional explanations in population genetics are acceptable only if the related compositional explanations in transmission genetics are acceptable. In this sense, the explanans of a total explanation in sociobiology is primarily transitional, derivatively compositional.

Debate over the conservative message of genetic explanations has suffered from imprecision with respect to the distinction between transmission and development. Just as the clash between preformationism and epigenesis contoured change in the Mendelian program, so we find a clash over transmission-oriented and development-oriented views of genes at work in coutouring changes in various programs of evolutionary research..

Strictly speaking, copies of genes are inherited, via processes typically involving DNA transcription and RNA translation. Phenotypes, characters, traits, observable features of organisms are not inherited. In sexually reproducing species, nothing but the characteristics of gene-copies as found in sperm and eggs are inherited, except for the nongenetic organized material of the spermatozoa and ova themselves. Not only are behaviors not inherited, neither are what most people consider to be paradigmatic genetic traits, such as eye color. Contrary to preformationism, not only is behavior "not in our genes," virtually nothing about us is "in our genes."

The phrase "nature versus nurture" blurs or fuses two distinct concept contrasts (Silverberg 1980). One is the relatives of influence of genes or environment on the development of single individuals. The other is sexual (genetic) transmission as opposed to social (communicative) transmission between individuals. All behavior of any individual is somehow a developmental product of genes and environments; in this sense "nature versus nurture" is a false dichotomy. Even so, some behavioral variants are spread genetically through sexual reproduction and others socially through communication. For a given behavioral variant, there is room for debate over whether we should treat it as a hereditary trait whose variation is primarily genetic or as a social tradition whose variation is primarily a result of learning. Enter the gene-culture programs, which vary in the respective roles they assign to social and genetic transmission in human and primate sociality. Genetic transmission requires compositional explanation; social transmission does not.

Under the spell of fear about "genetic determinism," evaluators have been tempted to treat explanation in developmental biology as falling into Kourany's category 'compositional explanation'. The temptation is predicated on the usual view that genes guide development, taking the developed organism as the whole and the genes as the controlling parts. Critics (e.g., Bleier 1984) fail to pry apart the fact that genes must play some role in evolutionary explanation, inherent in its explanatory ideals for full explanation and genotype-phenotype unification, from the extreme view that genes are overriding determiners of development. Genes control development. But so does the environment. Genes impart specificity. But so do other parts of the inner architecture of organisms. Genes affect the timing of various developmental stages. But cells under instruction from the lymph and neural systems affect when the genes are turned on. And so on (Hubbard 1982).

Of course, these are very general causative roles, and the actual determinative role of genes varies with the species being studied. Let us define a unique general causative role of genes as a role not shared by other parts of the organism or the environment. Our ideals of evolutionary explanation that put the life cycle into evolutionary focus require only one unique general role of genes in guiding development, namely, the role of genes in being transmitted across generations. They allow for any amount of diversity of genetic causation, of what stretches of DNA do, as a function of the diversity of organisms among different species or higher taxa. There is no reason for attributing genes causal primacy as part of a general life-cycle ideal. In development, nongenetic factors are ontologically on par with genetic factors in general.

It has been shown that assessment of sociobiology is unjustified when it fails to take account of the bearing of gene-culture programs on the unity of kinds of explanations in population and transmission genetics. In making this point, we drew some implications from sociobiology used as a case to test the adequacy of Kourany's classification of explanations. Although that scheme treats evolutionary explanation as a separate kind from transitional explanation, evolutionary theory explains in terms of transitions from one genetic state to the next. Although the scheme treats compositional explanation as a separate kind from evolutionary explanation, explanation of population changes in terms of iterated transitions of genetic states of populations requires explanation of genetic composition of zygotes in terms of the gamete pools. Although the scheme treats compositional explanations via the purely spatial relation of wholes and parts, the population orientation of transitional explanation requires that the whole/part relation of zygotes to their genome be related to the transmission of gametes, chromosomes, codons, nucleotides, and other genetic units across generations.

So, Kourany's survey of kinds of explanation in science fails to generalize from physics to a scheme of kinds of explanation general enough to subsume all sciences. It is unlikely, and at best an open question, whether a better classification scheme can be devised that subsumes biological and social sciences without favoritism to either. Recall that our criterion for whether two alleged rival explanations are genuine rivals is that they explain the very same thing using the very same kind of explanation. Little detailed inspection of explanations in social science is needed to see that they do not fall into the same kinds of explanation as the one found in sociobiology, however you classify them. In this research situation, it is prudent to regard the class of rival explanations to which judgements of acceptability are relative as consisting entirely of evolutionary explanations.

## Developmental Explanation

Human sociobiology needs to do justice to human development in order to say how culture is neither independent of nor inconsistent with evolution. However, even though all evolutionists recognize this fact, it has proven difficult to show that processes of development add a significant component of causality in evolutionary mechanisms. Even so, novel attempts are being made (Thomson 1984; Bechtel 1986).

Given the organization of the organism, we cannot treat observable traits as mapping in any simple scheme onto effects of gene-complexes. So we cannot treat natural selection as independently optimizing behavioral atoms corresponding to genetic atoms. Indeed, the origin of variation may reflect laws of molecular biology and laws of biological form. A dynamic explanation of trait distributions in terms of the change in variation over time due to selection has a different explanandum than a static explanation of variation itself in terms of the laws that govern the ranges of variation and stability of variant forms. Given the different explananda, selection-ist explanations and architectonic explanations are not rivals. The Gould-Lewontin emphasis on highly constraining channels of inner design should not be understood as "an equal partner to selection" (Gould 1982, 364), not because selection is more important, but because they are not rival explanations.

However, the mechanism of selection applies equally well to traits examined in terms of the organism's external environment and traits examined in terms of the organism's internal architec-ture. Any trait that yields an overall increased chance at success at survival and/or reproduction will be favored by selection, whether because it helps the organism adapt to its surroundings or because it helps the organism maintain a stable, functioning body. The extent that constraining channels of inner design are adaptive or neutral is crucial for evaluating adaptationist explanations.

Another key issue is how far the traditional life-cycle ideal just described must be changed to do justice to development. A the-oretically conservative response is to insist that the traditional ideal can accommodate cultural behavior merely by including the effects of members of the same species on each other's phenotype as part of an organism's developmental and social environment, arguing against the need for a dual inheritance program (Voorzanger 1987; Plotkin 1988; Kitcher 1988). A more drastic response is to hold that natural selection operates on developmental systems (Oyama 1985). To see the role of completeness in orienting substantive issues like this, consider the following objection. In her analysis of presupposi-tions in nature-nurture controversies, Oyama (1985) concludes that natural selection operates on developmental systems—a very differ-ent use of evolution from the sociobiological paradigm. In that framework, sociality is hardly the fatal flaw ultra-Darwinians and that thesis claim it to be; it is an integrated aspect of the evolution-ary process. Therefore, completeness is unimportant for analyzing sociobiology.

The confusion in this objection is instructive for proper evalua-tion. By identifying sociobiology with a certain theoretical stance, it straightjackets research in sociobiology. Research in sociobiology changes in orientation, now encompassing Oyama's conclusion rather than being an opposed doctrine, just as it can accommodate changes in its types of research programs (chapter 2), changes in problems like altruism and the units/levels of selection (chapter 3), and radically different strategies of domain specification (chapter 4). Sociobiology is based on testing the thesis that sociality is not a fatal flaw for evolutionary theory, hoping to show that evolutionary explanation can be made to completely cover all evolutionarily significant facts, even those recalcitrant facts involving social evolution. It is a positive response to the ultimate challenge that social facts are irrelevant to or inconsistent with evolutionary theory. By adopting an anticompleteness posture, it misconstrues the significance of its own conclusion. To show that and how development is integrated into the evolutionary process provides strong reason to conclude that evolutionary theory is relevant to and consistent with sociality, that is, that a holistic completion is being achieved.

Indeed, gene-culture theories explicitly treat the novel evolutionary situation in human sociality induced by our genetic capacity for flexible, situation-specific behavior. Recall from section 2.4 the three programs found in the early 1980s for reconciling the genetic basis of evolutionary change with social and cultural evolution: the epigenetic program, the coevolutionary program, and the dual inheritance program. Each has taken explicit account of development, albeit in controversial ways. Some evolutionists think that Wilson's epigenetic program is a disguised elaboration of Waddington's theory of epigenesis. Alexander's (1987, 33ff) coevolutionary program treats the way selection acts on the distribution of reproductive effort throughout the life cycle. Richerson's and Boyd's (1982) dual inheritance program treats the way various sorts of directed learning in human development combine with genetically evolved predispositions to yield behavior. Barkow's (1989c, 346ff) information-processing program posits that as children develop they process information about whether the father's involvement in child-caring is low or high, and adjust their ensuing reproductive strategies accordingly.

Now that genes are no longer viewed as super-causes, genetics and human behavior no longer need be conceived as irrelevant in order to give nongenetic causes their due. Behavioral geneticists have been "winning the war and losing our identity" (Scarr 1987). Behavioral geneticists have won the war to persuade others of the validity of their field in principle. As a result, behavioral genetics is being incorporated into mainstream psychology. Sociobiologists can strengthen their explanations by subjecting the behaviors explained to both traditional and the newer behavioral genetic methods. For explanations postulating genetic variations that correlate with behavioral variations, they need not be content to study behavior merely as an outcome of evolution. They can use quantitative genetics to study the process of evolution itself when present populations exhibit genetic variation (Arnold 1983; Mitchell-Olds and Rutledge 1986).

Critics of genetic influences on behavior have focused on the traditional methods, namely, family, twin, and adoption studies. Such studies continually tempt the usual criticism that cultural influences are systematically devalued. It is hard to show that the family members, the twins, or the biological and adopted children have not been raised in cultural environments more similar than those used in the control group. If so, conclusions that the behavioral differences studied are caused in part by genetic differences would be unwarranted. Such studies may merely reflect the truism that humans sharing more of a cultural environment behave more similarly than humans sharing less of one. When this criticism is well taken, it does not show that there are no genetic differences, just that their postulation is unjustified. Indeed, no one has identified any particular stretch of DNA as a hereditary factor specific to any human behavior, psychological mechanism, or behavioral predisposition. No one has shown that none exist. Criticism from the assumption that none exist is likewise unjustified. Currently, no explanation is unacceptable just because it conflicts with one's own favored presumption. The gene-versus-environment debate is an expression of our ignorance.

Promising genetical explanations have been reported (Martin et al. 1986) for psychopathological behaviors (e.g., mental illnesses such as manic depression or schizophrenia), cognitive abilities (e.g., intelligence, spatial discrimination), and personality (e.g., alcoholism, extraversion, activity level). Although criticisms like the foregoing will be raised again and again, these explanations are subject to critical testing in a more sophisticated manner using the newer methods in combination. They include structured models and model fitting, multivariate analysis, genetic change and continuity in development, shared and nonshared components of environmental variance, and genetic components of "environmental" variation (Plomin 1986). One allegedly robust finding is that most of the methods for studying such behavioral traits converge on heritabilities of .3 to .5. This would mean, to simplify, that although at least half of the variance is "environmental," up to half of the variance is "genetic." That is shockingly high. Whether the figures represent the facts or are just artifacts of "hereditarian" methods deserves further study (Plomin and Daniels 1987).

If the new methods of behavioral genetics can be legitimated in their own right, they can be used to test the three gene-culture research programs and successor programs as well. Large amounts of observed genetic variation are expected on the epigenetic research program, are not expected on the coevolutionary program, and are expected on some but not other theoretically possible scenarios on the dual inheritance program. Programs involving a complex psychology need to clarify the locus and extent of genetic variation for the cognitive predispositions they envisage.

Extreme critics assume that human populations do not exhibit internal genetic variation correlated with variation in social behavior, behavioral predispositions, learning rules, brain function, the nervous system, or any other precondition of observed sociality. They must explain how the human situation evolved from primate and presumably hominid situations in which they acknowledge the existence of such genetic variation. They must explain how innate psychological mechanisms yielding an unguided plasticity would not be evolutionarily fatal. They must develop their assumptions better than the opposed assumptions of, say, the Cosmides-Tooby gene-culture program. They must explain how general learning mechanisms or problem-solving abilities could be selectively favored over specific Darwinian rules specialized for situations encountered by hominid hunter-gatherers during the Pleistocene. Such explanations would count as rival sociobiological explanations, far less plausible than the existing ones.

Both advocates and critics hold the same broad ontological view, known as "interactionism" or "the epigenetic viewpoint": organismic development is guided by both genetic and environmental factors and their complex interactions. No one holds that genes or that environments (including culture) are the sole causes of human behaviors. Everyone accepts that neither genetic nor environmental factors acting in isolation can have any behavioral effect. Everyone accepts that neither genes nor environment determines an organism, but, rather, a unique and complex interaction between them. Interactionism, in the sense of those and related truisms, is defended by such critics as Lewontin, Rose, and Kamin (1985), Bleier (1984), and Kitcher (1985) and by such advocates as Wilson (1976), Barash (1979), Alexander (1987), and Barkow (1989c).

Wenegrat (1984, 11–12) rehashes ontological interactionism in an effort to discredit simple statistical approaches to gene-environment interactions:

> What many fail to realize, though, is that neither ethologic nor sociobiologic concepts imply a competitive relation between innate and

environmental behavioral determinants, a relation in which the greater efficacy of one implies the lesser efficacy of the other. A "competitive" framework of this sort is actually encountered more often in behavioral genetics than in modern evolutionary thinking (Alexander, 1979). . . . Within an interactionist framework of this sort it is as illogical to quantify the relative contribution of purely genetic and environmental factors to particular behaviors, whether that contribution is expressed in terms of statistical means or variability, as it is to assert that the operation of a radio is seventy percent determined by wire and thirty percent determined by transistors.

Here a denial of ontological interactionism is attributed to behavioral geneticists. However, whether it is logical or illogical to quantify the relative contribution of genetic and environmental factors depends on what is being studied. Some behavioral geneticists do emphasize that "Behavioral genetic methods are applicable only to the study of between-individual differences, not to single individuals or to the study of average differences between groups or to the study of species universals" (Plomin, 228, 1986). Wenegrat and Plomin are talking about different things. Ontological interactionism is a doctrine about single individuals; each organism develops as it does according to interactions of genetic and environmental factors. The statistical methods Plomin reviews apply to populations of individuals.

To simplify, for a given population in a given environment, some percentage of the variation is correlated with variation in genetic relationships among individuals (which does not require that the difference is solely caused by genes) and some percentage is correlated with variation in individual-environment relations among individuals (which does not require that the difference is solely caused by environments). The explanatory factors cited in the statistical methods of behavioral genetics are properly invoked when the explanandum is a population and improperly invoked when the explanandum is single individuals, groups, or all humans.

Heritabilities do not automatically record percentages of genetic variation. Actually, they record percentages of nonenvironmental variation which is then inferred to be genetic but could be due to variation in morphology or physiology, and that variation may or may not be under tight genetic control or correlate with genetic variation. Finally, heritabilities are calculated against a background of constancy, namely, for a given population in a given environment (Lewontin 1974b). No heritability has any automatic implication for a different population or a different environment or both. To study how different populations in different environments change the phenotypic effect of a gene, one must consult its (typically unknown) norm of reaction for a gene. We don't know whether or not our samples are representative. A trait with zero heritability may be under tight genetic control since heritabilities require individual variation and all the population members may share the same gene-complex coding for the trait. Heritabilities imply nothing for whether we can or cannot induce radical social change by changing our genes or our social environments. They are irrelevant to related ideas about "genetically determined human nature."

Such a reading fails to distinguish ontological interactionism from various methodological views about genes. Given ontological interactionism, genetic and environmental causes are on par; neither is more primary, privileged, direct, determinative, and so forth in individual development. Methodological separatism is the view that some developmental assumptions inherent in evolutionary claims need not be made precise or studied explicitly in order for the claims to be acceptable in the context of the present research situation where ignorance of the precise role of genes in development is rampant. Such limitations define the explanatory role of the ensuing explanations, that is, what they are or are not designed to do.

In conclusion, sociobiological explanations are committed to producing related developmental explanations in order to attain explanatory completeness. At present the research situation is both promising and disappointing. There are some interesting proposals about how to put development into an evolutionary focus and some new techniques for getting data about genetic variation important for the plausibility of explanatory hypotheses affiliated with various gene-culture research programs. Unfortunately, we still don't know the specifics of the role of genes in the development of behavior. We don't have the data to really test the variety of general but precise views of development, especially cognitive development, consistent with ontological interactionism.

## Variational Explanation

Kourany's summary scheme identifies and differentiates four kinds of explanation: compositional, evolutionary, functional, and transitional explanation. First, the categories are too narrow. All four kinds of these kinds of explanation are found in evolutionary biology, not just the one labeled "evolutionary." Second, the categories are not mutually exclusive. The scheme characterizes an evolutionary explanation as one in which "the properties of objects are explained in terms of the temporal development of those objects." It characterizes a compositional explanation as one whereby properties of wholes are explained in terms of properties of parts. The operative contrast is that 'evolutionary explanation' is defined in purely temporal terms, whereas 'compositional explanation' is defined in purely spatial terms. We have seen that explanation in developmental biology involves both spatial and temporal axes in this sense, falling into more than one category.

Moreover, the scheme fails to distinguish temporal explanations in which individual objects pass through stages of development from those in which populations of objects change according to changes in member variation. That is, it misses the basic character of what Mayr called "population thinking." We just saw that ontological interactionism is about the development of individuals, whereas hypotheses in behavioral genetics are about variations among members of a local population. Organisms develop but do not evolve. Populations evolve but do not develop. Developmental and variational explanations differ. One or the other sort is reasonable to pursue when the data has the following character, depending on whether the objects in the domain are construed as individuals or as populations:

> (Ei) If a domain is ordered, and if that ordering is one which can be viewed as the increase or decrease of the factor(s) on the basis of which the ordering is made, then it is reasonable to suspect that the ordering may be the result of an evolutionary process, and it is reasonable to undertake research to find such an answer (which we have called an evolutionary theory).
>
> (Eii) The reasonableness of such expectation is increased if there is a way (for example, by application or adaptation of some background information such as a theory from another domain, whether unrelated or (preferably) related) of viewing that sequential ordering as a temporal one, and still more if a way is provided of viewing that ordering as having a temporal direction. (Shapere 1977, 93)

Condition (Ei) suggests a logical requirement for the applicability of evolutionary explanation to the domain of social behavior: social behavior patterns exhibit an ordering involving the increase or decrease of values of descriptive variables. Evidence for this ordering is supplied by studies that show how primate social abilities increase as lineages evolve and reach their "height" with humans. An upshot is that those who think that animal sociobiology is, but human sociobiology is not, in principle legitimate must face a forceful objection. The same principles of reasoning (Ei and Eii) that legitimate the extension of evolutionary theory from nonsocial to social evolutionary explanations also legitimate its extension from animal sociobiology to human sociobiology.

Much early literature in sociobiology was dedicated to this sort of enterprise, namely, showing that the domains of animal and human sociality are so ordered that they fulfill preconditions for evolutionary explanation. For example, the function of Barash's (1979) loose language about genes is to show the relevance of genetic factors, and hence of evolutionary explanations to the extent that they rely on genetic factors, to animal and human sociality. Thus he concludes (1982, 45) that ontological interactionism "applies to behavior no less than to any other phenotype, thereby legitimizing the application of principles from evolutionary biology to the study of behavior."

Irons (1979) argued explicitly for the relevance of principles of evolutionary biology, explaining why they can be expected to apply to human behavior." These include principles dealing with phenotypic plasticity and sociality, including principles about genes and evolution by selection, group versus individual selection, kin selection, reciprocity selection, sexual selection and parental investment. To such theoretical arguments are added indirect empirical arguments. For instance, we have changed animal behaviors by changing animal genes. Hence, human behaviors are somehow connected to genes. Selection experiments over many generations have changed animal behavior in almost any direction of variation desired. Hence, human behaviors are somehow governed by selection. And so forth. If we combine conceptual, theoretical, and empirical relevance arguments, the reasonableness of giving evolutionary explanations for animal and human social behaviors is compelling, even if the difficulties in detail prevent us from being confident that the correct approach has been found.

Such relevance arguments, since they proceed from the current state of understanding of evolutionary theory, already incorporate a distinction among temporal explanations clarified by Sober. Sober (1984) captures the basic differences between developmental-stage explanations and evolutionary (variational) explanations. Organic diversity, the basic explanandum of evolutionary theory, is differently conceptualized in developmental and evolutionary explanations. The explananda of developmental theories are individual objects, whereas the explananda of evolutionary theories are local populations. In Sober's terms, Darwinian explanation is importantly novel in that it created a new object of explanation, a new contrastive context of explanation, and a new logic of explanation.

Given the population-level identification of the object of explanation, the status of variation became not only the primary object of explanation but an explanatory principle in its own right. Thus, the forces of evolutionary change produce evolutionary change by operating on the relative frequencies of various genotypic and phenotypic types in the population. Explanations in evolutionary genetics and evolutionary ecology explain variation among a generation of organisms in terms of variation among past generations and these forces of change. Recall our construal of evolutionary explanation as iterated transitional explanation. It is logically possible to iterate transitions from genetic states of a population over many generations in either a developmental stage or a variational way.

On a stage interpretation, the population would undergo a sequence of developmental stages as one generation begets another, just as individual organisms undergo a sequence of developmental stages throughout their lifetimes. Regarding species as populations, the evidence points against any natural sequence of stages in reproductively isolated populations, and so the stage interpretation is widely regarded as false. The stage interpretation models populations after individuals, which is sure to muddle evolutionary thinking. A stage interpretation would explain by appeal to the hypothesis that individuals in successive generations are different. On a variational interpretation, the population's state changes as a function of the variation among its members from generation to generation. Evolutionary forces act on existing variation to change the composition of the population. The change in the population is not due to the fact that members develop, but that they vary. A variational interpretation would explain, whether or not individuals in successive generations are different, by appeal to the hypothesis that variation in successive generations is different. Variation is not to be explained as a product of anything more basic, but functions as an irreducible explanatory principle in the explanans.

Sober contrasts variational evolutionary explanation with the natural-state model of explanation originating with Aristotle and still found in common-sense attitudes about explanation. In a natural-state or natural-type explanation, a natural state or type is postulated as a basic explanatory principle, and variation is to be explained by reference to deviation from the natural state or type under the influence of disturbing or interfering forces. The natural-state model has failed in application to development. No particular phenotype is natural since the norm of reaction concept in genetics maps a given genotype onto any number of phenotypes given the environment. The natural-state model has failed in application to speciation. Speciation is a macro-level consequence of iterated transitions of genetic states of populations (plus other factors) according to forces transforming variation among its members. So there is no natural phenotypic or genotypic type or genetic state in a given population.

Why have so many people persisted in interpreting sociobiological explanations as implying that "it is natural for humans to be such and such," or "human nature is such and such," where some state or type is adduced? Common-sense explanations continue to reason in terms of natural-state or natural-type explanations and superimpose them over quite alien evolutionary explanations. Debate over human nature takes the concept to be clear. Because crucial differences remain unclarified, miscommunication is rampant. The term 'human nature' falls into different categories of thought (1.4). It may mean widespread, invariant, or distinctively human attributes or else identity conditions for being human (an ontological or metaphysical term). It may mean aspects of humans that are especially revealing given the state of inquiry (an epistemological term). We can add here that it may indicate aspects of humans taken as basic in a kind of explanation (a methodological term).

Because talking about what is natural and about human nature in ways reflecting natural-state or natural-type explanations is so pervasive, sociobiologists must take special pains to prevent those interpretations. As a balancing overstatement, let us say that, for all the kinds of explanation in evolutionary biology, to explain something has no supporting relation at all to any natural-state (or natural-type) explanation. Sober's (1984, 159) comparison of variational and natural-state explanation is pertinent: "Here we see the natural state model stood on its head: Variability is 'natural,' whereas uniformity is the result of 'interfering forces'." Several reasons go to show that 'natural' here relates to what we expect, not to some quality of things in the world.

First, what Sober means by saying that variability is natural is that as a matter of fact, given Mendelian mechanisms of inheritance, populations normally have a great deal of genetic variability.

Now, Sober's logic in denying that there is a natural phenotype for a given individual or species is this: the alleged natural phenotype is from the point of view of theory only one possibility among many others, none different in ontological status. Actuality by itself confers no privileged status. However, the possibility of an earth with only asexually reproducing organisms forming uniform populations is one theoretical possibility on par with the possibility actualized in our present situation. So his own impeccable logic leads us to deny that variability is more natural than uniformity.

Second, the very idea of an automatic ontological interpretation of basic principles of a kind of explanation is vexed. True, variation is a given in variational explanations and cannot be reduced to a product of more basic evolutionary forces. All this means is that variation is methodologically basic to evolutionary explanation. Variation is to be expected in evolutionary explanation but is an oddity to be "explained away" in natural state explanations. To infer that variation is basic to the world because it is taken as a given in our explanation is to treat one kind of explanation as a privileged source of information about the world. To make the inference is to forget that there are different basic elements in other kinds of explanations, all of which must be reconciled and integrated to build a world view out of science, which cannot be done if the ontological commitments of each kind are finally given in isolation.

Third, to be pragmatic about actual linguistic usage, the word "natural" is so filled with connotations alien to or independent of variational explanation, that it would be imprudent to depend on it to interpret evolutionary explanations. Previous false theories of evolution and species incorporated a teleological element foreign to variational explanation into what is deemed natural. Aristotle's teleological conception that the purpose of all things is to fulfill their inner nature is incorporated into his view that each kind of physical object has a natural state and each species has a natural type. Lamarck's and Spencer's teleological conception that organic diversity is constrained by an inherent progressive tendency is incorporated into their view that adaptation to the environment is the natural state of organisms. To use the natural-state or natural-type model of variational explanation would be to raise the spectre of vulgar adaptationism and biological determinism (connotations the public gives to "It is natural for men to be promiscuous, women to be faithful").

Fourth, Sober's view of the structure of evolutionary theory as a theory of forces readily falls under the category of transitional explanation. So there is no reason to invoke Aristotle's alien natural-state or natural-type explanations to describe evolutionary theory so as to fulfill that aim.

Not only is evolutionary explanation antithetical to natural-type explanation, it is not intrinsically functional. This fact may surprise those who think of evolutionary explanation as explanation of evolutionary change by natural selection. Since natural selection increases the frequency of traits having a genetic basis which are adaptive in certain conditions, natural selection operates in a way that is functional in character. Iterated transitional explanations explain by appeals to forces of evolutionary change. Something counts as such a force independently of whether it is functional in character. There is nothing functional about genetic drift, meiotic drive, migration, or immigration, even though they are evolutionary forces. It is only the contingent truth that natural selection is an influential force of evolutionary change that makes evolutionary explanation functional. It involves functions because natural selection involves functions and counts as a force that changes frequencies of genes, genotypes, and phenotypes, not because of its status as iterated transitional explanation having a variational character.

In conclusion, assessment of sociobiology is unjustified when it fails to take account of the ways evolutionary explanation is committed to transitional, compositional, developmental, and variational explanations. This commitment reveals that there is no barrier between broad and narrow sociobiology. One cannot provide full explanations in evolutionary sociobiology without relying on work in a variety of fields that deal with organismic genes and genotypes: populations genetics, transmission genetics, behavioral genetics. Nor can full explanations in evolutionary sociobiology be provided without relying on work in a variety of fields that deal with orga-nismic traits and phenotypes: phylogenetic biology, evolutionary ecology, evolutionary ethology, and developmental biology. In this sense the internal structure of biology is a seamless web of studies that are integrated in order to do evolutionary biology but are not integrated by evolutionary biology. The difference shows that the impressive-sounding "evolutionary unification of biology" turns out to be a relatively modest idea.

A completed evolutionary biology would provide total explana-tions of evolutionarily significant nonsocial and social phenomena. As a holistic completion, it would work out particular explanations in all these categories so that they fit the available facts for those social phenomena and species that interest us, relying on the same explanatory scheme to give us a general view of social evolution as a whole. This vision of what a completed evolutionary sociobiology would be like is grounded in ideals which unify genotypic and phenotypic explanation through various accounts of the way that the life cycle of organisms fits into the evolutionary process. It views organisms as members of evolving populations, viewing life on earth in terms of an evolutionary time scale.

When applied to cultural organisms, such ideals change in interaction with gene-culture programs. The projection of actual behaviors from theoretical possibilities involving a complex psychology requires new methods for studying gene-behavior connections. They differ according to whether the genetic structure of evolving populations involves large amounts, moderate amounts, or small amounts of genetic variation underlying the abilities, dispositions, and skills used in adjusting to the natural and social conditions under which we live. They differ according to whether the behavioral mechanisms under study are considered to be selectively adaptive, maladaptive, or neutral in the face of culturally induced social motives. They differ according to the relationship between the processes and results of social transmission and genetic transmission of the evolved and culturally induced motives underlying behavioral variants. And so on.

Such theoretical decisions give rise to wide internal heterogeneity in human sociobiology. We cannot now predict how successor programs for achieving holistic completeness will differ from the present gene-culture programs. But our conceptualization of sociobiology as a discipline permits us to anticipate dramatic changes in the conceptualization of future explanatory hypotheses, theories, and programs. But no matter how their content and explanatory resources may differ, they are all oriented by the aim of extending the range of evolutionary explanations to cover social phenomena in cultural organisms so as to achieve explanatory completeness.


# 5.3 Evolved Functions


## Kinds of Functional Explanation

Kourany (1986 28) characterizes a functional explanation as one in which "relatively sophisticated capacities of objects are explained in terms of the sophisticated organization of relatively simple capacities of those objects or their components." To clarify the relationship between evolutionary sociobiology and nonevolutionary sociobiology, we need to capture the relationship between evolutionary and nonevolutionary functional explanations. In other words, what is the relationship between "ultimate" and "proximate" functional explanations? Some hold that all functional explanations are grounded in evolutionary explanations. Others wonder whether there are functional explanations at all. ". . . It is far from clear that there are separate questions about function begging to be answered once all the problems about evolution, mechanism, development, and inheritance have been addressed. What else would be left to know?" (Kitcher 1985, 114–15)

In fact, three theorists have described functions in such a way that (proximate) functional explanations do differ from (ultimate) evolutionary explanations. It is well known that Mayr used the example of male bird song to distinguish "functional and evolutionary biology." Cummins has developed the idea of functional explanation in psychology as "capacity explanation," the above account of function cited by Kourany. Horan has developed an account of functional explanation in sociobiology that clearly contrasts proximate functional explanation with evolutionary explanation, an account of functional explanation as "consequence explanation."

From a study of these three accounts, the following points will be argued. There is indeed nonevolutionary functional explanation in nonevolutionary sociobiology. Evolutionary sociobiology uses a related but distinct sort of functional explanation that we will call "evolutionary functional explanation." There are five main kinds of explanation involving functions that are found in sociobiology: component capacity explanation, composite capacity explanation, disposition explanation, consequence explanation, and normative explanation. The difference between functional explanation in nonevolutionary sociobiology and in evolutionary sociobiology comes to this: in nonevolutionary sociobiology, functions are identified independently of evolutionary processes, whereas in evolutionary sociobiology, functions are identified so as to be grounded in evolutionary processes.

Functional explanations are invoked to answer requests for functional information. To get a handle on these kinds of requests, let's consider what is involved in asking and answering the question, "Why do male birds sing in the spring?" We will use the intuitive correctness of the distinctions among kinds of functional explanation made here as their justification, and then use them to critically examine the views of function adopted by Cummins, Mayr, and Horan, among others.

First, we want to know, "How is it that male birds actually are able to sing in the spring?" To answer, we give a component capacity explanation. A component capacity explanation is an explanation of how the capacity in question is constituted by a number of different capacities. We answer by saying that the bird has the capacity to utter the particular sequence of sounds found in the song characteristic of its species. We analyze the song of a cardinal into its component sounds, characteristically a capacity to make a long ascending glissando from a lower note all the way up to the high note and the capacity to repeat this pattern in ways that vary in a predictable fashion. The function of the glissando is to contribute sounds that create a bird song. This is a functional explanation of the capacity to sing in the spring in terms of component capacities.

Second, we want to know, "When male birds are able to sing in the spring, what do that do that for?" To answer, we give a composite capacity explanation. A composite capacity explanation is an explanation of how the role of the capacity in contributing to one or a more general capacities. We say that male birds engage in various courtship rituals in order to attract mates, such as the capacity to sing in the spring, to preen their feathers when watched by potential mates, and to recognize the presence of females of their species ready for courtship. The functions of singing in the spring is to attract mates (mate selection) and intimidate rival males (male-male competition), each being a capacity constituted by the ways component capacities are organized. This is a functional explanation of the capacity to sing in the spring in terms of one or more composite capacities.

Third, we want to know, "What makes male birds disposed to sing in the spring?" To answer, we give a disposition explanation. A disposition explanation is an explanation of why the organism exercises the capacity in the conditions in which it does. We answer by saying that the disposition to sing depends on high levels of the hormone testosterone in the bird's blood, that increase in testosterone levels result from spring growth in testes size, and that the growth is triggered by an increase in the number of hours of sunlight per day in the spring. The function of increase in testes size and of increase in hormonal concentration is to trigger the production of the song in the spring. This is a functional explanation of the disposition to sing in the spring in terms of the cause of the exercise of the capacity to sing in the spring.

Fourth, we want to know, "Why is it that singing in the spring is something that male birds tend to do?" To answer, we give a consequence explanation. A consequence explanation is an explanation of why the capacity and disposition to exercise it is part of the behavioral repertory of the organism. We say that if the male bird sings in the spring, then it will attract female birds of the same species. Singing in the spring is a signal of courtship readiness to potential mating partners. The function of male bird song is to signal courtship readiness. This is a functional explanation of the tendency of the organism to act in a certain manner under given circumstances in terms of its survival or reproductive value, that is, an adaptive explanation.

Fifth, we want know, "On what grounds is the design of the bird song identified with its survival or reproductive value?" This is not a request for an explanation, but rather a request for a justification. Here, the relation between proximate and ultimate explanations comes into focus. If we can justify identifying design-problems independently of the fact that organismic capacities and dispositions are the products of evolutionary processes, then proximate functional explanations are autonomous from evolutionary explanations. If we cannot do so, then proximate functional explanations are not autonomous from evolutionary explanations, and either they depend on evolutionary functional explanations or evolutionary theory leaves no residual explanations that qualify as functional.

Sixth, we want to know, "How well designed is the male bird song?" To answer, we give a normative explanation. A normative explanation is an explanation of how well designed a behavioral disposition may be. It explains the quality of the behavioral disposition as a solution to a design-problem. Organisms are treated as problem solvers. Male birds face the general problem of being reproductively successful. Their reproductive success is very strongly positively correlated with finding appropriate mates. To solve the problem of choosing the right mate, they adopt a song with certain features. A song having those features is either optimal or suboptimal, given the constraints, for performing its function of finding appropriate mates. This is a functional explanation of the degree of success of the disposition to sing in the spring for reproducing.

Sixth, we want to know, "How or why did the capacity and tendency of male birds to sing in the spring, being adaptive to the extent it is adaptive, evolve?" To answer, we give an evolutionary explanation. An evolutionary explanation is primarily a transitional explanation, but includes the other categories of explanation we distinguished in section 5.2 in a secondary sense, one deriving from its association with a life cycle ideal. We say that the capacity and tendency of male birds to sing in the spring is an adaptation that evolved as a result of the way the totality of evolutionary processes acted on its selected function(s). This is a functional explanation of the way that natural selection enhances fitness, resulting in the evolution of adaptation. The first five explanations are nonevolutionary explanations, whereas this sixth sort of explanation is an evolutionary explanation.

## Capacity Explanation

Kourany draws her definition from Cummins. Although Cummins focuses on the idea in psychology that programs explain behavior, his definition (Cummins 1977, 97) is meant to apply to biology:

> Functional analysis in biology is essentially similar. The biologically significant capacities of an entire organism are explained by analyzing the organism into a number of "systems"—the circulatory system, the nervous system, etc.—each of which has its characteristic capacities. These capacities are in turn analyzed into capacities of component organs and structures.

Cummins's book (1983) on psychological explanation develops this account of functions in detail. It goes on to cite the applicability of this account to biology in the very same words as those above, except that it replaces "functional analysis in biology is essentially similar" with "functional analysis in physiology is essentially similar." Cummins does not explicitly speak to the relationship between proximate and ultimate explanations in biology, that is, between nonevolutionary and evolutionary explanations. A precondition for drawing the implications of Cummins's account for sociobiology is to recognize that capacity explanation is not a form of causal explanation. Cummins emphasizes this fact in contrasting transition theories, which provide causal explanations, with property theories, which provide noncausal explanations.

"The point of what I call a *transition theory* is to explain changes of state in a system as effects of previous causes-typically disturbances in the system" (Cummins 1983, 1). Evolutionary theory, as described in section 5.2, is primarily a transition theory in Cummins's sense. Subsumption under causal law is the natural explanatory strategy of evolutionary theory: one tries to fix on a set of state variables for the genotypic/phenotypic state of an evolving population that will allow one to exhibit each change of state as a function of a disturbing event, an event involving the operation of the forces of evolutionary change and the state of genotypic/ phenotypic state of the population at that time. The life cycle ideal describes the set of laws jointly necessary and sufficient to represent the transition from the state of the population in one generation to its state in the next generation. Evolutionary theory explains within-population evolutionary change via the strategy of subsumption of population-level events under causal laws. In Cummins's terms, it answers questions of the form "Why does population P from change states s-1 to s-2?", and of the form "How does the nth state (often the present state) of the population s-n reflect the cumulative effect of the prior state changes s-1, s-2, s-3, . . . , s-n-1?"

"The point of what I call a *property theory* is to explain the properties of a system not in the sense in which this means, 'Why did S acquire P?' or 'What caused S to acquire P?', but, rather, 'What is it for S to instantiate P', or, 'In virtue of what does S have P?'" (Cummins 1983, 15). Whereas transition theories explain changes, and therefore explain by appeal to a state before the change and a state after the change, property theories explain properties in a sense that do not appeal to temporal sequence. Whether we use the term "property theory" or not, the point is that some theories explain in such a way that the explained phenomena and the explanatory factors exist simultaneously. We can represent such explanations as subsumption of properties, not events, under laws of the following form: Anything having components C1, . . . , Cn organized in manner O—i.e., having analysis (C1, . . . ,Cn, O)—has property P; S has analysis (C1, . . . ,Cn,O); therefore, S has property P. This is not a state-transition, but rather a property constitution. S's having property P at a given time is constituted by S's having components C1, . . . , Cn organized in manner O at that time.

Functional explanations in sociobiology are not causal explanations, providing we understand the concept of causality to include the idea that the cause occurs before the effect in time. When we asked, "How is it that male birds are able to sing in the spring?" our question is about the constitution of that ability during the time the organism possesses the ability. By analyzing that relatively sophisticated ability into component abilities, we reveal constitution of the ability to sing as an organization of relatively less sophisticated abilities to sing each note in a sequence of notes at various rhythmically punctuated pitches.

Unlike Cummins, we distinguish component capacity explanations from composite capacity explanations. When we asked, "When male birds sing in the spring, what do they sing for?" our question is about the contribution of the ability to sing at the time the organism possesses it to a more sophisticated ability the organism also possess at that time. But this distinction adds nothing fundamental to Cummins's analysis of functions. He acknowledges that "Analysis is 'recursive,' since a given analysis may appeal to properties or components that themselves require analysis" (1983, 15). Thus, we may inquire into how birds are able to sing notes in sequences that vary in pitch and rhythm. That analysis eventuates in a structural explanation, where we talk about the physical constitution of the bird in terms of its vocal chords, beak size and shape, and so forth. If our original question were about the ability of birds to attract mates, we would answer by analyzing the ability to attract mates into the ability to recognize potential mates, sing in the spring, preen feathers, and so on, analyzing each of those abilities into their component abilities, and so on for their components, until we reach a structural explanation. That's the stuff of much of proximate biology: structure and function.

## Dispositional Explanation

Cummins does distinguish dispositional from nondispositional properties. Our view of proximate function makes this distinction in the following way pertinent to understanding organismic behavior. A capacity of an organism to do something is its ability to do it. Now, if organisms only had capacities but never exercised them, they would never survive. If they exercised capacities without regard to conditions of the natural and social environments, they would never survive. A disposition of an organism to do something is its tendency to behave, perform an action, or act in a certain manner under given circumstances. Organismic capacities, given that they do survive and survive because they are adjusted to their environments, are exercised in certain circumstances and not in others in characteristic patterns. Just what triggers the organism to manifest its disposition requires explanation. Why is it that when male birds sing, they do so in the spring? This is a question about what caused male birds to acquire the property of singing in the spring.

Mayr's well-known use of this example characterized functional biology in terms of this sort of explanatory request. Why do male birds sing in the spring? A proximate explanation would concern the direct mechanisms that brings something about, e.g., how the coming of spring induces song. Relevant explanatory information involves the facts that the song depends on high levels of the hormone testosterone in the bird's blood (internal structure, considered statically), that increase in testosterone levels results from spring growth in testes size (internal structure, considered dynamically), and that the growth is triggered by an increase in the number of daylight hours (response to environmental stimuli, considered statically or dynamically). Such explanatory information is integrated into an account of how the capacities of the animal are organized, given both the structure of the individual bird and the relevant environmental factors, so that they lead to a disposition to sing in the spring. That sort of explanation typifies what Mayr calls "functional biology."

On Mayr's account, an ultimate explanation would concern the adaptive significance of the male bird song, e.g., how the song enhances fitness. Relevant explanatory information here involves the facts that reproduction in birds is sexual and requires mating pairs, that mating pairs normally form in specific conditions which include effort on the part of the male to attract a female, and that the male bird song is only the first part of a complicated courtship ritual whose character is species-specific. Such explanatory information is combined into an account showing that the bird song is maintained by natural selection because of its utility in the attraction of mates and hence in promoting successful reproduction. That sort of explanation typifies what Mayr calls "evolutionary biology."

However, Mayr's proximate/ultimate contrast is very confused, according to Horan's account (1989; all page references to her account refer to her 1989 reply to commentators). First, biological explanations are responses to biological questions of four types: questions about immediate causation, development, function, or evolution (205). Functional explanations answer questions about the function of organisms' trait, questions about their adaptive significance, or survival value (205). Mayr's proximate/ultimate contrast is a contrast between immediate causation, which he calls "proximate causation" and evolutionary causation, which he calls "ultimate" causation (206). Mayr's contrast therefore fails as an exhaustive account of biological inquiry because it leaves no room for studies of development or studies of function.

Horan argues that Mayr's analysis runs together matters of

function and matters of evolution, as she thinks philosophical discussions of function have done for the past two decades (207). Because questions about functions and questions about evolution are distinct, one must distinguish statements describing the survival value of a trait from statements describing its evolutionary history (207). Mayr uses his proximate/ultimate contrast to make a distinction between proximate causes and ultimate causes. He recognizes four types of proximate causes: ecological causes, genetic causes, intrinsic physiological causes, and extrinsic physiological causes (206). He identifies as ultimate causes those proximate causes that currently exist in the organism because they have been present for thousands of generations in the past due to evolution by natural selection (206). Mayr's contrast between types of causes fails because it leaves unclear the role of the functions of traits, adaptive significance, or survival value as a cause in the sense of leaving indeterminate its role as a proximate cause or an ultimate cause. Indeed, fitness is not a cause of anything (Sober 1984).

These objections, on Horan's account, undermine the idea that Mayr's bird song example contains a clear contrast between proximate explanation and ultimate explanation. If the distinction between proximate and ultimate matters is confused, then so is the distinction between proximate and ultimate causation, and that confusion is transmitted to the distinction between proximate and ultimate explanation. The proximate explanation about the dependence of bird song on testosterone, testes size, and photoperiod is a causal explanation. It appeals to immediate causes. The ultimate explanation about the way bird song enhances fitness in terms normal mating patterns that derive from the evolutionary past is also a causal explanation. It, however, appeals to ultimate causes. Since Mayr divides biology in half, into functional biology and evolutionary biology, with functional biology treating proximate matters by citing proximate causes to yield proximate explanation, there is no room left for noncausal functional matters or noncausal functional explanations.

## Consequence Explanation

At this point we need to examine relations of autonomy and dependence between functional and evolutionary explanation. To distinguish between functional and evolutionary questions and answers, Horan gives an account of what is left out, namely, of functional explanations as "consequence explanations."

> Consequence explanations have the overall structure of a covering-law explanation. They differ from causal explanations in two respects: (1) the covering law is a "consequence law" instead of a causal law, and (2) the initial conditions contain a "functional fact" instead of a causal fact. The difference between a consequence law and a causal law is this. Causal laws state that one type of event, the cause, is sufficient for another type of event, the effect, and have the form, "If C then E.' Consequence laws state that the fact that one type of event, the cause, is sufficient for another type of event, the effect, is itself sufficient for the occurrence of the cause: 'If (if C then E), then C.' That is, consequence laws tell us that causes are brought about, or induced by the fact that they have certain effects. (Horan 1989, 136)

Why do male birds sing in the spring? Because singing signals courtship readiness. Let C stand for singing in the spring. Let E stand for signaling courtship readiness. A deductive-nomological explanation here would adopt the following reasoning. The functional fact that supplies the initial condition takes the form, if C then E: if male birds sing in the spring, then they signal courtship readiness. The functional regularity that supplies the consequence law takes the form If (if C then E), then C: If (if male birds sing in the spring, then they signal courtship readiness), then male birds sing in the spring. The functional fact that is derivable as a conclusion takes the form, therefore C: therefore, male birds sing in the spring. That's how adaptive explanations work in sociobiology.

Let us take 'signal courtship readiness' to be nonsignificantly different from 'attract female mates' in those species where courtship rituals are the mechanisms of mate selection. On Horan's view, the question "Why do male birds sing in the spring?" can be given two sorts of answers: (A) Some male birds sing in the spring *in order to* attract female mates, and (B) Some male birds sing in the spring *because* they attract female mates (208). Ordinary language is equivocal here, but the idea is the "in order to" of (A) is "forward-looking" whereas the "because" of (B) is "backward-looking" (207). In other words, (A) explains by appeal to functional design in the present whereas (B) explains by appeal to the results of selection for functional design in the past on the evolution of functional design in the present. (A) is a functional explanation, whereas (B) is a causal explanation in which the existence of functions are presupposed.

Since (A) explains by appeal to functional design in the present, it is a proximate functional explanation that is noncausal. In saying that "consequence laws tell us that causes are brought about or induced, by the fact that they have certain effects," the language is misleading. It seems to imply that the effect brings about the cause. That would violate the idea of causality, since, by definition, it is the cause that brings about the effect and not the effect that brings about the cause. However, the idea of 'bringing about' in the causal sense is predicated on the postulate that the cause exists before the effect in time. That future events cannot cause present events is one of the bedrocks of common-sense experience. To test the thesis that the idea of 'bringing about' in Horan's sense of proximate functional explanation violates common sense, it suffices to ask whether the cause C and the effect E in consequence explanation exist at the same time or whether C occurs before E. In fact, C and E are simultaneous in consequence explanation. This is obvious from our example. The act of singing by male birds and the act of signaling courtship readiness occur simultaneously.

Hence, we confront a choice here. Either we adopt Horan's terminology in which functions are effects and deny that causes must temporally precede their effects, or we retain the common-sense idea that causes must temporally precede effects and deny that what Horan describes as functions are effects. Since this choice would depend on considerations that go way beyond the issues raised by sociobiology, let us here finesse it by saying that in either case, the items that Horan describes as "effects" are radically unlike the sorts of effects we usually think in terms of. They would not be counted as functions on Cummins's account of functions because they occur simultaneously with their causes. In the sense of causality that requires temporal precedence, causal explanations explain the existence of something, that is, the existing cause brings about an effect that did not exist at the first moment the cause existed. In the sense of causality that requires temporal precedence, functional explanations explain the actuality of something, in the sense that, given the existence of the behavior and its function, the actual character or identity of the behavior is clarified in terms of its functional relationships.

To understand what it means for proximate functions to be effects without a reverse causal connection, let us distinguish between explaining the existence of something and explaining the identity of something. The ability to attract mates is constituted by the organization of a set of abilities, one of which is the ability of singing to potential mates. Thus, Horan's proximate functional analysis qualifies as a functional analysis in Cummins's sense, that is, as a capacity analysis. In the case of behavior, actions, or acts, to explain the identity or character of the ability at hand is to locate it in a nexus of organizational relations. The ability of male birds to sing in the spring is explained as identical with the totality of its component abilities and its contributive role with respect to the totality of its composite abilities. Thus, to explain the identity or character of some ability is to locate in a nexus of component relations, via component capacity explanations and composite capacity explanations. Causality comes into play because these are typically causal capacities, namely, capacities to do things that lead to successful survival and reproduction. The male bird's exercise of his capacity to sing leads to the female's being willing to be courted, which leads to the act of mating itself.

Proximate functional explanations are invoked when we already observe the behavior and need to explain it. The behavior is actual and the function is actual. That's part of how we know the latter explains the former, but it cannot be sufficient. As Cummins emphasizes, the justification of causal claims requires us to distinguish merely apparent from genuine causes and the justification of functional claims requires us to distinguish merely apparent from genuine functions. The usual scientific method for justifying causal claims requires that we manipulate both the causes and effects, e.g., to see if the cause invariably precedes the effect, if the effect invariably follows the cause, and so forth, in the conditions in which the phenomenon is observed. Causal claims are unjustified if there is no way to observe the causes independently of the effects. Sociobiological explanations are not justified, according to this criterion, since they posit some sort of causal relationship between genes and behaviors in their developmental explanations, and we have little idea of what these genetic causes may be.

To justify function claims, we cannot be required to manipulate behavioral capacities/dispositions and their functions in that way since they always exist together. Cummins recommends the requirement that the analyzed property should not reappear in the analysis as a criterion for distinguishing merely apparent from genuine functions. But even that is insufficient. We can dream up many ways of identifying the character of some behavioral capacity and the disposition to exercise it that invoke quite different functions. When male birds sing in the spring, they may attract mates, but they may also attract predatory birds. We assume that the function of bird song is to attract mates, not to attract predators. On what grounds do we identify the function of bird song as mate attraction, not as predator attraction? The obvious response is that mate attraction is their selected function, the function that increases their chances for success at survival and reproduction.

Ethology, now integrated into sociobiology as the biological study of the evolution and mechanisms of behavior, distinguishes capacities involved in the production of the bird song, capacities involved in the function of the bird song to attract mates, and capacities involved in the utility of mate attraction mechanisms for successful reproduction. We can apply a capacity analysis directly to the capacity to survive and reproduce. The relatively sophisticated capacity to survive and reproduce would be analyzed into a number of relatively simple capacities, such as obtaining food, securing mates, avoiding predators, and so forth. The capacity to secure mates would in turn be analyzed into a number of relatively simple capacities, such as the ability to sense the coming of spring, the ability to sing, and the ability to sense the presence of potential mates. We saw that developmental explanations gain evolutionary content by their import for deciding on what behavioral features natural selection acts. Similarly, functional explanations gain evolutionary content when recast to put the survival/reproductive capacities that give an organism its overall fitness into a different conceptual category than subsidiary behavioral capacities or dispositions.

## The Proximate/Ultimate Contrast

Millikan (1989) objected that Horan's account conflates two senses of function that should be kept distinct: one sense of function is what Millikan analyzes as 'selected functions' or 'proper functions' and the other sense of function is a Cummins-style function. Horan replies to Millikan's objection:

> I do think she recognizes the distinction between functional and evolutionary explanations I have tried to make, though she describes it in a different way,
> One kind of functional explanation, then, the kind that has to do with natural selection is intrinsically an "evolutionary explanation". [this quote is from Millikan]—

Her question, "What sense of function fits in here?" is required more by her decision not to separate evolutionary explanations from functional explanations than by my account, in which these are kept distinct. Of course, because Millikan makes the necessary compensation by then distinguishing what she calls the "proper" or "selected" function of a trait (what the trait was selected for that accounts for its presence in a population as opposed to that of an alternative) from what she calls its "Cummins function" (the contribution of a part to the capacities of the whole), the disagreement between us may be merely terminological.

There is more than a terminological issue here. But it is not a matter of choosing between two incompatible alternatives. We don't have to decide either that functional explanation ("proximate explanation") depends on evolutionary explanation ("ultimate explanation") or the reverse. We shall show that for each relation, there is a sense in which it holds.

(1) Functional explanation is independent of evolutionary explanation in an important sense. Male bird song has the function of attracting potential female mates. Male birds normally sing in the spring in order to attract females. The particular way they sing, the particular locations at which they sing, the particular time they sing, and so forth are designed or as if designed to attract females, given the particular strategies of mate choice adopted by those females at that time. This sense of function, designating the particularities of the relation between behavior and its immediate effects in particular circumstances, is standard in behavioral ecology and ethology. It is crucial for realistic, nonadaptationist explanations in sociobiology. Horan rightly emphasizes the particularity here, calling the particular actual behavioral effect under study "the proximate function of the behavior." Male birds don't just attract mates when singing in the same way for all species. They attract mates by engaging in various courtship rituals, and the specific character of these rituals varies across species. Explanations in terms of adaptive significance don't really explain if they don't capture the specific character of the behaviors at hand.

(2) Evolutionary explanation is dependent on functional explanation in an important sense. There is a distinction between "proximate function," the ways in which behaviors lead to certain effects in particular circumstances that enhance survival and/or reproductive success, and "ultimate function," survival success or reproductive success themselves. To say that "the function of male bird song is to enhance fitness" or "male bird song has survival or reproductive

value" does not explain anything by itself, but only in conjunction with a statement about how it increases fitness. Selection for survival value (mortality selection) or reproductive value (fertility selection) sorts among various proximate functions. If there were no proximate functions, there would be nothing for selectionist explanations to explain. Horan rightly brings attention to the "how," which adaptationist explanations are apt to leave out when they identify adaptive significance, e.g., when they say that a trait helps attract mates but do not say how.

(3) Evolutionary explanation is independent of functional explanation in an important sense. The name of the game in evolution is to do whatever it takes to project as many genes as possible into future generations, where those genes help construct bodies that perpetuate copies of those genes, via both direct reproduction and reproduction through relatives. If evolutionary change is wholly unaffected by selection, say, because all traits are adaptively neutral, and mutation and drift rule the day, then evolutionary explanation involves no functional explanation. Moreover, even when selection operates to cause evolutionary change, what is the operative concept of function? It is a trait that induces heritable variation in fitness. If there is no variation in fitness, then anything considered adaptively significant on some other grounds is irrelevant. If no proximate functions are correlated with ultimate functions so as to involve heritable variation, they are irrelevant to evolution.

(4) Functional explanation is dependent on evolutionary explanation in an important sense. One kind of function is a proximate function that currently has an ultimate function but did not have an ultimate function in the past which produced any evolutionary change by selection. Call that an "unselected function." Another kind of function is a proximate function which not only currently has an ultimate function, but that function which produced evolutionary change by selection in the past. Call that a "selected function." Unselected functions have no efficacy in affecting the character of the behaviors we find in organisms today. Selected functions are effective in affecting the character of the behaviors we find in organisms today. Therefore, the explanatory import of a selected function is far greater than that of an unselected function.

An unselected function of male bird song explains by permitting us to say that some male birds sing in the spring in order to attract female mates, but nothing more. A selected function of male bird song explains by permitting us to say that much, and also that some male birds sing in the spring because by singing they attract female mates. The selected function explains the presence of the trait in individuals in the present and previous generations in a sense unfulfilled by unselected functions. Selected functions are useful for answering questions of the form "How is the identity or character of the behavioral capacity/disposition we observe today a product of operative evolutionary processes?" The "because claim" presupposes causal efficacy in a sense in which the "in order to" claim does not.

To highlight the difference between evolutionary and nonevolutionary concepts of function, reconsider the definition of fitness. Concepts of function are related to adaptive significance. What counts as adaptive or maladaptive need not coincide in evolutionary and nonevolutionary sociobiology. A nonevolutionary concept of function might have us regard a behavior as adaptive just because it leads to reproductive success of the behaving organism. Suppose that trait leads its carrier to bear one more offspring at the price of leading to its close genetic relatives to bear many less offspring. In inclusive-fitness theory, it would decrease fitness relative to a trait that lead its carrier to bear one more offspring but also led to far greater overall reproductive output of both the organism possessing the trait and its close genetic relatives. Coefficients of relatedness aside, the evolutionary concept of function would have us regard the behavior as maladaptive.

Conversely, a nonevolutionary concept of function might have us regard a behavior as maladaptive because it lowers the reproductive success of its carrier, whereas an evolutionary concept of function would have us regard it as adaptive if it leads to greater reproductive output of its carrier plus close relatives. That is why evolutionary sociobiologists say that functional explanations have to be grounded in the proper evolutionary concept of fitness if they are to capture what adaptations are for. Otherwise, a measure of reproductive success need not measure what organisms are "as if designed" to accomplish. Otherwise, there is no reason for proximate, functional biology to regard organisms as "reproductive machines" rather than "survival machines." If we are sensitive to such differences in the identification of functional goal-states, actual behavior patterns (e.g., the sterile casts of social insects) make sense only in the light of evolution.

We will illustrate the significance of capacity explanation for evolutionary sociobiology by showing how it changes the way we understand the concept of "an adaptive strategy." In clarifying the relation of causal to functional explanation, Cummins contrasts a sense in which following a program explains behavior with a sense in which it does not. Sociobiologists conceptualize modes of behaviors promoted by selection as "adaptive strategies." A strategy is like a program. The fact that an organism follows an adaptive strategy explains its behavior by stating how the ability to survive and/or reproduce is enabled by the organization of subsidiary abilities, such as finding mates, avoiding predators, foraging for food, etc. It fails to explain why these subsidiary capacities so organized are actually exercised. The fact that an organism adopts an adaptive strategy does not explain why the organism is actually reproductively successful, except in the trivial sense in which it is given that the subsidiary capacities are actually operating. Of course, it is not trivial to identify which subsidiary capacities are actually operating. To think that following an adaptive strategy is sufficient to explain why it reproduces successfully both (a) confuses an analysis of a capacity or propensity with a cause of its exercise and (b) ignores the need to underwrite ultimate explanations with accounts of behavioral mechanisms.

A proximate causal explanation of an organism's behavior explains by appeal to causes of its behavior, where what counts as a cause is determined by events happening on an intragenerational time scale. An ultimate causal explanation of an organism's behavior appeals, given methodological decisions made in the light of identifying the organism through its membership in an evolving population, to causes of its behavior, where what counts as a cause is determined by events happening on an intergenerational time scale. Present-generation male birds sing in the spring as a result of past generations of male birds singing in the spring and the maintenance of that behavioral phenotype by natural selection from generation to generation.

So explanation in terms of natural selection involves both a functional and a causal aspect. To treat a behavior as adaptive involves a functional explanation applied at the level of individual organisms, namely, to analyze how a propensity for survival and/or reproductive success is enabled by a sophisticated organization of simpler behavioral capacities or dispositions. To treat a behavior as an adaptation involves a causal explanation applied at the level of populations of organisms, namely, that selection has operated in the past in relation to other evolutionary forces to cause an increase in the frequency of members of the population carrying that behavioral phenotype.

These results bear directly on the conceptualization of explanations provided by gene-culture programs. Both cognitive psychologists and sociobiologists who incorporate a complex psychology into their explanatory factors explain behaviors of organisms with minds. Both describe a "computational system" operating according to "programming rules," which can be identified by close analysis of the way people handle mental tasks (Cowley 1989). Traditional cognitive psychology tended to regard the mind as an all-purpose reasoning tool, equipotential in the sense of using some of the same basic procedures to process any information it receives. The work of Tooby and Cosmides falls into the grey area blurring the lines of sociobiology, evolutionary anthropology, and evolutionary psychology. The premise that mind is a biological adaptation leads to the explanatory postulates that (a) the mind did not evolve to solve arbitrary tasks, but tasks related to survival and reproduction; (b) these tasks are not solved by programming rules which yield logically optimal solutions, but pragmatically effective solutions that enhance fitness; (c) these tasks are not carried out by a small set or single overarching set of rules applicable to all inferences regardless of subject matter, but by a tremendously large number of rules particular to various recurrent adaptive problems involving information processing problems; and (d) since no organism can be preprogrammed to maximize fitness in every situation, natural selection in organisms with developed brains does not act directly on behavior, but on genes that assemble the organs that make behavior possible.

The theory of sexual selection is reconceptualized according to these postulates so that it acknowledges cultural diversity in sexual behavior but predicts that different culture-specific behaviors influenced according to these postulates have certain similarities. Tooby and Cosmides dramatize their point in the manner of pop sociobiology by saying that "the idea that culture (alone) explains sex differences will be taken seriously when female war parties start raiding villages to capture men as husbands" (Cowley 1989). Again, unwanted connotations of inevitability (involving necessity) arise from the fact that explanations of the past must have implications for the future in order to be tested.

Cummins's clarification of functional explanation reveals confusion in the usual understanding of what it means to say that "we do what we do because we are predisposed or preprogrammed by our genes to behave adaptively." We think in terms of cases like those in which someone follows a blueprint to build a house ("genetic blueprints"), follows a recipe to bake a cake ("genetic instructions"), or follows a computer program ("genetic programs"). These analogies mislead. Blueprints, instructions, or programs are taken to be objects in the environment which act as stimuli that direct behavior in addition to describing behavior and analyzing its direction. Yet

> ... an organism does not exercise its psychologically interesting capacities by consciously following an external program of instructions. This obvious fact has led some, presumably to preserve the analogy intact, to suppose that the required program is "there" all right, but "internally represented" in the brain, and "tacitly known and followed." Others, rightly suspicious of this talk of "internalization," have been led to reject the appeal to programs altogether. (Cummins 1977, 98)

Advocates like Barash think of adaptive programs as internally represented in the brain or in the genome and tell the public about "the whisperings within." The phrase assimilates genetic information to the imperatives of our conscience (or: a "humunculus" within the mind). Others reject such a "genetic determinism."

By realizing the way capacity explanations work, we see that the premise of this dispute is vexed. Whether a program is internally represented is irrelevant to the sort of explanation being offered. A functional explanation explains how sophisticated capacities are executed by means of simpler capacities but does not explain why these simpler capacities are exercised in the arrangements specified as adaptive. A functional explanation assumes the existence of the sophisticated and simpler capacities and merely exhibits their relation. It is another question as to why the sophisticated and simpler capacities exist in the first place. Part of the answer will be a mechanistic explanation, which invokes complex interactions between causes internal to the organism (including genes without ascribing them causal primacy over physiological or psychological or other internal causes) and causes external to the organism (including the physical, biological, social, cultural, historical environments not subordinated to genetic causes). Internal representation of an adaptive program does no explanatory work, making genetic determinism a pseudo-issue.

In sum, we have shown that explaining the character or the identity of something is different from explaining what caused it to exist, that both sorts of explanations are combined in subtle ways in evolutionary sociobiology which put functions into an evolutionary perspective, and that the evaluation of sociobiological explanations needs to take account of these differences and relationships.

## Normative Explanation

Let us return to Darwin's use of adaptive explanatory hypotheses without being tempted into extreme adaptationism. Whereas extreme adaptationists see in nature a balance of nature pervaded by perfect adaptations, Darwin emphasized that natural selection is no perfecting process and that organisms are adjusted to the conditions of their natural and social environments which reflect the operation of natural and sexual selection on historical contingencies that give the course of evolution no predictable outcome. He (1859, 42) describes the operation of natural selection by stating that, if behaviors arise which happen to be adaptive, if there are variant forms of those behaviors, and if the variants are inherited, then the favored variants should (ideally) be preserved in the population. Natural selection changes the frequencies of adaptive, neutral, and maladaptive traits, given their existence, in accord with differential fitness. This affects relative frequencies according to fitness taken to be an immediate better-or-worse and has not prevented almost all the species that have ever existed in the course of life on earth from going extinct.

Our gloss on Darwin's statement of natural selection describes an ideal case. If there is heritable variation in fitness, then the traits enhancing fitness should ideally increase in frequency according to the fitness differentials in the population. Why say "should ideally increase" rather than "will always increase"? Thomson (1984, 220–21) notes:

> As Hodge (1977) has shown, his (Darwin's) whole method was based on Hershel's treatment of vera causa (1830). Indeed, Hodge argued that each chapter of the Origin is arranged according to the three-fold content of vera causa: (1) the existence of a causal process, (2) the competence of that process to produce the effect to be explained, and (3) demonstration of the responsibility of the . . . mechanism for that effect, which then make it a possible source of explanation of other phenomena.

We know that the causal process of natural selection exists. Embedding procedures in sociobiology reveal the competence of natural selection to produce the effect to be explained, namely, diversity in social behavior across and within species. Projection procedures in sociobiology reveal the effective operation of natural selection as a cause of the observed social diversity. The nature of causal investigation itself sanctions our distinction between embedding and projection procedures. The purpose of (2) in sociobiology is to explain the possibility of social diversity, which demands that we understand how social diversity is theoretically possible. The purpose of (3) is to explain the actuality of social diversity, which demands that we understand why social diversity in all its particularity is the only actualized theoretical possibility.

Suppose selection is the only cause we are currently studying. The embedding of mating behavior is finished when we can show that the observed mating behaviors should increase in the population as a result of natural selection. The projection of mating behavior is finished when we can show that the actual conditions pertaining to the effectiveness of natural selection contradict every other sort of theoretically possible mating behavior than the actual one. Selectionist explanations help us understand the actuality of behavior in virtue of our understanding of how selection operates in an ideal setting and the relation between the actual setting and the ideal setting. This means that selectionist explanations have an idealized, normative character that demands further clarification. Evolutionary explanations are acceptable only if normative explanations in evolutionary ecology are acceptable, a kind of explanation not represented in Kourany's survey.

Ellis (1985, 55) characterizes a model theoretic explanation as one in which the properties of objects are explained in terms of "information about how (if at all) the actual behavior of some system differs from that which it should have ideally if it were not for some perturbing influences, and, where necessary, includes some information about what perturbing influences may be causing the difference." Taking theories to provide general schemata for giving explanations, he (1985, 55) characterizes model theories as those that "define norms of behavior against which actual behavior may be compared and (causally) explained." Model-theoretic explanations are normative explanations since they explain in terms of comparison to ideal norms. Since we should allow for normative explanations that do not use mathematical models, normative explanation is the more general category.

Optimality models in evolutionary ecology provide normative explanations, roughly, by specifying what counts as the optimal behavioral phenotype in an ideal situation in a way comparable to actual behavioral phenotypes in actual situations. We will clarify the sort of explanation provided by optimality models in three ways. First, normative explanation will be distinguished from the other sorts of explanation already discussed. Next, the structure of optimality models will be analyzed, viewed as tools of normative explanation. Then this structure will be used to interpret optimality models in a way that shows how they are useful even if Tooby, Cosmides, and critics of the adaptationist program are right that organisms do not solve adaptive problems in ways that typically yield logically optimal solutions.

Consider transitional explanation. The central concept in explanation in terms of natural selection is that of fitness, that is, expectation of success at survival and reproduction. The concept of success is a normative concept. Hence, we should suspect that evolutionary explanation is committed to normative explanation. The commitment accrues, not in virtue of its character of iterated transitional explanation, but in virtue of the status of natural selection as a force of evolutionary change.

Ellis's definition of normative explanation makes it grade imperceptibly into transitional explanation. However, they differ in their objects of explanation. Transitional explanations explain a change of state in an object, that is, a transition. In population genetics, a change of state of a population from one generation to the next is explained in terms of the earlier genetic state and the forces for genetic change. Normative explanations lay down norms determining an ideal state of an object. In evolutionary ecology, the ideal state of a variable behavior is determined, such as the optimal way to forage for food.

They also differ in modality. Transitional explanations stay within the actual world. Transitional explanations explain a change of object state by describing the prior actual state and posterior actual state, showing how the transition occurred in the way it did by appeal to forces of change of state actually at work. In population genetics, gene frequency change is explained by describing prior actual gene frequencies and posterior actual gene frequencies, showing how the frequencies change in the magnitude and direction they did by appeal to the actual magnitudes and directions of forces. Normative explanations relate the actual world to an ideal world of thought. In evolutionary ecology, an adaptive value of a variable behavior such as diet choice or mate choice is explained by comparing it to the optimally adaptive form the behavior would take in an ideal situation.

Consider causal explanation. Of course, population genetics also involves ideal models. The Hardy-Weinberg law describes a zero-force state, one in which no forces of evolutionary change operate on a population. Since some or all of the forces of migration, immigration, genetic drift, natural selection, and so forth are always in operation, the zero-force state is an ideal state. The strategy is to understand actual transitions by breaking them down into their components, which involves knowing what state transitions would occur if no forces operate, what state transitions would occur if each force operated alone, and what state transitions would occur as a result of interactions among multiple operating forces. With this background, the causal structure of change in actual situations can be understood.

Transitional explanation here is a kind of causal explanation, taking the actual prior state as an initial condition and the set of relevant principles about how forces act as causal laws. By contrast, normative explanation in evolutionary ecology via optimality models is not a kind of causal explanation since the optimal behavioral phenotype is an ideal and not supposed to cause anything. Normative explanation is used with causal explanation since we appeal to causal antecedents in order to understand why the actual behavior deviates in the way it does from the optimal behavior.

Consider functional explanation. Optimality models refine analyses of the functions of social behaviors exhibited by an individual of a particular species in a given environment. Every optimality model involves an optimality criterion, namely, a designation of some quantity that is maximized or minimized in a mathematical sense by the optimal phenotype. Normally, the modeler assumes that the quantity optimized varies proportionally with fitness, making its optimization a "proximate function." For example, it is assumed that foragers which maximize the rate of energy intake ($E/T$) maximize their fitness or that predators which maximize the food value to handling time ($V/T$) maximize their fitness. Fitness, as the chance of survival and reproductive success, is not explicitly present in the model. So an optimality model of male bird song would show how the optimal way to attract mates, where mate attraction is assumed to vary proportionally with fitness, is given by a certain combination of attributes of the song. The optimal capacity or disposition to attract mates is analyzed mathematically into contributing capacities, one of which is the spring song. The value of the optimality model is that we need not trust intuitive judgements of fitness. We can demonstrate via theorems derived from exact models that a certain behavior would or would not maximize fitness in the circumstances given by the assumptions of the model.

Consider natural-type or natural-state explanation. It is

tempting to interpret optimality explanations as natural-type or natural-state explanations. Just construe the optimal state of a variable behavior as the natural state or construe optimal foragers and optimal mate choosers as natural types. Then explain the properties of actual foragers and actual mate choosers as deviations from the natural type or natural state. We should resist this temptation, although it is nearly correct. A normative explanation is a natural-type or natural-state explanation, with the implication that the optimal phenotype is the natural type or state excised. A natural-type or natural-state explanation is a normative explanation overlaid with the interpretation that the type or state defined by the norm is natural.

The optimality criterion is grounded in evolutionary theory, that is, the theory leads us to identify the optimal phenotype as the one which maximizes fitness. Now, the structure of evolutionary theory and the logic of evolutionary explanation makes no commitments about the extent to which actual behaviors are adaptive. Whether the behavior is adaptive, maladaptive, neutral, or optimally adaptive, the frequency of the behavior in the population is explained as a result of interacting evolutionary forces and antecedent conditions. The tendency to view most important traits as adaptive or optimally adaptive involves a factual claim about the outcome of interacting forces. The claim is made in the context of evolutionary ideas, but independently of the structure of evolutionary theory and of the logic of evolutionary explanation. From the point of view of structure and logic, suboptimal phenotypes are just as natural as optimal phenotypes.

If we knew that all actual phenotypes were suboptimal, we would want a causal explanation, via iterated transitional explanation, of why they are suboptimal rather than optimal. If we knew that all actual phenotypes are optimal, we would want an explanation of similar form of why they are optimal rather than suboptimal. We expect that the truth lies between these two extremes. There is a rationale from theory structure and explanatory logic for making optimal phenotypes the norm and suboptimal phenotypes deviations from the norm. This rationale is not adaptationist since it involves no expectation of optimality in nature: selection maximizes average fitness or fixes the optimal phenotype in the simplest ideal conditions, as proven mathematically by Gale (1980).

Consider causal explanation again. Given the specification of the optimal phenotype as a matter of intuition or in an optimality model, normative explanation works by citing information about influences that are thought responsible for the discrepancy between the optimal phenotype and the actual phenotype. This involves causal explanation, but not exactly in the way Cummins (1977, 54) claims, which is that perturbing influences cause the difference between the actual and the ideal phenotype. More exactly, the discrepancy between the actual and the ideal phenotype is not an effect; causes operate to produce relations entirely within the actual world, not relations between the actual world and an ideal world. Instead, the discrepancy is rationally understood in terms of the network of causation from which the phenotype originates. Appeal to norms explains what the adaptive significance of the phenotype is, given the causal network. Appeal to the causal context explains the presence of the phenotype having a certain adaptive significance, given the normative comparison.

The causal network in which natural selection operates furnishes a variety of "obstacles to optimality," which count as "specific conditions that may get in the way of any idealized behavioral optimum" (Barash 1982, 50). Barash's phrase is well suited to normative explanation since it implies that optimality is an ideal norm to which actual phenotypes are referred in order that their degree of success be understood and that the specific conditions involve causal conditions. Gould and Lewontin (1979), Dawkins (1982a), Mayo (1985), and many others have their own preferred lists of these conditions. Suppose we have the total list of causal conditions that may produce deviations from any ideal optimal behavior. We combine information about the specific assumptions made in a given optimality model, about the species to which the model is to be applied, and about other relevant species using the comparative method. We use this information to decide which theoretical possibilities are plausible. Using our knowledge of the local conditions that act as constraints, we collect more information to decide which theoretical scenario is responsible for the actual behavior's deviation from the optimal design.

## The Structure and Use of Optimality Models

The structure of optimality models can be represented in several slightly different ways (Oster and Wilson 1978; Maynard Smith 1978; Beatty 1980; Horn 1978). No one has yet clarified the way the conceptual structure of optimality models embodies normative explanation. Their four-part structure is readily illustrated by a non-social example (Holcomb 1989c). The following scheme generalizes to social applications, e.g., studies of optimal foraging as a factor in why men hunt whereas women gather in hunter-gatherer societies (Hill et al. 1987; Winterhalder 1987).

In the logicomathematical part, a design-problem and design-solution are constructed whereby theorems can be deduced that identify the optimal design. If the problem is to decide in what proportion to eat different prey types upon encounter and the optimization criterion is to maximize the daily net rate of energy intake while foraging, then it can be deduced that the optimal forager maximizes fitness in situations of two prey types by behaving in accord with three conditionals: If $E1/T1 < E2/T2$, then eat prey type 2 exclusively; If $E1/T1 = E2/T2$, then eat prey types 1 and 2 in any proportion; If $E1/T1 > E2/T2$, then eat prey type 1 exclusively. The structural analyses cited above focus on the logicomathematical part but fail to do justice to the other parts that enable optimality models to yield normative explanations.

In the classificatory part, strategies are classified into types and, derivatively, organisms are classified on the basis of those types. Thus Shoener (1971) introduced the distinction between time-minimizers, animals having fixed energy requirements and which maximize fitness by minimizing the time needed to obtain a certain amount of energy, and energy-maximizers, animals having a fixed time in which to forage and which maximize fitness by maximizing the energy obtained from foraging. There is no one type of optimally designed organism for every design problem, every foraging design problem, every foraging design problem involving diet choice, and so forth. For every design problem there is a definition of a unique kind of organism.

In the advisory part, the optimal design theorem is interpreted as a prediction about how organisms of the appropriate kind should behave. Thus a robust theorem of several slightly different optimal foraging models is that the most valuable food type should always be accepted when encountered, but as its encounter rate decreases, the diet should expand to include the next most valuable food type. Notice that the generalization here, strictly speaking, applies to ideal organisms rather than to actual organisms. That is, it describes, not what organisms actually do, but what they should do in order to maximize fitness. The common usage of the term "should" reflects the fact that the model's "predictions" are normative.

Given information about actual organisms using the comparative method and other empirical methods, in the evaluative part, the rational efficacy of the the behavior of actual organisms is evaluated using the norm as the basis for evaluation. If we find that the actual organisms studied incorporate some low-profit prey into their diet even with a high encounter rate with the most valuable food type, then we have clarified the adaptive significance of the actual behavior. We then look to aspects of the causal situation that may furnish violations of the assumptions of the optimality model or other relevant factors not found in the model in order to explain the discrepancy between norm and fact. For instance, we may inquire into whether the actual organism is unable to discriminate food-type value in certain circumstances or whether its food-type sampling procedures is a relevant factor.

By tinkering with the model to take account of these exigencies, we can then see if the organism forages optimally with respect to a more realistic optimal design. By examining the similarities and differences between the way actual organisms do act and the way actual organisms would act if they were to act optimally, we learn something about the significance of causal constraints on organisms for their particular adaptive strategy.

This specification of how the structure of optimality models provides a basis for their function to deliver normative explanations contains important implications for the issue of adaptationism. To even pose the issue, we need to distinguish metaphysical from methodological adaptationism.

Gould and Lewontin (1979) charge that the very use of optimality models is based on a false metaphysical postulate that all organismic traits are either optimally adaptive or optimal compromises between conflicting optima. As such, their use "vulgarizes" evolutionary explanation by postulating that actual organisms are perfectly adapted organisms. But optimality models involve no such metaphysical adaptationism since the optimal behaviors are supposed to be ideal norms that may or may not have actual counterparts in virtue of their use in normative explanations.

Gould and Lewontin also charge that the purpose of optimality modeling is to find for each trait the optimization criterion and constraint set according to which the trait is optimized. If one choice does not exhibit the organism as perfectly adapted, the modeler looks for another choice. Even if the modeler is not rationalizing a belief in perfect adaptation, he is not really testing the model or the hypothesis of adaptation since by tinkering with the model long enough with enough imagination, he is guaranteed to arrive at an optimal design that seems to fit the actual behavior. But optimality models involve no such methodological adaptationism since the purpose of the tinkering with the models is to examine relations between ideal norms and actual facts about behaviors in order to understand their adaptive significance. We learn much more about organisms by studying the discrepancies between ideal norm and actual facts than from the few cases or ways in which they coincide. If all traits fit hypothetical optimal designs, optimality models would have no utility in providing normative explanations.

Horan (1989) continues the attack on the potential of optimality models to provide testable explanations. One point of attack is that the twin goals of optimality models to be realistic (literally true) and robust (sufficiently general to have explanatory and predictive success) are in conflict. The broader the generalizations about optimally designed behavior supplied by these models, the less likely are the models to provide true accounts of actual behavior in all its complexity. Tinkering with the models by introducing complex relations between given factors or new kinds of factors in order to capture the complexities of actual behavior succeeds at the price of sacrificing generality sufficient to explain and predict other related cases. But the significance of these insights is not a criticism of optimality modeling, as she thinks, since normative explanations based on these models are not supposed to be both realistic and general. The optimal phenotype is ideal, not realistic.

Another critical charge is that adequate evidence for hypotheses about the function of a trait cannot be provided by optimality analyses, but instead by the comparative method. But optimality models are a form of theory rather than evidence. Suppose we revise her point to charge that evidence for the functional claims of optimality models gained by testing the models hypothetico-deductively is much weaker than evidence for functional claims gained by examining actual behaviors using the comparative method.

Horan criticizes the hypothetico-deductive view of confirmation, which states that theories are tested by deriving predictions or explanations of observable phenomena from them and finding that these observable implications come true. This view succumbs to the old problem that one can logically construct a variety of rival theories for the domain of the theory to be tested, all of which can predict or explain the same observable phenomena. There is no way to choose between these rival theories. By hypothesis, they are confirmational equivalents. So we should add to the hypothetico-deductive view a criterion of independent warrant for weeding out the implausible from the plausible confirmationally equivalent rival theories, which states that the theory to be accepted should have a sufficiently high probability relative to background information. The comparative method, she says, offers us such background information whereas the method of deducing predictions from optimality models does not.

The logic of this argument, however, does not lead solely to the conclusion that optimality models are not sufficiently confirmable. It assumes that one must choose between the comparative method and optimality modeling. Not so (Krebs and Davies 1984, Preface). Optimality models are useful because they generate new explanations, provide testable hypotheses, link observations to general theory, refine explanatory hypotheses, and so forth (Smith 1987). In all these uses, information about the specific cases to which the models are applied, often gained from the comparative method, is incorporated into formulating and testing the mathematics of the model: an actor (who chooses or exhibits alternate states), a strategy set (the range of options), a currency (the cost-benefit measure maximized or minimized), and a constraint set (the factors determining the feasible strategy set and option payoff assignments). Empirical information about the frequency of certain kinds of situations in nature, often gained from the comparative method, is used to decide on various indices of how far a positive instance of the model confirms its adaptive hypotheses: whether the description of the strategy set is accurate, whether the description of the optimal strategy identifies the best available ancestral type, whether evolution has produced the best available ancestral type, and so forth (Kitcher 1987b).

In conclusion, disciplinary relations within sociobiology reflect the kinds of explanations being constructed. We saw earlier that evolutionary sociobiology generates primarily transitional explanations. Through affiliation with an ideal that puts the organismic life cycle into an evolutionary perspective, transitional explanations incur commitments to compositional, developmental, and variational explanations. Transitional explanation, and these derivative kinds of explanation, are kinds of causal explanations. Functional explanation is not causal explanation, but, rather, an explanation of something's character or identity (unless we allow that causes are simultaneous with their effects). Functional explanations presuppose operating causes and take the form of component functional explanations, composite functional explanations, dispositional explanations, consequence explanations, and normative explanations.

If the identification of functions is not made on evolutionary grounds, these are nonevolutionary explanations. If the identification of functions is made on evolutionary grounds, these are evolutionary explanations. Only evolutionary function is rooted in genetic fitness. Evolutionary sociobiology and nonevolutionary sociobiology therefore propose different kinds of functional explanation.

A completed evolutionary biology would require a synthesis of transitional explanation in population genetics, compositional explanation in transmission genetics, developmental explanation in developmental biology, variational explanation in behavioral genetics and phylogenetic biology, functional explanation in evolutionary ethology, and normative explanation in evolutionary ecology. The New Synthesis toward which evolutionary sociobiology strives is, first and foremost, a synthesis within biology, not a synthesis of biology and social science. Sociobiology has yet to achieve total explanations in which the discipline-laden connections between their explanatory commitments are well worked out. It is misleading for advocates to make grand claims about how the theoretical foundations of social science lie in sociobiology. Indeed, it is premature to make serious claims to the effect that sociobiology will place the social sciences on a firm theoretical foundation when a firm theoretical foundation that reorganizes the study of organismic sociality in the biological sciences in terms of an evolutionary time scale is still wanting. Given the array of explanatory resources and kinds of explanation involved, this inspiring task will absorb all the ambitious energy sociobiologists have generated in their problematic efforts to show how sociobiology illuminates matters beyond its limited domain.

# CHAPTER
# 6

## PERFORMANCE CONCEPTUALIZATION

### 6.1 Evaluative Perspectives

### Self-Reflective Methodology

We are now in a position to bring together our previous results in a way that informs the final component of conceptual frameworks in sociobiology, namely, the conceptualization of explanatory performance. To indicate where in this book these results are taken from, each result will be followed with a citation of the relevant chapter or section printed within parentheses. This convention enables the reader easily to refer back to the appropriate place in the book where the argument for the result was given.

From logical empiricist philosophies of the products of science, we have adopted the analysis of explanations into sentences stating the phenomena-to-be-explained and stating the explaining factors (1.2). From philosophies of scientific change, we have adopted the account of the dynamics of science in terms of changes in explanatory problems and explanatory solutions (3.3). Let us suppose that we have a body of explanatory work in sociobiology that implicitly makes decisions about the character of the problems posed by explanatory incompleteness (chap. 3), the character of the social phenomena in need of explanation (chap. 4), and the character of the explanatory factors for doing the explaining (chap. 5). Explanations of what makes sociality evolutionarily possible and of actual social diversity are constructed on the basis of an underlying theory (chap. 1) under the guidance of a research program (chap. 2), evaluated for their performance, and revised accordingly. That is how scientific research proceeds. How should we evaluate the effectiveness of sociobiology's explanatory performance?

This question moves us toward critically evaluating the way we conceptualize the research value of our explanatory hypotheses within the current research situation (1.5). More precisely, in the contextual background of our evaluation of scientific hypotheses lies a determination of their research value, given theoretical structure (chap. 1), programmatic structure (chap. 2), and conceptual structure (chaps. 3, 4, 5). Their research value with respect to their conceptual structure is expressible in terms of their underlying conception of the explanatory problem being addressed, their conception of the phenomena to be explained, and their conception of the factors doing the explaining.

Each particular explanation has its own specific way of conceiving the problem it addresses, the phenomena it explains, and the factors doing the explaining. In practice, of course, it is not explicitly formulated so as to wear its general conceptual role within sociobiology on its sleeve. Nevertheless, the research that exists today in evolutionary sociobiology is oriented by the quest for explanatory completeness (1.2). Our task is to defend the best version of evolutionary theory we have against its most severe challenges posed by animal and human sociality for completing the range of successful evolutionary explanation (3.3). The best available rival explanation is the one currently acceptable for purposes of further research (1.5). To justify claims that significant progress has been made as one currently acceptable explanation displaces another, the challenges posed by incompleteness in the explanations themselves must be met (2.3). Sociobiology is significantly progressive if, within the constraints of its research situation, its results meet a feasible standard of success in meeting its challenges. This idea incorporates a metascientific optimality model (5.3). Explanatory efforts are optimal within the constraints of a current research situation if they meet the challenge posed by manifest incompleteness in the most defensible manner, maximizing the severity of the challenge and minimizing revisions in our best version of evolutionary theory and our best version of evolutionarily significant social facts (3.3). A feasible standard of success is one that reflects a suitable compromise between defensibility, severity and revision.

A critically self-reflective methodology for evaluating sociobiology is a normative study of sociobiology that both analyzes its methods of explanation and critically examines the methods we use to evaluate the explanations proposed in that science (1.1). In order to decide whether our performance evaluations are conceptually well grounded, we ultimately find ourselves evaluating the methodological perspectives, criteria, standards, and rules by which explanations are evaluated. Having made the decisions involved in formulating the explanations according to the criteria found in specifying sociobiology's explanatory problems (chap. 3), domain (chap. 4), and disciplinary structure (chap. 5), we can judge the extent that they are well-articulated. Having made the decisions involved in testing the explanations so formulated according to the criteria found in theory-choice (chap. 1) and program-choice (chap. 2), we can judge the degree to which they are well-tested. Due to the interconnection of decisions about whether they are well-articulated and well-tested, a well-grounded evaluation makes appropriate use of all three units of analysis to discern an explanation's explanatory powers and explanatory limits. In this way we have elaborated the three-unit model of theory structure for evaluating science initially outlined (1.1).

We have shown that science involves many more sorts of trained judgement and decision making than are represented in simple appeals to "scientific method." A conclusion of acceptance or rejection is justifiable only if it applies the criteria of being well-tested and well-articulated in terms of the way the quest for completeness is embodied in all three units of analysis, namely, theories, research programs and conceptual frameworks. Our performance evaluations should take this fact into account in asking, "Has sociobiology on balance improved the degree of completeness by formulating the right sorts of explanations tested by the right sorts of evidence?"

Our decision-procedure for answering the question should be critically self-reflective, being aware of the terms in which it analyzes and evaluates science. An evaluative method is a tool. It detects the presence of varying qualities of scientific work. Like any detecting instrument, it allows you to find only that which the instrument is designed to detect. There may be other features of scientific work that affect their quality, but to these it is blind. To use a camera for judging the quality of music in a performance would be ludicrous. So we must make sure our evaluations of sociobiology are especially suitable for detecting the character of explanatory work within the research situation we have identified. Crucial to the conceptualization of performance evaluations is the question: "Are the choices of our evaluative tools and the manner in which we use them appropriate to what is being evaluated?"

Intuitively, the idea of appropriateness serves as a necessary condition for the adequacy of an evaluation. From the foregoing results, we therefore impose the following three conditions on an evaluation of sociobiology which can justifiably be claimed to be an adequate evaluation: (A) The evaluation operates from within an evaluative perspective that is truly appropriate to sociobiology's research situation; (B) the evaluation employs methodological standards and rules that are truly appropriate to sociobiology's research situation; and (C) the evaluation is framed in terms of evaluative criteria and units of analysis that are truly appropriate to sociobiology's research situation.

This chapter will tie our main previous results together by developing these conditions of adequate evaluation of sociobiology's performance. In this section we will treat (A) by showing how to justify an evaluative perspective. An evaluative perspective cannot be justified in the sense of adducing reasons for its truth since perspectives are not the sorts of things to be true or false. Instead, they are vindicated by showing that they can be articulated so that they lead to fruitful consequences, results which are backed up by their own special arguments. If we have made sense out of sociobiology, the perspective of this book has been vindicated by the results and arguments in the book as a whole. This is the perspective that emphasizes the following ideas: self-reflective methodology, irresolvability, evolutionary significance, quest for completeness, aim-oriented evaluation, prevalidated science, intradisciplinary diversity, scientific change, research value, image of science, presuppositions, units of analysis, and systematicness.

It takes far more work to show that one's evaluation is adequate for evaluating sociobiology than supplying reasons for making one's own pro or con comments. The rest of this chapter elaborates this idea by uncovering what is involved in showing that an evaluation is adequate according to conditions (A), (B), and (C). In the remainder of this section, we will show that another element of this perspective has been vindicated, namely, the emphasis on irresolvability.

In section 6.2 we will treat (B) by raising the problems of innovation, consensus, and dissensus in science in the context of sociobiology. If there is a unity to scientific method, scientists should share the same rules and standards, and so they should normally come to basically the same evaluative conclusions. If there is a diversity in scientific methods, scientists should operate with different rules and standards, and so they should normally come to basically different evaluative conclusions. In an emerging science, like sociobiology, which is not as rigorous as established science precisely because the research it engages in is innovative, how could its explanations ever be rational to accept?

Implications of the above perspective on how to evaluate innovative science will be drawn for coming to grips with the role of the pervasive criticism sociobiology has received, using Kitcher's influential and sophisticated critique as an example. It uses the sets of methodological rules imposed on sociobiology by Kitcher to raise the issue of how the tools of evaluation are to be properly chosen. It argues that the tools for evaluating explanatory adequacy are grounded both in particulars, standard examples of scientific practice as results, and in general orientations, the drive for explanatory unification inherent in the quest for completeness. It argues that the immediate target for applications of evaluative tools is the specific explanatory role a particular explanation has in the quest for completeness, that is, the contribution it makes to the synthesis or unification required for completeness.

Section 6.3 addresses (C) by assembling the requirements for a total adequate evaluation of sociobiology. A total adequate evaluation of sociobiology with respect to explanation would employ all the evaluative criteria and units of analysis found in the three-unit model of theory structure. This does not mean that everything about sociobiology would be evaluated, which would be an impossible task. Rather, it means that particular explanations are to be evaluated in terms of all the criteria affiliated with the explanation's surface structure, the way it answers variants of why or how questions, and its deep structure, which consists of its theoretical structure, programmatic structure, and conceptual structure. The questions to ask in order to determine the constitution of the surface and deep structure of explanations of sociobiological explanations will be enumerated in a manner easily generalizable to explanations in other sciences, particularly those in emerging sciences like sociobiology. This provides the final step in justifying our recommendation of the three-unit model of the units of analysis, making it usable and useful for evaluating science.

## Irresolvability: Genuine Issues

Evaluators cannot resolve or dissolve the sociobiology controversy as a whole. The reason it cannot be dissolved is that the issues are real. The main real issue is not over the existence of severely flawed explanations in evolutionary sociobiology that would have exciting implications for understanding us if relevant to and true of human sociality. That is an obvious fact. The main real issue is over how to evaluate their scientific worth with an eye to improvement in the match between goals and results. We have identified and explored quite a few of these real (genuine) issues. These results will be summarized.

Evaluations of the confirmational success of sociobiological explanations confront the following issues. Sociobiology is not testing evolutionary theory as such, but, rather, applications of evolutionary theory. Our decisions about confirmation are not attuned to this difference and are generally not attuned to the problems of confirmation special to the research situation of the principled extension of a science beyond its traditional or normal boundaries (1.2). Decisions about whether the statistically significant empirical generalizations, such as those reported by Betzig, provide definitive confirmation of hypotheses based on the theory of mate selection and mate competition are difficult on their own terms. They are doubly frustrating when the theoretical explanations they confirm have an illusion of empirical content because the data was not shown to be logically derivable from the theory (1.3). Decisions about what counts as sufficient confirmation for regarding them as acceptable scientific explanations turns on whether they are the best among rival available explanations, that is, if their acceptance possesses greater expectable value for promoting the aims of basic sociobiological research than does the acceptance of any rival available explanation. These decisions about aim-oriented research value go beyond simple appeals to confirming facts in ways that are going to be subject to continuing controversy (1.4).

Evaluations of successful resistance to attempts to disconfirm sociobiological explanations confront similar issues: becoming attuned to problems of extension posed for disconfirmation of hypotheses about genes, adaptation, natural selection, and fitness; the bearing of the lack of statistical significance on definitive disconfirmation of these hypotheses; inferences from disconfirmation to falsity or irrelevance; appropriate standards of sufficient disconfirmation for rejection (2.1). Evaluations of both confirmational success and success at resistance to attempted disconfirmation are affected by prior judgements of the plausibility of the explanatory hypotheses and theories under test (2.2). Evaluations of the plausibility of these hypotheses confront the issue of making decisions about the role of background beliefs involved in controversial ideologies (e.g., sexism) on the content of these hypotheses and on decisions to accept or reject them. It is doubtful that scientists will agree on decisions about plausibility, given the obvious continuation of dissensus on those background beliefs like sexism (2.2) and reductionism (2.3).

For instance, the Wilson-Lewontin exchange well illustrates the difficulty of coming to any agreement when judgements of acceptability are affected by holistic world views, encompassing differences over scientific method, strategies for gaining knowledge, the relation between science and ideology, human nature, and moral preferences (2.4). Evaluations of explanatory progress induced by underlying research programs confront the issue of making an impartial judgement about the record of successes and failures that determine whether the scientific work is progressive or regressive, when basic ideological and scientific orientations cannot help but contour these judgements (2.3).

Evaluations of the satisfactory regulation of the articulation and testing of explanations by guiding research programs confront the manifest difficulties in connecting the concepts and claims involving fitness, adaptation, natural selection, and genes to the available social data about cultural organisms. There have been rapid changes in research programs from those of early sociobiology, which did not supply a role for cultural transmission in the theory, to those of later sociobiology, which generated rival programs for reconciling and synthesizing genetic transmission with cultural transmission in a coherent scheme. Early programs include the epigenetic program of Wilson and Lumsden, the coevolutionary theory of Alexander, the dual-inheritance program of Richerson and Boyd, and the evolutionary mechanics program of Cavalli-Sforza and Feldman. These have been developed and are now a small subset of the current array of programs involving a complex psychology. We expect unpredictably different programs in the future (2.4).

Since sociobiology is to be evaluated in terms of its goals, a clear understanding of the goals and development of sociobiology's New Synthesis would have to employ a model of syntheses and a view of the Modern Synthesis less biased and more suitable than the one provided by Mayr. But agreement on this matter is unlikely, since people differ on how to understand sociobiology's explanatory aims in a historical context. Each significant change in or departure from the neo-Darwinian perspective reinterprets that perspective in terms of its own special proposals and interests (3.1). Since the fact that altruism is a precondition for observed sociality, evaluations of whether and to what extent we have progressed in solving the problem of altruism would have to speak to the cumulative, corrective, revolutionary, and gradual aspects of its further development. But we are far from having a model of scientific development which does justice to what is involved in the successive refinements that generate progress of this sort (3.2). To explain altruism and sociality, a good understanding of the relations between selection on genes, selection on individual organisms, and selection on groups is necessary, given the genetic basis of all evolutionary change and the need to explain individual interactions and social order. But the problem of the units/levels of selection has gone to the heart of the conceptualization of fitness, adaptation, selection, and evolution. At present the theorists involved cannot agree on a common set of concepts (3.3).

The very idea of including human behavior and human sociality in the evolutionary domain is so provocative to traditional scientific assumptions and common-sense world views that there is little consensus on whether we should adopt the strategies of domain restriction, domain extension, or domain transformation (4.1). In that circumstance, just how to carry out the procedures of domain extension will remain controversial. Claims that all the objections, e.g., to explaining such things as morality as evolved phenomena, can be overcome will not convince those already unpersuaded of the viability of human sociobiology (4.2). Just what it means to explain the evolution of some social behavior in such a way that it is revealed as actual or as possible or as necessary is a subtle point which we will not agree on (4.3).

It is going to be very difficult to figure out what difference social transmission and the development of behavior, psychological skills, and so forth makes to the ideals about sociobiology's resources that allow it to connect phylogenetic studies, studies in evolutionary ecology, sociobiology, and other related biological disciplines (5.1). There will be continuing disputes over the use of other ideals that determine the kinds of explanation found in sociobiology, such as the life cycle ideal which puts individual lifetimes into an evolutionary focus that provides the basis for integrating transitional, compositional, developmental, variational, functional, and normative explanations (5.2). The forms that rigorous functional explanations in sociobiology may take, the relation between evolution and functions, and the role of mathematical modeling techniques such as optimality modeling are subject to continuing problematic proposals within sociobiology (5.3).

Although the problems that confront sociobiologists—and these are just a few of them—are very intellectually demanding, they are potentially resolvable on their own terms. One reason that the scientific aspects of the sociobiology debate cannot be resolved in one fell swoop is that they turn on evaluative issues which call into question the adequacy of our ways of evaluating sociobiology. These evaluative issues, as the previous summary of our results show, involve too many sub-issues bearing complex and subtle relations to be solved in one fell swoop. In this sense, we should not expect an adequate evaluation of sociobiology to resolve the sociobiology debate. Kitcher began the preface to his (1985) book with the words, "In my optimistic moments I hope that the chapters that follow will put an end to the controversies that have beset sociobiology in the past decade." Instead, his philosophically sophisticated critique, very much in the spirit of Gould and Lewontin, became another milestone in the controversy. There is no getting round the fact that our views of what the controversy is and how to resolve it or dissolve it are themselves controversial.

## Irresolvability: Pseudo-Issues

In addition, we have pointed out a number of issues that are irresolvable on their own terms. These are the issues over biological determinism, biological reductionism, and extreme adaptationism, and the biologism of human nature. The basic reason they are irresolvable is that they involve externally imposed interpretations of sociobiology where sociobiology is caught in the crossfire among wide orientations that it can illustrate, for better or for worse, but not terminate. Every new sociobiological proposal becomes more grist for the mill of these biological philosophies. To extricate ourselves from this situation, we recommended the natural methodological and ontological attitude as expressed by Fine. He recommends that we just take these scientific problems on their own terms and try not to read things into science. He correctly infers that if one adopts this attitude, then the global interpretations, the "isms" of biological philosophies, appear as idle overlays to sociobiology: not necessary, not warranted and, in the end, probably not even intelligible. We will now show that this perspective has been vindicated by a number of our results.

First and foremost, the main aim of sociobiology has nothing to do with any of these biological philosophies. This is the aim of helping to achieve the completeness of evolutionary biology by making evolutionary theory applicable to and true of all the main kinds of phenotypic traits, including sociality in all the main kinds of species, including the social species (1.1). One can always interpret this aim with these biological philosophies. One can always undertake this aim using the social and intellectual ideals inherent in these philosophies. One can always interpret the specifics of projects that contribute to this end in terms of the biological philosophies. Any scientific aim or project in sociobiology can be treated in these ways. Therefore, such facts reflect on the all-embracing character of these biological philosophies, not the distinguishing character of this aim and project. The delicate issue of just why the aim of explanatory completeness has nothing to do with these biological philosophies has been a hidden theme of many of the ensuing discussions.

To achieve completeness with respect to the class of all evolutionarily significant social facts, sociobiology needs to provide an observational or descriptive language adequate for the expression of any evolutionarily significant social fact and to be able to explain every available fact expressed in this descriptive language (1.2). This aim is stated in terms neutral between the issues that divide opposing biological philosophies.

The dispute over the animal-human comparisons made in pop sociobiology is unnecessary since these comparisons have no evidential weight unless combined with the growing body of statistical evidence for explanations based on the general theory of sex-typical strategies of competing with members of their own sex for mates and choosing mates of the opposite sex (1.3). The dispute over sociobiology-as-science versus sociobiology-as-ideology is confused, as is revealed by the distinctions between the relation of explanatory products to themselves and to our explanatory acts, between the political and scientific status of an explanation, and between criteria and determinants of acceptability. The dispute over biologism is unnecessary since sociobiology is not intrinsically a theory of human nature, as revealed by appeal to the distinction between the ontology of a scientific theory and metaphysics of human nature (1.4). The dispute over the grounds for deciding how high the standards of evidence must be has turned on whether the social, political, and ethical consequences of accepting explanations are relevant to the determination of sufficient evidence. The dispute is confused since it fails to distinguish the contexts of use for purposes of inquiry, belief, and action as contexts of commitment, and so does not evaluate the acceptability of explanations according to use-specific acceptance (1.4).

The disputes over adaptationism and genetic determinism are

unintelligible since they have failed to employ a meaningful statement of what adaptationism and genetic determinism are that speaks to the comparisons which inform the complex relations denoted by "adaptiveness" or by "genetically determined" (2.1). The attribution of adaptationism to sociobiology is unwarranted since it has not done the work in showing not only that sociobiology offers adaptive explanations, but also that the only form of adaptive explanation it includes is an uncritical adaptationism (2.1). The judgement that the theory for the field of sociobiology is invalid because it is unfalsifiable has been vexed because it is not grounded in a hard-hitting sense of falsifiability in Popper's sense that is applicable to theories of adaptation or programs for investigating adaptive significance (2.1). The appeal to falsifiability is unnecessary since only particular versions of explanations are definitely verifiable or falsifiable in a pragmatic sense, although not in the logician's sense. But these are so transitory in research that their falsifiability does not make the difference for the path of research that proponents of falsifiability envisage (2.1).

The disputes over genetic determinism, adaptationism, biological reductionism are unnecessary since the statement of sociobiology's explanatory goals inherent in its New Synthesis has the form "social evolution can be explained in terms of specified explanatory factors; and observed evolutionary phenomena can be explained in a manner consistent with what is known about the way these factors operate in nature" (3.1). This form does not require that the factors of genetic changes are the only factors that determine individual development. It neither requires that the predominant force of evolutionary change is natural selection, nor does it require that everything is or was adaptive, nor does it rule out adaptive explanations which employ natural selection to explain the degree of adaptation in terms of the outcome of selection on adaptively positive, neutral, or negative traits. The minimal, unproblematic form of sociobiology's goal statement opens the way to go beyond orthodox population genetics and to incorporate gene-culture theories with a place for social transmission and a complex psychology. To do so involves resources taken from social science, and therefore does not reduce social science to biology. It is the responsibility of particular research projects to indicate which theoretical resources they use and to make proposals about which overall constellation of resources they conceive the New Synthesis to employ (5.1).

The dispute over sociobiology and sociopolitical questions are overstated, and thus quite misleading, when it comes to what is involved in an extension of the domain of evolutionary biology into the social realm, as found in the cumulative picture of sociobiology developed from chapters 1, 2, and 3 (4.1). The dispute over reductionism has ignored the possibility within sociobiology to apply evolutionary theory to humans in a way that encompasses the scientifically viable proposals by reductionists and antireductionists alike, namely, via the strategies of domain restriction, domain extension, and domain transformation (4.1). The disputes over reductionism are overly simplistic in their conception of what is involved in embedding even uniquely human qualities like morality into the evolutionary domain since they overlook the procedures of domain specification specific to a given domain strategy (4.2). The attribution of biological determinism to sociobiology is unwarranted on several grounds, most notably since it ignores the procedures of description, conceptualization, classification, expansion, and limitation on sociobiology's domain (4.3). The underlying conception of biological determinism is an incoherent hodgepodge of different kinds of explanations: cosmological, ideological, fatalist, essentialist, and determinist explanation. Since sociobiological explanation aimed at completeness transcends biological determinism in all these forms, that debate is also incoherent, unwarranted, and unnecessary (4.3).

The attribution of a reductionism that reduces social organization to individual behavioral interactions to sociobiology is unwarranted since the ideal of its totality of resources divides resources for studying behavioral interactions from resources for studying social order and since the specification of units of sociality is a normal part of its research (5.1). The dispute over sociobiology's disciplinary identity, as found in arguments over what is or is not biological, is vexed on several grounds that combine our previous results (5.1). Disputes over reductionism which envisage a rivalry between sociobiology and an autonomous social science are unnecessary since they ignore the fact that rival explanations must be of the same general kind and same general category. Allegedly opposed kinds of explanation in sociobiology and social science fall into different kinds. They typically do so because sociobiological explanations have a conceptual apparatus designed to express and explain social facts using an evolutionary time scale and categories that apply across the various taxa of organisms (5.1). Disputes over reductionism that pit what is biological against what is cultural violate the sociobiology's practice of developing a variety of gene-culture programs. They ignore the fact that disciplines are organized in terms of their ideals of explanatory resources (5.1) and ideals of kinds of explanation (5.2, 5.3).

These results collectively go to show that the questions raised by proponents and opponents of sociobiology are not to be answered by falling into the trap of taking them on their own terms. They go to show that the answer is neither "a defense of adaptationism" nor "antiadaptationism," "for a biologism of human nature" nor "against a biologism of human nature," neither "pro-reductionism" nor "con-reductionism," neither "human sociality is determined by its biological basis" nor "human sociality has no biological basis," and so on, for any variant of these "isms" or for other "isms" which express biological philosophies. These results provide convincing argument, as convincing as is possible for such matters, that such biological philosophies are unnecessary, unwarranted, and, in the end, probably unintelligible. The answer, then, is not to fall into the trap of interpreting the scientific problems that face sociobiologists, including the set of genuine evaluative issues previously identified. Treat the genuine issues on their own terms and do not try to draw from or project onto sociobiology such "isms." The biological philosophies are only tempting illusions.

## The Scientist's Perspective in Perspective

This is a normative proposal, with its own limits. If it did not have its own limits, it would become another "ism," namely, anti-interpretationism. There is a need that gives rise to our refusal to adopt the natural methodological and ontological attitude in doing science. The phrase "in doing science" suggests these limits. The need arises because the natural methodology and ontological attitude is an attitude in science, and science isn't everything. Scientific explanation starts with ordinary questions and ends with ordinary explanations. If its explanations could not be used to inform our ordinary ways of thinking about things and our ordinary explanations, it would be an idle overlay to common sense. For instance, people will continue to think about the biological, genetic, and evolutionary determination of why we do what we do in ways that create sympathetic or antagonistic evaluations of human sociobiology, in no small part because the forms of explanation found in common-sense views of the world will not go away just because of various analyses of biological determinism. The answer to the proposal

"Take science on its own terms and don't try to interpret it, don't try to externally impose something onto it" meets its own limits in the response "We have to take science on our own terms, we cannot help but conduct it and interpret it according to our own common-sense ways of representing nature and ourselves, and there is an externally generated need to bring the meaning of science home."

Fortunately, yesterday's science is often incorporated into today's common sense. So we feel an undeniable need to make sense of the validity and significance of science in ways that speak to our common-sense attitudes. It is from this need that pop sociobiology and sophisticated sociobiology both emerge and eventually must return. In this sense, there is no demarcation of science from common sense or society at all. All the boundaries eventually dissolve. It is their transiency that gives rise to impossible attempts to once-and-for-all demarcate science from nonscience; or to try to define the scientific method, the scientific outlook, or the evolutionary perspective; or to try to capture the essence or meaning or practice of science. It would be hubris to try to legislate how people should try to interpret science in ways that inform their common-sense views. The only proposal that our cumulative results justify is this: when you do so, don't ignore the scientific character of sociobiology, but instead interpret sociobiology in a way that takes into account all that is involved in its role in the quest for explanatory completeness in evolutionary biology pertinent to your interests.

In this way, the self-reflective methodology for evaluating science eventuates in the recognition of its own limits. Within those limits, we have vindicated the present evaluative perspective with respect to two of its main ideas—self-reflective methodology, irresolvability—in ways that actually incorporate all the rest of its ideas. We will close by adding one more facet to the idea of the natural methodological and ontological attitude. Whom is it natural for? It is natural for the working scientist when she or he is thinking in terms of a distinction between science and nonscience. It is natural for the working scientist thinking of herself or himself as being busy at the practice of doing science, not at the practice of wondering about its external implications for common sense.

The philosophies of scientific change have shown us that when we claim to adopt a purely disinterested objective starting point, our alleged "view from nowhere" is a "view from here" or a "view from there" in disguise. Every "general philosophy of science" reflects its own historical period and special concerns, inviting the response "Whose rationality? Which knowledge?" The present theory has not been argued by starting from uncritical acceptance of any particular point of view in the sociobiology debate, pro or con. A test of whether philosophy of science can clarify current science is whether it helps arbitrate scientific disputes. Such arbitration cannot proceed from a perspective totally divorced from sociobiology, i.e., philosophy of science in general without regard for the specific character of the special sciences. That would leave it unable to penetrate into live issues of scientific importance. Neither can it proceed from a perspective totally immersed in those disputes. That would make it too partisan, ad hoc, and idiosyncratic for worthwhile general implications.

The present theory of the pivotal nature of the quest for completeness for evaluating sociobiology was generated from repeatedly analyzing and critically examining claims and arguments on both sides, pushing the issues to a point where what is at stake in the debate has been totally overhauled. Thus, by treating the case of sociobiology as one instance of a general kind of science, it adopts the "view from somewhere." The method by which it has been constructed treats the relation between science and philosophy of science as a "chicken-or-the-egg" relation. Given standard philosophies of scientific method, what are their implications for the sociobiology debate? This procedure adopts the philosophies of science as fixed and uses them to critically examine the views of disputants in the sociobiology debate. Given the special character of sociobiology and its debate, what are the implications for standard philosophies of scientific method? That procedure adopts the research situation of sociobiology as a given and uses it to critically examine philosophies of method. The combination is a bootstrap procedure whereby neither science nor philosophy of science is taken as validated independently of the other, but each can inform the other.

By adopting the point of view of the working sociobiologist, we have constructed a novel point of view. It differs from that of the working scientist not attuned to philosophical concerns. It differs from that of the working philosopher not attuned to sociobiological concerns. Such a point of view can deliver novel results. Adopting it, we have identified the quest for completeness as what's at stake in the sociobiology debate. We have drawn out its import for traditional analyses in terms of theories and recent analyses in terms of research programs, especially by calling attention to a third unit of analysis, a conceptual framework. This theory of evaluative method has been argued for by showing that it makes sense of the debate and that the proposed criteria, conceptions of standards, and units of analysis are needed to speak to issues of live scientific moment. It has been argued using a case study that this conception is needed to adjudicate the more subtle considerations about explanatory acceptability which underlie scientific debate. This theory of method does not collapse into an "anything goes" relativism or an "a priori philosophy" since the evaluative methods used by scientists are revealed as unjustifiable for not taking proper account of what's at stake in the sociobiology debate.

Nickles (1987) outlines the methodological benefits that arise from adopting the working scientist's own point of view. Since the concept of acceptability captures the way evaluation should be sensitive to the working sociobiologist's own point of view, Nickles provides the following reasons for the kind of assessment proposed in this book:

1) Assessment benefits from a change in focus from the products of science to the process of scientific study. ". . . [T]o confine assessment to static or retrospective analysis is to ignore half of scientific methodology" (Nickles 1987, 45). Practitioners of sociobiology evaluate explanations both retrospectively and prospectively (recall Laudan's criteria).

2) Assessment benefits from a change in focus from solutions to problems, from theory choice to problem choice. Issues over "what problems are, where they come from (how they arise), and how scientists generate or choose their problems, projects, and research programs are fundamental to methodology" (Nickles 1987, 45). Practitioners of sociobiology have chosen their problems and programs according to a vision of the problematic induced by incompleteness. Their production of explanatory problems is an important achievement.

3) Assessment benefits from a change in focus from truth to solved problems. "Adopting the solved problem and the reliable result, rather than the certifiably true result, as the immediate goal of inquiry is not to throw away something that we ever had" (Nickles 1987, 46). Science does not strive for any old truth, but the interesting truths involved in problem posing and problem solving. Practitioners of sociobiology adopt the usual norms involving truth—test for the truth and falsity of theories—in the act of confronting problems posed by the seeming inconsistency or irrelevance of evolutionary theory and social data. Knowing the truth status of all aspects of the explanations produced so far is unnecessary for research to proceed. The status of explanations as certifiably true beliefs is bracketed by the status of explanations as acceptable in the current problem situation.

4) Assessment benefits from change in focus from logic and justification to heuristics and discovery.

> Heuristic appraisal is the evaluation of the future prospects of a theory, hypothesis, research proposal, or program, its generative potential, i.e., its apparent ability to handle problems still outstanding and to generate interesting new questions for research. The urgent question which working scientists have for a given theory or program which they are actively using or considering is not 'What have you done for me?'. . . but rather, 'What can you do for me tomorrow?' (Nickles 1987, 47)

The concept of acceptability implicit in the assessment of practitioners of sociobiology incorporates the logic of justification. Being well-tested and well-articulated are two basic facets of acceptable scientific explanations. The logic of justification has been included within the broader notion of generative potential. Being the best among rival available explanations for improving the state of completeness is a measure of generative potential.

5) Assessment benefits from change in focus from unlimited resources to economy of research. "Our rationality is 'bounded'; time and resources (and expertise) are limited" (Nickles 1987, 48). The methods of assessment associated with criteria involving theories and programs cannot be guaranteed to achieve completeness or make it likely. Instead, trained judgement is called for in determining which criteria should be given more weight in the current research situation in deciding which explanation is acceptable, i.e., which explanation has the highest expectation of improving the state of completeness. If we have limited time, effort, and expertise, why not use our best available rival explanation to frame heuristics about how to and how not to conduct future research? Let us frame aim-oriented heuristics about procedures involved in assessing confirmation, disconfirmation, plausibility, progress, problem solving, domain specification, ideals of the totality of explanatory resources in the discipline, resource choice specification, ideals of the totality of kinds of explanation in the discipline, and explanatory-kind choice specification. Let us extend self-reflective methodology to critically reflect on heuristics in choosing evaluative perspectives, evaluative rules and standards, evaluative criteria, and units of analysis that are appropriate to the research situation in which scientific explanations are to be evaluated.

In sum, our evaluative perspective gains important benefits when it shifts from a change in focus on products to process, solutions to problems, truth to problem posing and problem solving, unlimited resources to and economy of research, logic to heuristic procedures. These benefits gain even more importance when our evaluations of sociobiological explanations are aware of what issues count as real issues and what issues count as pseudo-issues, so that we focus on the real issues. We need to discipline our evaluations of sociobiology so that our evaluations of sociobiology's performance are just as rigorous as the kind of research we expect from sociobiology as a science. What we need, then, are procedures for specifying what counts as an adequate evaluation of sociobiology in terms of the appropriateness of our choice of evaluative perspectives, rules, standards, criteria, and units of analysis for capturing the research value of explanations in sociobiology.

This section has indicated three procedures for specifying what counts as an appropriate evaluate perspective: the procedure of vindicating the main guiding ideas of the evaluative perspective, the procedure of showing how that vindicated perspective distinguishes real issues from pseudo-issues, and the procedure of putting limits on the scope and utility of the distinctions made by that vindicated perspective.

## 6.2 Methodological Rules and Standards

### The Problem of Innovation

An adequate evaluation of sociobiology would employ methodological standards and rules that are truly appropriate to sociobiology's research situation. To see how our cumulative results bear on the adequacy of actual evaluations of sociobiology in terms of their rules and standards, let us see how the evaluative problems of disagreement, agreement, and innovation are made concrete in one historical case and in sociobiology. The study of these problems by Laudan and Laudan (1989) will provide our point of departure. They characterize these problems as follows.

The problem of disagreement is that, if there is a unity of scientific method, then why are there so many cases in the history of science of longstanding disagreements among scientists about which of rival explanatory theories give us knowledge? The problem of agreement is that, if such disagreement is due to disagreement among scientists about the specific standards and aims of their science, then why are there so many cases in the history of science of longstanding consensus about which of the rival explanatory theories give us knowledge? The cases of agreement and cases of disagreement thus seem to invoke conflicting rational explanations. If there is a unity of scientific method, then agreement is rational but disagreement is irrational. If there is a diversity of scientific methods that are in conflict, then disagreement is rational but agreement is irrational.

The problem of innovation poses these problems in their most intense form, a problem that permeates the sociobiology debate. How can research be both creative and disciplined in moving into uncharted territory? If standards for accepting a theory should be demanding, then how could it ever be rational for scientists to accept new theories which are less well-tested and well-articulated than their older and better established rivals? How could it be rational to accept new explanations in sociobiology that, in the nature of the situation, are poorly tested and articulated as compared to those in evolutionary theory generally? And how could it ever be rational to accept new explanations in human sociobiology which, in the nature of its research situation, faces a far greater skepticism, given the intrinsically problematic status of any sociobiology of human social behavior?

Laudan and Laudan (1989) propose to explain all three facts about the history of science at once, without giving up the presumption that all the scientific positions adopted are rational. Here is their solution.

Scientists cannot agree on what counts as a good reason for accepting a scientific theory. Disagreement about standards and rules obviously explains why dissensus is rational; scientists cannot agree in their assessments of rival theories because they operate from different standards and rules. Disagreement about standards and rules also explains why consensus is rational; scientists agree that one theory among rivals is acceptable when that theory best satisfies all the rival sets of standards and rules. They come to the same conclusion for different reasons. Disagreement about standards and rules explains why innovative sciences are accepted by some scientists and not by others: the scientists who accept the theory operate with one set of standards and rules, and the scientists who reject the theory operate with a conflicting set of standards and rules.

The theory of continental drift in geophysics is a case in point.

In 1915 Wegener published his theory that lateral motions of the earth's crust (including the continents) exist and cause many of the major tectonic features of the earth. Although some scientists accepted the drift theory at the time, most did not. Dissensus continued until 1967, when scientists reached a consensus accepting the drift theory. Laudan and Laudan describe the kind of rationality relative to evaluative assumptions in this episode for which there are obvious parallels in the sociobiology debate.

It was rational for the scientists who accepted the theory in 1915 to accept it, given their rules and standards of acceptability. They regarded a variety of instances as a sufficient criterion for acceptability and regarded broad and impressive post-hoc explanatory credentials as the standard of a sufficient variety of instances. No other theory exhibited such a wide explanatory range: why there is a transatlantic fit of the continents, why there are similar transatlantic flora and fauna, why mountain chains are foreshortened, and why the poles have changed in position.

It was rational for the scientists who rejected the theory in 1915 to reject it, given their rules and standards for acceptability. They regarded a variety of instances as a necessary but insufficient criterion for acceptability. The additional criterion is that the theory has to make surprisingly true predictions, where the standard of truth is unambiguous confirmation. During the period from 1915 to 1965, drift theory only accounted for phenomena already known. Since it was devised to explain known phenomena, the variety of instances were not as impressive as the early acceptors thought. In 1966 startling predictions of new kinds of effects made by drift theory were unambiguously confirmed: mirror-image magnetic reversals showed up on opposite sides of oceanic ridges and a submarine fracture zone had a specific direction of movement. By 1967 the consensus was reached that drift theory is worthy of acceptance. The consensus was rational since it is the only theory that satisfied both sets of criteria and standards.

The situation in sociobiology involves some differences and some similarities. Whereas drift theory was a new theory in 1915, evolutionary theory is accepted by all parties in the dispute over sociobiology. However, we can formulate the theory for the field of sociobiology in its most general form, roughly, as a causal, transitional theory (5.2). This is the theory that evolutionary processes involving sociality exist and cause evolutionary changes that are reflected in many social phenomena, phenomena which vary within and between the social species, whether nonhuman or human.

Moreover, the case of continental drift seems to be described in terms too simple to capture the evaluative situation in sociobiology. Notice that the standards of the advocates of drift theory were a subset of the standards of the critics. Advocates employed the standard of variety of instances. Critics employed that standard plus the standard of surprisingly true predictions. When the shared standard was met but the unshared standard was violated, there was dissensus. When both the shared and unshared standards were met, there was consensus. In sociobiology there are not only disputes involving shared and unshared standards, but also disputes over whether shared standards are met. For instance, advocates and critics may share the standard of a respectable amount of confirmational success, but the same confirming data is viewed as sufficient confirmation by some and insufficient confirmation by others. Again, advocates and critics may share the standard that plausible explanations are modest, but use very different conceptions of what counts as a modest explanation that spans nonhumans and humans. Finally, the controversy of the relation between sociobiology as a science and as an ideology cannot be captured merely in terms of shared and unshared standards.

Nevertheless, we can see how the Laudan and Laudan analysis can be used to make sense of the fact that critics find the advocates' acceptance of sociobiological explanations irrational ("they just don't think") and the advocates find the critics' rejection of the explanations irrational ("they resist applying evolution to humans for no good reason"). As representatives of widely influential evaluative views of sociobiology, reconsider the positive evaluations of Wilson, Barash, and Alexander and the negative evaluations of Bleier, Lewontin, and Kitcher.

It is rational for scientists like Wilson, Barash, and Alexander to accept the causal explanations of both animal (that is, nonhuman) and human sociobiology, given their rules and standards. Evidently, like the early acceptors of drift theory, the view that a variety of instances is sufficient for acceptability is implicit in their acceptance. They argue that no other theory than evolutionary theory as we know it can explain social behavior in all species. Wilson (1975) shows how evolutionary theory explains group size, social communication, aggression, territoriality, dominance systems, roles and castes, mating and parenting in animals. His last chapter extends these explanations to similar phenomena in humans. Barash (1979) shows how evolutionary theory explains animal and human mating, parenting, altruism, and competition through explicit animal-human comparisons. Alexander (1987) shows how the same inclusive-fitness theory that explains behavioral diversity among animal species also explains within-culture behavioral diversity in the human species.

It is rational for scientists like Lewontin and Bleier to reject the causal explanations in both animal and human sociobiology, given their rules and standards. Lewontin's rejection of the theory of both fields is implied by his exclusive use of the term sociobiology, which purposely does not distinguish them. Lewontin requires that acceptable explanations of sociality do not promote biological determinism, reductionism, adaptationism, sexism, or biologism of any form. For example, anthropomorphic animal-human comparisons are made in both fields which apply terms specific to human sociality to animals in ways that distort differences between animal and human behaviors. Both fields combine to devise explanations of human social behaviors by deriving them as special cases of the social behaviors of nonhuman organisms. The general categories and their applications are conditioned by preconceptions specific to the scientist's own society. In practice these categories and applications embody the faulty preconceptions found in those "isms," preconceptions Lewontin and Bleier have been fighting for years. The ensuing explanations are unacceptable as science and as ideology.

It is rational for scientists who agree with Kitcher to accept explanations in animal sociobiology and reject explanations in human sociobiologists, given their rules and standards. Kitcher requires that explanations in sociobiology exemplify the high standards of rigor found in the best evolutionary explanations. He found that some explanatory work in animal sociobiology meets these high standards but other work in animal sociobiology does not. Since all the explanatory work in human sociobiology he examines uses dubious assumptions or faulty explanatory methods, he found no rigorous explanatory work at all in human sociobiology.

These negative verdicts perfectly express the problem of innovation. The results of innovative science are uneven and only sometimes adequate if the new science extends an established science beyond its traditional boundaries in a principled extension that is intrinsically controversial.

Reference to the conceptual framework in sociobiology adds new dimensions to the way Laudan and Laudan propose to make sense of innovative science. First, there is a reason why a diversity of instances is especially important in sociobiology. If evolutionary theory is to cover its domain completely, it has to explain the possibility and actuality of organic diversity. Since organic diversity involves diversity of social behavior and social organization across all species, the criterion of a diversity of instances is necessary to achieve a completed evolutionary theory. Hence, the early proponents such as Wilson, Barash, and Alexander are right to speculate about how evolutionary theory might explain social diversity, although the achievement of completeness involves many more criteria. Here we have a close connection between explanation and unification. Evolutionary theory is supposed to explain the diversity of life. Diversity within and between species over evolutionary time is the product of the same underlying evolutionary processes in different circumstances. Thus, to explain social phenomena is to exhibit the unity underlying social diversity by subsuming them under common natural processes. The sort of knowledge sociobiology is after is process knowledge.

There is more to understanding the rationality of consensus, dissensus, and innovation than showing that scientists' assessments are rational, given their rules and standards. The rules and standards themselves must be rational. Otherwise, one could arbitrarily adopt any old rule or standard, even "accept any theory that strikes one's fancy," and come to a rational assessment. Perhaps Laudan and Laudan assume that the rules and standards they find in science are rational because "prominent philosophical defenders can be found for each of the relevant standards" (1989, 228) and their arguments contain good, but inconclusive, reasons. The present study concurs that the tradition in philosophy of science makes all the criteria endorsed in this book prima facie rational, which does not lead to an "anything goes" relativism. Rationally justifiable assessment of sociobiology uses all of these criteria unless it supplies especially good reasons for eliminating some of them. The rational use of rules and standards will be discussed in section 6.2.

The unity-of-science hypothesis that Laudan and Laudan actually attack is not the one found in sophisticated logical empiricism, which is primarily normative. It held that theories need to satisfy certain logical and empirical conditions to be worthy of acceptance and these conditions are the same throughout all science. Naive empiricism reads a description of science directly from these norms; theories are actually accepted or rejected in all sciences throughout history according to these conditions. Sophisticated logical empiricists like Carnap, Hempel, and Popper never advocated naive empiricism. Given the actual diversity of rules and standards, they asked which rules and standards are the most rationally justifiable and answered by introducing new ones or revising old ones. They claimed that satisfaction of these conditions qualified theories as knowledge, not that scientists used their own analyses. They knew that in different areas of science and in different episodes in the history of science, different norms were proposed, and saw themselves as having a place in that ongoing enterprise. Since Laudan and Laudan just describe the rules and standards used by scientists and supply no arguments drawing implications from descriptive to normative diversity, their analysis is irrelevant to the normative unity of science thesis.

Similarly, given that different evaluators arrive at different assessments of sociobiology because they start with different criteria and standards, we need to assemble the criteria and standards most rationally justifiable for its proper assessment. The main thesis here is normative for all natural science of a certain sort. The rival available explanation that best satisfies the entire set of criteria involving theories, programs, and frameworks makes it worthy of acceptance. This holds for natural science, assessed in the context of research, which extends established theory into a new part of its domain but whose explanations are not yet established.

The concept of acceptance used by Laudan and Laudan is left unanalyzed. Since acceptance is acceptance relative to some purpose or use, evaluators must decide whether the explanations they regard as acceptable are acceptable as bases of action, belief, or research. Evidence that Laudan and Laudan (1989, 223) implicitly tie acceptance to the context of belief is given in their statement "The epistemic challenge is to account for the presumed rationality of that process (of innovation) without abandoning tough standards for acceptable beliefs." Since explanations in human sociobiology are far less well-tested and less well-articulated than the best explanations in animal sociobiology and in evolutionary biology generally, it is not rational to believe that they are true even though some are rational to adopt for further research.

Since explanations produced so far in human sociobiology are not established explanations, critics reject them. Since the explanations are the only available ones, proponents accept them. To do justice to both facts, we need to distinguish two sorts of assessments, one suitable for evaluating an explanation as a finished product of research and one suitable for evaluating an explanation as an unfinished product of research used in future research. First, each explanation that fulfills all the proper criteria relating to theories, programs, and frameworks achieves a reduction of incompleteness posed by the phenomena in need of explanation. Second, given a set of rival explanations for the evolution of some social phenomenon, one (unless there is a tie) will best satisfy the criteria, and so is the best result to date. That one provides a model for future research for reducing incompleteness.

People who are not practitioners of human sociobiology need only be concerned with the former sort of assessment since they are not using the explanation to guide their future work. People who are practitioners of human sociobiology must be concerned with both sorts of assessment since efforts to achieve completeness must carry a conception of what a completed evolutionary theory would be like and of what result should guide their future work. Since we, taking the attitude of the working practitioners of human sociobiology, have to start with something, what could be more rational than to start with our best result to date for the explanandum under study? That is the pragmatic content of the concept of acceptability used here. We may agree or disagree on which result is best.

The very meaning of acceptability depends on which kind of evaluation underlies the use of rules and standards for arriving at a verdict about acceptability. So when practitioners of human sociobiology assert and nonpractitioner critics deny that "the explanations so far produced in human sociobiology qualify as acceptable scientific explanations," they only seem to assert and deny the same proposition. In this sense, disputes over the acceptability of sociobiological explanations are vexed due to equivocation, and so they are unnecessary, unwarranted, and ultimately incoherent.

This is yet another point indicating that the rationality of adopting certain criteria, standards, or rules as tools for evaluation depends on the conceptualization of performance evaluations. Since the performance conceptualization component of sociobiology's conceptual framework governs its own evaluation, it carries its own controls for evaluation. Because the disputants do not employ self-reflective methodology for evaluating sociobiology and ignore its conceptual framework, they create incommensurable debates. In the case of sociobiology, their starting points needlessly pit internal evaluation against external evaluation. Because they do not argue why their own starting point is superior to that of the their opponents, the ensuing evaluations time and time again beg the question. What is needed is a self-reflective methodology in which the critical awareness of one's own starting points is incorporated into the way the justifications for one's evaluative conclusions are communicated to one's peers. To improve our evaluations of the performance of innovative sciences like sociobiology, we can overhaul our image of science. We need to expand it to encompass conceptual frameworks and our conceptions of how the performance of innovative sciences are to be evaluated.

In conclusion, if we evaluate the effectiveness of sociobiology's performance by treating it the same way we treat established sciences, we are sure to arrive at a negative verdict. We would say that its performance has been ineffective and that its explanations have no explanatory power. Rather than discrediting sociobiology, that conclusion would discredit our demanding standards of explanatory adequacy as sufficient tools for its proper evaluation, even if they are necessary. Our evaluative method would fail to come to grips with the problem of innovation. Instead, our use of methodological rules and standards should be grounded in the evaluative perspective of the scientist who knows that his or her innovative science is not established and is working to make it established.

## Exemplars and Rules of Method

The critical attitude inherent in the rationality of science not only uses criticism of past explanations to guide the construction of new explanations. It also generalizes the lessons drawn from examples of good and bad scientific practice to generate methodological rules for how explanatory work in sociobiology should or should not proceed. We need to ask of the last statement, "Should or should not proceed in order to accomplish what task?" There are two ways to ground decisions about which set of methodological rules is appropriate and decisive for evaluating the effectiveness of explanatory work in sociobiology. One, well known, is to ground general rules in particular results. The other, unfamiliar but equally important, is to ground general rules in general objectives. We will illustrate the former and introduce the latter, so that rules are grounded both in exemplars and in objectives.

Many people ignore a crucial difference between Kuhnian programs and any set of general background expectations. Research programs (paradigms, disciplinary matrices), says Kuhn, contain positive exemplars, examples of scientific practice in a new field that sets the standard for future work in the field (Eckberg and Hill 1980). Positive exemplars and methodological rules are related since evaluation via positive exemplars precedes and results in evaluation according to rules of method. Positive exemplars are concrete examples of scientific practice that count as achievements. Methodological rules are generalizations about how to conduct further inquiry in the tradition introduced by a positive exemplar. When scientists learn how to conduct science by emulating the sort of research orientation found in the positive exemplar, they generalize a lesson about what sort of explanatory research they should conduct.

Many think Kuhn viewed scientific development as initiated by a dogmatic phase of normal science devoted to following in the footsteps of a publicly applauded positive exemplar. It remains unclear how far Kuhn went in deemphasizing the critical attitude. For example, Kitcher calls on practitioners of sociobiology to emulate and apply the sort of evolutionary research found in Hamilton's theory of inclusive fitness and Maynard Smith's game theory. Kitcher gives this advice, not because of any blind acceptance explainable solely in psychosociological terms, but because his highly developed critical standards of success identify the work of Hamilton and Maynard Smith as innovative, successful, and worthy of emulation. Kuhn, when pushed on the issue of whether a field counts as science just because it is empirical and enjoys consensus, emphasizes that to have a paradigm involves naming a consensus because the paradigmatic approach is worthy of consensus.

There is no consensus that any effort at explanation in human sociobiology deserves the status of a paradigm or exemplar of good scientific practice as yet. In any case, it seems to follow from Kuhn's model of scientific development that human sociobiology is in a prescientific state, given that fundamental issues about how to conduct research are unsettled. In the present terminology, human sociobiology is an extension of an established science that is not yet established. This is a new category of science, one that violates our usual distinctions. Is it science? No, it is not established, unlike evolutionary biology in general. Is it non-science? No, it has something of a scientific character, unlike English. Is it pre-science? No, it extends an established science, unlike early astronomy. Is it pseudo-science? No, the science it extends is tried and true, not a sham, unlike astrology. The fact that sociobiology violates our usual distinctions is the basis for its challenge to our image of science, and thereby to the appropriateness of our usual evaluative techniques which are designed primarily for established science.

Kitcher has responded to this research situation by locating positive exemplars for doing human sociobiology in animal sociobiology. He finds in animal sociobiology a few examples of explanatory practice that succeed in emulating the best work in evolutionary theory generally (Kitcher 1985, chap. 5). These are Parker's study of copulation time in dung flies (Parker 1978) and the study by Woolfenden and others of helping at the nest in the Florida scrub jay (Woolfenden 1975; Woolfenden and Fitzpatrick 1978; Emlen 1978, 1984). Until human sociobiology produces work equally as rigorous as that work, Kitcher concludes that human sociobiology will remain only a possible science. As long as it remains only a possible science, no significant progress has occurred. In effect, the standards and rules of good science satisfied in such cases operate as Kitcher's standards for significant progress in human sociobiology. Even if today's currently best available explanation of human mating patterns is better than yesterday's best available one, unless these rules and standards are satisfied, no significant progress has occurred.

Whereas Kuhn recognized only positive exemplars, Kitcher (1985, chap. 5) identifies exemplars of good science, bad science, and ugly science in animal sociobiology. Examples of bad science and ugly science are worth studying since from them we can draw lessons for how not to conduct future research. The category of ugly science is a "gray area," devised, presumably, because the distinction between legitimate science and pseudo-science is a matter of degree. If so, it is less important to decide whether human sociobiology is really or only pretends to be a science than to locate in precise but general terms the way it has so far failed to live up to the rigor of the best explanatory work in evolutionary biology.

Orian's effort to explain mating systems in birds and mammals constitutes a negative exemplar, an example of bad science according to Kitcher. Wilson's efforts to explain the vertebrate defensive behavior and animal sexual behavior constitute even worse negative exemplars, examples of ugly science according to Kitcher. Such science is so bad that it grades into pseudo-science. By making methodological distinctions between good, bad, and ugly science grounded in concrete examples about which we should have a consensus, future research in both animal and human sociobiology will be guided by examples and methodological rules for how to and how not to conduct explanatory research.

The following questionnaire enables anyone to employ the rules of method Kitcher derives from these positive and negative exemplars. The questionnaire makes explicit one way to reconcile the universality of scientific method in general with the special methods specific to each scientific field. One set of rules determines the distinctions of rigor between good, bad, and ugly science (Kitcher, chap. 5). These rules embody two of Kitcher's criteria, namely, confirmational success and fecundity. They are sufficiently abstracted from evolutionary theory to apply to natural science in general. Another set of rules applies to the structure of evidential arguments he attributes to Wilson, which he calls "Wilson's Ladder" (Kitcher, 126, 242). That set locates assumptions implicit in explanations about fitness, selection, genes, and human nature. That set is specific to evolutionary theory. Rather than address the difficult problem of the normative unity and diversity of scientific method(s) outright, Kitcher evaluates explanations in sociobiology by supplementing criteria for natural science in general with criteria for evolutionary biology in particular.

## I. Aspects of Scientific Method in General

(Each rule is expressed so that assent to most or all of the questions in a quality category indicates that the work evaluated falls into that category.)

1. Qualities of Good Science: a) Does it formulate precise mathematical models to explain the phenomenon? b) Does it use experiment or observation to determine the quantitative values of crucial variables and parameters for applying the general theory to the specific phenomenon? c) Does it make detailed observation of the behavior to be explained? d) Is it wary of stopping explanatory work too soon, so that research is open ended? e) Does it investigate all discrepancies of reasonable error in the match of explanatory hypothesis to data? f) Is it part of an ongoing effort to combine precise theoretical analysis and detailed field research? g) Does it announce explanatory conclusions with caution? h) Does it structure our ignorance by identifying precise explanatory questions to be answered if the analysis is to be taken one step further? i) Does it attempt to overcome difficulties in explanation, not to hastily trumpet final, grand conclusions?

2. Qualities of Bad Science: a) Is the explanatory account not articulated with precision? b) Are some but not all explanatory factors considered, yet a plausible explanation is heralded as the sole, total, or correct explanation? c) Does the attempt to remedy deficiency in the theory-data match blot out a host of interesting theoretical possibilities? d) Do efforts at explaining discrepancies between theoretical expectation and data not really account for the actual relevant data? e) Are anomalies confronting the explanation resolved by

invoking new explanatory factors, whose role is not studied or which subvert the original explanation? f) Does it explain away lack of theory-data fit by claiming the fit results from conflicting multiple factors even though the conflict is not studied and tested? g) Does it stop research when the anomalies are explained away? h) Does it fail to identify further explanatory questions for study? i) Does it fail to confirm explanatory hypothesis by elimination of rival hypotheses using good data that makes use of case-specific conditions?

3. Qualities of Ugly Science: a) Does it use no mathematical models at all? b) Does it substitute spur-of-the-moment thoughts about theoretical possibilities for rigorous analysis? c) Does it omit uncomfortable facts, discrepancies between theory and data relevant to the explanation? d) Does it misreport other relevant findings? e) Does it ignore or devalue complications confronting simple explanation? f) Does it exhibit looseness of discussion and lack logical reasons for explanatory claims or connections among explanatory claims? g) Does it make no serious attempt to explore main components of the account in detail? h) Does it make explanatory claims that break down upon serious, careful examination? i) Is it proposed in order to trumpet hasty, final, grand explanatory conclusions, not to overcome difficulties in achieving successful explanations?

## II. Aspects of Scientific Method Specific to Evolutionary Biology

(Each rule is expressed so that assent indicates an omission or fallacy.)

1. Step 1 of Wilson's Ladder—a Fitness Hypothesis: a) Does it fail to clarify its fitness hypothesis? b) Does it supply weak grounds for claiming that animals whose behavior is described in the same terms are doing the same thing? c) Are unexamined evolutionary assumptions implicit in the description of the behavior that identifies the behavior's function? d) Is language used in the fitness hypothesis vague or ambiguous or misleading? e) Does the fitness hypothesis slide between claims about groups and about individuals? f) Does the fitness hypothesis extend the application of a concept that makes sense only in a narrower context? g) Does the fitness hypothesis exhibit other qualities of vulgar anthropomorphism or vulgar reductionism?

2. Step 2 of Wilson's Ladder—a Natural Selection Hypothesis: a) Does it fail to clarify its natural selection hypothesis? b) Does it neglect general problems in viewing natural selection as a process that optimizes fitness, especially those involving genetic complexity? c) Does it neglect general problems in the interaction of selec-

tion and other factors of evolution, especially those involving complex interactions? d) Does it neglect the possibility of rival selection hypotheses? e) Does it supply no good reason for an inference from the hypothesis that the behavior promotes fitness to the hypothesis that the behavior is maintained by natural selection? f) Does it neglect other problems in treating a promising fitness hypothesis as signaling a history of natural selection?

3. Step 3 of Wilson's Ladder—a Genetic Hypothesis: a) Does it fail to clarify its genetic hypothesis? b) Does it neglect our ignorance of the genetic details? c) Does it assume that further study of proximate factors would not affect the interpretation of what the organisms are doing? d) Does it neglect the possibility of rival genetic hypotheses? e) Does it supply no good reason for the inference from the hypothesis that the behavior is maintained by natural selection to the hypothesis that the behavior has a genetic basis specific to it? f) Does it neglect other problems in treating a promising selection hypothesis as signaling that the behavior has a specific genetic basis?

4. Step 4 of Wilson's Ladder—a Human Nature Hypothesis: a) Does it fail to clarify its human nature hypothesis? b) Does the human nature hypothesis imply that the behavior explained is difficult to modify by modifying the social environment alone? c) Does the human nature hypothesis imply that the behavior is modifiable in the way desired only by modifying others in an undesirable way? d) Does the human nature hypothesis assert something else that smacks of biological determinism and has potentially harmful political consequences? e) Does it neglect the possibility of rival human nature hypotheses? f) Does it supply no reason for the inference from the hypothesis that the behavior has a specific genetic basis to the hypothesis that the behavior is built into human nature? g) Does it neglect other problems in treating a promising genetic hypothesis as signaling that the behavior is part of human nature?

Now, the formulation of rules in such general terms is inherently risky. One hardly knows what they mean or how to apply them to additional cases unless one is familiar with the cases from which they were extracted. In this sense, rules of method must be grounded in particular cases. Moreover, it is one thing to see how Kitcher decided that the exemplar satisfied or violated a given rule from his reasoning about the work evaluated. It is quite another to have a sense of the standard for applying the rule that easily decides whether work unexamined by Kitcher satisfies or violates the rule. It has been found difficult to generalize Kitcher's results into a method whereby we can mechanically apply these rules to new explanatory work and know whether a yes or a no answer to these questions is justified. So, standards are ultimately grounded in cases in ways that prevent dissensus from arising over whether unexamined work is good, bad, or ugly science and from whether it successfully climbs Wilson's Ladder. In sum, it is necessary to ground methodological rules in pertinent cases in order for the evaluations that use them as evaluative tools to be appropriate to what they are evaluating, but it is hard to abstract them sufficiently from exemplary cases which provide a consensus on previously unexamined work (see, e.g, Seyfarth and Cheney 1988).

Moreover, the cases in which the rules are grounded must be relevantly similar to new cases where the rules are applied in order for their application to be justified. For example, the sort of explanation that tries to climb Wilson's Ladder contains a fitness hypothesis about a behavior. It treats that behavior as evolving directly under the influence of natural selection, as having a genetic basis specific to the behavior on which natural selection operates and as being an unchangeable part of human nature. The sorts of explanations that issue from most gene-culture theories which envisage a complex psychology do not provide that sort of explanation. For instance, Tooby and Cosmides envisage fitness hypotheses about domain-specific psychological skills, not about behaviors. Alexander's research program generates fitness hypotheses about behaviors and our abilities to assess the consequences of behaviors in the light of other people's expected reactions to them. If we treat a behavior as enhancing fitness, his program leads us to deny that natural selection operates directly on the behavior and to deny that the behavior has a genetic basis specific to it. Then the question of that behavior being an unchangeable part of human nature does not even arise. In sum, many of the rules associated with the program inherent in Wilson's Ladder would not be appropriate for evaluating explanations issuing from other programs. To use any specific set of rules indiscriminately with respect to research programs would lead to unjustified evaluations. Explanations need to be evaluated using standards appropriate to their affiliated research programs.

## Aims and Methodological Rules

The grounding of evaluative rules in relevant exemplary cases is necessary but insufficient to decide the significance of the evaluative results. Suppose we find that explanations in human sociobiology typically violate the rules of proper method. Suppose we find that, again and again, particular explanations turn out to be bad science according to the rules of evidence in science in general. Suppose they contain the fallacies and omissions of Wilson's Ladder or of other program-specific sets of evaluative rules. What would be the significance of this result, the result at which Kitcher arrived?

An appropriate evaluation is one that adopts the point of view of the scientist working in conscious awareness of the research situation oriented by the aim of completeness. This requires our evaluation to be sensitive to the difference between retrospective and prospective evaluation. We will let Kitcher speak for himself (the ensuing quotations are from his 1985 book), showing that his language makes the significance of his result ambiguous, at least, to his readers. As a matter of fact, some read his book as burying human sociobiology once and for all, while others found in it a vindication of the possibility of human sociobiology.

"Triumph for sociobiology . . . would consist in showing that the present range of schemata enables us to explain all cases of social behavior" (120). On one hand, if "explain" means "potential to explain," then the violation of evidential rules shows that human sociobiology has no promise. Indeed, he said by critiquing numerous examples of explanations, ". . . I hope to scotch the impression that pop sociobiological research promises us new insights about ourselves" (244). On the other hand, if "explain" means "explains adequately in the present," then the violation shows that the field is not established science. Indeed, he concluded his book by saying, "In the case of Homo sapiens the first rigorous analyses still await us." Established science and rigorous science come to the same thing. Rigor consists in satisfying appropriate and decisive methodological rules. So this conclusion is trivially true from the point of view of the scientists working in the quest for completeness who know the power and limits of their explanatory work.

"Narrow sociobiology is a legitimate part of evolutionary theory only if the explanations that its proponents offer are as well supported by the evidence as those in evolutionary theory generally" (120–21). On one hand, if "legitimate" means "follows a method that contains potential for delivering sound results," then the violation shows that human sociobiology is not just ineffective in its performance, but is incompetent to produce improved performance. On the other hand, if "legitimate" means "contains rigorous results," then the standard of conforming to the standards met in evolutionary theory generally seems appropriate and decisive. But, then, "legitimate" will coincide with "established" and the conclusion is similarly uninformative from the point of view of the scientist.

". . . when the difficulties loom, there is a temptation . . . to settle for lower standards" (124). On one hand, the best available explanation will be the one which satisfies the highest standards that are appropriate and decisive. We do want human sociobiology to pass the standards of the best work in animal sociobiology and in evolutionary biology in general. On the other hand, this seems to beg the question of which rules and standards are appropriate against those who use less narrow rules and standards that yield positive verdicts, as if "broadened" meant "lower." Our study of criteria related to theories and programs contains arguments against narrow views of validity. Standards are not fixed as high or low, but are flexible and situation-specific. If the standards satisfied are those of a related science that contains examples of established science, then the standards are rigged. We found in section 3.3 that we have no gene-culture theories which put human sociobiology on theoretical foundations as firm as theories of altruism associated with inclusive-fitness theory put animal sociobiology decades ago. To be fair to human sociobiology today, we would compare it to animal sociobiology before inclusive-fitness theory. Then, both animal and human sociobiology would fail evidential standards. That result would not tell us which results to accept, that is, as the best of current rivals for bringing together evolutionary theory and social facts. Use of absolute standards in the absence of relative standards does not advance scientific research. Indeed, probably the only universal rule of method applicable to all sciences over all history is the vague rule "Do not block the path of research."

"Even when sociobiologists offer accounts of the evolution of a behavior that do not conform to the high standards we rightly demand of accounts in evolutionary biology, their claims may nonetheless be taken as useful suggestions for further research" (134). But, of course, that is all they are when evaluated from the point of view of scientists evaluating in the context of exploratory research. By projecting a higher expectation onto human sociobiology than is appropriate, finding that the expectation is not met and criticizing the sociobiologists themselves and their work, the critique reduces that expectation to absurdity.

"The battles are fought around local issues of a general type: do the sociobiologists instantiate their preferred patterns of explanation so as to produce correct accounts of the evolution of animal behavior?" This is not a real issue for human sociobiology since its practitioners do not normally claim in their research reports to have achieved correct explanations. The negative verdict is doubly misleading since even his examples of "good science" in animal sociobiology try to overcome difficulties and are beset by so many difficulties that their explanations are unworthy of belief.

Why is it important to distinguish the good, the bad, and the ugly? "Danger looms only when we confuse ourselves into thinking that there is some undifferentiated mass of studies, all equally well supported, which goes by the general name 'sociobiology'. The stage is then set for the reporting of these findings as matters of 'scientific fact'—that is, as if they were well-confirmed scientific hypotheses—in works that argue for the application of nonhuman sociobiology to human" (134). Who is we? Not scientists, including practitioners of sociobiology, since scientists are trained to make distinctions in evidential success. Kitcher has made no effort to show that popularizers like Wilson, Alexander, and Barash and nonpopularizers like Betzig, Borgerhoff-Mulder, and Turke are victims of such confusion. Of course, they know better. Evidently, Kitcher is not adopting the perspective of the working scientist in his evaluation, but the perspective of the champion of rigor protecting the gullible public, and thus loses the benefits previously described.

Any performance evaluation must contain a representation of the argument used in constructing well-tested and well-articulated explanations. Kitcher identifies pop sociobiology with any sociobiology that connects evolutionary explanations to claims about human nature. He reconstructs the argument of Wilson's pop sociobiology in the image of science according to a confirmationist methodology. It goes as follows: we confirm fitness hypotheses, infer confirmed selection hypotheses from confirmed fitness hypotheses, infer confirmed genetic hypotheses from confirmed selection hypotheses, and infer confirmed human nature hypotheses from confirmed selection hypotheses (126–27). This is misleading with respect to human sociobiology since Kitcher fails to distinguish between human sociobiology and pop sociobiology. As a genre of literature, pop sociobiology is an attempt to weave together common sense and scientific approaches to understanding human behavior. A whole different set of standards apply to pop sociobiology than to science. We want a sociobiological science of humans to be as rigorous as a sociobiological science of nonhumans, taking into account the extra difficulties in reconciling evolution with human behavior, action, and acts. We want a pop sociobiology of animals and humans to be as rigorous as pop social science, taking into account the extra difficulties of saying anything worthwhile about human nature.

The idea of basing a view of human nature on science is incorrect when taken to be a logical argument. In Wilson's Ladder (constructed by Kitcher, not by Wilson), an argument is constructed in which purely scientific premises (premises about fitness, selection, and genes) lead to a metaphysical conclusion (a conclusion about human nature). But science has no way of telling whether some fact about humans is or is not a fact about human nature. In particular, sociobiology has no way of telling whether a fact about human genes is or is not a fact about human nature. Kitcher assumes that what is genetic is part of human nature, but that assumption has no place in evolutionary theory. That is Kitcher's own metaphysics, a metaphysics so pervasive it normally goes unrecognized as such. In general, no scientific argument can lead to a conclusion about human nature in the sense of a sound argument backed up by scientific method.

So what is the relationship between sociobiology and human nature? Before doing or hearing about sociobiology, we already have some view of what makes our lives human lives, whether we use the term "human nature" or not. Sociobiology reaches explanatory conclusions, framed in terms of the central concepts used to express the observations it explains, such as adaptation, and the theory that explains them, such as fitness, natural selection, genes and genotypes, characters and phenotypes. We then ask ourselves what difference, if any, these conclusions would make if they were true (and do make if we regard them as true) for our antecedently held views of human nature. In that case, our view of human nature is not based on sociobiology. The most we can claim is that a difference in our view of human nature is based on sociobiology. This result substantiates the proposal that implications for human nature arise externally to a sociobiology aimed at completeness. If we want to draw implications for human nature, we overlook the goals of the Modern Synthesis and the New Synthesis at the price of ignoring the scientific enterprise in sociobiology.

If we represent the justification of this 'difference' claim as an argument, then the premises contain both scientific statements and statements about human nature and the conclusion contains both scientific statements and statements about human nature. Such an argument is logically irrelevant to the arguments of the form found in Mayr's statement of the Modern Synthesis and the corresponding statement of the New Synthesis. When we adopt the point of view of the working scientist, the quest for a New Synthesis is the ultimate aim. The soundness of the arguments needed to make the hypotheses of the New Synthesis into substantiated conclusions does not turn on the soundness of the arguments about human nature. In that sense, sociobiologists can ignore the task of drawing the implications for human nature. As scientists, we do not try to climb Wilson's Ladder or any Ladder up from nature to human nature. Any evaluation that takes sociobiology to be a theory of human nature is irrelevant to what we are trying to do, inappropriate to the work being evaluated, and therefore inadequate.

Of course, the rules for "good, bad, and ugly science" can be fruitfully applied to many sciences, and some of the rules identifying fallacies or omissions of "Wilson's Ladder" are good for pointing out what not to do in sociobiology. Yet any statement can be evaluated in terms of evidence. What is distinctive of explanation in sociobiology is that it tries to unify a theory with its domain. Kitcher's evaluation is blind to the distinctive research situation in sociobiology. It cannot detect the specific unifying role of each study's explanatory work. We should judge the effectiveness of its performance relative to that role since that role governs what it does and does not attempt to accomplish.

Kitcher (1981) wrote an influential article about the nature of explanation. It began with the idea that although Hempel's official view is that the nature of explanation is given by the covering-law model, Hempel's unofficial view is that the nature of explanation is unification. There is no discrepancy here (recall 1.3). We used Hempel's model of explanation to make the point that an explanation should not only be well-tested, it should be well-articulated. Scientific explanations are associated with arguments. Explanatory arguments are ideally sound. In sound arguments, to blur the line between deductive and nondeductive standards, all statements are true and correct reasoning connects the explanans and explanandum. Given that ideal explanatory arguments contain all true statements and no false statements, we want them to be well-tested since being well-tested is our route to finding out that they are true and not false. Given that ideal arguments contain correct reasoning, we want them to be well-articulated since being well-articulated is our route to finding out that their internal reasoning is correct. The "official" and "unoffical" views coincide in the idea that explanatory unification is achieved by means of good explanatory arguments.

The idea of unification is inherent in the idea of explanatory completeness. Ontologically, a complete evolutionary picture of life (with respect to sociality) is one that can unify social evolution with the evolution of other aspects of the organism. Epistemologically, a complete book of evolutionary knowledge is one, to borrow Hempel's phrasing (Kitcher 1971, 167), that achieves a systematic unification which exhibits social and nonsocial phenomena as products of common, underlying processes that conform to specific testable, basic principles. Kitcher argued persuasively that to explain is to unify. At stake in the sociobiology debate is the unification of evolutionary knowledge. We could develop the analysis of explanation and evaluation of sociobiology accordingly. Why not ground methodological rules in both exemplars and specific research objectives, ground specific objectives in the aim of completeness, and ground the aim of completeness in the nature of explanation as unification?

That project, to be reserved for future work, dovetails with the question of proper rules in an interesting way. What sorts of methodological rules are appropriate for evaluating explanations in sociobiology? They are rules associated with standards for satisfying certain criteria of acceptability. Everyone has their favorite list of methodological rules. The purpose of these rules is to evaluate the performance of explanations in completing the main overall picture of evolution in a unified, holistic manner. To unify evolutionary theory and social facts, we have to develop new theory and new data pertinent to sociality: both the theory and the data have to be completed. Our research programs are programs for developing new theory and new data that will achieve epistemological unification. We should evaluate the utility of our methodological rules as rules for deciding when apparent unification is genuine or spurious, according to a theory of explanatory unification.

# Rules of Domain Specification

We need, then, to reinterpret our old rules of method and develop new rules of method pertinent to criteria associated with the sorts of conceptualization found in specifying sociobiology's explanatory problems, domain, and disciplinary structure. Many common nonevidential rules concern domain specification. Good criticisms of sociobiology invoke rules whose violation creates spurious unification of domain. For example, recall Barash's explanation of the double standard in terms of selection for relative male promiscuity as opposed to female faithfulness (1.1).

Following Lewontin (1979), we would argue that the description of animal and human behavior as "promiscuous" in the same sense leads us to think that phenomena fall within the sociobiology's domain which in fact fall within the domain of social science. Spurious unification occurs when there is arbitrary agglomeration (behaviors of different sorts are lumped under one arbitrary heading), reification (promiscuity rules are mental constructs, not material items that evolve by selection in their own right), conflation (a relation of metaphor or analogy is mistaken for a special-case relation), and confusion of levels (gender-typical social roles are collapsed into collections of behavioral interactions among individuals).

Following Silverberg (1980), we would argue that Barash's explanation creates spurious unification of domain by obscuring behavioral diversity through a number of means: violation of phylogenetic relationships, minimization of intraspecies variation, overgeneralization of findings, taking the culturally familiar or widespread to be universal or species-typical, taking social rules as actual behaviors, prematurely attributing genetic significance, and using overly general or simple or evaluative labels which imply conscious motivations. Following Bleier (1984), we would argue that the description 'promiscuity' creates spurious unification of domain through the use of categories permeated by the concept of a society dominated by men: inappropriate use of language, lack of definition of the behavior, and the ethnocentric, androcentric, and anthropocentric biases underlying the questions asked and explanatory answers given.

Moreover, many of the criticisms of sociobiology pertaining to its genetic hypotheses are profitably construed as criticisms of its procedures of domain specification. Consider in this regard a widespread criticism stated quite bluntly by Lewontin, Rose, and Kamin (1985, 251):

> The central assertion of sociobiology is that human social behavior is, in some sense, coded in the genes. . . . The relation between gene and trait is direct and determinative. Those who possess one form of the gene have the trait; those who carry a different form lack the trait or have it in smaller degree. . . . The trouble with the simple determinative model of gene control is that the manifest traits of an organism, its phenotype, are not in general determined by the genes in isolation but are a consequence of the interaction of genes and environment in development. Sociobiologists are aware of this fact, so sometimes they hedge.

Now, we saw in section 5.2 that explanations in evolutionary sociobiology are primarily transitional explanations and that the life cycle ideal articulates these transitional explanations according to commitments about developmental explanations. Therefore, human sociobiology is committed to the thesis that there is some connection between human social behavior and genes. The life cycle ideal leaves open what this connection may be and does not imply that the relation between gene and trait is direct and determinative.

In practice, talk of "genes for behaviors" is often shorthand for the specific indirect, nondeterminative relations sociobiologists and their critics know to exist. It is used in a sense designed to be neutral as to what the indirect, nondeterminative relation may turn out to be for the species studied and the trait studied. In other cases, sociobiologists say things about genes that go all over the board. In particular, we will show that the treatment of genes in Barash's (1979) *Whisperings Within* offers a wide variety of mutually contradictory ways of treating the role of genes. The function of his talk about genes is to describe human behavior in such a way that provides the first step in embedding it in the evolutionary domain; maintaining that some sort of gene-behavior connection exists is vital to achieving explanatory completeness. The following quotations are from Barash.

"Or, to describe it from the gene's viewpoint, genes that are able to construct bodies with characteristics that make them successful will themselves be successful" (21). Let us call this 'unlimited gene constructionism' because it ignores all nongenetic causes and places no limits on the role of genetic composition or genetic transmission in the construction of organismic bodies or production of their behaviors.

"Behavior patterns develop gradually, through an interaction between the instructions encoded on an organism's genes and the environmental realities it encounters" (27). Let us call this 'contextualist gene constructionism' because it makes nongenetic causes into merely contextual conditions for the operation of genetic causes.

"In other cases, the path (from genes to behavior) may be very diffuse, and environmental influences play a major role, as in the development of artistic sense or one or another personality trait" (29). Let us call this 'multiple cause gene constructionism' because it acknowledges both genetic and environmental conditions as causes without any relative weighting.

"Biology and culture undoubtedly work together, but it is tempting to speculate that our biology is somehow more real, lying unnoticed within each of us, quietly but forcefully manipulating much of our behavior. Culture, which is overwhelmingly important in shaping the myriad details of our lives, is more likely seen as a thin veneer, compared to the underlying ground substance of our biology" (14). Taking "biology" to refer to that which is involved in genetic causation, let us call this 'metaphysical gene constructionism' because it uses metaphysical language to draw attention to operation of genes in a dramatic way.

"Proximal analysis deals with immediate factors that operate within an individual to produce a particular behavior. Evolutionary analysis asks about the behavior's adaptive significance: why do the proximate mechanisms occur in the first place? . . . As sociobiologists view behavior, there may be many different proximate means to the same ultimate, evolutionary end, which is the maximization of fitness" (33). Let us call this 'ultimate cause gene constructionism' because it assigns genes no unique status among other proximate causes except whatever is involved in fitness maximization.

"As Samuel Butler pointed out, a chicken is but an egg's way of making more eggs. A more modern view might be that the chicken is a device invented by chicken genes to enhance the likelihood of more chicken genes being projected into the future. People are similar devices—temporary, skin encapsulated egos, serving as complex tools by means of which their potentially immortal genes replicate themselves" (21). Let us call this 'teleological gene constructionism' because it construes organisms or bodies as means to ends intended by and caused by genetic agents.

"Genes can literally go outside the body; in that sense, they have an independent existence" (27). Let us call this 'asymmetric dependence gene constructionism' because it views organisms as dependent on genes but takes genes to be independent of organisms, due to the transitory existence of phenotypes and /or genotypes in relation to the persistence of single genes or alleles according to an evolutionary time scale.

"Genes are merely blueprints, and sometimes remarkably incomplete ones. This is because in the evolution of life genes have progressively given up direct control of their affairs. . . . Instead, as we have seen, genes began to produce devices we call bodies to look out for their affairs. Their evolutionary fate is not determined by the bodies they have helped to create" (27). Let us call this 'symmetric dependence gene constructionism' because it views genes and organisms as mutually dependent.

"When we say that bone structure is somehow "in our genes",

we mean that genes carry directions for producing bone structure, although with considerable room for modification depending upon the environment encountered during the building process. When we say that a behavior is "in our genes", we mean exactly the same thing, except that bones depend largely on the distribution of certain compounds of calcium and phosphorus and brains depend largely on the distribution of nerve cells" (28). Let us call this 'preformationist gene constructionism' because it regresses to the preformationist conception that traits are somehow inherent in genes.

"Actually, there are only two things genes can do: provide directions for the manufacture of proteins, and make more genes" (27). Let us call this 'minimal gene constructionism' because it asserts severe limitations on the role of genes in the construction of developed organisms.

No wonder careful thinkers like Lewontin chastise sociobiology for its loose, contradictory claims about the role of genes. No wonder political fears lead them to focus on the worst, most damaging interpretation, treating sociobiology as a pseudo-science whose only well-executed function is to reinforce the conservative political vision of an inherent, genetically determined human nature. Such loose talk is neither a serious metaphysics of human nature, nor a serious science of gene-behavior relations, nor a serious politics of social problems. So why take it seriously in the first place? Because the ignorant masses may take it seriously. We need people who act as political watchdogs—like Bleier, Kitcher, Lewontin, Rose, and Kamin—to see that they don't get away with it. In this sense, their evaluations are truly appropriate to what is being evaluated.

Scientists need to clarify their choices of the form "we shall treat genes as if they were such and such." The risk to science is that genetic viewpoints created as methodological tools to get on with the project are corrupted as false ontologies created in in the image of those tools. The risk to the public is that by not ruling out any attitude toward genetic control of development, scientists perpetuate preconceptions they know to be factually wrong and politically repugnant. Scientists do have an intellectual and moral duty not to mislead the public, e.g., by disciplining their own epistemic, metaphysical, and political claims. Most scientists could use their speculations to make grand claims about human nature but did not do so because they knew that the public would treat them as if they had a unique insight into human nature. By overstating their case, sociobiologists were asking for trouble and created an equal and opposite reaction by critics who overstated their own case. The public has a similar duty not to exaggerate the status of reports about science and to not be so naive as to believe self-advertising and propaganda just because it comes from scientists. The risk to sociobiology as a science and to common sense is that the project of attaining evolutionary completeness in a disciplined manner gets lost, and so the opportunity to use the results of that project to inform common sense in a disciplined manner gets lost as well.

The public dissemination of methodological rules typically lags behind the public presentation of the work the rules are directed against. Thus, we anticipate new counterpart rules pertinent to new and improved work (e.g., the anthology by Betzig, Borgerhoff Mulder, and Turke). We also need rules for how to formulate the explananda properly, with respect to the procedures of description and classification used in both expanding and limiting sociobiology's domain. In any case, the significance of criticism according to rules of method and the selection of the rules themselves is to be grounded in the way the quest for completeness orients theories, research programs, and conceptual frameworks in sociobiology.

## 6.3 Evaluative Criteria and Units of Analysis

### Specific Explanatory Roles

An adequate evaluation of sociobiology is framed in terms of evaluative criteria and units of analysis that are truly appropriate to sociobiology's research situation. Its research situation is oriented by the quest for completing evolutionary explanation in a New Synthesis. To evaluate explanatory work in sociobiology properly, the immediate target of assessment is the specific role particular studies have in the quest for explanatory completeness. This is a new unit of analysis. We will try to identify it in actual studies and to communicate its importance in a preliminary fashion, thereby fulfilling a vital precondition for giving it the more precise and detailed analysis it deserves.

This point about adequate evaluation is normative in an important sense. Think of how hard it would be to evaluate whether explanations in a field were falsifiable, prior to working scientists' appreciation of the importance of falsifiability and prior to attempts by working scientists to test for the falsity of their hypotheses. Such evaluation would be hard to construct. But that would not take away from its importance. We are in a similar position with respect to the criteria pertinent to conceptual frameworks. In the future, scientists need to design their explanatory work and evaluations so as to target specific explanatory roles. Without rules and standards created deliberately with conceptual frameworks in mind, our evaluations are impoverished.

Fortunately, we can do more than lament the current impracticality of references to specific explanatory roles in the context of underlying conceptual frameworks when faced with existing scientific practice that does not recognize them. In the meantime, we can use the author's statement of what the study is about together with sets of methodological rules to identify what it did and did not accomplish. Then we can identify the explanatory power and limits of the explanation being worked on relative to those sets of rules. Human sociobiology now contains a significant body of results. Let us apply Kitcher's rules to three typical research reports found in *Ethology and Sociobiology* in order to identify their explanatory roles, and the explanatory power and limits that derive from those explanatory roles. We will use three examples in order to give a sense of the variation in the quality individual studies and their specific explanatory roles.

Some research reports contain elements of good science, elements of bad science, and elements of ugly science, according to Kitcher's rules. Daly and M. Wilson (1985) explain the fact that child abuse is greater in households with a stepparent than with both natural parents as a fitness effect: theory leads us to expect that parental feeling varies as a function of prospective fitness value of the child, one determinant being the link of biological parenthood. Did they formulate precise mathematical models? No, the theory was stated qualitatively, not quantitatively. Did they use experiment or observation to determine the value of crucial parameters? No, the theoretical parameters were unspecified. Did they make detailed observation of behavior? Yes, from a population-at-large survey, a child abuse sample, and a police sample they obtained statistics on family structure, family income, frequency of child abuse, relatedness of child to cohabitants, maternal age and their relationships. They showed that other predictors of child abuse—socioeconomic status, family size, maternal age—did not account for the stepparent-abuse association. Did they study flaws in match of hypothesis to data? No discrepancy was visible. Is the work part of an ongoing effort at a marriage of precise analysis and detailed field research? Yes, they have studied discriminative parental solicitude (Daly and Wilson 1980), child abuse and neglect (Daly and Wilson 1981a, 1981b; Wilson and Daly 1980, 1983, 1987), infanticide (Daly and Wilson, 1984), and more. Their research follows up unanswered questions with admirable specificity. Did they announce conclusions with caution? Yes, they discussed possible sources of error in the statistics and difficulties in justifying the rival explanation in terms of stepparenthood roles and problems of ambiguity and newness. Did they structure our ignorance by identifying questions for future work? Yes, the preceding discussion contains them implicitly. Is their purpose to overcome difficulties, not to trumpet grand conclusions? Yes, they conclude that "as predicted from Darwinian considerations, stepparents evidently constitute a risk factor for child abuse" (their 1981a, 1983, found cases of less child abuse by adoptive than nonadoptive parents).

Is the work good sociobiology? Yes and No. Yes, the child abuse explanation fits all the qualities of good sociobiology except two. No, it fails to use precise mathematical models and fails to study hypothesis-data discrepancies. Is the work bad sociobiology? Yes and No. Yes, the failure to make the explanation theoretically precise leads to a critically important quality of bad sociobiology; the account is not articulated with precision. No, other related bad qualities were not applicable because discrepancies were not noticed; they were not even in a position to attempt to remedy the deficiency by blotting out possibilities, by failing to account for actual data, by subverting the old explanation, or by illicitly explaining away the lack of theory-data. Is the work ugly sociobiology? Yes and No. Yes, in failing to study discrepancies, it has two qualities of ugly sociobiology: the omission of uncomfortable facts and discrepancies, and no serious attempt to explore main components of the account in detail. No, it lacked other qualities of ugly sociobiology: substitutes spur-of-the-moment thoughts for rigorous analysis; misreports other relevant findings; ignores or devalues complications; engages in loose, sloppy discussion; makes claims that break down upon scrutiny; and trumpets hasty, final, grand conclusions.

Thus, Daly and Wilson's explanation of child abuse has some qualities of good sociobiology, some of bad sociobiology, and some of ugly sociobiology. Yet our own trained intuitions tell us that their explanatory work is good scientific work. Why the difference? While ideal explanations are both theoretically refined and empirically refined, Daly and Wilson were not trying for theoretical refinement but only for empirical refinement. Their study had a specific purpose: "This study was undertaken to quantify various risks to children as a function of the identity of the person(s) in loci parentis" (197). They intended to do so with respect to observed risks, not theoretically expected risks. Their own explicit aims partially define the explanation's explanatory role. Since they executed their specific, chosen task well, their explanatory work was successful. Since the risks were not developed in quantitative theory, we recognize that their explanatory work was less than the ideal inherent in the grading scheme, which demands both theoretical and empirical precision. If the explanatory hypothesis they investigated were the best-articulated and the best-tested among rivals, then it would be an acceptable but not a correct explanation.

Ideally, the predictive content of evolutionary explanations should be exact—quantitative, not just qualitative. Unlike the exemplars from which the Kitcher's methodological rules are abstracted (Krebs and Davies 1978, 1984), most behavioral predictions from basic theory are inexact. So the work by Daly and M. Wilson is on par with normal evolutionary work in this respect. Appropriate rigor is not ideal rigor but feasible rigor. Any field can be made to look bad by invoking inappropriate standards. The issues are "How did the work go beyond the best relevant study to date?" and "How does the work open up a viable direction for future research?" What counts as rigor and as "high" or "low" rigor is relative to the study's particular aims. The schema for good, bad, and ugly science expects each work to achieve the ideal and assigns qualities of bad or ugly science to the extent it falls short. While this schema may be appropriate for the issue of whether we should believe the explanation (to be believable it must be theoretically and empirically refined), it is inappropriate for evaluating work that hones in on some aspects of explanation to the exclusion of others.

No individual study is a total science, one that successfully captures all the aspects of explanation, satisfies all the criteria and rules according to ideal standards. Evaluations predicated on the expectation of finding a total explanation, or even one that satisfies all the requirements of Kitcher's qualities of good science and the confirmational ability to climb Wilson's ladder, create negative verdicts which reduce to absurdity their own evaluative technique. That is why the determination of specific explanatory roles is indispensible for appropriate evaluation. By ignoring the explanatory role of the explanation—it contributes to empirical refinement but not theoretical refinement of the explanation—the method ignores the explanation's design and point.

Moreover, when a given explanation has some qualities of all categories, the grading scheme breaks down. The verdict of whether the explanation is good, bad, or ugly science is less informative and less important than identifying what it achieved and did not achieve, that is, to note the power and limits of the explanation. The power and limits of a piece of explanatory inquiry are calculated, practically, according to the relevant criteria, rules, and standards pertinent to the specific role in explanatory inquiry the work was designed to accomplish.

Wilson's Ladder locates fallacies in supporting fitness, natural selection, genetic, and human nature hypotheses. Fallacies for fitness hypotheses center on anthropomorphism and reductionism in behavioral description, but none were present in Daly and Wilson (1985). Since they explain behavior as reflecting a history of selection, some connection between fitness and selection is required. No just-so adaptationist story, the hypotheses treat child abuse as maladaptive since it is not efficient to allocate parental effort by damaging children one also invests in. What evolved by natural selection is 'child-specific parental solicitude', whose relation to child maltreatment and a child's expected contribution to parental fitness were discussed in previous articles. No genetic hypothesis or human nature hypothesis was made. By failing to go into detail on the fitness, selection, and genetic hypotheses to which the explanation is committed, the explanation is theoretically vague. Rather than call it bad or ugly sociobiology because it is theoretically vague, as the Wilson Ladder schema suggests, we should note that the elimination of such vagueness is not part of the explanatory role of that version of the explanation.

For each study in human sociobiology, there is at least one fallacy, at least one "guilty suspect," as Kitcher says, according to his piecemeal method for evaluating particular explanations. Notice, though, that some suspects are guilty more often than others. The failure to test predictively exact hypotheses is the norm, the failure to pursue discrepancies happens often, and the failure to explore rival hypotheses occurs sometimes.

Some research reports turn out to be mainly bad science, according to Kitcher's rules. For instance, a study of sex differences (Babchuk, Hames, and Thompson 1985) tests a hypothesis that does not state an exact prediction but does try to eliminate a rival hypothesis. They follow Symons (1979) and Daly and Wilson (1983) in developing the theory that different selective pressures on males and females have led to the development of psychological differences between them. They cite cross-species evidence and provide cross-cultural evidence spanning tribal and industrial societies to show that infant mortality has been high throughout our evolutionary history and that women have been the sex which expends the greater effort at infant caretaking. Hence, recognition of infant needs is an important selective pressure. This theory and data jointly motivate the qualitative prediction that "women will be quicker and more accurate in their identification of infant expression of emotion than men." The study's purpose was to rule out the rival explanation that women have had more experience with child care throughout their lives.

They selected a group of people to provide a "crucial experiment" for differentiating the two explanations. The group was divided into four groups of subjects with ten members each and of similar ages: males with no caretaking experience, males with caretaking experience, females with no caretaking experience, females with caretaking experience. Women identified infant facial expression more accurately (mean of 74 percent correct responses) than men (mean of 61 percent correct responses). Women identified infant facial expression faster (mean of 3.94 seconds) than men (4.90 seconds). In both cases there was no significant main effect for the amount of prior caretaking experience and no interaction between sex and experience according to two-way analyses of variance techniques. The one exception was the speed of noting infant disgust, but this discrepancy was not pursued. Thus, the selective hypothesis was supported in relation to the rival. Yet we don't know whether a 10 percent difference in correct recognitions or a one-second difference in speed of recognition between men and women is of an order of magnitude that violates or fits sexual-selection theory.

Other research reports turn out to be mainly good science, according to Kitcher's rules. Blurton Jones (1987) explains the features of bushman birth spacing on the assumption that the fitness benefits accruing from more births are balanced against the fitness costs incurred in caring for each child. This paper far surpasses the previous two papers with respect to both the good, bad, and the ugly and to Wilson's ladder. It develops further an optimization model for the cost/benefit relationship of female reproduction under certain ecological-economic constraints. There is no need to present the model, since it is cited, but the modifications utilized are stated (183, 184). Predictions from the improved model are listed together with the rationale for each (185–88). Results of the application of the improved model upon previously collected demographic data are thoroughly discussed (193–96). Results that appear contrary to prediction and possible reasons for discrepancies are fully and frankly discussed (193, 194). The author is quite circumspect concerning the results of his modifications to the model, the possible limits, false confirmations, and conclusions that can be drawn from it. This work falls prey to hardly any of Kitcher's criticisms of fitness and selection hypotheses (see Blurton Jones and da Costa 1987).

Further applications reveal a trend: studies in human sociobiology fit or violate the schema for Good, Bad, and Ugly Science and the Ladder to Human Nature in myriad ways, with each study having its own constellation of virtues and vices. Each study works on something unique in reducing the incompleteness of evolutionary explanation posed by social behavior. Kitcher's piecemeal method springs from the fact that it is tailored to weed out a particular type of research, namely, that which (1) treats a subject as though it has the final judgement on interpretation of that subject (as opposed to pursuing difficulties and opening up future lines of research) and (2) fails to include the biological and mathematical rigor necessary to insure the logic of the argument. Much work escapes (1) but succumbs to (2), and thus fails to achieve well-tested and well-articulated explanations. Each study has a specific objective in doing so, an objective only dimly revealed by treating any particular set of evidential standards as necessary and sufficient for capturing the effectiveness of explanatory performance. Confirmation, we may recall, is only one of many criteria of acceptability.

Human sociobiology is being tried in a court where the law is outdated and ill designed for cases of emerging fields that aim to extend past work in various situation-specific ways. Instead, two sorts of trained judgement inform evaluation: judgements of acceptability, given the specific explanatory role of the explanatory work in the current research situation, and judgements as to what that role is. Mainstream philosophy of science has shown that assessments of evidential success cannot be successfully formalized. There can be no algorithms for computing evidential success. Acceptability is a complex, informal function of a variety of criteria, only one of which is evidential success. Evidential success itself involves many criteria, each with their own standards, but standards such as "detailed observation" or "reasonable error" must be applied according to trained judgements, not formal rules. Even if we were to construct standards for applying standards, we would need standards for applying those standards, and so forth. To ward off a regress, generalizable rules have to come to an end in trained judgements specific to the research situation. Rules are empty without judgement, and judgement is blind without rules.

These endpoint judgements necessarily assume a stance on what the explanatory work is trying or not trying to do, on what the explanatory role of the explanation investigated is supposed to be, on what specific contribution it is supposed to make toward completing evolutionary explanation. We would like equal rigor in judging explanatory roles as in judging evidential success and so should devise general rules for doing so. But these rules would have to be applied, in the end, according to trained judgement specific to what is being assessed. Evaluations must be appropriate to what is being evaluated. Acceptance is relative to a specific context and purpose, and so appropriate judgements must judge explanatory work within the context and purpose of the work itself. Since judgements of appropriateness are notoriously unformalizable, it is naive to hanker after mechanical rules. Trained judgement can be expected to deliver verdicts of success subject to consensus or disagreement in unpredictable ways. Rather than lament the fact that we cannot scientifically predict the course of science or the course of evaluation, we can put our own expectations into critical perspective and enjoy the humor found in the ways the practice and evaluation of science continually goes against the grain of our expectations.

As sociobiology has developed, it continues to be an exciting field that won't stand still and let itself be evaluated by a single rigid set of specific expectations for acceptability. Sociobiology, like other sciences, is no monolithic perspective with work of a single qualitative grade, but an ongoing investigation. It takes the form of many types of research at a given time that fit together in complex and subtle ways. The repertoire of research types and relations changes as it develops. The general criteria for well-tested and well-articulated explanations collected together as a single package in this book will continue to apply, but the specific standards and rules will change in response to the research situation.

## The Three-Unit Model

An adequate evaluation of sociobiology, then, is to be framed in terms of evaluative criteria and units of analysis that are truly appropriate to sociobiology's research situation. We can assemble our cumulative results pertaining to evaluative criteria and units of analysis by organizing them by means of the three-unit model of theory structure (theories, programs, and frameworks). The basic argument for the appropriateness of the present evaluation of sociobiology is that the evaluative criteria and units of analysis employed here speak to and make sense of real dimensions of sociobiological practice. To show how this argument has been made concrete would be to rehearse the entire book all over again. In lieu of that, we can summarize our results by showing how they bear on evaluating explanations in terms of their specific explanatory roles.

The three-unit model is based on the insight that the problems of the validation of scientific claims and the units of thought used for analyzing science are connected. Validation operates in terms of criteria for validity, in the broad sense, and these criteria pertain to various units of thought. The three-unit model postulates that the unit of achievement and the object of validation is the particular explanation (or explanatory hypothesis). It postulates that the commitments arising from accepting an explanation are induced by the explanation's specific role in the quest for completeness. It is a "three-unit model" of theory structure for evaluating sciences that extend an established theory beyond the boundaries of its traditional or normal domain. The term "three-unit model" calls attention to the postulate that evaluation of this specific role is to be informed by knowledge of theory structure. An explanation in such a science has a structure given by its basis in the theory to be extended itself and the facts it currently covers, in research programs for extending the theory and the facts it is supposed to be explain when it is extended, and in conceptual frameworks for orienting the way decisions are made about the way research programs extend the theory and the facts.

The three-unit model, stated in these terms, is perfectly general, since it applies to a class of sciences without mentioning or using any term that applies to any particular science. By elaborating it using the case of sociobiology, we have put flesh on its bare bones. The first step in doing so was to identify the rationale for extending the theory as a quest for explanatory completeness. From that idea, everything else followed, though not in a deductive sense. The present evaluation of sociobiology in terms of the three-unit model has been designed to expand our image of the scientific enterprise. It delivers the following picture, generalizable in principle and grounded in one historical case as a precondition for generalization. The various places in which parts of this picture are taken from will be cited.

A particular sociobiological explanation's specific explanatory role is given, first, by its use in the activities of science traditionally studied by logical empiricist philosophies of scientific knowledge. These activities center on, but are not exhausted by, the use of logic and facts to verify or falsify an hypothesis or theory; more precisely, setting up plausible explanatory hypotheses or theories and then checking them against observed facts to see whether the hypothesis is confirmed or disconfirmed.

In order to clarify an explanation's specific explanatory role in the quest for completeness with regard to the criteria pertaining to theories, we ask questions that fall into the following categories:

A) We ask questions about the conception of the project of completeness (1.2): 1) In what way does the explanation contribute toward making the basic theory complete in a historical sense (i.e., the third phase of the completion of the Darwinian revolution)? 2) In what way does it contribute toward making the basic theory complete in an intuitive sense (i.e., making evolutionary theory applicable to and true of all the main kinds of phenotypic traits in all the main kinds of species, by facilitating a synthesis of evolutionary theory and the recalcitrant social facts? 3) In what way does it contribute toward completeness in a sense analogous to completeness in a metalogical sense (i.e., constructing a theoretical system containing an observation language adequate for the expression of any evolutionarily significant social fact and constructing a body of theory which can explain every available fact so expressed)?

B) We ask questions about the conception of the explanation employed (1.2): 1) How does the conception of the explanation relate to the inferential, causal, and question-answer models of explanation, among others? 2) In what way, say, given the inferential conception, does the explanation contribute toward explanatory reasoning having a sound inferential structure? 3) Is the explanation currently developed as an explanatory insight or hypothesis, an explanation-sketch, a well worked out explanation, or an ideally correct explanation?

C) We ask questions about the way the explanation instantiates this conception of explanation so as to be confirmable (1.3): 1) What assumptions does the explanation make concerning claims involving central concepts of the basic theory, (i.e., evolutionary theory, such as about fitness, adaptation, natural selection, and genes? 2) What assumptions does the explanation make about the connection between the recalcitrant data and the theory (i.e., between social behavior and these components of evolutionary processes?

3) Given the inferential conception, is the explanation supposed to contribute to fulfilling the condition of derivability, of lawhood, empirical content, or of truth as required in its conception of a correct, well-reasoned explanation? 4) As a predictive explanation, how is it supposed to relate to other kinds of explanation generated by using standard methods (i.e., by using the comparative method, such as historical, evaluative, and correlational explanations)?

D) We ask questions about the way the explanation fulfills the criterion of being given some confirmation (1.3): 1) What empirically testable expectations are suggested by, although are not logically derivable from, this explanation? 2) What kinds of confirmational tests are these expectations being given, such as direct tests of causal factors, analogical tests of relevantly similar cases, and indirect tests of predictive implications? 3) Given indirect tests, what kinds of empirical generalizations are being carried out, and what empirical generalizations do they confirm as being statistically significant? 4) In what respects do these tests justify claims about the theory being employed, whether expressed in quantitative or qualitative models or without explicit models? 5) In what respects do these tests justify methods of data collection? 6) In what respects do these tests justify test results?

E) We ask questions about the way the explanation fulfills the criterion of being given sufficient confirmation (1.5): 1) Is the explanation sufficiently confirmed in the sense of deserving use as a basis for further inquiry, belief, or action? 2) Is the explanation sufficiently confirmed to be acceptable, with respect to its inquiry-specific acceptance, in the sense of being the best of available rival explanations of the same phenomenon and of the same general kind of explanation? 3) Is the explanation sufficiently confirmed to be acceptable, both for reducing incompleteness with respect to that phenomenon and that kind of explanation, and for informing common-sense views with that specific result in reducing incompleteness?

F) We ask questions about the way the explanation fulfills the criteria relating to disconfirmation (2.1): 1) In what way is the explanation supposed to be subject to attempted disconfirmation? 2) In what way is it being subjected to attempted disconfirmation? 3) Is it in some respect resistant to attempted disconfirmation? 4) Is it sufficiently resistant to attempted falsification to be acceptable in any of the senses paralleling those above, and if so, which? 5) What rival possibilities are being ruled out?

G) We ask questions about the way the explanation fulfills the criteria relating to plausibility (2.2): 1) In what way is the explanation designed to be plausible, that is, to what extent is it supposed to be conservative, modest, simple, general, or disconfirmable? 2) In virtue of what background information are these judgements of plausibility being made? 3) In what ways do ideologically problematic judgements tacitly enter into judgements of plausibility, and derivatively, into the above judgements involving confirmation and disconfirmation? 4) In what ways do research programs, (e.g., adaptationism) enter into judgements of plausibility, and derivatively, into the above judgements involving confirmation and disconfirmation? 5) In what respects are judgement of plausibility predicated on a distinction of scientific and social issues or lack of it?

A particular sociobiological explanation's specific explanatory role is given, secondly, by its use in the activities of science recently studied by historical presuppositionist philosophies of scientific change. These activities center on, but are not exhausted by, the continual changing of hypotheses; more precisely, continually proposing, revising, or discarding plausible explanatory hypotheses or theories as motivated by evidential and nonevidential considerations under the guidance of a research program.

In order to clarify an explanation's specific explanatory role in the quest for completeness with regard to criteria pertaining to research programs, we ask questions that fall into the following categories:

H) We ask questions about the way the explanation fulfills the criteria relating to progress (2.3): 1) In what way is the predictive content of the explanation able to cover novel facts, facts either unexpected from rival explanations or anomalous to rival explanations? 2) In what way is the determination of whether a fact is familiar or novel based on the expectations given by an underlying research program? 3) How does the facet of the item being explained relate to those facets being explained in ways guided by other research programs in the same science (i.e., evolutionary biology)? 4) How does the facet of the item being explained relate to those facets being explained in ways guided by other research programs in other sciences (i.e., the social sciences)? 5) Is the underlying research program progressive or regressive in terms of the goal of extending the domain to connecting the basic theory with the recalcitrant facts? 6) What background information is employed in making judgements about progressiveness and regressiveness? 7) What background information, including both scientific matters and extrascientific matters and views of their relation, is employed in making judgements about whether to continue work under the guidance of that program, given its state of progressiveness or regressiveness?

I) We ask questions about the way the explanation fulfills the criteria relating to the regulative function of research programs (2.4): In what way is the explanation regulated by one or more (e.g., gene-culture) research programs in terms of its choice of: 1) what phenomena are properly included in such a specialized study: 2) what aspects of the phenomena are problematic; 3) what the importantly basic aspects of the phenomena are; 4) what statements regarding the phenomena are observational as opposed to theoretical; 5) what meanings the observational and theoretical terms possess; 6) what counts as a properly interpreted observation; 7) counts as a plausible explanatory hypothesis; 8) what counts as a good test of the confirmational status and of the disconfirmational status of the explanation; 9) what counts as the general range of rival explanations to which judgements about acceptance and rejection are relative; 10) what significance the test results have for the decision to retain, revise, or discard the explanation under test; 11) and in what general manner it is reasonable or unreasonable to revise an explanation?

J) We ask questions about the way the explanation fulfills the criteria relating to the problem-solving efforts of research programs (2.5): 1) What considerations are at work in classifying the explanatory problem addressed by the explanation as solved, actual, or anomalous? 2) What considerations are at work in classifying the conceptual problems pertaining to that problem? 3) What considerations are at work in connecting the theoretical core of an underlying research program with the methods based on that theoretical core and the objectives those methods are designed to achieve? 4) How is the entire observational, theoretical, and programmatic basis of the explanation structured into various levels of generality of concepts and assertions and how do those concepts and assertions fit together?

A particular sociobiological explanation's specific explanatory role is given, thirdly, by its use in the activities of science currently studied by aim-oriented, systematic philosophies of scientific research, as called for by the present study. These activities center on, but are not exhausted by, the determination of the research value of hypotheses within the current situations; more precisely, the determination of the conceptual character of explanatory hypotheses, theories, or research programs in terms of their underlying conception of the explanatory problem addressed, the phenomena to be explained, and the factors doing the explaining.

In order to clarify an explanation's specific explanatory role in the quest for completeness with regard to criteria pertaining to conceptual frameworks, we ask questions that fall into the following categories:

K) We ask questions about the aims and projected course of problem-solving activities directed toward explanatory completeness (3.1): 1) To the extent that the explanation is based on theories and research programs unfit for achieving any respectable set of aims, what unrespectable aims do they appear to serve (e.g., the biological philosophies)? 2) To the extent that the explanation is fit to contribute something toward achieving the goal of completeness, how is this goal to be grounded in a historically accurate understanding of the previous development of the science into an established science (e.g., the grounding of the aims of the New Synthesis in the updated legacy of the Modern Synthesis)? 3) What is the expected course of research development in which the explanation is located toward the present goals (e.g., the state of the area before the synthesis, the factors bringing about the synthesis, the factors delaying the synthesis, and the character of the actual achievement of the synthesis)?

L) We ask questions about the sort of progress found in the course of problem solving in removing obstacles to completeness (3.2, 3.3): 1) In what respect does the explanation contribute to cumulative development in problem solving, such as the of accumulation of explanations, problem-identification, identification of new explananda as special cases of older categories, and the conception of completeness (e.g., as found in the development of the altruism problem); 2) In what respect does the explanation contribute to corrective development in problem solving, such as the correction of past theories by later theories in terms of the details of theory structure (e.g., the altruism problem); 3) In what respect does the explanation contribute to revolutionary or gradual development in problem solving viewed on different time scales, such as solutions gained through new evidence obtained through new methods applied in relation to new theory, as made possible by new fundamental concepts and reevaluations of old fundamental concepts (e.g., the transformation of the altruism problem and its generation of the units/levels of the selection problem); 4) In what respect does the research role of the explanation contribute to progress-as-refinement of aim-oriented efforts to achieve the most defensible response to the most severe challenge to completeness that revises antecedent basic commitments in the least damaging way?

M) We ask questions about the conceptualization of the phenomena to be explained so as to place them within the scope of the basic theory to be extended so that it completely covers its domain (4.1): 1) What tactics of domain extension guides the explanation? (e.g., animal sociality); 2) For explanations of phenomena that are intrinsically problematic, is the explanation guided by a strategy of domain restriction, domain extension, or domain transformation (e.g., human sociality)? 3) What procedures of framework-laden description are used to embed the phenomena into the extended domain, such as explanatory goal procedures and point of departure procedures? 4) What procedures of program-laden description are used to embed the phenomena into the extended domain, such as presupposition procedures? 5) What procedures of theory-laden description are used to embed the phenomena into the extended domain, such as levels of description procedures, intradomain relevance procedures, problem identification procedures, theory extension procedures, theory combining procedures, explananda identification procedures, and explanation revision procedures? (e.g., the framework, program, and theory-laden description in Alexander's explanation of the morality of monogamy).

N) We ask questions about the conceptualization of the phenomena to be explained in relation to the ideas opposing a principled extension on behalf of completeness (4.2, 4.3): 1) What reasons for constructing such an explanation defeat the justification of antithetical viewpoints, such as by showing them to make arbitrary restrictions on the domain (e.g., the substantive, methodological, conceptual, and epistemic incoherence of objections to Alexander's explanation)? 2) What limits on the extended domain are implicit in the explanation, and on what grounds are they determined (e.g., limits on what counts as evolutionarily significant human social behavior)? 3) What conception of the character of the explained phenomena is implicit in the explanation (e.g., showing why and how social behavior is theoretically possible and empirically actual, but not necessary in the sense of biological determinism)?

O) We ask questions about the conceptualization of the resources and kinds of explanatory factors to be used in doing the explaining so that the basic theory is complete (5.1, 5.2, 5.3): 1) What choice of resources from the ideal of the total set of available explanatory resources is implicit in the explanation (e.g., Wilson's table of disciplinary connections reflecting the basic structure of evolutionary explanation)? 2) How does the explanation reflect an understanding of the internal disciplinary structure and the external disciplinary relations of the field that determine the potential range of rival explanations (e.g., broad and narrow sociobiology, sociobiology and social science)? 3) What selection among kinds of explanation from the ideal of the total set of available kinds of explanation is implicit in the explanation (e.g., transitional, compositional, developmental, variational, and functional explanations found in the life cycle ideal of biological laws)?

P) We ask questions about the conceptualization of what would count as an adequacy evaluation of the explanation's performance in carrying out its specific explanatory role in contributing to explanatory completeness (6.1, 6.2, 6.3): 1) What choice of explanatory perspectives would count as an appropriate evaluation of its explanatory performance (e.g., the perspective stressing the ideas stated in 1.1); 2) What typical opinions about its performance concern real issues and what typical opinions about its performance concern pseudo-issues (e.g., the quest for completeness as opposed to the scientific philosophies hotly debated as "isms")? 2) What choice of explanatory rules and standards would count as appropriate for determining its performance as a scientific explanation and its worth for informing common sense (e.g., the pertinence of rules and standards for sciences whose research situation poses the problem of innovation)? 3) What choice of explanatory criteria and units of analysis would count as appropriate for determining its overall scientific status or character as a scientific explanation (e.g., the set just described).

One obvious, compelling, and remarkable fact about the scientific enterprise evident from the results in this book is that science contains its own array of controls which govern its appropriate evaluation. These controls apply not only to the obvious content, style, and form of the explanations, but extend to the deep structure of scientific thought on which they are based, namely, theory, research programs, and conceptual frameworks. Self-reflective methods for evaluating explanations are the outcome of the self-control by which scientists both carry out a systematic purposeful activity (making, evaluating, and revising explanations) and are critically and constructively aware of what they are doing.

## Conclusion

We have come to the end of a journey that began with puzzlement about how to assess the claims made for and against the principled extension of an established science beyond its normal boundaries. Sociobiology has offered us an instructive opportunity to reflect again on old problems such as the acceptability of hypotheses, the validation of theories, the character of explanation, reductionism, and the like. These old problems stay fresh, especially when a vigorous newcomer, human sociobiology, arouses responses that reflect deeply held convictions about the nature of science and its domain.

This book is an attempt to work out a systematic perspective that opens to us an integrated picture of the units of analysis involved in evaluating sociobiology. Examination of theories of validation led to the conclusion that acceptability of an explanation is essentially connected to the goal of completeness in a science's domain. Tracking the role of completeness, we were led to the fundamental unit of analysis: a conceptual framework of commitments that regulate the direction of an explanatory hypothesis, theory, or research program as it provides a system of intellectual controls over the conceptualization of an explanation.

Sociobiology's conceptual framework sets a background of expectations with interacting components: successfully refined problems (problems induced in completing evolutionary knowledge by unifying evolutionary theory with social facts), specifications of domain (extensions and limitations); disciplinary relations (disciplines connected with the Modern Synthesis and associated with the goal of a New Synthesis); and performance evaluations (performance in completing evolutionary knowledge). Explanations always have their theory-laden and program-laden conditions, and it is the background of expectation within sociobiology's framework that controls the construction, revision, and contextual evaluation of explanations. So it turned out that an explanation in sociobiology is an acceptable scientific explanation within the context of inquiry only if it more nearly fulfills sociobiology's aim at completeness in that context than does any available rival explanation. All of sociobiology's explanations are revisable, and it has no fixed, unchanging categories immune from self-critical revision.

To evaluate science-in-process in order to capture the sorts of decisions working scientists have to make, we need a concept of acceptability in addition to standard philosophical ideals of explanatory adequacy, one that is appropriate to the research situation of the science in question (6.1, 6.2, 6.3). We have shown that an acceptable scientific explanation is: the best of available alternative explanation (1.5) for solving problems (2.5, 3.2, 3.3) in satisfying sociobiology's goals (3.1) induced by its quest for explanatory completeness (1.2, 1.4). To carry out this vital mission, it constructs progressive (2.3) research programs (2.4) for constructing theoretical explanations that are confirmed (1.3), resistant to attempts at disconfirmation (2.1), and plausible (2.2), whose phenomena to be explained are well-described (4.1), well-classified, and delimited (4.2, 4.3) and whose explanatory factors contain the right choice of resources (5.1) appropriate to the kind of explanation being proposed (5.2, 5.3).

To test the evaluative approach proposed here, one may test the various postulates of the three-unit model of theory structure for evaluating scientific explanation. Evaluators should incorporate into their background information the following facts, and by doing so, their evaluative reasoning will be improved. Proper evaluation targets specific explanations (not whole fields). Particular explanations are to be assessed in terms of whether they are well-tested and well-articulated (not well-tested alone). Criteria for being well-tested and well-articulated include those pertaining to theories, research programs, and conceptual frameworks (not only theories). These criteria are to be applied according to standards fixed in principle by considerations of completeness (not only something external to the field). Evaluations according to this principle are obtained by evaluating explanatory work according to its specific explanatory role (not something external to the point of the work itself). As the science develops, so do its data, methods, theories, research programs, and conceptual frameworks (not just its data, methods, and theory). The most basic progress in understanding the significance of explanatory work for research is progress in conceptual frameworks (not data, methods, and theories, and research programs). Conceptual frameworks consist in the way we conceive the problems, domain, disciplinary relations, and performance evaluations pertinent to explanations (nonidentical to theories or research programs in a fine-grained analysis of the basic units of scientific thought).

Have these notions been of any service in understanding sociobiology as science-in-progress? Have they pushed the discussions of testability, biological philosophies, the goals of evolved creatures, gene-culture programs, human nature, and differences in the way males and females select their mates along even an inch or two? This book invites reflection in the hope that others will see the utility of fields like sociobiology for constructing, testing, and revising general views about how science works. This book will have succeeded in its task if it inspires us to replace the impoverished image of the scientific enterprise most people employ in reasoning about science with one that does justice to the richness of its characteristic structures and procedures of decision making.

# REFERENCES

Alexander, R. D. 1971. "The Search for an Evolutionary Philosophy of Man." *Proceedings of the Royal Society of Victoria, Melbourne* 84:99–120.

———. 1979a. *Darwinism and Human Affairs*. Seattle: University of Washington Press.

———. 1979b. "Evolution and Culture." In N. Chagnon and W. Irons, eds., *Evolutionary Biology and Human Social Behavior: An Anthropological Perspective*. North Scituate, Mass.: Duxbury.

———. 1987. *The Biology of Moral Systems*. Hawthorne, N.Y.: Aldine.

Alexander, R. D., and Borgia, D. 1978. "On the Origin and Basis of the Male-Female Phenomenon." In M. F. Blum and N. Blum, eds., *Sexual Selection and Reproductive Competition in Insects*. New York: Academic Press.

Arnold, S. J. 1983. "Morphology, Performance and Fitness." *American Zoologist* 23:347–61.

Arnold, S. J., and Wade, M. J. 1984. "On the Measurement of Natural and Sexual Selection: Theory." *Evolution*, 38:709–19.

Babchuk, W.; Hames, R.; and Thompson, R. 1985. "Sex Differences in the Recognition of Infant Facial Expressions of Emotion: The Primary Caretaker Hypothesis." *Ethology and Sociobiology* 6:89–101.

Barash, D. 1979. *The Whisperings Within*. Dallas: Penguin.

———. 1982. *Sociobiology and Behavior*. 2d ed. Amsterdam: Elsevier.

Barkow, J. 1989a. "The Elastic Between Genes." *Ethology and Sociobiology* 10:111–30.

———. 1989b. "Overview." *Ethology and Sociobiology* 10:1–10.

———. 1989c. *Darwin, Sex, and Status: Biological Approaches to Mind and Culture*. Buffalo: University of Toronto Press.

Barlow, G. 1980. "The Development of Sociobiology: A Biologist's Perspective." In Barlow and Silverberg 1980.

Barlow, G., and J. Silverberg, eds., 1980. *Sociobiology: Beyond Nature/Nurture? Reports, Definitions, and Debate*. Boulder, Colo.: Westview.

Bateman, A. J. 1948. "Intrasexual Selection in Drosophila." *Heredity* 2:349–68.

Bateson, W. 1894. *Materials for the Study of Variation*. London: McMillan.

Beatty, J. 1980. "Optimal-Design Models and the Strategy of Model Building in Evolutionary Biology." *Philosophy of Science* 47:532–61.

Bechtel, W., ed. 1986. *Integrating Scientific Disciplines*. Boston: Martinus Nijhoff.

Beckwith, J. 1981–1982. "The Political Use of Sociobiology in the United States and Europe." *The Philosophical Forum* 13:311–21.

Berkson, W. 1987. "Research Problems and the Understanding of Science." In N. Nersessian 1987.

Betzig, L., M. Borgerhoff Mulder, and P. Turke, eds. 1988. *Human Reproductive Behavior: A Darwinian Perspective.* Cambridge, Mass.: Cambridge University Press.

Betzig, L. 1988. "Mating and Parenting in Darwinian Perspective." In Betzig, Borgerhoff Mulder, and Turke 1988.

————. 1989. "Rethinking Human Ethology: A Response to Some Recent Critiques." *Ethology and Sociobiology* 10:315–24.

Bleier, R. 1984. *Science and Gender: A Critique of Biology and Its Theories on Women.* New York: Pergamon.

————, ed. 1986. *Feminist Approaches to Science.* New York: Pergamon.

Blurton Jones, N. 1987. "Bushman Birth Spacing: Direct Tests of Some Simple Predictions." *Ethology and Sociobiology* 8:183–203.

Blurton Jones, N., and da Costa, E. 1987. "A Suggested Adaptive Value of Toddler Night Waking: Delaying the Birth of the Next Sibling." *Ethology and Sociobiology* 8:135–42.

Boyd, R., and Richerson, P. J. 1985. *Culture and the Evolutionary Process.* Chicago: University of Chicago Press.

Brandon, R., and Burian, R., eds., 1984. *Genes, Organism, Populations.* Cambridge, Mass.: MIT Press.

Brandon, R. 1990. *Adaptation and Environment.* Princeton: Princeton University Press.

Brody, B., ed. 1970. *Readings in the Philosophy of Science.* Englewood Cliffs, N.J.: Prentice-Hall.

Burian, B. 1989. Review of *Vaulting Ambition,* by P. Kitcher. *The Journal of Philosophy* 385–91.

Burns, J.; Cheng, K.; and McKinney, F. 1980. "Forced Copulations in Captive Mallards: I, Fertilization of Eggs." *Auk* 97:875–79.

Buss, D., and Barnes, M. 1986. "Preferences in Human Mate Selection." *Personality and Social Psychology* 12:559–70.

Caplan, A., ed. 1978. *The Sociobiology Debate.* New York: Harper and Row.

Caro, T. M., and Borgerhoff Mulder, M. 1987. "The Problem of Adaptation in the Study of Human Behavior." *Ethology and Sociobiology* 8:61–72.

Cavalli-Sforza, L. L., and Feldman, M. W. 1981. *Cultural Transmission and Evolution: a Quantitative Approach.* Princeton: Princeton University Press.

Chagnon, N., and W. Irons, eds. 1979. *Evolutionary Biology and Human Social Behavior: An Anthropological Perspective.* North Scituate, Mass.: Duxbury.

Clutton-Brock, T. H., and P. Harvey, eds., 1979. *Readings in Sociobiology.* San Fransisco: Freeman.

Clutton-Brock, T. H. 1983. "Selection in Relation to Sex." In King's College Sociobiology Group, eds., *Current Problems in Sociobiology.* London: Cambridge University Press.

————. 1988. "Reproductive Success" in T. H. Clutton-Brock, ed., *Reproduc-*

*tive Success: Studies of Selection and Adaptation in Contrasting Breeding Systems.* Chicago: University of Chicago Press.

Cowley, G. 1989. "How the Mind Was Designed." *Newsweek* 113 March 56ff.

Crawford, C., M. Smith, and D. Krebs, eds., 1987. *Sociobiology and Psychology: Ideas, Issues, and Applications.* Hillsdale, New Jersey: Erlbaum.

Cummins, R. 1977. "Programs in the Explanation of Behavior." In Kourany 1987.

———. 1983. *The Nature of Psychological Explanation.* Cambridge: MIT Press.

Daly, M., and Wilson, M.I. 1980. "Discriminative Parental Solicitude: A Biological Perspective." *Journal of Marriage and the Family* 42:277–88.

———. 1981a. "Abuse and Neglect of Children in Evolutionary Perspective." In R. D. Alexander and D. W. Tinkle, eds., *Natural Selection and Social Behavior.* New York: Chiron.

———. 1981b. "Child Maltreatment from a Sociobiological Perspective." *New Directions for Child Development* 11:93–112.

———. 1983. *Sex, Evolution, and Behavior.* 2d ed. Belmont, Calif.: Wadsworth.

———. 1984. "A Sociobiological Analysis of Human Infanticide." In G. Hausfater and S. B. Hrdy, eds., *Infanticide: Comparative and Evolutionary Perspectives.* New York: Aldine.

———. 1985. "Child Abuse and Other Risks of Not Living with Both Parents." *Ethology and Sociobiology* 6:197–210.

Darlington, C. D. 1969. *The Evolution of Man and Society.* New York: Simon and Shuster.

Darwin, C. 1859. "Origin of Species." In Ruse 1989.

———. 1871. *The Descent of Man and Selection in Relation to Sex.* New York: Random House.

———. 1872. *The Expression of the Emotions in Man and Animal.* 1896 ed. New York: Appleton.

Dawkins, R. 1976. *The Selfish Gene.* New York: Oxford University Press.

———. 1982a. *The Extended Phenotype.* San Francisco: Freeman.

———. 1982b. "Replicators and Vehicles." In King's College Sociobiology Group, eds., *Current Problems in Sociobiology.* Cambridge, Mass.: Cambridge University Press.

Dobzhansky, T. 1937. *Genetics and the Origin of Species.* Reprint. New York: Columbia University Press, 1982.

Donovan, A.; Laudan, L.; and Laudan, R. 1988. *Scrutinizing Science: Empirical Studies of Scientific Change.* (Synthese Library, Studies in Epistemology, Logic, Methodology, and Philosophy of Science, vol. 193) Boston: Kluwer Academic Publishers.

Dretske, F. 1988. *Explaining Behavior: Reasons in a World of Causes.* Cambridge, Mass.: MIT Press.

Duhem, P. 1954. "Physical Theory and Experiment." In Kourany 1987.

Durham, W. H. 1976a. "Resource Competition and Human Aggression, Part I: Review of Primitive War." *Quarterly Review of Biology* 51:385–415.

———. 1976b. "The Adaptive Significance of Cultural Behavior." *Human Ecology* 4:89–121.

———. 1979. "Toward a Coevolutionary Theory of Human Biology and Culture." In N. Chagnon, and W. Irons, eds., *Evolutionary Biology and Human Social Behavior*. North Scituate, Mass.: Duxbury.

Eckberg, D. L., and Hill, L. 1980. "The Paradigm Concept and Sociology: A Critical Review." In G. Gutting, ed., *Paradigms and Revolutions*. Notre Dame, Ind.: University of Notre Dame Press.

Edelman, M., 1981–82, "Human Behavior and Sociobiological Models of Natural Selection." *The Philosophical Forum*, 1–42.

Eible-Eiblesvelt, I. 1989. *Human Ethology*. Hawthorne, N.Y.: Aldine.

Eldredge, N. 1985. *Unfinished Synthesis*. New York: Oxford University Press.

Ellis, B. 1985. "What Science Aims To Do." In P. Churchland and C. Hooker, eds., *Images of Science: Essays on Realism and Empiricism*. Chicago: University of Chicago Press.

Emlen, S. T. 1978. "The Evolution of Cooperative Breeding in Birds." In Krebs and Davies 1978.

———. 1984. "Cooperative Breeding in Birds and Mammals." In Krebs and Davies 1984.

Fausto-Sterling, A. 1985. *Myths of Gender: Biological Theories about Women and Men*. New York: Basic Books.

Fetzer, J. H., ed., 1985. *Sociobiology and Epistemology*. Dordrecht: Reidel.

Fine, A. 1984. "And Not Anti-Realism Either." In Kourany 1987.

Fisher, R. A. 1958. *The Genetical Theory of Natural Selection*. 2d ed. New York: Dover.

Gale, J. S. 1980. *Population Genetics*. New York: Halsted Press.

Giere, R. 1983. "Testing Theoretical Hypotheses." In Kourany 1987.

Good, I. 1967. "The White Shoe is a Red Herring." *British Journal for the Philosophy of Science* 17:322.

Gould., S. J., and Lewontin, R. C. 1979. "The Spandrels of San Marco and the Panglossian Paradigm: A Critique of the Adaptationist Programme." In E. Sober, ed., *Conceptual Issues in Evolutionary Biology*. Cambridge, Mass.: MIT Press. 1984.

Gould, S. J. 1980. "Sociobiology and the Theory of Natural Selection." In M. Ruse, ed. *Philosophy of Biology*. 1989. New York: Macmillan.

———. 1981. *The Mismeasure of Man*. New York: Norton.

———. 1982. Darwinism and the Expansion of Evolutionary Theory." *Science* 216:380–87.

Gribbon, J., and Gribbon, M. 1988. *The One Per Cent Advantage: The Sociobiology of Being Human*. New York: Blackwell.

Hacking, I. 1981. *Scientific Revolutions*. Oxford: Oxford University Press.

Hamilton, W. D. 1964. "The Genetical Evolution of Social Behavior: I and II." *Journal of Theoretical Biology* 7:1–52.

———. 1971a. "Geometry for the Selfish Herd." *Journal of Theoretical Biology* 7:1–52."

———. 1971b. "Selection of Selfish and Altruistic Behavior in Some Extreme Models." In J. F. Eisenberg and W. S. Dillon, eds., *Man and Beast: Comparative Social Behavior*. Washington, D.C.: Smithsonian.

———. 1972. "Altruism and Related Phenomena, Mainly in the Social Insects." *Annual Review of Ecology and Systematics* 3:193–232.

Harraway, D. 1984. "Primatology Is Politics by Other Means." In Bleier 1986.

Hawkes, K.; O'Connell, J.; Hill, K.; and Charnov, E. 1985. "How Much Is Enough? Hunters and Limited Needs." *Ethology and Sociobiology* 6:3–15.

Hawkes, K. "Limited Needs and Hunter-Gatherer Time Allocation." 1987. *Ethology and Sociobiology* 8:87–91.

Hempel, C., and Oppenheim, P. 1948. "Studies in the Logic of Explanation." In Kourany 1987.

Hempel, C. 1981. "Turns in the Evolution of the Problem of Induction." *Synthese* 46:389–404.

Hershel, J. F. W. 1830. *A Preliminary Discourse on the Study of Natural Philosophy*. London: Longmans.

Hill, K.; Kaplan, H.; Hawkes, K.; and Hurtado, M. 1987. "Foraging Decisions Among Ache Hunter-Gatherers: New Data and Implications for Optimal Foraging Models." *Ethology and Sociobiology* 8:1–36.

Hinde, R. A. 1974. *Biological Bases of Human Social Behavior*. New York: McGraw-Hill.

———. 1982. *Ethology: its Nature and Relations with Other Sciences*. Oxford: Oxford University Press.

Hodge, M. J. S. 1977. "The Structure and Strategy of Darwin's 'Long Argument'." *British Journal of the History of Science* 10:237–46.

Holcomb, H. 1986–87. "Causes, Ends, and the Units of Selection." *Philosophy Research Archives* 12:519–39.

———. 1987a. "Criticism, Commitment, and the Growth of Human Sociobiology." *Biology and Philosophy* 2:43–63.

———. 1987b. "Logicism and Achinstein's Pragmatic Theory of Scientific Explanation." *Dialectica* 41:239–48.

———. 1987c. "Circularity and Inconsistency in Kuhn's Defense of His Relativism." *The Southern Journal of Philosophy* XXV, no.4, 467–80.

———. 1987d. "Kuhn." *The Encyclopedia of World Biology, Supplement for Twentieth Century People* 14:345–46.

———. 1988a. "The Modern Synthesis and Lewontin's Critique of Sociobiology." *History and Philosophy of the Life Sciences* 10:315–41.

———. 1988–89. "Constraints on Defining the 'Level' and 'Unit' of Selection." *Theoria: Segunda Epoca* (Spain), 107–38.

———. 1989a. "Interpreting Kuhn: Paradigm-Choice as Objective Value Judgement." *Metaphilosophy* 20:51–67.

———. 1989b. "Rational Progress in Science and Meta-Science." *The Philosophical Forum* 20:286–310.

———. 1989c. "Expecting Nature's Best: Optimality Models and Perfect Adaptation." *Philosophy in Science* 4:124–47.

———. forthcoming in 1993. "Sociobiologia." *Storia del Secolo XX (History of the 20th Century* 4 Biologia). Roma, Italia: Istituto Della Enciclopedia Italiana.

Horan, B. 1989. "Functional Explanation in Sociobiology." (Including Open Peer Commentary and Author's Response.) *Biology and Philosophy* 4:131–234.

Horn, H. 1978. "Optimal Tactics of Reproduction and Life-History." In Krebs and Davies 1978.

Hrdy, S. 1986. "Empathy, Polyandry, and the Myth of the Coy Female." In Bleier 1986.

Hubbard, R. 1982. "The Theory and Practice of Genetic Reductionism—From Mendel's Laws to Genetic Engineering." In S. Rose, ed., *Towards a Liberatory Biology*. London: Allison and Busby.

Hull, D. L. 1980. "Individuality and Selection." *Annual Review of Ecology and Systematics* 11:311–32.

Hunter, G. 1971. *Metalogic: An Introduction to the Metatheory of Standard First Order Logic*. Berkeley: University of California Press.

Hutchison, M. 1990. "Sex on the Brain." *Playboy* 37(4):76ff.

Huxley, J. S. 1942. *Evolution: The Modern Synthesis*. London: Allen and Unwin.

Irons, W. 1979. "Natural Selection, Adaptation, and Human Social Behavior." In Chagnon and Irons 1979.

Jeffrey, R. 1956. "Valuation and Acceptance of Scientific Hypotheses." In Brody 1970, 547–58.

Kitcher, P. 1985. *Vaulting Ambition: Sociobiology and the Quest for Human Nature*. Cambridge, Mass.: MIT Press.

———. 1987a. "Precis of *Vaulting Ambition: Sociobiology and the Quest for Human Nature*." (Including Open Peer Commentary and Author's Response). *Behavioral and Brain Sciences* 10:61–100.

———. 1987b. "Why Not the Best?" In Dupre 1987.

———. 1988. "Imitating Selection." in M. Ho and S. Fox, eds., *Evolutionary Processes and Metaphors*. New York: Wiley & Sons.

———. 1990. "Developmental Decomposition and the Future of Human Behavioral Ecology." *Philosophy of Science* 57:96–117.

Kleiner, S. 1985. "Darwin's and Wallace's Revolutionary Research Programme." *The British Journal of Philosophy of Science* 36:367–92.

Kourany, J., ed. 1987. *Scientific Knowledge: Basic Issues in the Philosophy of Science*. Belmont, Calif.: Wadsworth.

Krebs, J. R. and Davies, N. B., eds., 1978. *Behavioral Ecology: An Evolutionary Approach*. Oxford: Blackwell.

————. eds., 1984. *Behavioral Ecology: An Evolutionary Approach*. 2d ed. Sunderland, Mass.: Sinauer Associates.

Kuhn, T. 1962. *The Structure of Scientific Revolutions*. Chicago: University of Chicago Press.

————. 1970. *The Structure of Scientific Revolutions*. 2d ed. Chicago: University of Chicago Press.

Lack, D. 1954a. *The Natural Regulation of Animal Numbers*. Oxford: Oxford University Press.

————. 1954b. "The Evolution of Reproductive Rates." In J. S. Huxley, A. C. Hardy, and E. B. Ford, eds., *Evolution as a Process*. London: Allen and Unwin.

Lakatos, I. 1970. "Falsification and the Methodology of Scientific Research Programmes." In I. Lakatos and A. Musgrave eds., *Criticism and the Growth of Knowledge* 91–196. Port Chester, N.Y. Cambridge University Press. Reprinted in part in Kourany 1987.

Lancaster, J. 1985. "Evolutionary Perspectives on Sex Differences in the Higher Primates." In A. S. Rossi, ed., *Gender and the Life Course*. Hawthorne, N.Y.: Aldine.

Laudan, L. 1981. "A Problem-Solving Approach to Scientific Progress." In Hacking 1981.

————. 1984. "Dissecting the Holist Picture of Scientific Change." In Kourany 1987.

Laudan, R., and Laudan, L. 1989. "Dominance and the Disunity of Method: Solving the Problems of Innovation and Consensus." *Philosophy of Science* 56:221–38.

Leeds, A., and Dusek, V. 1981–82. "Editor's Note." *Philosophical Forum*, i–xxxv.

Leigh, E. G. 1977. "How does Selection Reconcile Individual Advantage with the Good of the Group?" *Proceedings of the National Academy of Sciences in the United States* 74:4542–46.

Lewontin, R. C. 1970. "The Units of Selection." *Annual Review of Ecology and Systematics* 1:1–18.

————. 1974a. *The Genetic Basis of Evolutionary Change*. New York: Columbia University Press.

————. 1974b. "The Analysis of Variance and the Analyis of Cause." *American Journal of Human Genetics* 26:400–11. Also in N. Block and G. Dworking, eds., *The IQ Controversy*. New York: Random House. 1976.

————. 1976. "Sociobiology: A Caricature of Darwinism." In F. Suppe and P. Asquith, eds., *Proceedings of the Philosophy of Science Association* 2:22–31. East Lansing, Mich.: Philosophy of Science Assn.

————. 1977a. "Caricature of Darwinism." *Nature* 266:283–84.

————. 1977b. "Biological Determinism as a Social Weapon." In Sociobiology Study Group 1982.

————. 1979. "Sociobiology as an Adaptationist Program." *Behavioral Science* 24:5–14.

——. 1981. "Sleight of Hand." *The Sciences* (July–August) 23–26.

Lewontin, R. C.; Rose, S.; and Kamin, L. J. 1985. *Not in Our Genes: Biology, Ideology, and Human Nature*. New York: Pantheon.

Levi, I. 1960. "Must the Scientist Make Value Judgements?" In Brody 1970.

Lopreato, J. 1984. *Human Nature and Biocultural Evolution*. London: Allen and Unwin.

Lumsden, C., and Wilson, E. O. 1981. *Genes, Mind and Culture*. Cambridge, Mass.: Harvard University Press.

Lumsden, C. 1989. "Does Culture Need Genes?" *Ethology and Sociobiology* 10:11–28.

MacDonald, K. 1989. "The Plasticity of Human Social Organization and Behavior: Contextual Variables and Proximal Mechanisms." *Ethology and Sociobiology* 10:171–94.

Martin, N. G. et al. 1986. "Transmission of Social Attitudes." *Proceedings of the National Academy of Science* 83:4364.

Masterman, M. 1970. "The Nature of a Paradigm." In Lakatos and Musgrave 1970.

Maynard Smith, J. 1978. "Optimization Theory in Evolution." *Annual Review of Ecology and Systematics* 9:31–56.

——. 1982. *Evolution and the Theory of Games*. Port Chester, N.Y.: Cambridge University Press.

——. 1984. "Group Selection." In Brandon and Burian 1984.

Mayo, D. G., and Gilinsky, N. L. 1987. "Models of Group Selection." *Philosophy of Science* 54:515–38.

Mayo, O. 1985. *Natural Selection and its Constraints*. New York: Academic Press.

Mayr, E. 1942. *Systematics and the Origin of Species*. New York: Columbia University Press.

——. 1980. "Prologue: Some Thoughts on the History of the Evolutionary Synthesis." In E. Mayr and W. Provine, eds., *The Evolutionary Synthesis: Perspectives on the Unification of Biology*. Cambridge, Mass.: Harvard University Press.

——. 1985. "What is Darwinism Today?" In P. Asquith, P. and P. Kitcher, eds., *PSA 1984* (Proc. of the 1984 Biennial Meeting of the Philosophy of Science Assn.). Ann Arbor, Mich.: Philosophy of Science Assn.

McGill, T., D. Dewsbury, and B. Sachs, eds. 1978. *Sex and Behavior: Status and Prospectus*. New York: Plenum.

Midgely, M. 1978. *Beast and Man: The Roots of Human Nature*. Ithaca, N.Y.: Cornell University Press.

——. 1979. "Rival Fatalisms: The Hollowness of the Sociobiology Debate." In A. Montague, ed., *Sociobiology Examined*. New York: Oxford University Press. 1980.

Millikan, R. 1989. "On Ambiguity in the Notion of Function." In Horan 1989.

Mitchell-Olds, T., and Rutledge, J. J. 1986. "Quantitative Genetics in Natural Plant Populations: A Review of the Theory." *American Naturalist* 127:379–402.

Morris, S. 1980. "Darwin and the Double Standard." *Playboy* 27 109ff.

Nersessian, N., ed., 1987. *The Process of Science: Contemporary Philosophical Approaches to Understanding Scientific Practice.* Boston: Martinus Nijhoff.

Nickles, T. 1987. "'Twixt Method and Madness." In Nersessian 1987.

Oster, G. F. and Wilson, E. O. 1978. *Cast and Ecology in the Social Insects.* Princeton: Princeton University Press.

Oyama, S. 1985. *Ontogeny of Information: Developmental Systems and Evolution.* Cambridge: Cambridge University Press.

Parker, G. A.; Baker, R. R.; and Smith, V. 1972. "The Origin and Evolution of Gamete Dimorphism and the Male-Female Phenomenon." *Journal of Theoretical Biology* 36:529–53.

———. 1978. "Searching for Mates." In Krebs and and Davies 1978.

Partridge, L., and Halliday, T. 1984. "Mating Patterns and Mate Choice." In Krebs and Davies 1984.

Pierce, G. J., and Ollason, J. G. 1987. "Eight Reasons Why Optimal Foraging Theory is a Complete Waste of Time." *Oikos* 49:111–17.

Plomin, R. 1986. "Behavioral Genetic Methods." *Journal of Personality* 54:226–61.

Plomin, R., and Daniels, D. 1987. "Why are Children in the Same Family so Different from One Another?" (Including Open Peer Commentary and Author's Response.) *Brain and Behavioral Sciences* 10:1–60.

Plotkin, H. C., ed., 1988. *The Role of Behavior in Evolution.* Cambridge, Mass.: MIT Press.

Pollock, J. 1986. *Contemporary Theories of Knowledge.* Totowa, N.J.: Rowman and Littlefield.

Popper, K. 1963. "Science: Conjecture and Refutations." In Kourany 1987.

Putnam, H. 1974. "The 'Corroboration' of Theories." In Hacking 1981.

Quine, W. V., and Ullian, J. S. 1978. *The Web of Belief.* 2d ed. New York: Random House.

Reed, E. 1978. "Sociobiology and Pseudoscience." In E. Reed, ed., *Sexism and Science.* New York: Pathfinder.

Reynolds, V. 1980. *The Biology of Human Action.* Oxford: Freeman.

Rhindos, D. 1985. "Darwinian Selection, Symbolic Variation, and the Evolution of Culture." (Including Open Peer Commentary and Author's Response) *Current Anthropology* 26:65–88.

Richardson, R. 1984. "Biology and Ideology: the Interpenetration of Science and Values." *Philosophy of Science* 51:396–420.

Richerson, P., and Boyd, R. 1989. "The Role of Evolved Predispositions in Cultural Evolution: Or, Human Sociobiology Meets Pascal's Wager." *Ethology and Sociobiology* 10:195–220.

Rifkin, J. 1983. *Algeny: A New Word—A New World.* New York: Penguin.

Rosenberg, A. 1980. *Sociobiology and the Preemption of Social Science.* Baltimore: Johns Hopkins University Press.

———. 1985. *The Structure of Biological Science.* New York: Cambridge University Press.

Rosenkrantz, R. 1977. *Inference, Method, and Decision.* Dordrecht: Reidel.

Rudner, R. 1953. "The Scientist Qua Scientist makes Value Judgements." In Brody 1970.

Ruse, M., ed., 1989. *Philosophy of Biology.* New York: Macmillan.

———. 1979. *Sociobiology: Sense or Nonsense?*, 1st ed. Dordrecth: Reidel.

———. 1987. "Is Sociobiology a New Paradigm?" *Philosophy of Science* 54:98–104.

———. 1989. *The Darwinian Paradigm: Essays on its History, Philosophy, and Religious Implications.* New York: Routledge.

Salmon, W. 1984. Scientific Explanation and the Causal Structure of the World. Princeton: Princeton University Press.

Scarr, S. 1987. "Three Cheers for Behavior Genetics: Winning the War and Losing Our Identity," *Behavior Genetics* 17:219–228.

Schilpp, P. A., ed. 1974. *The Philosophy of Karl Popper.* The Library of Living Philosophers Vol. 14, Books 1 and 2. La Salle, Ill.: Open Court.

Segerstrale, U. 1985. "Colleagues in Conflict: An 'In Vivo' Analysis of the Sociobiology Controversy." *Biology and Philosophy* 1, 53–88.

Seyfarth, R., and Cheney, D. 1988. "Empirical Tests of Reciprocity Theory: Problems in Assessment." *Ethology and Sociobiology* 9:181–87.

Shapere, C. 1977. "Scientific Theories and Their Domains." In Suppe 1977 and in Kourany 1987.

Shoener, T. W. 1971. "Theory of Feeding Strategies." *Annual Review of Ecology and Systematics* 2:369–404.

Shubert, G. 1989. *Evolutionary Politics.* Carbondale, Ill.: Southern Illinois University Press.

Simpson, G. G. 1944. *Tempo and Mode in Evolution.* New York: Columbia University Press. Reprint 1982.

Silverberg, J. 1980. "Sociobiology, the New Synthesis? An Anthropologist's Perspective." In Barlow and Silverberg 1980.

Smith, E. A. 1987. "On Fitness Maximization, Limited Needs, and Hunter-Gatherer Time Allocation." *Ethology and Sociobiology* 8:73–85.

Smith, J. W. 1984. *Reductionism and Cultural Being: A Philosophical Critique of Sociobiological Reductionism and Physicalist Scientific Unificationism.* Dordrecht: Martinus, Nijhoff.

Sober, E. 1984. *The Nature of Selection.* Cambridge, Mass.: MIT Press.

———. 1985. "Methodological Behaiorism, Evolution, and Game Theory," In Fetzer 1985.

———. 1986. "Reply to George Williams." *Biology and Philosophy* 1:122–24.

———. 1987a. "Explanation and Causation." *British Journal of Philosophy of Science* 38:243–57.

———. 1987b. "What is Adaptationism?" In Dupre, 1987.

———. 1988. "What is Evolutionary Altruism?" In M. Matten and B. Linsky, eds. *Philosophy and Biology, Canadian J. of Philosophy* 14, Calgary: University of Calgary Press.

Sober, E., and Lewontin, R. C. 1984. "Artifact, Cause and Genic Selection." In Brandon and Burian 1984.

Sociobiology Study Group (Allen, E. et al.). 1975. "Against 'Sociobiology'." In Caplan 1978, 259–64.

———. 1976. "Sociobiology: Another Biological Determinism." *BioScience* 26:182–86.

———. (affiliated with The Ann Arbor Science for the People Editorial Collective), eds., 1978a. *Biology as a Social Weapon*. Minneapolis: Burgess.

———. 1978b. "Sociobiology: A New Biological Determinism." In their *Biology as a Social Weapon*, 133–49.

Spuhler, J. N., ed. 1959. *The Evolution of Man's Capacity for Culture*. Detroit, Michigan: Wayne University Press.

Stearns, S.C. and Schmid-Hempel, P. 1987. "Evolutionary Insights should not be Wasted." *Oikos* 49, 118–25.

Suppe, F., ed., 1977. *The Structure of Scientific Theories*. 2d ed. Champaign, Ill.: University of Illinois Press.

Symons, D. 1979. *The Evolution of Human Sexuality*. New York: Oxford University Press.

———. 1989. "A Critique of Darwinian Anthropology." *Ethology and Sociobiology* 10:131–44.

Thompson, K. S. 1985. "Essay Review: The Relationship Between Development and Evolution." In Dawkins and Ridley 1985.

Tooby, J., and Cosmides, L. 1989. "Evolutionary Psychology and the Generation of Culture, Part I: Theoretical Considerations." *Ethology and Sociobiology* 10:29–50.

Tooby, J., and DeVore, I. 1987. "The Reconstruction of Hominid Behavioral Evolution." In W. Kinzy, ed., *The Evolution of Human Behavior: Primate Models*. Albany, N.Y.: State University of New York Press.

Tooby, J. 1985. "The Emergence of Evolutionary Psychology." In D. Pines, ed., *Emerging Syntheses in Science*. Santa Fe: Rio Grande Institute.

Toulmin, S. 1961. "Ideals of Natural Order." In Kourany 1987.

Trivers, R. L. 1972. "Parental Investment and Sexual Selection. In B. Campbell, ed., *Sexual Selection and the Descent of Man*. Hawthorne, N.Y.: Aldine.

Turke, P. 1988. "Helpers at the Nest: Childcare Networks on Ifaluk." In Betzig, Borgerhoff Mulder, and Turke.

Van Balen, G. 1987. "Conceptual Tensions Between Theory and Program: The Chromosome Theory and the Mendelian Research Program." *Biology and Philosophy* 2:435–61.

Van der Steen, W. J., and Voorzanger, B. 1984. "Sociobiology in Perspective." *Journal of Human Evolution* 13:25–32.

Vehrencamp, S. L., and Bradbury, J. W. 1984. "Mating Systems and Ecology." In Krebs and Davies 1984.

Voorzanger, B. 1984. "Altruism in Sociobiology: A Conceptual Analysis." *Journal of Human Evolution* 13:33–39.

———. 1987. Methodological Problems in Evolutionary Biology VIII. Biology and Culture. *Acte Biotheoretica* 36:23–34.

Wade, M. J. 1979. "Sexual Selection and Variation in Reproductive Success." *American Naturalist* 114:742–47.

Wade, M. J., and Arnold, S. J. 1980. "The Intensity of Sexual Selection in Relation to Male Sexual Behavior, Female Choice, and Sperm Precedence." *Animal Behavior* 26:446–61.

Watkins, J. 1984. *Science and Scepticism*. London: Hutchinson.

Wenegrat, B. 1984. *Sociobiology and Mental Disorder*. Menlo Park, Calif.: Addison-Wesley.

Williams, G. C., and Williams, D. C. 1957. "Natural Selection of Individually Harmful Social Adaptations among Sibs with Special Reference to Social Insects." *Evolution* 11:32–39.

Williams, G. C. 1957. "Pleiotropy, Natural Selection, and the Evolution of Senescence." *Evolution* 11:398–411.

———. 1966. *Adaptation and Natural Selection*. Princeton: Princeton University Press.

———. 1985. "A Defense of Reductionism in Evolutionary Biology." In R. Dawkins and M. Ridley, eds., *Oxford Surveys in Evolutionary Biology*. Vol 2. Oxford: Oxford University Press.

———. 1986. "Comments on Sober's *The Nature of Selection*." *Biology and Philosophy* 1:114–22.

———. 1989. "A Sociobiological Expansion of *Evolution and Ethics*." In *Evolution and Ethics: T. H. Huxley's Evolution and Ethics, With New Essays on Its Victorian and Sociobiological Context*. Princeton: Princeton University Press.

Wilson, D. S. 1979. *The Natural Selection of Populations and Communities*. Palo Alto, Calif.: Benjamin.

Wilson, E. O. 1975. *Sociobiology: The New Synthesis*. Cambridge, Mass.: Harvard University Press.

———. 1976. "Academic Vigilantism and the Political Significance of Sociobiology." New York Review of Books. Reprinted in Caplan 1978.

———. 1978. *On Human Nature*. Cambridge, Mass.: Harvard University Press.

———. 1980. "A Consideration of the Genetic Foundations of Human Social Behavior, in Barlow and Silverberg 1980.

Wilson, F. 1985. *Explanation, Causation, Deduction*. (The University of Western Ontario Series in Philosophy of Science 26.) Dordrecht: Reidel.

Wilson, M. I.; Daly, M.; and Weghorst, S. J. 1980. "Household Composition and the Risk of Child Abuse and Neglect." *Journal of Biosocial Science* 12:333–40.

Wilson, M. I., and Daly, M. 1983. "Differential Maltreatment of Girls and Boys." *Victimology* 6:249–61.

————. 1987. "Risk of Malteatment of Children Living with Stepparents." In R. J. Gelles and J. Lancaster, eds., *Child Abuse and Neglect: Biosocial Dimensions*. 1987. New York: Aldine.

Wimsatt, W. C. 1984. "Reductionistic Research Strategies and Their Biases in the Units of Selection Controversy." In Brandon and Burian 1984.

Winterhalder, B. 1987. "The Analysis of Hunter-Gatherer Diets: Stalking an Optimal Foraging Model." In M. Harris and E. Ross, eds., *Food and Evolution: Toward a Theory of Human Food Habit*. 1987. Philadelphia: Temple University Press.

Woolfenden, G. 1975. "Florida Scrub Jay Helpers at the Nest." *Auk* 92:1–15.

Woolfenden, G., and Fitzpatrick, J. 1978. "The Inheritance of Territory in Group-Breeding Birds." *BioScience* 28:104–8.

Wynne-Edwards, V. C. 1962. *Animal Dispersion in Relation to Social Behavior*. New York: Hefner.

————. 1988. *Evolution Through Group Selection*. Oxford: Blackwell.

# INDEX OF NAMES

# INDEX OF SUBJECTS